Discourse Analysis

Discourse Analysis provides an essential and practical introduction for students studying modules on the analysis of language in use. It explores the ways in which language is used and organised in written and spoken texts to generate meanings and takes into account the social contexts of production, and the social roles and identities of those involved.

Investigating the ways in which language varies according to subject, social setting, and communicative purpose, this book examines various forms of speaking and writing, including casual conversation, speeches, parliamentary debate, computer-mediated communication, and mass media articles. It discusses topics including how we convey more than we actually say or write, the role of politeness and impoliteness in communication, and what makes texts cohesive and coherent. It also shows how particular aspects of discourse analysis can be assisted by corpus methods and tools.

Taking students through a step-by-step guide on how to do discourse analysis that includes the collection of data and presentation of results, the book also documents a text analysis project from start to finish. Featuring a range of examples and interactive activities, as well as additional online support material, this book is key reading for those studying discourse analysis modules.

Patricia Canning is an assistant professor at Northumbria University, Newcastle (UK). Her recent publications include journal articles on the linguistic construction of domestic abuse police reports (2022; and with Nick Lynn, 2021). She is co-author of an independent report into what went wrong at the Champions League Final in Paris (2022) and has published research on the narrative evidence following the Hillsborough Football Stadium disaster (2018; 2021; 2023). She is author of *Style in the Renaissance: Language and Control in Early Modern England* (2011).

Brian Walker is a visiting scholar in the School of Arts, English and Languages at Queen's University Belfast, Belfast (UK). His published research focuses on corpus stylistics and using corpus linguistic approaches in the analysis of discourse.

LEARNING ABOUT LANGUAGE

Series Editors:
Brian Walker, Queen's University Belfast, UK; **Willem Hollmann**, Lancaster University, UK; and the late **Geoffrey Leech**, Lancaster University, UK

Series Consultant:
Mick Short, Lancaster University, UK

Learning about Language is an exciting and ambitious series of introductions to fundamental topics in language, linguistics and related areas. The books are designed for students of linguistics and those who are studying language as part of a wider course.

Also in this series:

Analysing Sentences
An Introduction to English Syntax, Fourth Edition
Noel Burton-Roberts

The History of Early English
An Activity-based Approach
Keith Johnson

An Introduction to Foreign Language Learning and Teaching, Revised Third Edition
Keith Johnson

The History of Late Modern Englishes
An Activity-based Approach
Keith Johnson

Analysing Sentences
An Introduction to English Syntax, Fifth Edition
Noel Burton-Roberts

An Introduction to Sociolinguistics, Sixth Edition
Janet Holmes and Nick Wilson

Critical Discourse Analysis
A Practical Introduction to Power in Language
Simon Statham

Introducing Linguistics
Edited by Jonathan Culpeper, Beth Malory, Claire Nance, Daniel Van Olmen, Dimitrinka Atanasova, Sam Kirkham, and Aina Casaponsa

Discourse Analysis
A Practical Introduction
Patricia Canning and Brian Walker

For more information about this series, please visit: www.routledge.com/series/PEALAL

Discourse Analysis

A Practical Introduction

PATRICIA CANNING AND BRIAN WALKER

LONDON AND NEW YORK

Designed cover image: © Getty Images

First published 2024
by Routledge
4 Park Square, Milton Park, Abingdon, Oxon OX14 4RN

and by Routledge
605 Third Avenue, New York, NY 10158

Routledge is an imprint of the Taylor & Francis Group, an informa business

British Library Cataloguing-in-Publication Data
A catalogue record for this book is available from the British Library

Library of Congress Cataloging-in-Publication Data
Names: Canning, Patricia, author. | Walker, Brian (Linguist), author.
Title: Discourse analysis : a practical introduction / Patricia Canning and Brian Walker.
Description: Abingdon, Oxon ; New York, NY : Routledge, 2023. | Series: Learning about language | Includes bibliographical references and index. | Summary: "Discourse Analysis provides an essential and practical introduction for students studying modules on the analysis of language in use. It explores the ways in which language is used and organised in written and spoken texts to generate meanings and takes into account the social contexts of production, and the social roles and identities of those involved"—Provided by publisher.
Identifiers: LCCN 2023024794 (print) | LCCN 2023024795 (ebook) | ISBN 9781138047082 (hardback) | ISBN 9781138047099 (paperback) | ISBN 9781003351207 (ebook)
Subjects: LCSH: Discourse analysis.
Classification: LCC P302 .C338 2023 (print) | LCC P302 (ebook) | DDC 401/.41—dc23/eng/20230808
LC record available at https://lccn.loc.gov/2023024794
LC ebook record available at https://lccn.loc.gov/2023024795

ISBN: 978-1-138-04708-2 (hbk)
ISBN: 978-1-138-04709-9 (pbk)
ISBN: 978-1-003-35120-7 (ebk)

DOI: 10.4324/9781003351207

Typeset in Sabon
by Apex CoVantage, LLC
Access the Support Material: www.routledge.com/9781138047099

To Simon and to Jacqui; enjoy – there'll be a test later.

Contents

Acknowledgements

Writing a book is hard. It can also be lonely but it's never a lone effort. In this case, there were two of us but there were more people behind the glossy cover who helped. Friends and colleagues advised us and offered invaluable feedback on chapters and we would especially like to thank Billy Clark, Dan McIntyre, Sarah Duffy, Robert McKenzie, and Michael Burke for giving up their time and lending us their expertise. Their constructive feedback improved the book. You should've seen it before. That said, any errors or anomalies are our own and we'll pass the blame for each one to the other.

Getting timely permission to use copyrighted material is always a challenge. Also, paying for permission to use a text snippet can be costly. And we quite like living in houses and, you know, eating. So, a big thanks to Eve Canning whose original artwork got us out of a potential legal quagmire. Viva la Absorbent Andy. If we go down for that, we are taking Eve with us. We are also sincerely grateful to Sebastian Hoffman for granting us permission to use screenshots from *BNCweb* in our supplementary online materials.

We would also like to thank the many staff at Routledge for their help and infinite patience, in particular Nadia, Bex, Sarah, and the rest of the team that helped us get this book into your hands (or on your screens).

Nobody writes a book between the hours of 9am and 5pm. There were many weekends and evenings and Christmases and Easters that were lost to writing this one. Thanks are due to our friends and families – particularly Jacqui, Simon, and Eve – for supporting and patiently suffering with us during the writing, editing, editing, editing, and editing of this book.

Finally, Patricia would like to thank Brian for being a writer, a reader, a critic, and a mate. It's been a blast (EMOTIONS ARE EVENTS[1]). I'll let you go now[2]. Brian would like to say 'Ight Imma head out'[3].

PC and BW
May 2023

Notes

1 See Chapter 8
2 Not really
3 See Chapter 6

List of figures

List of tables

List of activities

List of QR codes

IPA chart

THE INTERNATIONAL PHONETIC ALPHABET (revised to 2015)

CONSONANTS (PULMONIC)

© 2015 IPA

	Bilabial	Labiodental	Dental	Alveolar	Postalveolar	Retroflex	Palatal	Velar	Uvular	Pharyngeal	Glottal
Plosive	p b			t d		ʈ ɖ	c ɟ	k ɡ	q ɢ		ʔ
Nasal	m	ɱ		n		ɳ	ɲ	ŋ	ɴ		
Trill	ʙ			r					ʀ		
Tap or Flap		ⱱ		ɾ		ɽ					
Fricative	ɸ β	f v	θ ð	s z	ʃ ʒ	ʂ ʐ	ç ʝ	x ɣ	χ ʁ	ħ ʕ	h ɦ
Lateral fricative				ɬ ɮ							
Approximant		ʋ		ɹ		ɻ	j	ɰ			
Lateral approximant				l		ɭ	ʎ	ʟ			

Symbols to the right in a cell are voiced, to the left are voiceless. Shaded areas denote articulations judged impossible.

CONSONANTS (NON-PULMONIC)

Clicks	Voiced implosives	Ejectives
ʘ Bilabial	ɓ Bilabial	ʼ Examples:
ǀ Dental	ɗ Dental/alveolar	pʼ Bilabial
ǃ (Post)alveolar	ʄ Palatal	tʼ Dental/alveolar
ǂ Palatoalveolar	ɠ Velar	kʼ Velar
ǁ Alveolar lateral	ʛ Uvular	sʼ Alveolar fricative

VOWELS

Front — Central — Back

- Close: i • y — ɨ • ʉ — ɯ • u
  - ɪ ʏ — ʊ
- Close-mid: e • ø — ɘ • ɵ — ɤ • o
  - ə
- Open-mid: ɛ • œ — ɜ • ɞ — ʌ • ɔ
  - æ — ɐ
- Open: a • ɶ — ɑ • ɒ

Where symbols appear in pairs, the one to the right represents a rounded vowel.

OTHER SYMBOLS

ʍ Voiceless labial-velar fricative

w Voiced labial-velar approximant

ɥ Voiced labial-palatal approximant

ʜ Voiceless epiglottal fricative

ʢ Voiced epiglottal fricative

ʡ Epiglottal plosive

ɕ ʑ Alveolo-palatal fricatives

ɺ Voiced alveolar lateral flap

ɧ Simultaneous ʃ and x

Affricates and double articulations can be represented by two symbols joined by a tie bar if necessary. t͡s k͡p

SUPRASEGMENTALS

ˈ Primary stress

ˌ Secondary stress — ˌfoʊnəˈtɪʃən

ː Long eː

ˑ Half-long eˑ

˘ Extra-short ĕ

| Minor (foot) group

‖ Major (intonation) group

. Syllable break ɹi.ækt

‿ Linking (absence of a break)

DIACRITICS Some diacritics may be placed above a symbol with a descender, e.g. ŋ̊

̥ Voiceless	n̥ d̥	̤ Breathy voiced	b̤ a̤	̪ Dental	t̪ d̪
̬ Voiced	s̬ t̬	̰ Creaky voiced	b̰ a̰	̺ Apical	t̺ d̺
ʰ Aspirated	tʰ dʰ	̼ Linguolabial	t̼ d̼	̻ Laminal	t̻ d̻
̹ More rounded	ɔ̹	ʷ Labialized	tʷ dʷ	̃ Nasalized	ẽ
̜ Less rounded	ɔ̜	ʲ Palatalized	tʲ dʲ	ⁿ Nasal release	dⁿ
̟ Advanced	u̟	ˠ Velarized	tˠ dˠ	ˡ Lateral release	dˡ
̠ Retracted	e̠	ˤ Pharyngealized	tˤ dˤ	̚ No audible release	d̚
̈ Centralized	ë	̴ Velarized or pharyngealized	ɫ		
̽ Mid-centralized	e̽	̝ Raised	e̝ (ɹ̝ = voiced alveolar fricative)		
̩ Syllabic	n̩	̞ Lowered	e̞ (β̞ = voiced bilabial approximant)		
̯ Non-syllabic	e̯	̘ Advanced Tongue Root	e̘		
˞ Rhoticity	ɚ a˞	̙ Retracted Tongue Root	e̙		

TONES AND WORD ACCENTS

LEVEL		CONTOUR	
e̋ or ˥	Extra high	ě or ˩˥	Rising
é ˦	High	ê ˥˩	Falling
ē ˧	Mid	e᷄ ˦˥	High rising
è ˨	Low	e᷅ ˩˨	Low rising
ȅ ˩	Extra low	e᷈ ˧˦˧	Rising-falling
↓ Downstep		↗ Global rise	
↑ Upstep		↘ Global fall	

Typefaces: Doulos SIL (metatext), Doulos SIL, IPA Kiel, IPA LS Uni (symbols)

1 Discourse

Language, context, and choice

Introduction

In this first chapter we explain what we mean by discourse and discourse analysis and introduce some of the key concepts and linguistic terminology that we will use throughout this book. We will discuss the notions of **text**, **context**, and **co-text**, before going on to explore the differences between spoken and written discourse. We will also examine the idea of a **standard language** and that some language varieties hold more **prestige** than others. We will discover that when analysing discourse, analysts consider the *form* of language (see levels of language in Figure 1.2), its *function* (e.g. the purpose to which it is put; how it works to achieve certain goals), and the *context* in which the **language event** occurs (e.g. a conversation between friends; a political debate, an opinion piece in the press). Our starting point, perhaps unsurprisingly, is 'discourse'.

What is discourse?

Discourse does not have one single definition and has different meanings even within linguistics. According to the *Oxford English Dictionary* online edition ('Discourse' 1989), discourse can mean:

- a detailed and lengthy spoken or written discussion of a particular topic;
- spoken communication, interaction or conversation;
- a connected series of utterances by which meaning is communicated.

Although non-technical, these definitions nonetheless provide important information about what discourse *is*. Discourse is connected chunks of spoken or written language (e.g. utterances; sentences) used in interactions for meaningful communication. Discourse, then, is language being used in all its forms (including signed languages) to communicate, interact, inform, and get things done. Simply put, and to quote two pioneers of discourse analysis, discourse is "language in use" (Brown and Yule 1983: 1). Consequently, discourse analysis is <u>not</u> the study of linguistic forms in isolation; it is, as Brown and Yule explain, the study of how linguistic forms **function** when they are **used** in different contexts. Simpson and

DOI: 10.4324/9781003351207-1

Mayr (2009: 5) echo this distinction between linguistic forms and the function of forms in use when they contrast **language** (as a system) with **discourse** (as language in use):

> Whereas language refers to the more abstract set of patterns and rules which operate simultaneously at different levels in the systems [. . .] discourse refers to the instantiation of these patterns in real contexts of use.

Importantly, they go on to say that:

> discourse works above the level of grammar and semantics to capture what happens when these language forms are played out in different social, political and cultural arenas.

The definition above chimes with that of another discourse pioneer, Mike Stubbs, who described discourse as "language above the sentence or above the clause" (Stubbs 1983:1). Therefore, while discourse is, of course, made up of the building blocks of language, it is greater than the sum of its parts. It is what results when these language forms combine and connect in different ways in different contexts.

Figure 1.1 captures the preoccupations of language and discourse and their relationship to each other. Discourse concerns all of that which pertains to language (such as syntax, lexis, and morphology – see Figure 1.2) but, in addition, it involves the **context** in which language is used (we will say more about context

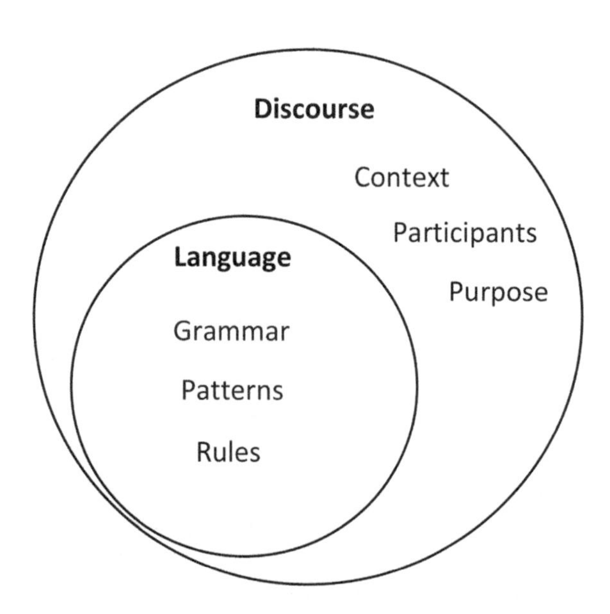

Figure 1.1 Relationship between language and discourse

later in this chapter), the **people** using the language, and the **purpose** served by the language in that context. Discourse, then, is **structural** because it involves the linguistic building blocks set out in Figure 1.2, **cognitive** because it incorporates the mental representations language users hold about the world (we explore this further in Chapter 8), and **social** because "language users engaging in discourse accomplish *social acts* and participate in *social interactions* [that are] embedded in social and cultural contexts" (van Dijk 1997: 2, original emphasis) (we say more about acts in Chapter 4).

What is discourse analysis?

As we established in the previous section, discourse analysis is not the study of language rules and components in isolation; it is not just about considering clauses and other structures and establishing what words or phrases go where. Instead, discourse analysis studies how language is used in real-life, everyday settings. When we 'do' discourse analysis we are looking at how meaning is conveyed between those producing the language and those receiving the language. However, that is not to say an understanding of the language system is not essential for analysing discourse, because it is! Discourse analysis concerns analysing language *forms* and appreciating their *function* in the context in which they occur. Moreover, it involves investigating whether forms combine to create larger units of language, whether these have their own structural patterns, and whether any such patterns relate to meaning. In short, discourse analysis examines how meanings are made and interpreted through linguistic and non-linguistic behaviour in a given situational context. As you might imagine, given the almost endless number of different situational contexts, this makes discourse analysis a broad area of study. Indeed, in the preface to his 1997 edited volume, *Discourse as Social Interaction*, Teun van Dijk acknowledges that given the vast number of discourse **genres** (e.g. argumentation, storytelling), **modes** (e.g. spoken, written, imagistic), and **social domains** (e.g. medical, legal, political), the remit for discourse analysts is so wide that "even two volumes [of his edited collection] are unable to cover everything" (xi). Twenty-five years on, the information and communication technology revolution has increased the scope of 'everything' still further, with online interactions and social media now a commonplace way of 'doing' discourse.

The nuts and bolts of language and discourse

In this section, we introduce some of the 'nuts and bolts' of a language. This is because for us to be able to analyse discourse in linguistic detail, we need to know how language is constructed. This section will also provide a vocabulary that will enable us to describe language and discourse. Language operates on several levels from the smallest units through to discourse. Figure 1.2 below shows these structural levels, which we describe below.

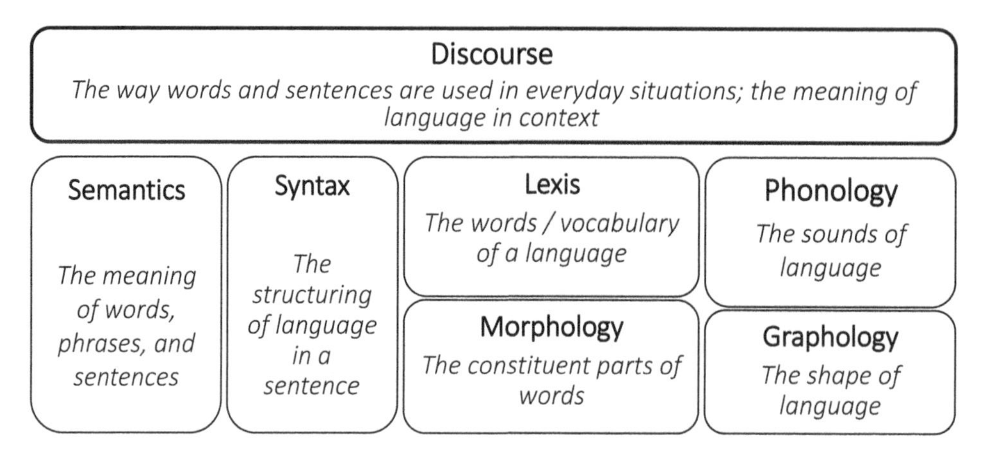

Figure 1.2 The levels of language

Morphology

Morphology is the study of the smallest units of meaning in language, known as **morphemes**. Words comprise one or more morphemes. For example, 'books', contains the morphemes 'book' and 's' (see Figure 1.3). The morpheme 'book' is what's known as a **free morpheme** because it can stand on its own as a word. The morpheme 's' that is attached to 'book' is known as a **bound morpheme** because even though it carries meaning (in this case, it means 'plural') it cannot stand alone and have meaning; it must be bound to another morpheme. For example, we would not say 's' to answer the question 'what are libraries full of?'

'books'		
book	+	s
free morpheme	+	*bound morpheme*

Figure 1.3 Free and bound morphemes in 'books'

The addition of the bound morpheme 's' to the free morpheme 'book' is an example of affixation. In the example in Figure 1.3, the morpheme 's' is a suffix because it attaches to the end of 'book'. This specific type of suffix is known as an **inflectional suffix** because it carries grammatical information (in this case 'number'). Inflectional suffixes can also signal tense,'possession, or comparison (e.g. '-est'). Bound morphemes can also function as **derivational suffixes**. For example, the verb 'assassinate' is created by adding the bound morpheme '-ate' to the free morpheme 'assassin' (a noun). When the suffix is added, there is a change in grammatical class from noun to a verb, so a new verb ('assassinate') is *derived* from a noun ('assassin'). Some bound morphemes attach to the front of a free morpheme and are known as **prefixes**. These carry a variety of meanings but nonetheless cannot stand on their own as words. For example, the bound morpheme, and prefix, 'dis' means 'not' or 'the opposite of' so when attached to, say, 'respect', a new word is derived ('disrespect') that means the opposite.

Morphological rules can be manipulated in discourse for a range of different effects. For example, the poetry of E. E. Cummings often plays with morphology in creative ways. For instance, in the poem 'Love is more thicker than forget',[1] Cummings describes love as 'moonly' and 'sunly' which are unusual constructions that, through the addition of the suffix '-ly', change the word class of 'sun' and 'moon' from nouns to adjectives (you can find the full poem at the *Poetry Foundation* website).

QR 1.1 Link to E. E. Cummings's poem

New words can also be formed by the merging of two **free** morphemes to form compound words. For example, 'bookworm' is a combination of 'book' + 'worm'. In 2020, the Oxford Dictionary's 'word of the year' was expanded to account for an "unprecedented" year and introduced new compounds that included 'bushfires', 'Covid-19', 'lockdown', 'circuit-breaker', 'support bubble', and 'keyworker'. As you can see, the words of the year can tell us much about how we use existing language for new concepts, but it can also tell us about the events of that year!

Phonology

Phonology is the study of the sound system of a language and is concerned with the different sounds that carry meaning, known as **phonemes**. A phoneme is a distinctive sound in any language that, when uttered, makes a difference to meaning and therefore contrasts with other sounds. For example, the vowel sound in the word 'pip' is different to the vowel sound in 'pup'; indeed, it is the only difference between those two words, and it is that difference that affects the meaning of the words. In phonology, 'pip' and 'pup' are an example of a **minimal pair**, which is a pair of words that differ in one sound only. Therefore, 'pip' and 'pat' are not a minimal pair because they differ by two sounds. The idea of a minimal pair is to contrast particular sounds to show that they make a difference to meaning. Phonologists aim to identify and quantify the phonemes that comprise a language. For example, with Received Pronunciation of English (see below), there are said to be 20 vowel sounds (Cruttenden 2001: 91) and 24 consonants (Cruttenden 2001: 149). There are, therefore, many more sounds in spoken English than there are letters in written English, which has just five vowels (aeiou) and 21 consonants (bcdfghjklmnpqrstvwxyz). Consequently, phonologists use an expanded set of symbols (including the letters we know and recognise) to represent the sounds of a language which together make up the International Phonetic Alphabet (IPA). You can find a copy of the IPA at the start of this book.

Table 1.1 presents a series of words and aims to demonstrate the 20 different vowel sounds in English (assuming Received Pronunciation!) along with the IPA symbol that represents that sound. The IPA symbol is placed between slashes, which is the convention for phonemic transcription.

Table 1.1 The 20 vowel sounds in standard pronunciation (RP) of British English

pap	/æ/	Parp	/ɑ:/	pos*er*	/ə/	poise	/ɔɪ/
pep	/e/	Perp	/ɜ:/	pun	/ʌ/	pope	/əʊ/
pip	/ɪ/	Peep	/i:/	pain	/eɪ/	pow	/aʊ/
pop	/ɒ/	Paw	/ɔ:/	peer	/ɪə/	pair	/eə/
pup	/ʊ/	Poop	/u:/	pipe	/aɪ/	poor	/ʊə/

When we talk about speaking 'standard' English, we mean the variety of the language that is conventionally accepted as the 'norm'. In the IPA, the 'norm' is Received Pronunciation of British English or 'RP' for short. The 'received' in RP means 'accepted' or 'approved' and it is therefore the version of spoken English approved by arbiters of the language (in this case, those policing it in the late 1800s). RP then is the point of reference or model that the IPA is based on. This might seem odd given that very few people actually use RP (around 3 per cent of the UK population). In other words, RP's approval or acceptance is more to do with perceived social status than correctness (we say more about this later). Use QR code 1.2 to find out more about RP at the British Library website and hear what it sounds like (think 1950s English TV/radio announcer at the BBC and you are there).

QR 1.2 Received Pronunciation

Of course, English is spoken in many different regional accents across the world and different accents have a slightly different inventory of phonemes (due to differences in pronunciation) and differ in which phonemes contrast in meaning. For example, with some accents it is doubtful that the difference between /ʌ/ and /ʊ/ is meaningful – e.g. in parts of the North of England, /pʊb/ and /pʌb/ are both places to buy and consume beer (among other things).

According to Crystal (1995: 239), the most frequent vowel sound in English is /ə/, which is known as **schwa** and represents a sort of short 'uh' sound. The first 12 vowel sounds in Table 1.1 are known as monophthongs (or pure vowels) because their sound remains fairly constant when they are spoken. The remaining eight vowels are diphthongs because there is perceivable movement (known as a **glide**) between two different sounds. It is also possible to have triphthongs (e.g. words such as 'power', 'prior' and 'player'). Such triphthongs involve a diphthong with the addition of a schwa (/ə/) at the end. For example, 'power' is pronounced /paʊə/ in standard (RP) English.

In Hiberno-English such as that spoken in the north of Ireland, some triphthongs are spoken as monophthongs. For example, 'power' is often pronounced in Belfast as 'par' /pɑ:r/. Irish humour can often be self-reflexive and has given rise to many books on what is affectionately called the language of 'Norn Iron', itself a non-standard phonological rendering of standard 'Northern Ireland'. You cannot go far in Belfast without seeing some form of this rich Hiberno-English variant marketed as T-shirts, mugs, and more, as the following example in Figure 1.4 from T-shirt retailer Norn Iron Tees shows.

Figure 1.4 An example of Hiberno-English: 'power shower'

Lexis

This is the linguistic term given to the words (or vocabulary) of a language and their different forms. Words can be divided into two general types: **lexical words** that refer to things in the world (ideas, concepts, entities); and **function words** (also known as grammatical words) that help to link the lexical words together to make clauses and sentences (Freeborn 1995: 36). Lexical words are known as **open class**, because they are being added to all the time as new words are coined to encode new experiences and new 'things'. Function words are known as **closed class** because they are static (but not totally fixed – consider the more recent introduction of 'Mx' as a substitute for the more conventional 'Ms' pronoun for women). Words are traditionally assigned to what are known as **word classes** (also known as Parts of Speech) based on what task they are performing in the text they occur. The different word classes with some examples are shown in Tables 1.2 and 1.3. There are four open word classes: verbs, nouns, adjectives, and adverbs, and six closed word classes: prepositions, pronouns, determiners, demonstratives, conjunctions, and modal verbs. Note that the same word can perform a different role in different texts and so can be assigned to different word classes. For example, 'flower' can be a noun (as in 'what a lovely flower'), but if you ask, 'has your agapanthus started to flower yet?', then 'flower' is doing the job of a verb.

Table 1.2 Lexical word classes

Nouns	thinker, book, worm, shelf, case . . .
Verbs	think, book, saw . . .
Adjectives	sunny, bookish, booky, quick . . .
Adverbs	gingerly, bookishly, hurtfully, quickly . . .

Table 1.3 Function or grammatical word classes

Pronouns	her, they, it, we, them, his, Mr, Mx . . .
Prepositions	in, at, above, on, beside . . .
Determiners	a, an, the, some, any, all . . .
Conjunctions	for, and, but, so . . .
Demonstratives	this, that, those, them . . .
Modal verbs	should, shall, would, could, can, may, might, must, ought

Lexical creativity

New concepts require new words, known as **neologisms**. Neologisms are typically achieved by compounding and blending existing words or by novel affixation. For example, the new word 'staycation' (meaning to go on holiday without going abroad) is a blend of 'stay' and 'vacation'; 'crowdfunding' is a compound of 'crowd' and 'funding'; and 'metaverse' (meaning a virtual meeting space), is formed by replacing the prefix 'uni' (meaning 'one') in 'universe' with 'meta' (meaning 'beyond' or 'higher order'[2]). An alternative to neologising is to give existing words new, additional meanings. It was not so long ago that 'mouse' and 'virus' referred only to living organisms, yet now they refer to inanimate objects or concepts as well. If we said to you 'We cannot get our mouse to work', we doubt you would think we were exploiting our pet rodent for material gain.

Poets and writers are often creative with language and will neologise willy-nilly to suit their needs. An extreme example is the poem 'Jabberwocky' by Lewis Carroll, in which there are so many neologisms that the poem seems totally nonsensical (at first). However, linguistic conventions are being adhered to, particularly word-class conventions. In Activity 1.1 below, the first activity in this book, see if you can tell what word classes (noun, verb, adjective, adverb) the neologisms belong to. What do you base your guesses on? How does what you know about language help you to interpret the poem?

Activity 1.1 Making sense of neologisms

'Jabberwocky', by Lewis Carroll

'Twas brillig, and the slithy toves
Did gyre and gimble in the wabe:
All mimsy were the borogoves,
And the mome raths outgrabe.

"Beware the Jabberwock, my son!
The jaws that bite, the claws that catch!
Beware the Jubjub bird, and shun
The frumious Bandersnatch!"

He took his vorpal sword in hand;
Long time the manxome foe he sought—
So rested he by the Tumtum tree
And stood awhile in thought.

And, as in uffish thought he stood,
The Jabberwock, with eyes of flame,
Came whiffling through the tulgey wood,
And burbled as it came!

One, two! One, two! And through and through
The vorpal blade went snicker-snack!
He left it dead, and with its head
He went galumphing back.

"And hast thou slain the Jabberwock?
Come to my arms, my beamish boy!

O frabjous day! Callooh! Callay!"
He chortled in his joy.

'Twas brillig, and the slithy toves
Did gyre and gimble in the wabe:
All mimsy were the borogoves,
And the mome raths outgrabe.

There are linguistic patterns in 'Jabberwocky' that indicate that the conventions of English are being followed. Your knowledge of how sentences are constructed (syntax) might help you to interpret 'toves' as a noun (and perhaps a material thing), whereas your knowledge of morphology might lead you to conclude that 'slithy' is an adjective that is constructed from 'slith+y' (much in the same way that 'curl' becomes 'curly'). To take another example, you might have never heard of 'The frumious Bandersnatch' but it will not take much effort to discern that 'frumious' is an adjective that describes the noun following it, and that the noun is in fact a noun because it follows a determiner (the definite article 'the'). You might also have deduced that the 'Bandersnatch' is a specific name/has a specific referent as it is capitalised (and so graphologically marked – we introduce graphology below). These are just some of the consistent patterns in this neologistically rich text.

One neologism that gained traction in 2017 was the word 'covfefe', used in a viral tweet on 17 May 2017 by the then president of the United States, Donald Trump. The full tweet read "Despite the constant negative press covfefe". Widely acknowledged as a typo for 'coverage', Trump refused to confirm his error and instead deleted the tweet. When probed by reporters about the nonsensical reference, Trump's spokesperson, Sean Spicer, replied "I think the president and a small group of people know exactly what he meant" (Estepa 2017). Sometimes discourse communities are *really* small, it seems.

Graphology

Written language exists as marks on a page (or some other medium). This is known as graphology and refers specifically to such things as typography, punctuation, and the arrangement of any marks that constitute the discourse. The word *really* in the preceding paragraph is graphologically marked as it is enclosed within asterisks. Some fonts, for example, carry meaning and/or are associated with particular discourse types. For instance, this book is written using **Times New Roman** font because this is seen as a 'serious' font that is suitable for this sort of text. The **Comic Sans MS** font, however, with its comic book associations would probably be seen as not suitable for a serious academic book. In some discourses, such as social media and other computer-mediated communication, upper-case letters can be meaningful where they communicate SHOUTING and/or anger. When we refer to the way the text is arranged visually, we are also talking about graphology, and this includes all the meaningful elements of that text (images, colour, space, etc.). The poster in Figure 1.5 is an artistic representation of one that appeared on a few online vegan sites in 2015.

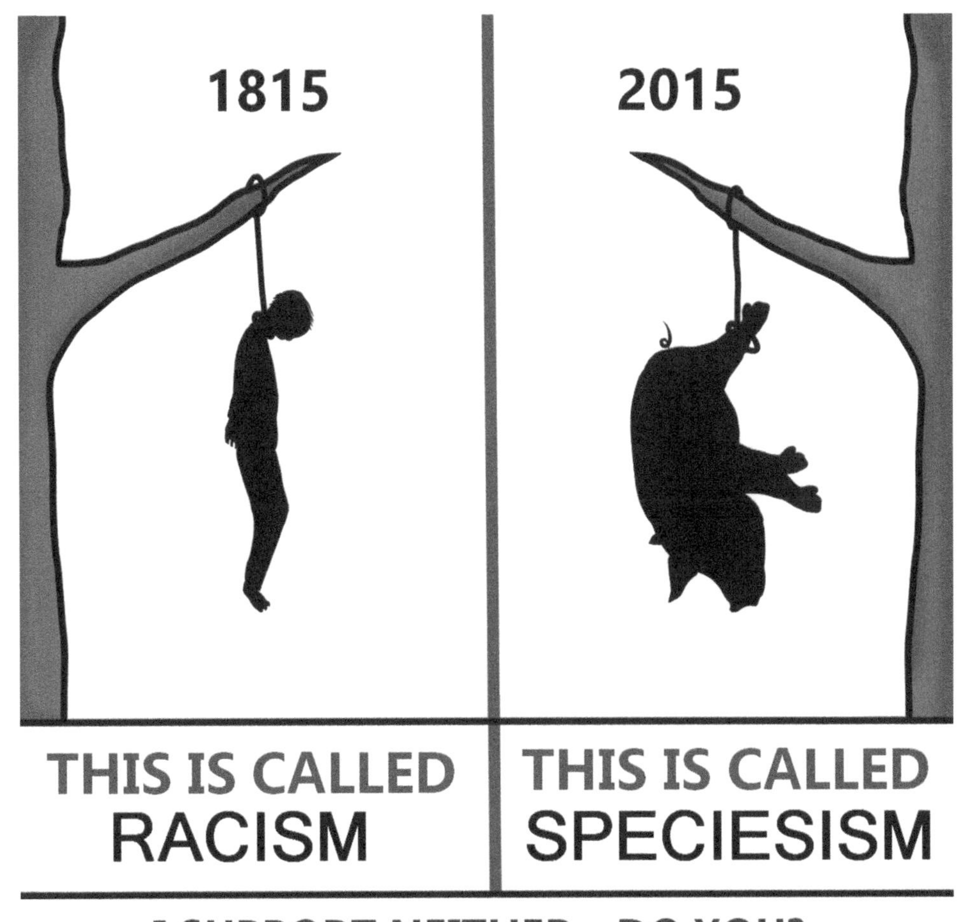

Figure 1.5 Vegan propaganda poster

Writing about the projected equivalence between racism and 'speciesism', Twitter user and blogger, Claire Heuchan, shares the poster (citing @veganoso Twitter account as the source) in her article condemning the use of "slavery as a tool to promote vegan values" (2015). Heuchan argued that such comparisons were akin to "vegan activists mak[ing] clear that vegan spaces are frequently racist spaces". The poster uses graphology to promote a relationship of semantic equivalence between two disparate practices to persuade non-vegans to go vegan or in Heuchan's terms, to "trigger a dietary epiphany". The division of the space into two equal parts sets up a parallel between the two images, the two dates, and the two concepts 'racism' and 'speciesism'. This nudges the reader to tease out a connection between them (regardless of whether or not it exists in reality). By making the perceived connection implicit through the graphological arrangement, the text producer relies on the reader picking up the inferential connection. After all, we are more likely to be persuaded by an argument we have helped construct than one that we have invested no time in formulating.

Syntax

This is the linguistic term for clause structure. A clause is an organisational unit of language that is made up of a subject and predicator. 'We write' is an example of a clause. The linear line that comprises most European modern languages, as well Southeast Asian, Indian, North American, and South American, is written from left to right, syntactically speaking. Syntax refers to the different structural slots occupied by language tokens such as nouns, adjectives, verbs, adverbs, and grammatical words like conjunctions and so on. Conventionally, these syntactic slots follow a conventional order, so a clause like 'the dog ate the bone' follows the conventional Subject-Predicator-Object pattern in English. Sometimes, the syntactic order switches, and we get constructions like that in Figure 1.6 'the bone, the dog ate'.

(a)

the dog	**ate**	**the bone**
Subject	Predicator	Object

(b)

the bone	**the dog**	**ate**
Object	Subject	Predicator

Figure 1.6 Conventional and unconventional syntax

Both constructions in Figure 1.6 mean the same thing. However, when we encounter construction (b), it seems to communicate more than simply its **propositional** meaning, which is the basic meaning of the clause relating to the entities involved and their relationship to each other (see Chapter 5). Indeed, it implies that the addressee already knows that the dog ate *something*, just not what it was. We explore syntactic ordering and its effects in Chapter 2.

Semantics

Semantics is the study of meaning. An important concept in semantics is denotation, or the thing, idea, action or concept that a word refers to. The denotive meaning of a word is sometimes called its primary, core or literal meaning. A word may have a set of possible denotive meanings one of which may be triggered by the surrounding co-text and/or the context in which a word is produced. So, returning to our sentence, 'the dog ate the bone', 'dog' refers to a domesticated canine animal, 'bone' refers to part of an animal skeleton and 'ate' refers ingesting (chewing and swallowing) food via the mouth. A word can also come with associated meanings, which are to do with the feelings or psychological connections a word (or the concept it refers to) evokes. For example, 'dog' is sometimes associated with concepts such as loyalty and devotion or companionship. Another aspect of meaning is literal and non-literal (figurative) meanings a word can have. For example, a person can be 'dogged' by bad luck, and you might need to 'bone up' before an exam. With these uses, 'dog' and 'bone' no longer refer to their primary meanings but to metaphorical meanings. In Chapter 5, we talk more about semantics including presuppositions and entailments, and in Chapter 8 we deal with figurative meaning.

Discourse

This brings us back to where we started this chapter – discourse. We defined discourse as 'language in use'. It concerns meaning above the level of the clause and sentence (syntax). This sentence is a piece of discourse. This book is a bigger piece of discourse characterised by academic writing, with an instructional purpose, with a high percentage of domain-specific lexis (the phrase 'domain-specific lexis' being a case in point). In fact, we are actively trying to avoid an overly academic register, and so we hope that this chapter and the rest of this book is NOT characterised by long, embedded sentences, passive structures, third-person pronouns, and lots of what are known as 'logical operators' (Sinclair 2004: 7), which include, for example, 'therefore', 'so', and 'consequently'. (Okay, apart from that overly long embedded sentence.) Our purpose is to inform, not impress. We failed at the latter long ago.

Text

When we analyse discourse, we inevitably study texts because, as Halliday and Matthiessen (2014: 3) point out, "[w]hen people speak or write, they produce text". Halliday and Matthiessen (2014: 3) go on to define text as "any instance of language, in any medium, that makes sense to someone who knows the language". Text, then, is a single language artefact or "unit of language" that can be spoken, written, signed or otherwise (e.g. image) that is defined by "meaning" (i.e. it makes sense to someone) rather than "form" (i.e. there are no formal restrictions on what counts as a text) (Halliday and Hasan 1976: 1–2). Texts in written form are the typical object of analysis for discourse analysts, which means to study and analyse spoken and signed texts, we must record them in some way and create written transcriptions to allow repeated scrutiny. Audio and video recordings can also be analysed using special software, such as *Praat* (Boersma and Weenink 2023; 'praat' means 'speak' in Dutch), but this is not something we will deal with in this book. Text, then, is the object of study but, as Bloor and Bloor (2013: 8) point out, as discourse analysts we must also appreciate that language is used within a particular context and texts emerge from **language events**.

Language event is a general term often used (but less often defined) by linguists ('speech event' and 'communicative event' are also sometimes used). A language event is any event where language has a fundamental role or any event where language happens. For example, chatting to a friend is a language event; it is difficult to chat without using language (in whatever form it might take). Giving a speech is a language event because it would be very difficult to give a speech without using any language. Going for a run, however, is not a language event

Activity 1.2 HAVE YOU SHEETED?

Consider the example in Figure 1.7, which is a photograph of a real sign board situated somewhere in the UK. Think about the words on the sign and consider their meaning in combination. Do you understand the meaning (or message) that the sign is aiming to convey? What do you need to know to understand the sign? Have you ever sheeted?

Answer these questions before reading on.

Figure 1.7 HAVE YOU SHEETED?

because it does not require language, just working legs, fitness, and a certain amount of willpower. Language events might well occur during a run though. If you run with a friend, you might chat (in which case, kudos), or if you get lost you might stop to ask someone for directions.

A discourse can involve one or more texts and, importantly, other factors including the producer and intended receiver of the text, the location and date of production, and purpose. Essentially, discourse is text and context. When we do discourse analysis, we combine detailed linguistic analyses of formal features of text(s) with an examination of context. By considering both language and its context of use we can gain a greater understanding of how meaning is communicated in everyday settings. To illustrate this point, try Activity 1.2.

'HAVE YOU SHEETED?' – discussion

This text forms part of a discourse. Indeed, to understand the text, we need to know about the discourse it is part of. Moreover, we need to understand something about the **context** in which the discourse occurs (we discuss context in more detail later in this chapter). This text is printed on a sign at the exit of a quarry in the north of England. The sign, which is made up of white words on a blue background with a white border, contains a single sentence in the form of an interrogative. It is asking whether the intended recipient of the text has done something. However, the text might not make much sense, or communicate very much to readers who are not the intended recipients. It is probably the word 'sheeted' that is hard to understand because it might not be clear what action it refers to. The sign uses the word 'sheet' as a verb, but what is 'to sheet' and what does it mean in this context? Quite simply, it means to cover the back of tipper-trucks that leave the quarry fully loaded with gravel with a tarpaulin sheet.[3] The sheet is stretched taut over the back of the trucks to keep the gravel in the hopper. Sheeting is therefore an important safety measure that all truck drivers should do before they drive out of the quarry and on to the public highway.

Notice that the text is an interrogative and as such it asks a question probably on the behalf of the quarry owners. However, the question is not intended to elicit a verbal response from the truck driver. That is, the truck driver is not meant to go and find the quarry owner and reply: 'yes, I have sheeted'/'no I have not sheeted'. Instead, the interrogative **functions** as a reminder for the driver leaving the quarry with a fully loaded truck to pause and check that their truck is sheeted. The presence of the sign at the quarry exit might be because in the past some drivers left the quarry without sheeting and this caused a problem, or that there is a legal obligation on the quarry to remind drivers to sheet. Whatever the reasons that led to the placing of the sign, it is a text that is part of a discourse between quarry owner and driver, and to understand the text we need an appreciation of the context and the place the sign takes in the discourse.

Discourse communities

The positioning of the text at a quarry exit and its lexically specific terminology might have led you to conclude, correctly, that it is directed towards a particular group of people (quarry workers/truck drivers) who know what it means 'to sheet'. Such groups of people are known as a **discourse communities** (Swales 1988) because members participate in and communicate through similar textual practices such as specialist lexis (e.g. 'sheeting'), and pragmatic meanings (e.g. 'reviewer 2' in academia).[4] Although some scholars argue that discourse communities share common goals or are "unified by a common focus" (Porter 1992), this is slightly misleading because there are many examples of discourse communities (e.g in academia or government) where people frequently have different goals and are often not unified! We can, of course, be members of many different discourse communities, which means we adopt different language practices depending on which community we are interacting with (and therefore part of) at any particular time.

Meaning potential

The example in Figure 1.7 serves to demonstrate that as discourse analysts, we are interested in how people use language in different settings to make meaning. Indeed, meaning-making and meaning potential[5] (Allwood 2003) is a topic we will deal with in some detail over the course of this book. The example helps to show that **context** is crucial to the notion of discourse and its analysis. The aim of our next section, therefore, is to understand better what we mean by context and how we can incorporate it into discourse analysis.

Understanding context

Language – and, by extension, meaning – does not exist in a vacuum. Language is used by people in different locations, at different times, involves different participants and is used for different purposes. In short, language occurs in different **contexts**. Context refers to the various situational parameters that coincide with language and which work together with language to create meaning. Language and context are inseparable components in meaning making. J. R. Firth (a key figure in linguistics) made the following observation about the importance of context: 'meaning' is to do with "the function of a complete locution in the context of situation, or typical context of situation" (Firth 1935: 72). In other words, the intrinsic meaning of an utterance (i.e. locution) only means what it means in relation to its context.

Brown and Yule (1983) discuss context at considerable length and in this section, we summarise some of their main points. Citing Hymes (1962) and Lewis (1972), they set out several situational parameters that help to delimit context. These parameters can be thought of as answers to a set of questions that we can ask about the discourse under analysis.

What is happening?
This question concerns the **activity** or **event** that the discourse is part of. The answer might be, for example, a conversation with a friend, a university lecture, an advertisement, a political speech, a celebrity interview.

Where is it happening?
The **location** of the discourse can be an important contextual factor and includes, for example, the geographic location (e.g. country, town, street), the building or physical space (e.g. university lecture theatre, conference hall, television studio), or the virtual space (e.g. Snapchat, TikTok, Instagram).

When is it happening?
This question concerns the **time** of the discourse: hour, minute, second, year, month, day.

What is being talked about?
This question refers to the **topic** of the discourse: medicine, shampoo, state health provision, 'my latest movie'.

What job is the language doing?
The **purpose** of the discourse: e.g. teaching, informing, selling, persuading, entertaining.

Who is involved?
The people or **participants** involved: the addressor/speaker/producer, addressee/hearer/receiver, and any observers or overhearers (audience). Also, the social relationship between participants (e.g. friends, family, colleagues), and power relations (is one participant more institutionally powerful?) e.g. lecturer and students, advertisers and social media users, politician and delegates, interviewer, interviewee and audience.

How is it happening?
This question considers the **mode** of the discourse – whether it is spoken (produced orally by vocal cords and received aurally by ears), written (produced graphically and received visually), or signed (produced gesturally and received visually) or a combination (multimodal). The question also includes the means of conveyance, or the **medium** of communication (e.g. phone message, email, webpage, print). There might not be any media involved, of course, such as with face-to-face communication.

A further possible consideration relating to how the discourse is happening is whether spoken or signed discourse is happening spontaneously or involves some level of planning. For example, political speeches are typically carefully prepared and written out prior to their delivery whereas naturally occurring conversations tend to be unplanned and spontaneous.

Examples of how discourse is happening include: face-to-face spoken conversation, spoken telephone conversation, video lecture via (say) Zoom or

Microsoft Teams, printed handouts, slides projected on-screen, on-screen advert with words and pictures, speaking from a script, participating in a face-to-face spoken Q&A, participating in an online written Q&A.

Which language (variant) is being used?

For this aspect of context, Hymes (1962) uses the term **code**, which includes language varieties and dialects such as, for example, American English, Haitian Creole, British Sign Language, Hiberno-English, Yorkshire dialect.

These questions and their answers help to pin down contextual factors that are potentially important for meaning making. For example, different contextual factors influence our language choices including the words we use (lexis), the way we say them (phonology) and the way we arrange them (syntax). These choices, which are made both consciously and subconsciously, help to tailor our language according to what it is being used for, where it is being used, who is involved, and how the communication is being mediated. Context is also important because it influences our understanding of language.

Expanding context (the role of background knowledge)

Consider this language event based on the experience of one of the authors, whom we will refer to in the third person as person B.

> On Wednesday 18 May 2022, at 06:45, B embarked on a train journey from Inverness to Edinburgh (both in Scotland). B travelled alone and sat at one end of a carriage. There were other people in the carriage. In particular, there were four people travelling together who were sat at the opposite end of carriage being very loud. Two were wearing bright orange sunhats (which is quite unusual for Scotland). The conductor of the train entered the carriage to check people's tickets. He spoke to the four loud people and then came to the end of the carriage where B was sat and addressed the people sat there. The conductor said that he had asked the loud people not to be too loud; to let him (the conductor) know if they got too rowdy; and that the train was quite empty so people could move to another quieter carriage if they wished. The conductor finished by saying: "Oh dear. I feel sorry for Seville."
>
> B was confused. What did he mean by that? Clearly, B was lacking essential information which the conductor seemed to be assuming his hearers shared. B asked his close friend, Professor Google, for help and soon all became clear. He simply typed in 'seville' on Google search on his telephone, and the first result was a news story headline: "Rangers in Seville: Police say 100,000 fans expected".

All became clear: "Oh dear, I feel sorry for Seville" was said in the context of the 2022 UEFA Europa cup final that was to be played in Seville on the evening of Wednesday 18 May 2022 between German club, Eintracht Frankfurt, and (importantly) Scottish football club, Rangers. This was a Big Deal for Rangers fans (apparently) and more generally for Scottish football, and Scotland. B is not a football fan and is not Scottish – a perfect storm for non-understanding in this context. However, once B had this important missing piece in the discourse jigsaw, he understood that the loud people were Rangers fans and the significance of their orange hats (Rangers are strongly associated with the colour orange). Notice though that the search for meaning had to go beyond the local context (location, time, participants, mode, purpose) of the train. The sentence was uttered in a national and international context that relied on shared knowledge outside the carriage of the train. In this instance, B did not share the knowledge of the football **discourse community** ordinarily required to enable him to correctly interpret the reference to Seville.

Context and relevance

One issue with context that Brown and Yule (1983) highlight is how analysts (and indeed language users) narrow down the particular contextual factors that are important for understanding discourse. For relevance theorists (see, for example, Sperber and Wilson 1986; Clark 2013) this issue is addressed by the notion of – yes, you've guessed it – 'relevance' and the crucial role it plays in constraining contextual factors and analysing discourse. Relevance theory posits that we make sense of discourse largely through adhering to a principle of local interpretation, which basically means that we only use what is relevant in the discourse situation to derive meaning. Where local interpretation is insufficient (as we saw in the train example above), we might need to draw on a wider context to fill gaps in local knowledge. So, we may use our own background knowledge in determining what is meant. We also draw on our experience of discourse in different situations that develops over time and use that to delineate basic patterns in discourse, which help us make sense of interactions.

Co-text

Co-text is a specific type of context that is not covered by any of the questions set out above. It refers to the immediate linguistic environment of an utterance and concerns how the meaning of a particular unit of discourse (word, phrase, sentence, utterance) is influenced by the rest of the discourse. Co-text constrains or influences meaning of lexical items and is particularly important for the interpretation of utterances in time and space. The following sentences relate to the football event we mentioned above. Consider the meanings of the words 'teams' and 'goal' in the following invented sentences.

(i) Football fans arrive in Seville to support their teams.
(ii) Seville's citizen security commissioner, Juan Carlos Castro Estevez, set his teams the goal of calmly dealing with any problems that might emerge.

(iii) Joe Aribo scored a goal in the 57th minute putting Rangers ahead.
(iv) Rangers did not achieve their goal of winning the Europa League cup.

Hopefully, you will have noticed that 'teams' and 'goal' refer to different things in the sentences above. In (i) the word 'teams' refers to 'football teams', and we reach that conclusion because of the mention of 'football fans' at the start of the sentence. In (ii) however, 'teams' refers to 'security teams' rather than 'football teams' and we reach that conclusion because these are the teams of Seville's security commissioner. The pronoun 'his' in front of 'teams' references the security commissioner (see Chapter 3 for more on reference) and signals belonging. It would make no sense for multiple football teams to belong to the commissioner; the logical conclusion therefore is that he has within his control some other sorts of teams relating to security. Similarly, the word 'goal' in (ii) does not refer to getting a ball between two posts; rather, it means 'objectives' or 'desired outcomes'. However, in (iii), the co-occurrence of 'scored', '57th minute' and 'Rangers' leads us to read 'goal' as the 'getting-the-ball-into-the-net' type. Additionally, if you know the names of the people playing for football teams, then 'Joe Aribo' might also be a clue. In (iv), however, we understand 'goal' to mean 'objective' once again, and this is because of its co-occurrence with the verb 'achieve' and its post-modification by the prepositional phrase 'of winning the Europa League cup', which identifies the goal. We can see then that the words 'teams' and 'goal' have different meanings in the sentences and co-text helps us to discern those meanings.

Spoken and written discourse

Discourse is often divided into two **modes** – either spoken or written – or a combination of both (i.e. multimodal). The spoken/written division characterises our ability to physically produce language either orally using our vocal cords[6] or, with the right tools and materials, graphically. With the latter, combinations of symbols (graphemes) convey meaning by representing the sounds of language visually (a system referred to as orthography). Signs and symbols convey meaning in language systems, including pictures. Additionally, we can communicate visually using gestures and facial expressions, both of which are crucial for sign languages.

The spoken/written division also marks other important differences. For instance, we learn to speak before we write and, certainly, human beings evolved to speak first. We are able to acquire spoken language through exposure to speech, but we must be instructed on how to read and write. Naturally occurring speech is produced dynamically and spontaneously and when in conversation, we must listen and comprehend and plan our next turn. We cannot look back at what was said earlier, we cannot flick forward to see what is coming up and we cannot backspace or delete because we produce and transmit simultaneously – the words are out there as soon as we have said them. Unless recorded in some way, they exist only in the moment they are produced, disappearing as soon as the air molecules set in motion by our vocal cords cease to vibrate, surviving only in the (imperfect and limited) memories of the discourse participants.

Following Miller and Weinert (1998), we can summarise the features of unplanned, spontaneous spoken language as follows:

- produced in real time, so without any planning and without editing;
- typically face-to face communication, so production and reception synchronous with interlocutor;
- involves changes in voice pitch, amplitude (loudness), rhythm, speed of delivery, shortening/lengthening of words and voice quality;
- also involves gestures, gaze, facial expressions, and body posture;
- influenced by the limitations of our short-term memory.

(Adapted from Miller and Weinert 1998: 22–23)

According to Miller and Weinert (1998), these features of speech production set out above result in:

- information being produced in small chunks;
- low information density; for example, short phrases;
- a limited range of vocabulary and lexical repetition;
- simple embedding of clauses, one after another;
- interactive markers, back channels, fillers, discourse markers (see below);
- grammatically incomplete utterances;
- constructions and organisational features that are particular to unplanned speech.

(Adapted from Miller and Weinert 1998: 22–23)

In contrast to (non-recorded) spoken discourse, written discourse is not transient; its production immediately creates a record which can be referred to (albeit not indefinitely). For this reason, written discourse is traditionally the object of study, and the point of reference on which grammars of English are written and against which spoken language is compared. If we wish to study spoken discourse, we must first record it and then transcribe it into written form (see Chapter 4).

There are marked differences between spoken and written discourse. Consider the following made-up examples A and B below which contain phonological markers (explained below).

A. So (.) I says to °her° eh, like, are YOU g-gonna, like, pick me up this avo or what like?

B. So I said to her, "are you going to pick me up this afternoon or not?"

It's not difficult to tell which is which. The first example (A) shows characteristic markers of spoken discourse including false starts (g-gonna), pauses which are signalled with a standard notation of parenthesis with a period in between (.), non-standard contractions ('avo' for 'afternoon'), fillers (a type of discourse marker) ('eh' and 'like'), emphasis (YOU) and quiet pitch signalled by degree signs (°her°), all of which can all be marked in written format using transcription notations (see Chapter 4). In contrast, the written version (B) contains standard English grammar and lexis. None of the prosodic features apparent in A are discernible in B.

Discourse markers

One of the defining features of spoken communication, and which are present in the above speech example, is the use of fillers or '**discourse markers**' (Schiffrin 1987; McCarthy 2004) such as 'er' and 'um' or 'so', 'right', 'yeah'. Although such lexical items may not carry much semantic meaning, they serve the **pragmatic** function of showing our addressee or interlocutor that we are, in fact, listening to them (we deal with pragmatics in Chapters 6 and 7). The linguistic term for this is 'backchannelling' and these little markers are more broadly understood as a type of language that is used to maintain social connection (known as 'phatic communion', Malinowski 1923). Next time you are chatting with a friend on the phone try not to 'backchannel' and see how quickly your interlocutor asks 'Are you still there?'

Standard English (or the issue of convention)

Earlier we introduced the notion of a 'standard' form when it comes to thinking about a language. In written, spoken, and multimodal texts, linguistic behaviour is varied and ranges from strict adherence to conventional grammatical and lexical forms, to non-conventional grammar and lexis that incorporates vernacular forms, dialectal markers and, in recent years, emoji, gifs, memes, and more. The choices we make are context-dependent. This raises the issue of a reference point in terms of which form of a language is considered the 'norm' or 'standard' against which different variants of that language are assessed. That is to say, what do we mean by 'standard form'? When we speak, we often use language that suits the discourse situation we are in. For example, suppose you are giving a talk in class for one of your courses. You are likely to be more aware of the 'correct' forms of pronunciation and strive to adhere to the 'rules' of language in front of an audience, particularly one that may be judging your intelligence! Therefore, you might make more effort to enunciate your words.

The issue over what counts as 'standard' is typically one of **prestige** masquerading as 'correctness'. The advent of print in the 1400s meant that (English) language producers needed linguistic uniformity or a standard form of the language in order to decode written texts. The area of England that was chosen as the 'standard' form was the southeast of England, named 'Estuary English' after the river Thames and its estuary. 'Estuary English' was adopted as the new 'normal' as far as language was concerned. The reason for this geographical variant was simply that London and the surrounding area was the location of the courts, the government, and other socially and politically important institutions, and garnered prestige based solely on this connection to its learned users. The standardisation process took years of elaboration and implementation but once codified, the notion of a normative standard variant stuck (Haugen 1972). Estuary English involved pronunciation that is now known as 'Received Pronunciation' ('RP'), which we introduced earlier in the chapter. More colloquially, RP referred to as 'BBC' or 'Queen's English' (or now King's), but in reality, not many people talk like that.

In casual conversation, which is less rule-governed, adherence to Standard English (SE) is less expected and non-standard forms abound. For instance, take the use of '-ing' in spoken words like 'having', we may well shift from a voiced velar nasal [ŋ] to a voiced alveolar nasal [n] and say, for example, 'havin' [hævɪn]. The social situation you are in might encourage you to use more non-standard forms as a way of socially bonding to the people with whom you are interacting (this is known in linguistics as '**covert prestige**'). In such interactions we may use more slang terms, or omit grammatical elements, include expletives, and so on. Here is a complete spoken exchange between two English speakers who come from the same family:

> A: Lift'll be in five minutes, K?
> B: Are you ACTUALLY?

The second speaker (B) appears to have asked an unfinished question, but the utterance is complete as B's intention is to convey surprise at the timing of the 'lift' in A's message. Note also that A uses non-standard grammar by omitting some elements of the message. If it were SE, it would read '**Our/Your/The** lift **will** be **here** in five minutes, **O**K?' (bold elements are omitted in the actual example).

Social attitudes underpin linguistic notions of prestige. Activity 1.3 asks you to consider the ideological or attitudinal responses to how people use language in certain situations and whether you consider their version of the language to be appropriate (or not) in the context.

Activity 1.3 G-droppin'

To get a sense of how ingrained rules about standardisation are and the social snobbery that exists among prescriptivists and language pedants in the UK, consider the criticisms levelled at Priti Patel (the UK Home Secretary in the early part of 2022) on a popular internet forum, mumsnet, because of her 'G-dropping' (conventionally known as '-ing dropping') during national briefings and interviews (or should that be 'briefins and interviews'?). You can find the thread here, https://www.mumsnet.com/Talk/pedants_corner/2077339-Priti-Patel-and-her-dropped-Gs, or use QR code 1.3).

QR 1.3 Link to G-droppin' discussion on mumsnet

To give you a flavour of what is written on the forum, here are a few isolated comments from the 'reviews' of Patel's speech: "intensely irritatin'", "absolutely awful", "Gordon Bennett!",[7] "causing me much stress", "idiot".

Do you think these criticisms of Patel's linguistic behaviour are justified? If so, why? On what linguistic grounds? What might your response say about your own attitudes to language variants? Our discussion below will help you to think about how you might answer some of these questions.

Having considered Patel's speech style, you might be interested to know that popular British television presenter, Alex Scott, was criticised on Twitter in 2021 by businessman and politician Digby Marritt Jones for habitually using the same non-standard form in her broadcasts of the Tokyo 2020 Olympic games. Jones bemoaned that Scott's -ing-dropping (more specifically, /ŋ/) "ruins the Olympics" and further claimed – incorrectly – that -ing dropping was "wrong".[8] Simply put, 'correct' language is synonymous with SE or the standard variant of a given language. This 'correct' variant is the one that is used in official situations or situations where conventions dictate that the language matches the agreed standard. It will be characterised by strict adherence to standard grammatical structures and lexis. It is important to note that what counts as standard can vary geographically. Indeed, if we consider English, we would be more correct to think about different Englishes based on their geographical location: British English, American English, Australian English, Indian English, Hiberno-English, for example. Informal language usually includes some non-standard forms and is what we use in everyday situations where social conventions do not dictate that we adhere to the standard forms.

Sociolinguistic variables

While SE may garner more prestige on the whole than non-Standard variants, there are times when the latter is preferred. Therefore, different sociolinguistic variables (also known as situational factors) influence linguistic choices. **Interpersonal distance**, for example, can be a motivating factor in the decision to use non-standard or standard forms. For instance, you might say 'gimme me that book' to your mate, but 'would you mind handing me that book' to a stranger or a more socially powerful interactant (see Chapter 7).

To offer another example, if you are chatting to friends over a messaging forum such as WhatsApp, your linguistic choices are likely to reflect, among other things, the equal nature of your social relationship including your relative social proximity, your generational status, and very likely your current mood. This might be manifested linguistically via responses such as 'K' for 'okay' or acronyms with multiple punctuation marks such as 'WTF??!!!', and orthographic duplication, e.g. 'see yaaaaaaa' or 'niiiiiiiice', or misspellings like 'noice' for 'nice'. Non-Standard examples like these would be well-received by your friends and indicate a high degree of familiarity between you and them. However, email messages to, say, your teacher are likely to adopt standard forms and be much less familiar; after all your teacher would probably not take kindly to being addressed: 'hiiiiiii P-Dawg'. This is because the **power** relations between friends and peers are usually equally distributed, whereas between you and your teacher they are asymmetrical, and this has an impact on what is conventionally expected in interactions (we return to this in Chapter 7). In messages to your friends, **politeness** markers like 'thanks', non-standard **lexis**, like 'gimme', or even the length or share of the conversational '**turns**' (see Chapter 4) need not be so important because, to use a term from sociology, you are on an equal **footing**. However, you are not on an equal footing with your teachers and so politeness will be more important (student readers please take note!) as will standard lexis. So, instead of saying 'gimme (more time to complete my essay)' you might opt for the more standard form 'give me' when communicating with your teacher.

Age is another sociolinguistic variable that impacts how we communicate. Your lexis may also show generational differences, so 'spill the tea', 'boomer', or 'woke' may mean very different things to a much older teacher than to your fellow students (unless, of course, your teacher is woke). And as one of our own students taught us, even micro-features such as punctuation can carry social or contextual (**pragmatic**) meaning as well as grammatical meaning. One of us gave lengthy positive feedback to a student during a face-to-face tutor meeting where they thought they had not done so well in their other classes. Their misunderstanding was fuelled by another teacher's answer to an online question on how they were progressing in that teacher's course. The teacher had answered (positively) with the following:

> Fine.

The student was horrified. When asked why, their response was 'because it says "Fine PERIOD"!' Clearly, the presence of a period (full stop) at the end of a message shows that the sentence has been completed (grammatically speaking), yet pragmatically, it can signal displeasure or anger, depending on the context (we return to the punctuated period in Chapter 6). For what it's worth, this was not the intended meaning! The student was indeed fine (no period needed).

Professional occupation is yet another sociolinguistic variable that can determine what language choices we make. Where we work can determine what way we use language. Profession-specific lexis, such as 'sheeted' in Activity 1.2, is one such example. Some socioeconomic domains are more likely to adhere to a standard form of the language than others. For example, university and educational websites are likely to use standard forms because the social and cultural context demands greater adherence to standard linguistic conventions, not least so that they are uniformly understood by most people in a wide geographical area. Because there is also a higher level of social value or **prestige** attached to the standard form, its use in education is advocated over non-standard or slang forms. So much so, that some schools and educational organisations have taken to a form of language policing, proscribing what students can and cannot say. One example is the policy (or should that be 'policing') of preferred and dis-preferred language choices at Ark All Saints Academy, a high school in southeast London which was the subject of a feature in the *Guardian* newspaper in the UK (Booth 2021) for proscribing its students' language choices. The school banned such phrases as 'he cut his eyes at me', which means 'throwing a bit of shade' and 'giving side-eye' (for the Boomers, this roughly translates as dismissing a person by lowering the eyes and turning the head to the side).

Conclusion

In this chapter, we have touched on some of the important elements of discourse analysis in everyday examples of communication. We have shown how the discourse situation can impact on the language used, its meaning, and its **meaning potential**. We also introduced the idea that what works in one discourse situation does not always work in another and that part of our linguistic competence is knowing when to use what and with whom. We also highlighted some of the differences and commonalities between spoken and written discourse and acknowledged that the boundaries between both modes are not so absolute, as our WhatsApp example showed.

Throughout this book we will highlight the key fact: **language is choice**. When we choose to say something in a particular way, we are choosing from a varied, socially, ideologically, and politically inflected set of possible words and grammatical structures to say it. Such choices are not always consciously made, but nonetheless we have access to several ways of saying something, and how we say it is governed by what we know about the world, our social expectations, and so on, all of which motivates those selections. This knowledge of the world includes knowledge of interpersonal relationships (e.g. friend vs teacher), age, and the discourse context. As we will show in upcoming chapters, power relationships also have a lot to do with how and why we make such choices. It is the remit of discourse analysis to tease out these relationships between language and choice and to explore to what extent, and to what effect the factors noted above shape discourse, and how discourse can shape our knowledge of the world.

The remaining chapters present a toolkit for analysis that incorporates relevant theories and methodological frameworks from linguistics that are instrumental for analysing discourse. To help you practice discourse analysis, there will be activities and tasks that explore the concepts, models, and frameworks we introduce. Answers to activities will be either in the text immediately following the activity or at the end of the chapter.

Notes

1 Cummings's poems usually don't have titles, so the first line of the poem often becomes the proxy title.
2 We're not actually sure what 'meta' means in this context – we'd need to ask Mark Zuckerberg.
3 Thanks to Simon Garner of Hanson Aggregates for confirming the meaning of the sign and giving us permission to use it as an example.
4 The phrase 'reviewer 2' sends fear through the bones of academics. When submitting an article or other academic publication for review prior to it being accepted for publication, the author usually receives two 'blind' and anonymous reviews from academics. Think of this like 'good cop, bad cop'. One will invariably be constructive and kind (known affectionately as 'reviewer 1') whereas the other will trash the fruits of your hard labour, destroy any hope or self-worth left in your fragile ego-trodden soul, making you question your very existence in your academic discourse community. Hello, reviewer 2.
5 While we prefer Allwood's term 'meaning potential', Croft and Cruse (2004) use the term 'purport' but this sounds like somewhere you'd park your cat.
6 Also referred to as vocal folds.
7 Gordon Bennett is a phrased commonly used instead of a curse in some discourse communities.
8 In fact, he called it 'g' dropping. The correct term is '-ing dropping'. Jones is not a linguist. You might be interested in Peter Trudgill's (2021) piece on this specific example. Peter Trudgill is a linguist.

Further reading

Leech, Deuchar, and Hoogenraad (2006) provide an accessible introduction to the model of grammar we use in this book.

For more on J. R. Firth, see Chapman and Routledge (2005: 80–86).

For more on language policing, see Cushing (2020) and Lampropoulou and Cooper (2021).

Clark (2013) is a good place to find out more about relevance theory.

Nørgaard (2010) provides a useful introduction to graphological analysis of texts.

For an analysis of forensic discourse through relevance theory, see Lynn and Canning (2021).

Resources

International Phonetic Alphabet with sounds: https://www.internationalphoneticalphabet.org/ipa-sounds/ipa-chart-with-sounds

References

Allwood, J. (2003) 'Meaning potential and context. Some consequences for the analysis of variation in meaning'. In H. Cuyckens, R. Dirven, and J. Taylor (eds), *Cognitive approaches to lexical semantics*, pp. 29–65. Berlin: Mouton de Gruyter.

Bloor, T. and Bloor, M. (2013) *The functional analysis of English: A Hallidayan approach*. London: Routledge.

Boersma, P. and Weenink, D. (2023) *Praat: Doing phonetics by computer* [Computer program]. Version 6.3.06. Accessed 31 January 2023. http://www.praat.org/

Booth, R. (2021) 'Oh my days: linguists lament slang ban in London school', *Guardian*, 30 September. Accessed 30 September 2021. https://www.theguardian.com/education/2021/sep/30/oh-my-days-linguists-lament-slang-ban-in-london-school?CMP=Share_iOSApp_Other

Brown, G. and Yule, G. (1983) *Discourse analysis*. Cambridge: Cambridge University Press.

Carroll, L. (2001) [1871]. 'Jabberwocky', *Jabberwocky and other poems*. Dover Thrift Edition. New York: Dover.

Chapman, S. and Routledge, P. (eds) (2005) *Key thinkers in linguistics and the philosophy of language*. Edinburgh: Edinburgh University Press.

Clark, B. (2013) *Relevance theory*. Cambridge: Cambridge University Press.

Croft, W. and Cruse, D. A. (2004) *Cognitive linguistics*. Cambridge: Cambridge University Press.

Cruttenden, A. (2001) *Gimson's pronunciation of English* (6th edition). London: Edward Arnold.

Crystal, D. (1995) *The Cambridge encyclopedia of the English language*. Cambridge: Cambridge University Press.

Cushing, I. (2020) 'The policy and policing of language in schools'. *Language in Society*, 49(3): 425–450.

'Discourse' (1989) *The Oxford English dictionary* (2nd edition) OED Online. Oxford University Press. Accessed 30 April 2020. http://dictionary.oed.com

Estepa, J. (2017) 'Sean Spicer says "covfefe" wasn't a typo: Trump knew "exactly what he meant"', *USA News Today*. Accessed 3 June 2022. https://eu.usatoday.com/story/news/politics/onpolitics/2017/05/31/sean-spicer-says-covfefe-wasnt-typo-trump-knew-exactly-what-he-meant/102355728

Firth, J. R. (1935) 'The technique of semantics'. *Transactions of the Philological Society*, 34(1): 36–73.

Freeborn, D. (1995) *A course book on English grammar* (2nd edition). Basingstoke and New York: Palgrave.

Halliday, M. A. K. and Hasan, R. (1976) *Cohesion in English*. London: Longman.

Halliday, M. A. K. and Matthiessen, C. (2014) *An introduction to functional grammar* (4th edition). London: Routledge.

Haugen, E. (1972) [1966]. 'Dialect, language, nation'. In J. B. Pride and J. Holmes (eds), *Sociolinguistic*, pp. 97–111. Harmondsworth: Penguin. (Originally published in *American Anthropologist*, 68: 922–935.)

Heuchan, Claire (2015) 'Veganism has a serious race problem'. *Media Diversified*. Accessed 22 October 2021. https://mediadiversified.org/2015/12/16/veganism-has-a-serious-race-problem

Hymes, D. (1962) 'The ethnography of speaking'. In Thomas Gladwin and William C. Sturtevant (eds), *Anthropology and human behavior*, pp. 13–53. Washington, DC: Anthropological Society of Washington.

Lampropoulou, S. and Cooper, P. (2021) 'The "grammar school pressure": From tolerance to distance, to rejection of "Scouse" in middle-class Merseyside schools'. *Linguistics and Education*, 66: 1–13.

Leech, G., Deuchar, M., and Hoogenraad, R. (2006) *English grammar for today* (2nd edition). Basingstoke: Palgrave.

Lewis, D. (1972) 'General semantics'. In D. Davidson and G. H. Harman, *Semantics of natural language,* pp. 169–218. Dordrecht: Reidel.

Lynn, N. and Canning, P. (2021) 'Additions, omissions, and transformations in institutional "retellings" of domestic violence'. *Language and Law/ Linguagem e Direito,* 8(1): 76–96.

Malinowski, B. (1923) 'The problem of meaning in primitive language'. In C. K. Ogden and I. A. Richards (eds), *The meaning of meaning*, pp. 296–336. London: K. Paul, Trend, Trubner.

McCarthy, M. (2004) 'Spoken discourse markers in written text'. In G. Fox, M. Hoey, and J. M. Sinclair, *Techniques of description: Spoken and written discourse*, pp. 186–198. Abingdon: Routledge.

Miller, J. and Weinert, R. (1998) *Spontaneous spoken language: Syntax and discourse*. Oxford: Oxford University Press.

Nørgaard, N. (2010) 'Multimodality: Extending the stylistic tool kit'. In D. McIntyre and B. Busse (eds), *Language and style*, pp. 433–448. Basingstoke and New York: Palgrave Macmillan.

Porter, J. (1992) *Audience and rhetoric: An archaeological composition of the discourse community*. Englewood Cliffs, NJ: Prentice Hall.

Schiffrin, D. (1987) *Discourse markers* (No. 5). Cambridge: Cambridge University Press.

Simpson, P. and Mayr, A. (2009) *Language and power: A resource book for students*. London: Routledge.

Sinclair, J. M. (2004) 'Written discourse structure'. In G. Fox, M. Hoey, and J. M. Sinclair (eds), *Techniques of description: Spoken and written discourse*, pp. 22–47. Abingdon: Routledge.

Sperber, D. and Wilson, D. (1986) *Relevance: Communication and cognition*. Oxford: Blackwell Press.

Stubbs, M. (1983) *Discourse analysis: The sociolinguistic analysis of natural language*. Chicago: University of Chicago Press.

Swales, J. (1988) 'Discourse communities, genres and English as an international language'. *World Englishes*, 7(2): 211–220.

Trudgill, P. (2021) 'Digby Jones' attack on Alex Scott's accent wasn't just snobbish, it was wrong'. *The New European*. Accessed 29 September 2021. https://www.theneweuropean.co.uk/digby-jones-attack-on-alex-scotts-accent-wasnt-just-snobbish-it-was-wrong

van Dijk, T. A. (1997) *Discourse as social interaction* (Vol. 2). London: Sage.

2 Organising discourse

Thematic and information structure

Introduction

An important aspect of discourse analysis is considering how we structure the information we are communicating when we speak and write. This might be at the clausal level or at a broader, macro-level beyond the clause. In this chapter, we discuss the organisation of information in the clause because the way the clause is structured inevitably "fits in with and contributes to the flow of the discourse" (Halliday and Matthiessen 2014: 88). One of the functions of the clause is to convey information, or 'message' (Halliday and Matthiessen 2014). The way information is organised in clauses is constrained by the grammar of a language but there is nonetheless some freedom within the grammar that allows the text producer room for choice. These choices influence how information is organised, how it is received, and the meaning that is conveyed. For example, different syntactic structures can emphasise (and de-emphasise) different clausal elements and focus our attention on specific parts of the message. It is these and other choices and their (potential) effects that are of interest to the discourse analyst. In this chapter, we will discuss information structure using ideas from Systemic Functional Linguistics: Theme and Rheme, and Given and New.

Organising discourse

Typically, when we communicate, whether in speech or in writing, we try to organise what we say in a way that helps the other person (the reader/hearer) understand. Indeed, we sometimes need to work extremely hard to structure the information in discourse to make it understandable for the receiver. The interest of the discourse analyst, then, is investigating "how speakers [and writers], having a given quantum of information to impart, identify and package that information." (Brown and Yule 1983: 176). What Brown and Yule are alluding to is that there are different ways, linguistically, of delivering the same information and speakers and writers make linguistic choices from the available possible alternatives within the rules of language. These choices can affect meaning and reception.

DOI: 10.4324/9781003351207-2

The structuring and organisation of information in discourse was studied by scholars at the Prague School of Linguistics[1] (founded by Vilem Mathesius), who showed that information structure shapes meaning and guides interpretation. Their insights were adopted by Michael Halliday in, for example, his explorations of transitivity (Halliday 1967) (see Chapter 9 of this book) and later his Systemic Functional Grammar (e.g. Halliday and Matthiessen 2014). In Systemic Functional Grammar there are two interrelated systems of analysis of the message: **thematic structure** and **information structure**. The former involves what are known as **Theme** and **Rheme**, and the latter **Given** and **New** information. These systems will be described in this chapter. However, before we get to that, we first need to introduce the structure of the English clause.

Structure of the English clause

Simply put, the clause is an organisational unit of language that comprises (at least) a grammatical Subject and a Predicator (e.g. 'we write'). In Chapter 1, we briefly introduced some of the 'nuts and bolts' of discourse including grammatical parts of speech, which categorise words according to their grammatical class (e.g. noun, verb, adjectives). We also briefly introduced syntax and noted that English is a Subject-Predicator-Object language (SPO), where the Subject comes before the Predicator and the Object comes after. Figure 2.1 shows these relationships using a made-up clause, 'the donkey ate a carrot'.

Clausal function	Subject		Predicator	Object	
Clause	**The**	**donkey**	**ate**	**a**	**carrot**
Grammatical class	determiner	noun	verb	determiner	noun

Figure 2.1 Clausal and grammatical terminology

The labels Subject, Predicator and Object relate to **function** within a clause, and Thompson (2013:19) suggests thinking of them as slots that are filled by particular words and categories of words. Sometimes, instead of Predicator, the category label Verb is used, reflecting the fact that the Predicator slot is always filled by a verb or verb phrase. However, this conflates two different but nonetheless interrelated systems: grammatical class and clausal function (Thompson 2013:20). In this chapter, we will use Predicator to mean the clausal function and verb to mean grammatical class (or part of speech).

Subject and Predicator

In English grammar, the Subject and the Predicator are the two main parts of a clause. The Predicator is always realised by a verb or verb phrase (VP) containing a lexical verb (e.g. 'eat') and, optionally, one or more auxiliary verbs (e.g. 'is eating', 'has eaten', 'has been eating'). The Predicator expresses some sort of action (physical, verbal, cognitive) or state of being relating to the Subject and, where there is one, the Object.

The Subject is typically a noun ('donkey'), a pronoun ('it', 'he', 'she'), or a noun phrase ('the hungry little donkey') which can be structurally large containing, for example, coordination (e.g. 'the hungry little donkey and the child') or a relative clause (e.g. 'the donkey who ate the carrot'). The canonical (prototypical) Subject is who/what the clause is about, and/or who or what performs the action or takes on the state realised by the Predicator. As we will see later in this section (and in Chapter 9), this is not always the case. The position of the Subject in a clause differs depending on clause type: declarative, interrogative, imperative. The different positions are summarised in Table 2.1.

Table 2.1 Clause types and Subject position

Clause type	Subject position	Example
Declarative	Before the Predicator	*The donkey eats* *The donkey can eat* *The donkey has eaten*
Interrogative	Between a form of the verb 'do' (or other auxiliary verb) and the main verb of the Predicator, or immediately after the Predicator when main verb is a form of 'be'	*Does the donkey eat?* *Did the donkey eat?* *Can the donkey eat?* *Has the donkey eaten?* *Is the donkey hungry?*
Imperative	Subject is elided but typically understood to be 'you'	*Eat!*

Non-canonical Subjects

Subjects are prototypically noun phrases (NPs), but they can be realised by a variety of other grammatical categories. For example:

1

(i) | To motivate a donkey | requires | a carrot
S P O

(ii) | Having a carrot to eat | was | the donkey's dream |
S P C

(iii) | In the field | is | where the donkey ate the carrot |
S P C

(iv) | Yesterday | is | when the donkey ate the carrot |
S P C

In clause 1(i), the Subject is realised by a to-infinitive clause, in (ii) a gerund clause (a gerund is an '-ing' form of a verb which acts as a noun), in (iii) a prepositional phrase (PP), and in (iv) the Subject is an adverbial. In 1(ii), (iii), and (iv), a form of the verb 'be' is the Predicator, and this is followed by a Complement which tells us more about the Subject. We will say more about Complements after we have introduced Object.

Object

Objects, like Subjects, are typically realised by pronouns, nouns, or noun phrases. While the Subject is usually (but not always) the thing that performs the action or embodies the state expressed by the Predicator, the Object is the thing that the action is performed on. For example:

2

(i) | The donkey | ate | the carrot |
S P O

(ii) | The hungry donkey | was eating | the juicy carrot |
S P O

In example 2(i), the noun phrase 'the donkey' (which comprises a determiner and a noun) is the Subject of the clause and the eater of the carrot, the verb 'ate' is the Predicator, and the noun phrase 'the carrot' is the Object and the thing that is eaten. This type of Object is known as the **direct Object** (Od) because it is acted on directly by the Subject. Some clauses also involve **indirect Objects** because some Predicators (and therefore some actions) can involve more than one Object. For example, 'gave' typically involves something or other being given to someone/something. Consider the following examples.

3

(i) | The child | gave | the donkey | a carrot |
S P Oi Od

(ii) | The child | gave | a carrot | to the donkey |
S P Od Oi

The examples demonstrate that the thing being given (a carrot) is being acted on directly and is therefore the direct Object (Od), while the recipient (the donkey) is the indirect Object (Oi). In 3(i), the indirect Object is realised by a noun phrase ('the donkey') which is the canonical situation. Example 3(ii) shows a non-canonical but nonetheless common situation where a prepositional phrase, which is made up of the preposition 'to', the determiner 'the' and the noun 'donkey', acts in a similar way to an indirect Object.[2]

Complement and Adjunct

As well as Subject, Predicate and Object, there are two other clause slots known as Complement (C) and Adjunct (A). The Complement functions to tell us more about the Subject and is typically an adjective, noun phrase, or prepositional phrase. The Adjunct expresses extra information concerning, for example, where or when the action happened. Adjuncts are typically adverbial or prepositional phrases. In the following examples 'A' labels the Adjuncts and 'C' the complements.

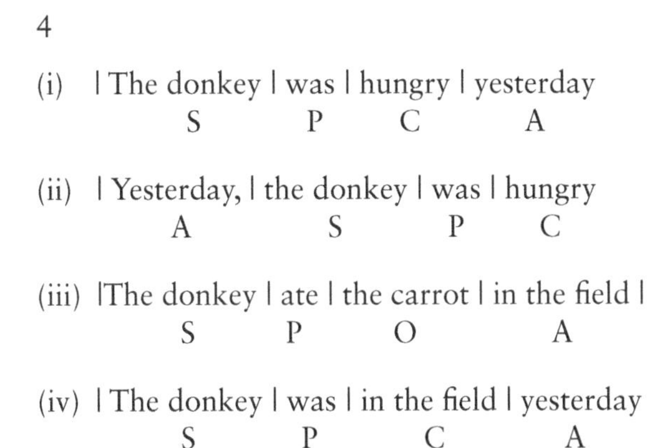

4

(i) | The donkey | was | hungry | yesterday
S P C A

(ii) | Yesterday, | the donkey | was | hungry
A S P C

(iii) |The donkey | ate | the carrot | in the field |
S P O A

(iv) | The donkey | was | in the field | yesterday
S P C A

In 4(i) and (ii), the adjective 'hungry' provides more information about the Subject, 'the donkey'. Examples 4 (i), (ii), and (iii), contain Adjuncts that provide information about when ('yesterday') and where ('in the field') the action takes place. Example 4 (iv) shows that the Complement can also be a prepositional phrase when the Predicator is a form of the verb 'be'. In this example, the Complement tells us where the carrot eating took place, and the Adjunct tells us when. The position of Adjuncts is flexible. The Adjuncts in 4(i) and (iii) are at the end of the clause, while in 4(ii) it is at the beginning. Also, Adjuncts are not necessary for the clause to be grammatically complete (we say more on this in Chapter 9). So, deleting the adverb, 'yesterday', from 4 (i), (ii), and (iv) or the prepositional phrase, 'in the field', in 4(ii) leaves a grammatically complete clause. Removing 'the donkey' from any example, however, leaves a grammatically incomplete and nonsensical clause. The moveability/removability (or otherwise) of a clausal element is often a good test for whether it is an Adjunct.

Adjuncts tend to be adverbs, adverbial phrases (AdvP), and prepositional phrases (PP). They can also be single words (e.g. brightly), phrases (e.g. very brightly), or a clause (e.g. even though the sun shone brightly). The latter type of adjunct, known as the clausal adjunct, consists of a **dependent clause.** A dependent clause is one that cannot stand on its own and needs the support of another, **independent clause.** For example:

5

(i) To motivate a donkey, **you have to give it a carrot**
(ii) **The donkey was content,** because it had eaten a carrot
(ii) Having eaten a carrot, **the donkey was content**

In each example, the underlined section is a dependent clause, and the bold section is independent. The independent clauses can stand alone and still make complete sense while the dependent clauses cannot.

Passive clauses

Clauses in the 'passive voice' are created using a form of the verb 'be' and the past participle of a lexical verb. A passive clause structures the message so the thing being acted on, which would be the direct Object in a conventional SPO structure, becomes the Subject. The thing doing the acting is not a necessary part of the clause but could be added as an optional Adjunct. For example:

6

(i)	The donkey	ate	the carrot
	S	P	O
(ii)	The carrot	was eaten	by the donkey
	S	P	A

Examples 6(i) and (ii) communicate the same (or similar) information – one entity (the donkey) acts on another entity (a carrot) in a particular way (eat). However, in 6(ii), 'the carrot' is Subject even though it is the thing being acted upon, while the doer of the eating, 'the donkey', is now part of a prepositional phrase, 'by the donkey', and is an Adjunct.

Either direct or indirect Objects can be Subject in a passive clause. Consider examples 7(i), (ii), and (iii), all of which communicate a similar message. In 7(ii) 'the donkey' (the receiver of the carrot) is Subject, 'the child' (the giver) is part of prepositional phrase which functions as an Adjunct, and 'a carrot' (the Object being given) is the direct Object. In 7(iii) 'a carrot' is the Subject while both 'the donkey' and 'the child' become embedded in prepositional phrases both of which act as Adjuncts. In both examples, the Adjuncts can be removed, and the clauses will still be grammatically complete – although in 7(iii), the clause would nonetheless 'feel' incomplete.

7

(i)	The child	gave	the donkey	a carrot
	S	P	Oi	Od
(ii)	The donkey	was given	a carrot	by the child
	S	P	Od	A
(iii)	A carrot	was given	to the donkey	by the girl
	S	P	A	A

Note that when the Adjuncts are removed, the clause no longer communicates who or what carried out the action – eating in 6(ii) and giving in 7(ii). Removing the doers of actions is a topic we return to in Chapter 9, where we discuss the participants in clauses and their roles.

Summary of clause structure

Subject, Object, Complement, Predicator, and Adjunct are labels given to elements of the clause by virtue of their function within the clause. Particular grammatical entities typically perform these functions: the Predicator of a clause is a verb or verb phrase; nouns and noun phrases can be seen as the 'norm' for Subject and Object; Complements are usually realised by adjectives, nouns/noun phrases, and prepositional phrases; and Adjuncts are typically prepositional phrases and adverbs. However, this is only what is typical, and as we have seen throughout this section, Subject, Object, Complement, and Adjunct can be realised by other grammatical entities. A summary of clause structure is shown in Table 2.2. The bottom row of the table indicates the grammatical categories that **typically** realise the clausal function.

Table 2.2 English clause structure and typical grammatical realisations

Subject	Predicator	Object (indirect)	Object (direct)	Complement	Adjunct
The donkey	is eating		the carrot		in the field
The donkey	is			asleep	in the field
The donkey	is			a mammal	
The child	gave	the donkey	a carrot		yesterday
The donkey	was given		a carrot		by the child
Noun phrase	***Verb phrase***	***Noun phrase***	***Noun phrase***	***Adjective; noun phrase***	***Prepositional phrase; adverb; adverbial phrase***

Activity 2.1 Label the clausal elements

In the following examples, taken from a variety of sources, label the clausal functions (SPOCA) and say how they are realised by grammatical categories (NP, VP, PP, etc.)

a) I volunteer at Andy's care centre

Dementia UK website, Sarah's story, 28/07/2021
https://tinyurl.com/j3x2shzr

b) Oesophageal squamous cell carcinoma is the predominant subtype of oesophageal cancer in Asian populations

BMJ 2022; 377: e068714, 19/04/2022
https://tinyurl.com/mtdttxfa

c) Kim Kardashian has broken the internet for the thousandth time in her life

Cosmopolitan.com UK, 29/06/2018
https://tinyurl.com/35ruwhwb

d) Improving how colleagues treat each other is a critical prerequisite to improving how the department treats the public

Windrush Lessons Learned Review, March, 2020[3]

e) In our analysis, we have attempted to mitigate this limitation [reporting autonomy] in a number of ways

Cancer Immunology Research, 25/07/2019
https://www.ncbi.nlm.nih.gov/pmc/articles/PMC6066474

f) Cedars-Sinai, like every other hospital in California, is overwhelmed with COVID-19 patients

The Jerusalem Post (online), 14/01/2021
https://tinyurl.com/4rtwu6dd

g) Global macroeconomic developments and commodity supply factors will likely cause boom-bust cycles to continue in commodity markets

World Bank Press Release, 11/01/2022
https://tinyurl.com/5ykkvt52

h) As a donkey owner, you need to be prepared for the cold winter months

The donkey sanctuary website, care of donkeys through winter, 18/12/2022
https://tinyurl.com/2v4ppb36

i) Coronavirus, also called COVID-19, is part of a family of viruses that includes the common cold and more serious respiratory illnesses such as SARS.

Age UK website, Information about coronavirus, 07/04/2022
https://tinyurl.com/5mbjzvtc

We give our answers at the end of the chapter.

Thematic structure

Now that we have established how the English clause is structured and familiarised ourselves with the labels and functions of clausal elements, we can now move on to another way of analysing clauses. This next framework focuses on thematic structure. It separates the clause out into two parts that serve two functions called Theme and Rheme.[4] Together, Theme and Rheme make up the message of the clause.

Theme and Rheme

In both spoken and written English, **Theme** is the first component or the starting point of a clause. It is therefore defined by its initial position in a clause. Everything that follows the Theme is known as the **Rheme**. The term 'Rheme', which was introduced by the Prague School, is derived from the Greek word 'rhema', meaning 'that which is said'. Theme, in its primary position, "serves as the point of departure of the message" (Halliday and Matthiessen 2014: 89) and consequently becomes the lens through which the rest of the clause is read and understood. Consequently, Theme can have a focusing function, highlighting certain information. The Rheme is what the text producer has to say about the Theme and contains the main message of the clause. Rheme, then, realises the communicative goal of the clause. Figure 2.2 shows a simple example of how Theme and Rheme work. In the example, 'The donkey' is the Theme and the rest of the clause is the Rheme.

The donkey	ate a carrot in the field
Theme	**Rheme**

Figure 2.2 Simple example of Theme and Rheme

Theme in declarative clauses

Subject as Theme

The example in Figure 2.2 is a declarative clause and it demonstrates the prototypical situation where grammatical Subject and Theme are conflated. We noted in the previous section that English is an SPO (Subject, Predicator, Object) language and when Subject and Theme coincide, this is said to be conventional and **unmarked**. That is not to say that Subject and Theme are the same because they are not; Subject is a clausal function whereas Theme relates to the message of the clause and is simply the part of the message that comes first.

The Subject of a clause can be structurally large and include, for example, coordinated words and phrases, and pre-/post-modified noun phrases. In such cases, all parts of the Subject count as the Theme. Below are some (made-up) examples to illustrate this point (in these and all subsequent examples, Theme is underlined).

8

(i) A carrot and an apple was eaten by the donkey
(ii) A carrot or an apple was eaten by the donkey
(iii) The donkey, equus asinus, is a carrot-loving hoofed mammal.
(iv) Bonnie, the donkey, loves a carrot
(v) The donkey who ate the carrot is in the field.
(vi) The donkey, which had a reputation for being a greedy asinus, ate the carrot.

In examples 8(i) and (ii), the Subjects are realised by two noun phrases joined by conjunctions ('and' and 'or'), and in each case the whole Subject is the Theme. In examples 8(iii) and (iv), both Subjects are realised by two noun phrases separated by commas. This type of structure is known as **apposition** whereby two noun phrases referring to the same entity are juxtaposed with the second noun phrase providing further information. In 8(iii) the noun phrase, 'the donkey' refers to the species generally, as does 'equus asinus' but provides an alternative label. In 8(iv) both noun phrases have the same referent (Bonnie) with the second noun phrase providing further information about the referent.

The Subjects in examples 8(v) and (vi) include relative clauses that provide more information about the referent of the noun phrase. The noun phrase in 8(v) involves what is known as a **defining relative clause** which helps to identify a specific donkey; 8(vi) has a **non-defining relative clause** which simply provides more, non-essential information about the referent of the noun phrase. In each case, these relative clauses are included in the Theme.

Marked Themes

In principle, any part of the clause can be Theme, but when a clause constituent other than Subject is Theme, then this is **marked** (Halliday and Matthiessen 2014: 98). It is worth noting, though, that some non-Subject Themes are more marked than others. It is not unusual, for example, to see an Adjunct as Theme since this clause constituent has more moveability than others (Thompson 2013: 149). For example:

9

(i) In the middle of the field, the donkey ate the carrot.
(ii) Later that day, the donkey ate the carrot.

You will probably agree that the sorts of Themes above are common in English providing, as they do, a useful starting point and focus for the Rheme. A similar type of marked Theme that is also common is when a dependent clause occurs first in a multi-clause sentence. For example:

10

(i) As the sun rose, the donkey ate the carrot.
(ii) Having eaten the carrot, the donkey had a snooze.
(iii) Without pausing, the donkey ate the carrot.

In each example, the underlined section is a dependent clause and the Theme; what follows is the independent clause and the Rheme. A more marked (and much less frequent) situation is when the Object or Complement is Theme, as follows.

11

(i) This carrot the donkey ate.
(ii) Always hungry was the donkey

A clause can start from any point and this starting point is chosen by the text producer/speaker. The choices made by text producers can be influenced by the context of the discourse. For example, the context might require a marked Theme to direct attention to a particular part of the clause. As Thompson (2013: 150) explains:

> Subject is chosen as Theme when there is no good reason to choose anything else; but when there are contextual pressures, such as the speaker's wish to establish a contrast or signal a particular form of organization in their discourse, another element – Adjunct or Complement – may be chosen as Theme instead.

A marked Theme, therefore, is an emphasised Theme and can be meaningful. The more marked a Theme is the more potentially meaningful (and noticeable) the choice is. A summary of the marked/unmarked Themes in declarative clauses is shown in Table 2.3.

Activity 2.2 uses examples from real texts (which you might recognise from Activity 2.1) and aims to demonstrate a range of Themes.

Table 2.3 Summary of unmarked and marked Themes in declarative clauses

Status of Theme	Function	Constituent	Example
Unmarked	Subject	Pronoun	**She** ate the carrot
		Noun phrase	**The donkey** ate the carrot
Marked	Adjunct	Adverb	**Hungrily,** she ate the carrot
		Preposition	**In the field,** the donkey ate the carrot
		Clause	**Rather than feel hungry,** she ate the carrot
	Object	Pronoun	**This** the donkey ate
		Noun phrase	**This carrot** the donkey ate
	Complement	Adjective	**Always hungry** was the donkey

Activity 2.2 Theme and Rheme in declarative clauses

In each of the following examples identify the Theme.

(i) I volunteer at Andy's care centre
(ii) Kim Kardashian has broken the internet for the thousandth time in her life
(iii) Improving how colleagues treat each other is a critical prerequisite to improving how the department treats the public
(iv) Global macroeconomic developments and commodity supply factors will likely cause boom-bust cycles to continue in commodity markets.
(v) Cedars-Sinai, like every other hospital in California, is overwhelmed with COVID-19 patients
(vi) In our analysis, we have attempted to mitigate this limitation [reporting autonomy] in a number of ways.
(vii) As a donkey owner, you need to be prepared for the cold winter months.
(viii) Coronavirus, also called COVID-19, is part of a family of viruses that includes the common cold and more serious respiratory illnesses such as SARS.

We give our analysis at the end of the chapter.

Theme in interrogative and imperative clauses

Interrogative clauses prototypically ask a question to seek information but as we saw in Chapter 1 ('Have you sheeted?') and as we will see in later chapters this is not always the case (e.g. consider the question 'Can you please be quiet?'). There are two types of questions: those that seek a yes/no response; and those that seek information using a wh- word (i.e. who, when, where, why, what, how). For yes/no questions, the unmarked Theme is an auxiliary verb + Subject, for example:

12

(i) Did the donkey eat the carrot?
(ii) Has the donkey eaten yet?

For Wh-questions, the unmarked situation is for Theme to be a wh-word, for example:

13

(i) What did the donkey eat?
(ii) Where did the donkey eat the carrot?

Imperatives typically instruct (or order!) someone to do something. The other person (the Subject) is usually elided from an imperative clause. The exception is where the imperative involves both the text producer and receiver and starts with 'let' (e.g. 'let us go/let's go'). For imperatives, then, the Theme is the Predicator or 'let's/let us'. When the imperative is negative or emphatic then 'do' or 'don't'/'do not' are also included, for example:

14

(i) Eat the carrot
(ii) Let's eat the carrot
(iii) Don't eat the carrot
(iv) Do eat the carrot

Marked Themes

It is possible for interrogatives and imperatives to have marked Themes, for example where an Adjunct takes Theme position, as shown in 15.

15

(i) After the carrot, what did the donkey eat?
(ii) Yesterday, did the donkey eat a carrot?
(iii) Once in the field, give the donkey a carrot.

Table 2.4 summarises unmarked and marked Themes in interrogative and imperative clauses.

Table 2.4 Unmarked and marked Themes in interrogative and imperative clauses

Type of clause	Theme	Examples
Interrogative	**Unmarked**	
yes/no	Aux verb + Subject	Did she eat the carrot? Is she eating the carrot? Has she eaten the carrot?
	Marked	
	Adjunct	Afterwards, did she eat a carrot?

(Continued)

Table 2.4 (Continued)

Type of clause	Theme	Examples
wh-	**Unmarked**	
	wh-word	Who ate the carrot?
	Marked	
	Adjunct	Afterwards, what did she eat?
Imperative	**Unmarked**	
	Predicator	Eat the carrot!
	'let us'	Let's eat the carrot!
	Aux verb + 'let us'	Do let's eat the carrot!
	Aux verb + Neg + 'let us'	Don't let's eat the carrot!
	Aux verb + Predicator	Do eat the carrot!
	Aux verb + neg + Predicator	Don't eat the carrot!
	Marked	
	Adjunct	Afterwards, eat the carrot!
		Tomorrow, let's eat the carrot!

Test your knowledge of Theme and Rheme in imperative clauses by completing Activity 2.3.

Activity 2.3 Theme and Rheme in imperative clauses

Identify the Themes in the following sentences typical of those you would find in a recipe.

Preheat the oven to 180°C/160°C Fan/Gas 4.
For the sauce, heat the oil in a small frying pan over a medium heat.
Fry the onion and garlic in the oil. After five minutes, add the spices.

Answers are at the end of the chapter.

Theme in complex sentences

When a sentence consists of more than one independent clause, then each clause is analysed separately. For example:

16

(i) The donkey liked carrots, but carrots were a rare treat.
(ii) The donkey ate the carrot and then it had a snooze.

Compound Themes

In the examples we have used so far, the Themes have simply contained the Subject, Object, Complement, Predicator, or an Adjunct. Themes can also contain other elements that can form part of the Theme yet cannot by themselves constitute the Theme. An inventory of the possible additional elements is set out by Halliday and Matthiessen (2014: Section 3.4), which we summarise below.

Continuatives

These are also known as discourse markers and can be used for emphasis or to mark a change in the direction of the discourse. The examples provided by Halliday and Matthiessen (2014: 107) are: 'well', 'yes', 'oh', 'now'. For example:

17

Well now, the donkey ate the carrot.

The continuative 'well now' is bundled together with 'the donkey' to create a compound Theme.

Conjunctions

These are linking words and include, for example: 'and', 'but', 'then', 'when', 'while'. These can be placed in Theme position, but do not form the Theme on their own. For example:

18

But the donkey ate the carrot.

Conjunctive and modal adjuncts

While some Adjuncts can form the Theme on their own (e.g. 'in the field'), Halliday and Matthiessen (2014) identify two types of adjunct that do not. These are conjunctive and modal Adjuncts and are grouped in with the next element in the clause to form a compound Theme. Conjunctive adjuncts include: 'however', 'meanwhile', 'likewise', 'therefore', 'nevertheless', 'to sum up'. Modal adjuncts include: 'regrettably', 'probably', 'surely', 'usually', 'apparently', 'to my mind' (for a comprehensive inventory, see Halliday and Matthiessen 2014: 109). For example:

19

(i) However, the donkey ate the carrot
(ii) Regrettably, the donkey ate the carrot
(iii) Surely, the donkey ate the carrot

Vocatives

These are personal names or other terms of address, such as: 'madam', 'sir', 'your honour'. For example:

20

Madam, your donkey ate my carrot.

Multiple elements

The Theme can contain any or all the elements set out above, as the following examples demonstrate:

21

(i) But then suddenly to my surprise the donkey ate the carrot in the field
(ii) And so, madam, as expected the carrot was eaten by the donkey

Special Themes

In this section we discuss four syntactic structures that create marked Themes that have the effect of manipulating, emphasising, and prioritising (Jeffries 2010: 77) the starting points of the message.

Clefting

Cleft clauses separate out a clause constituent from the rest giving it prominence. Clefts consist of an impersonal pronoun (e.g. 'it') which is known as the cleft pronoun, a copular verb (usually 'be'), a noun phrase, known as the cleft phrase, and a relative clause, known as the cleft clause. All these constituents – the cleft pronoun, copular verb, and cleft phrase – combine to make the Theme in the cleft structure. Example 22 demonstrates cleft structures:

22

(i) It was the carrot that the donkey ate.
(ii) It was the donkey that ate the carrot.

With 22(i), the Theme includes the Object, while in (ii) the Subject. Cleft structures foreground the Theme and signal the cleft phrase as being newsworthy (in our examples 'the carrot' and 'the donkey'). This emphasis might be to show that the cleft phrase has been singled out from other possibilities and/or create a contrast between the actual situation and what might have been asserted previously (e.g. it was the donkey that ate the carrot – not the rabbit).

Pseudo-clefts

Pseudo-clefts (also known as wh-clefts) are cleft structures that consist of a relative clause at the start of the sentence, followed by a copular verb, followed by a noun phrase. For example:

23

(i) What the donkey ate was a carrot.
(ii) What ate the carrot was the donkey.

Like the cleft clauses in 22 above, these pseudo-cleft constructions can also be used to indicate a contrast in assumed knowledge in a discourse or to contradict a previous assertion (we will see how this relates to Given and New in the next section). Additionally, they might be used to answer imagined questions for the hearer/reader and help to prepare the hearer/reader for what comes next, therefore guiding the hearer/reader (Thompson 2013: 155). Wh-clefts can also be inverted so that the relative clause is at the end of the sentence, for example:

24

(i) The carrot is what the donkey ate.
(ii) The donkey is what ate the carrot.

These can serve a similar sort of purpose as pseudo-clefts, but also tend to refer to previously mentioned elements in the discourse or commonly held assumptions/ knowledge (see Given and New in the next section).

Fronted or preposed Themes

A further way in which the starting point of a sentence can be changed is by a special structure known as a **fronted** or **preposed** Theme. Fronting (or preposing) refers to any construction where the Object, Complement or Adjunct of a clause is placed before the verb. Fronting can emphasise different parts of the clause (it can also help with cohesion – the topic of our next chapter). For example:

25

(i) This carrot, the donkey ate.
(ii) In the field, the donkey ate the carrot.
(iii) Hungry was the donkey

A further type of fronting is where Theme is separated from the rest of the clause by putting it first in a dislocated phrase. This phrase is then followed by a clause that contains a pronoun that refers back to the Theme. Here are some made up examples (Thematic referent is underlined and the corresponding pronoun is in bold font):

26

(i) A carrot, **that**'s what the donkey ate.
(ii) The donkey, **it** ate the carrot.
(iii) In the middle of the field, **that**'s where the donkey ate the carrot.

In each case above, the fronted Theme is non-canonical and so is **marked** and has prominence.

Passive clauses

Passive clauses, as we noted earlier in this chapter, put the entity that would canonically be the direct Object (the thing acted upon directly) into Subject position. Thematically, therefore, passive clauses bring the affected entity into Theme position, and therefore into prominence. In example 27, the carrot is the thing acted upon – it has been eaten by the donkey – but it is the Theme of the clause.

27

The carrot was eaten by the donkey in the field.

Now, try identifying Theme and Rheme for yourself by completing Activity 2.4.

Activity 2.4 Theme and Rheme in a news report

Below is a short extract from the beginning of an article from a British regional newspaper, the *Northampton Chronicle and Echo*, reporting on the outcome of a court case involving domestic violence (18 March 2021). The extract starts with the headline for the piece (in bold).

> **Drunk dad-of-two who set fire to his partner and threatened to kill her spared jail by Northampton judge.**
>
> A phone engineer went on a 24-hour New Year's vodka binge before threatening to kill his partner, a court has been told.
>
> Dad-of-two [name redacted], 39, had been drinking heavily after struggling to cope with the demands of the long hours he was working to provide for his family, Northampton Crown Court heard yesterday (Tuesday, March 16).
>
> [Redacted name], a father of two children with additional needs, had been working 'obsessively' in the run up to the incident and had found it difficult to relax.
>
> He had been drinking bottles of vodka for 24 hours and taking his son's ADHD medication in when his partner went to visit her family, which he said invoked feelings of 'paranoia and jealousy'.

Identify the Theme and Rheme. What might the choice of Theme indicate about what the text producer deems important or 'newsworthy'? How might the choice of Theme influence the way you process the information in terms of perpetrator culpability?

Information structure: Given and New

In this section, we continue our examination of how the information in the messages we communicate is structured by looking at another of the insights of the Prague School: the information in a message can be divided into **Given** and **New** (we use capitals to show the technical status of these words). In this section we will describe what is meant by **Given** and **New** (hereafter Given-New) and show how information status is signalled in discourse.

What is Given-New information?

Haviland and Clark (1974: 513) make the point that the primary purpose of language is to impart information; speakers/writers use language to tell their hearers/readers something. That 'something' is typically information that the hearers/readers did not already know. However, when speakers/writers do impart information, the message will inevitably contain things that the hearers/readers do know. To communicate successfully (i.e. to impart information) speakers/writers must make assumptions about what their hearers/readers do and do not know, and they must choose their language accordingly. Information that the speaker/writer assumes **is already known** by their addressees is **Given** information, while information that is assumed **not to be known** is **New** (Brown and Yule 1983: 154).

Signalling Given-New information

The status of information in discourse (i.e. the **Givenness** or **Newness**) is signalled by language choices made by the speaker/writer based on their assumptions about the hearer's/reader's knowledge. Information can be assumed to be **known** to their addressee and therefore **Given** if it has already been mentioned in the discourse or is physically present in the immediate context. Information can be assumed to be **not known** to their addressee and therefore **New** if it is not obvious in the context or has not already been introduced. Givenness can be (but not always) signalled by the definite article ('the') or pronouns, whereas Newness can be (but not always) signalled by indefinite reference, which usually involves the grammatical articles 'a' and 'an'. For example:

28

Look at **that** donkey. **It** is eating <u>a carrot</u>. **The** carrot looks tasty.

In our invented (and rather thrilling) example, the demonstrative pronoun 'that' (highlighted in bold type) indicates that the donkey is physically present in the context and so is taken as Given by the speaker. The pronoun 'it' refers to the previously mentioned donkey so is also Given (we deal with reference in more detail in the next chapter). Similarly, the definite article 'the' signals that the speaker assumes that the carrot in question is known to the addressee because it has already been introduced in the discourse. The first mention of the carrot, though, is preceded by the indefinite article 'a' indicating that (even though the hearer might be able to see the carrot) the speaker assumes (and signals) it is New information.

Givenness can be indicated in other ways; consider the two examples in 29.

29

(i) The carrot that the donkey ate was very tasty.
(ii) Q: Where's Bonnie your donkey?
A: At the coast for the day.

In 29(i), the information in the subordinate clause that forms part of the Subject ('that the donkey ate') is assumed to be known and therefore Given (see also presupposition in Chapter 5). The New information in that clause concerns the tastiness of the carrot. In (ii), Bonnie the donkey is elided from answer (A) completely, and this absence signals Givenness.

Notice that in 29(ii) the definite article in the noun phrase 'the coast' signals a different kind of Givenness: the speaker assumes the referent is common or shared knowledge. Other examples of this sort of Givenness include 'the sun', 'the moon', and 'the equator', each of which might be assumed to be known to the hearer even though they have not been mentioned previously in the discourse. In our invented example, the referent of 'the coast' will differ from discourse community to discourse community and location to location. In some situations, the assumption might be misplaced; for example, if the conversation in 29(ii) happened in Nepal, then the next question might well be 'Which coast?' The general assumption concerning the existence of coasts still stands, though.

Another observation we can make about 29(ii) is that the Given-New distinction is complicated. This is because that while 'the coast' is signalled as assumed shared knowledge, it is nonetheless New information with regard to the whereabouts of Bonnie. It is, after all, the information sought in the question (Q), which explicitly communicates it as being not known to the question asker. The New information is therefore the circumstantial relationship (see Chapter 9 for more on circumstances) between Bonnie and the coast: Bonnie is at the coast. The example therefore combines what Gundel and Fretheim (2004: 176–177) call **referential Given-New** and **relational Given-New**. The former concerns what is referenced, and the latter is what we find out about the relationship between the things referenced. In 29(ii) it is what is asserted about Bonnie the donkey that is the New information.

To summarise, Given can be seen as information that is recoverable (Halliday and Matthiessen 2014: 118) from the immediately preceding discourse, the immediate context (discourse situation) or from shared knowledge and means that 'this is not news'. New information is not recoverable and means 'this is news' (Halliday and Matthiessen 2014: 118). Over the rest of the chapter, we will look at Given-New in relation to Theme and Rheme and examine how New information can also be signalled by syntactic and/or phonological prominence (Halliday and Matthiessen 2014: 118). A summary of Given-New information can be found in Figure 2.3.

Activity 2.5 Given-New in a spoken interaction

Consider the following short extract of a conversation taken from the spoken section of the **British National Corpus (BNC)**. The conversation is between two people discussing photographs (turns numbered for ease of reference):

1 Stuart: That's a good one.
2 Alison: Well where's the one I took of you in the tree?
3 Stuart: It might be on the other ones. Oh the two of us in the tree?
4 Alison: Yeah. Look at him there. Oh my god.
5 Stuart: Look at me leg!

a Which information is signalled as Given and which as New?
b What are the signals?
c What do you think are the reasons for the speakers assuming Givenness-Newness?

We give our answers at the end of the chapter.

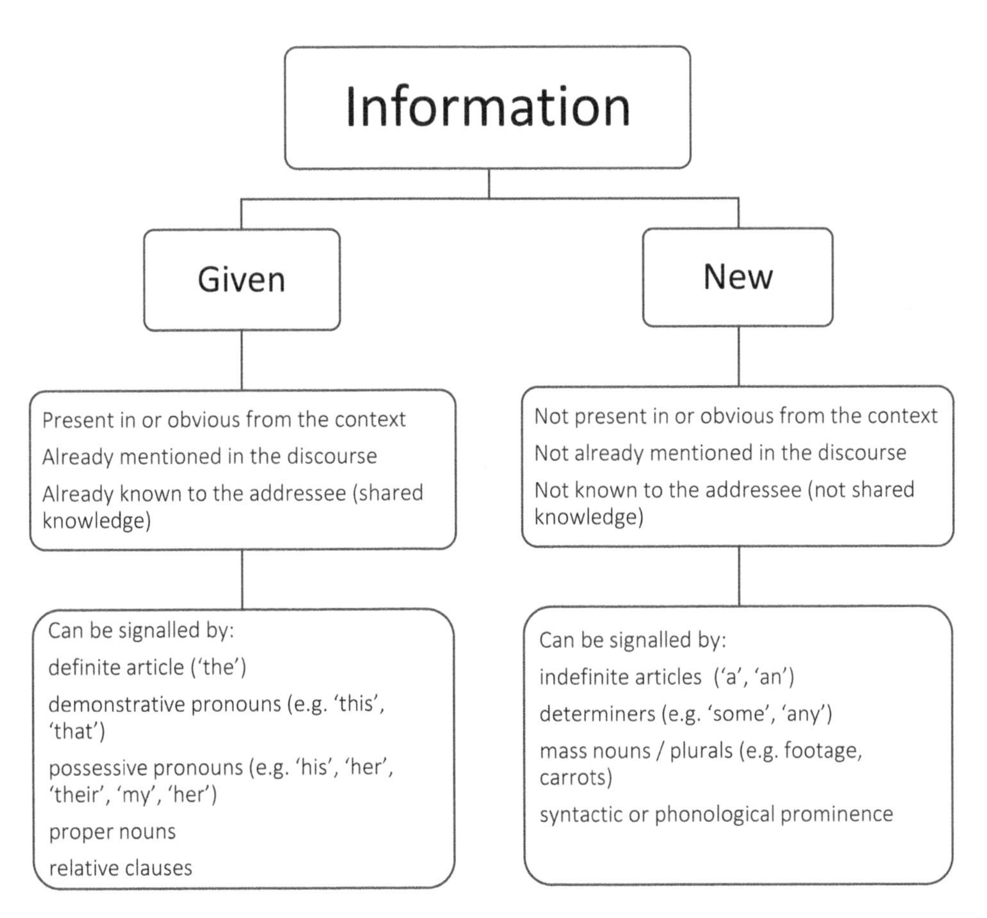

Figure 2.3 Given and New information

Given-New and Theme and Rheme

The prototypical and unmarked situation is for Given information to coincide with Theme, and New with Rheme (Halliday and Matthiessen 2014:120). However, this is not always the case, not least because the start of any discourse will contain mostly new information. Indeed, the clauses in a discourse may contain a complex sequence of Given-New information rather than the two-way division that we saw with Theme and Rheme. Given-New status depends on what is decided as being known to the text-recipient and what is not. Consider the information on Covid19 taken from a UK Government website. The information has been divided into Theme and Rheme; New information has been underlined.

Table 2.5 Theme and Rheme, Given and New

Theme	Rheme
Coronaviruses	are <u>a large family of related viruses that cause diseases in animals and humans</u>.
Some	<u>cause less severe disease</u>, such as the common cold,
and others	<u>cause more severe disease</u>, such as Middle East respiratory syndrome (MERS) and severe acute respiratory syndrome (SARS).
They	are <u>a different family of viruses</u> to the influenza viruses that cause seasonal influenza.

The Government article that the information in Table 2.5 is drawn from provides details about the history of Covid-19. By the time the reader gets to the first clause shown in the table, the concept of 'coronaviruses' contained in the Theme is assumed (quite reasonably) to be known. The Rheme in the first clause contains New information which is indicated by the indefinite article 'a' at the start of the long noun phrase.

The Theme of the second clause is the word 'some'. As a determiner, 'some' can indicate indefiniteness and sometimes signal Newness (e.g. 'I want some carrots' vs 'I want the carrots'). In our example, 'some' is acting pronominally, referring to the Theme of the first sentence ('coronaviruses'). In this case, we suggest that it signals Givenness. The Rheme of the second clause contains a combination of New information and Given; the presence of the definite article in 'the common cold' suggests that text producer is assuming this is shared knowledge.

The third clause is similar, with the Theme referring back to the Theme of the first clause, and the Rheme containing New information, but with MERS and SARS being taken as Given.

The fourth clause is also similar – the Theme refers to 'Coronaviruses', so is Given, the Rheme contain a combination of New and Given. Indeed, the noun phrase 'the influenza viruses' is post-modified by a subordinate clause 'that cause seasonal influenza' assumes the existence of influenza viruses and that they cause seasonal influenza. All that is taken as Given by the text producer and links to the notion of presupposition which we discuss in Chapter 5.

The example in Table 2.5 does indeed have a pattern of Theme coinciding with Given, with successive Themes point back to information established in the first Theme. It also shows that the Rhemes are a combination of New and Given. Readers may well find different patterns with different texts. News stories, for example, are likely to necessarily start with all New information before a pattern is established.

Given injustice: the case of Derek Bentley

Derek Bentley was the last man to be hanged in Britain. His crime – which he didn't commit and was (much) later pardoned for – was the murder of a police officer. The judge made a great deal about Bentley's (later disputed) confession, which contained the phrase "I didn't know he was going to use the gun" (Coulthard 2006). The phrase concerns Bentley's 'accomplice', Chris Craig – the person who actually murdered the officer – and the gun that Craig was carrying and used to shoot the officer. The judge claimed that if Bentley was telling the truth, that he did not know Craig had a gun, then why would he refer to it as 'the gun' and not 'a gun'? The answer, of course, is that once Craig used said gun to shoot the police officer it was completely obvious to all that Craig did indeed have a gun! By using the definite phrase 'the gun' (even though it was the first mention in the confession), Bentley appears to be assuming, quite reasonably, that the gun is **Given** information because by that point, it is known to all concerned with the case.

Given-New in spoken English

Given and New information is introduced (or brought to the attention of the addressee) in discourse via definite/indefinite expressions. In spoken English, Givenness-Newness can also be signalled by intonation. Use of prosody can make information New even if it is in Theme position and Given information can be signalled even when it is in Rheme position. In the spoken data they analysed, Brown and Yule (1983: 166) found that, by and large, New information was introduced with phonological prominence, while Given information lacked phonological prominence. Brown and Yule (1983) explain, though, that there is not a one-to-one correspondence between phonological prominence and new information because there are other reasons why a speaker might choose to make part of what they say phonologically prominent, such as contrast or emphasis. Similarly, not all discourse that lacks phonological prominence is Given. While the pattern described by Brown and Yule (1983) indicates that there is a strong relationship between phonological prominence and New, it is down to the speaker to decide what to emphasise, and to judge whether something is obvious by the context or to be in the conscious of the hearer. Given-New, therefore, is decided by the speaker and their "moment-to-moment assessment of the relationship between what he [*sic*] wants to say and his [*sic*] hearer's informational requirements" (Brown and Yule 1983: 168).

Stress and prominence

Stress can also be used to give prominence to a part of an utterance compared with the rest of the utterance. Such prominence is achieved by choices made by the speaker about pitch, loudness, and length of syllables (O'Grady et al. 1996: 48). In the following examples prominence is indicated by bold type and underlining.

30

i) **I** thought you were singing tomorrow (someone else did not think it)
ii) I **thought** you were singing tomorrow (and I was right)
iii) I thought **you** were singing tomorrow (not someone else)
iv) I thought you **were** singing tomorrow (but apparently, you're not)
v) I thought you were **singing** tomorrow (and not dancing)
vi) I thought you were singing **tomorrow** (not another day)

The prominence afforded to the underlined words in the examples above suggest that alternative scenarios are possible or have been suggested during the discourse. In all examples, 'I' is in Theme position, but it is not always Given. Instead, the stressed word has New status, while the rest is assumed to be known and therefore Given. (We look at the meaning potential of intonation further in Chapter 4.)

Given-New and special Themes

As we saw earlier in the chapter, cleft clauses are a special structure where the cleft phrase forms part of the Theme and the cleft clause is the Rheme. However, in cleft structures the Theme is what is New, and the Rheme is what is Given (and, as we will see in Chapter 5, also presupposed). Clefting therefore brings a clause constituent to Theme position, and also marks it as New information. For example:

31

Theme	Rheme
It was the Donkey	that ate the carrot
New	**Given**

Fronting also brings the New information into Theme position. This therefore prioritises the newsworthy information and makes it prominent.

32

	Theme	Rheme
(i)		Eat the carrot		that's what the donkey did in the field	
(ii)		In the field		that's where the donkey ate the carrot.	
(iii)		The carrot		that's what the donkey ate.	
(iv)		The carrot		the donkey ate it.	
(v)		Ate the carrot		The donkey did	
	New	**Given**

The sorts of fronted structures shown in 32 are likely in a question-and-answer situation: What did the donkey do? Eat the carrot, that's what the donkey did. In such situations, it is possible to elide the Given information (and therefore the Rheme), because the information is recoverable from the discourse situation. Note that in spoken discourse, phonological emphasis leaves the information structure unchanged. Instead, it provides contrast. For example (emphasis indicated by underlining and bold type):

33

(i) Eat a carrot, **<u>that's</u>** what the donkey did.
(ii) Eat a carrot, that's what the **<u>donkey</u>** did.

In 33(i), even though 'that' is stressed, 'eat a carrot' is still New information. You could imagine (i) answering the question: 'I wonder what the donkey did in the field?' or contradicting the statement: 'I heard that the donkey ate an apple in the field'.

Similarly in 33(ii), emphasising 'donkey' phonologically does not change the information structure; 'eat a carrot' is still New. The emphasis makes clear that it was the donkey, but it is nonetheless Given. The example could answer the imaginary question: 'I wonder what the donkey did?'

Activity 2.6 Given and New in a news report

Consider again the news report from Activity 2.4 and identify Given and New information in it. Focus on the following three sentences.

(i) A phone engineer went on a 24-hour New Year's vodka binge before threatening to kill his partner, a court has been told.
(ii) Dad-of-two [name redacted], 39, had been drinking heavily after struggling to cope with the demands of the long hours he was working to provide for his family, Northampton Crown Court heard yesterday (Tuesday, March 16).
(iii) [Redacted name], a father of two children with additional needs, had been working 'obsessively' in the run up to the incident and had found it difficult to relax.

Our answers are at the end of the chapter.

Conclusion

In this chapter we have looked at how information is organised in the clause. The thematic structure of a clause is divided into Theme and Rheme, and the information structure is divided into Given and New. We examined how the choices available to text producers, whether speaking or writing, can influence what information is taken as Theme, and what is Given (shared) and New (assumed not to be known by the other person). We looked at the difference between marked and unmarked Themes, which assumes a structural 'norm' in English whereby the Subject of the clause comes first and therefore realises the Theme. Marked Themes can emphasise different clausal elements and bring into focus a particular part of the message that the clause is communicating. This may raise the importance of what is contained in the Theme and frame how the rest of the message (in the Rheme) is understood. The prototypical arrangement is that Given information comes before New information, and that Given coincides with Theme, and New with Rheme. However, we saw that marked Themes can contain New information meaning that it is highlighted as newsworthy. The choices made by the text producer can therefore influence how information in the clause is marked as news or taken for granted, and this may influence how that information is received.

Further reading

For clear and accessible introductions to Theme and Rheme, and Systemic Functional Linguistics more generally, see Thompson (2013) and Bloor and Bloor (2013).

Answers to activities

Activity 2.1 Label the clausal elements

a) **[S]** I **[P]**volunteer **[A]** at Andy's care centre
S = pronoun; P = verb; A = Prepositional phrase (PP)

b) **[S]** Oesophageal squamous cell carcinoma **[P]** is **[C]** the predominant subtype of oesophageal cancer **[A]** in Asian populations
S = Noun Phrase (NP); P = verb; C = NP; A = PP

c) **[S]** Kim Kardashian **[P]** has broken **[Od]** the internet **[A]** for the thousandth time in her life
S = NP; P=verb phrase (VP) made up of auxiliary verb, 'has' and past participle 'broken'; Od = NP; A = PP

d) **[S]** Improving how colleagues treat each other **[P]** is **[C]** a critical prerequisite to improving how the department treats the public
S = NP (Present participle 'improving' functions as a noun and is known as a participle noun or gerund; this type of NP also known as a Gerund Phrase); P=verb; C = NP

e) **[A]** In our analysis, **[S]** we **[P]** have attempted **[Od]** to mitigate this limitation **[A]** in a number of ways.
A = PP; S=pronoun; P = VP; Od = is not a prototypical NP, but an infinitive clause; A=PP

f) **[S]** Cedars-Sinai, **[A]** like every other hospital in California, **[P]** is **[C]** overwhelmed **[A]** with Covid-19 patients.
S = NP; A = PP; P = verb; C = participle adjective (i.e. past participle of 'overwhelm' acting as an adjective); A = PP
This example is not a passive construction; it is describing a state of being.

g) **[S]** Global macroeconomic developments and commodity supply factors **[P]** will likely cause **[Od]** boom-bust cycles to continue in commodity markets.
S = two NPs coordinated by 'and'; P = VP which includes adverb 'likely'; Od = is a non-finite, to-infinitive clause which consists of NP+VP+PP.

h) **[A]** As a donkey owner, **[S]** you **[P]** need to be prepared **[A]** for the cold winter months
A = adverbial phrase; S = pronoun; P = 'need' acts as an auxiliary and is followed by a passive infinitive; A = PP.

Activity 2.2 Theme and Rheme in declarative clauses

Theme	Rheme
I	volunteer at Andy's care centre
Kim Kardashian	has broken the internet for the thousandth time in her life
Improving how colleagues treat each other	is a critical prerequisite to improving how the department treats the public
Global macroeconomic developments and commodity supply factors	will likely cause boom-bust cycles to continue in commodity markets.
In our analysis,	we have attempted to mitigate this limitation [reporting autonomy] in a number of ways.
As a donkey owner,	you need to be prepared for the cold winter months.

Activity 2.3 Theme and Rheme in Imperative clauses

Themes are underlined:

(a) Preheat the oven to 180⁰C/160⁰C Fan/Gas 4.
For the sauce, heat the oil in a small frying pan over a medium heat.
Fry the onion and garlic in the oil. After five minutes, add the spices.

Activity 2.4 Theme and Rheme in a news report

	Theme	Rheme
1	Drunk dad-of-two who set fire to his partner and threatened to kill her	spared jail by Northampton judge
2	A phone engineer	went on a 24-hour New Year's vodka binge before threatening to kill his partner, a court has been told.
3	Dad-of-two, [name redacted], 39,	had been drinking heavily after struggling to cope with the demands of the long hours he was working to provide for his family, Northampton Crown Court heard yesterday (Tuesday, March 16).
4	[Redacted name], a father of two children with additional needs,	had been working 'obsessively' in the run up to the incident and had found it difficult to relax.
5	He	had been drinking bottles of vodka for 24 hours and taking his son's ADHD medication in when his partner went to visit her family, which he said invoked feelings of 'paranoia and jealousy'.

In each case, we have just analysed the main clause in each sentence. The sentences are numbered in the table. In sentences 1, 3, and 4, apposition is used in the Theme to provide more information. The three Themes the noun phrase 'dad-of-two' is used twice and 'a father of two children with additional needs' once. Themes are the starting point of the message and serve to frame the message, so the information in the Rheme is framed by the 'dad/father-of-two' Theme on three occasions. In sentence 2, the starting point is 'a phone engineer'. The Thematic pattern focuses on the social roles (father and engineer) of the perpetrator.

What might such an analysis indicate regarding the perpetrator's culpability? Well, the reader first encounters the perpetrator not as a violent abuser, but as a 'dad', or 'father of two children with additional needs', 'drunk', 'a phone engineer'. In every case, his crime is backgrounded syntactically, while his familial and professional status is brought to the fore. This might serve to mitigate the criminal activities by suggesting he is a hardworking parent, rather than a violent abuser. Moreover, the reference to him being 'drunk' could be read as excusing his violent behaviour.

Activity 2.5 Given-New in a spoken interaction

1	Stuart:	That's a good one.
2	Alison:	Well where's the one I took of you in the tree?
3	Stuart:	It might be on the other ones. Oh the two of us in the tree?
4	Alison:	Yeah. Look at him there. Oh my god.
5	Stuart:	Look at me leg! <laugh>

Given is double underlined; New is single underlined.

Definite reference is being used to refer to Objects that are **physically present** in the immediate context of the conversation or known to both participants. When Stuart uses the demonstrative 'that' he is referring (and maybe even pointing) to a photo in close proximity. When Alison refers to 'the one I took of you in the tree', she assumes Stuart will know the photo and remember the tree. She is therefore assuming **shared knowledge** and memories. The noun phrase 'the other ones' again presumably refers to more photographs which both participants are aware of. Definite reference is being used to refer to things that are physically present in the immediate context and which form part of the shared knowledge of the interlocutors. This information is taken as **Given** in the discourse by the participants. In turn 1, 'a good one' uses indefinite reference and is New information. Turn 3 answers a 'where' question. The answer provides information that Alison seeks, but uses referentially Given information ('the other ones'). The relationship between 'the one of you in the tree' and 'the other ones' is New.

Activity 2.6 Given and New in a news report

(i) A phone engineer went on a 24-hour New Year's vodka binge before threatening to kill his partner, a court has been told.

(ii) Dad-of-two, [name redacted], 39, had been drinking heavily after struggling to cope with the demands of the long hours he was working to provide for his family, Northampton Crown Court heard yesterday (Tuesday, March 16).

(iii) [Redacted name], a father of two children with additional needs, had been working 'obsessively' in the run up to the incident and had found it difficult to relax.

The news article is written discourse where the text producer (a journalist) is sharing information with a temporally and spatially displaced text receiver (a reader). The journalist must make assumptions about what the reader does and does not know and therefore about what is Given-New. The indefinite articles in (i) indicate that the information is assumed not to be known by the reader and therefore **New**. This is entirely reasonable since this is the opening of the article and the first mention of the people and events and is what we would expect at the start of a news article (and other texts). The Subject and Theme of (ii) has the same referent as (i), but we are nonetheless provided with more New information about the 'phone engineer'. This is a relational connection we must make, along the lines of 'the phone engineer is a dad-of-two / is called . . . / is 39', where the 'phone engineer' is Given, and the extra details about him are New. Similarly, in (iii) the repetition of the perpetrator's name is Given, but we are provided further information about the referent (underlined), which is New. Notice in (ii) the NP that begins 'the demands of . . .' (double underlined). The use of the definite article signals Givenness, even though the reader cannot possibly know this information, and imbues 'demands' with the status of common or shared knowledge (rather like 'the coast' example we discussed). The NP also presupposes these things to exist, which is a topic we take up in Chapter 5.

Notes

1 The Prague School refers to Vilém Mathesius, Nikolay Trubetskoy, Roman Jakobson, and other scholars based in Prague in the 1930s.
2 This position is not agreed. Huddleston and Pullum (2002: 248), for example, say that the PP is not an Object at all but a Complement.
3 This independent review authored by Wendy Williams is licensed under the terms of the Open Government Licence v3.0 which can be viewed at: nationalarchives.gov.uk/doc/open-government-licence/version/3
4 Following Halliday and Matthiessen (2014), both Theme and Rheme have an initial capital to show their status as a technical term.

References

Bloor, T. and Bloor, M. (2013) *The functional analysis of English: A Hallidayan approach*. London: Routledge.
Brown, G. and Yule, G. (1983) *Discourse analysis*. Cambridge: Cambridge University Press.
Coulthard, R. M. (2006) '"And then . . .": Language description and author attribution'. Sinclair lecture. Birmingham: ELR (Birmingham University).
Gundel, J. K. and Fretheim, F. (2004) 'Topic and focus'. In L. Horn and G. Ward (eds), *The handbook of pragmatics*, pp. 175–196. Oxford: Blackwell.

Halliday, M. A. K (1967) 'Notes on transitivity and theme in English: Part 2'. *Journal of Linguistics*, 3(2): 199–244.

Halliday, M. A. K. and Matthiessen, C. (2014) *An introduction to functional grammar* (4th edition). London: Routledge.

Haviland, S. E. and Clark, H. H. (1974) 'What's new? Acquiring new information as a process in comprehension'. *Journal of Verbal Learning & Verbal Behavior*, 13(5): 512–521.

Huddleston, R. and Pullum, G. K. (2002) *The Cambridge grammar of the English language*. Cambridge: Cambridge University Press.

Jeffries, L. (2010) *Critical stylistics: The power of English*. London: Palgrave.

O'Grady, G., Dobrovolsky, M., and Katamba, F. (1996) *Contemporary linguistics: An introduction*. London: Longman.

Thompson, G. (2013) *Introducing functional grammar*. London: Routledge.

3 Organising information in discourse

Cohesion

Introduction

One of the important aspects of discourse analysis is understanding the ways in which information is structured and links together, whether at a macro (whole text) or micro (clause/sentence) level. In the previous chapter, we introduced key grammatical concepts and terminology which are necessary to understand the relationship between discourse and its structure. In this chapter, we continue by considering how structure influences the coherence and interpretation of discourse. We will look at Halliday and Hasan's (1976) influential notions of coherence and cohesion and how, when we produce language, we make it fit in with what has gone before and what is coming up, as well as making it situationally relevant. We will see that cohesion and coherence are created (in part) by organising and sequencing information as the communication event (written or spoken) progresses (Thompson 2013: 145).

Coherence and Cohesion in discourse

When discourse is seen as logical, consistent, and understandable, has continuity, and makes sense then it is said to be coherent. **Coherence** is achieved by organising and structuring the information in discourse using the available language resources. **Cohesion** refers to the lexical and grammatical choices (the language resources) that combine to make a discourse a connected whole. Whereas coherence is a matter of judgement by the reader/hearer, and so is a logical, common-sense phenomenon, cohesion is a language and discourse phenomenon. Coherence and cohesion in discourse were first examined in detail by Halliday and Hasan (1976), who proposed and described a system of cohesion in English. According to Halliday and Hasan (1976), cohesion incorporates the following devices.

1 reference
2 ellipsis and substitution
3 conjunction
4 reiteration (lexical cohesion)

DOI: 10.4324/9781003351207-3

In the next four sections we will briefly describe these cohesive devices. In our discussion, we will refer to both Halliday and Hasan's (1976) original model, as well as to the revised model described in Halliday and Matthiessen (2014).

Reference

Reference is the use of pronouns (e.g. 'she', 'her'), demonstratives (e.g. 'this', 'that'), and comparatives (e.g. 'more', 'less') to point backwards or forwards to things that have already been or that are about to be mentioned in the discourse. For example, consider this short extract from a report commissioned by the UK Government on racist immigration policies.

1

> Veronica was invited to undertake work at The University of the West Indies as a coordinator and lecturer of a number of social work programmes. She took up the opportunity as she was delighted to use her expertise in a new context, however, she eventually decided to return to the UK conscious of her responsibilities, growing debt and gaps in NI contributions.
>
> *Windrush Lessons Learned Review*, 19/03/2020[1]

In example 1, the same entity, Veronica, is referred to again and again. Veronica is first identified by name and then the pronouns, 'she', and 'her' (highlighted in bold), refer back to Veronica. Halliday and Hasan (1976: 32) suggest that pronouns (and other reference words) are signals that indicate the relevant information is to be retrieved from elsewhere in the discourse. By relevant information, they mean "the identity of the particular thing being referred to" which, in the case of example 1 above, is 'Veronica'. The pronouns are semantically empty until filled by the thing they each refer to, known as their "referential meaning" (Halliday and Hasan 1976: 32). In 1, the pronouns all refer to 'Veronica' and cohesion is created via this relationship of co-referentiality. Thinking back to our previous chapter, we can also notice that pronominal reference signals **Given** information, i.e. information that has already been introduced in the discourse and is therefore known to the hearer/reader.

Endophoric versus exophoric reference

The link between a reference word (pronoun, demonstrative, and comparative) and the thing being referenced is cohesive only if the 'thing' is introduced elsewhere in the language of the discourse. This is the case in example 1 where 'Veronica' is introduced at the start of the story. The pronouns therefore point to something mentioned within the text, and this type of reference is known as **endophoric**. Reference to things external to the language of the discourse is known as **exophoric reference** and is not a cohesive device because it relies on context rather than co-text for meaning (cohesion is a **textual** phenomenon). To help understand the difference between endophoric and exophoric reference, let's return to the extract of a conversation we met in Chapter 2 that is taken from the spoken section of the **BNC**. Recall that the conversation is between two people discussing photographs (emphasis added; turns numbered for ease of reference):

2

1. Stuart: That's a good one.
2. Alison: Well where's the one I took of you in the tree?
3. Stuart: It might be on the other ones. Oh the two of us in the tree?
4. Alison: Yeah. Look at him there. Oh my god.
5. Stuart: Look at me leg!

In example 2, Stuart and Alison refer to the photos in a few ways including the demonstrative pronouns 'that' and 'there', and the noun phrases 'the one' and 'the other ones'. Additionally, when Alison says, 'Look at him', the pronoun 'him' references a person in a photograph. These noun phrases and pronouns are all examples of **exophoric** reference because they point to and reference things in the immediate context (the situation) in which the discourse, the conversation, occurs. They do not point inwardly to the language of the discourse and to things already or about to be mentioned. Consequently, the referents are only apparent and known to the people sharing the same immediate physical context and visual perspective. Readers of the transcription or hearers of the audio recording of the conversation can only imagine the referents of the noun phrases and pronoun.

In turn 3, however, Stuart's use of the pronoun 'it' is an example of **endophoric** reference because it refers backwards within the conversation to something previously mentioned by Alison in turn 2. The pronoun points inwardly to the language of the discourse and establishes a co-referential link between 'it' and 'the one I took of you in the tree' creating cohesion between the two lexical items. Notice, though, that when Alison says, 'the one I took of you in the tree', this is **exophoric** reference because it points outwards from the conversation and references a photograph that exists somewhere in the situation of the conversation. It is, as we saw in Chapter 2, also assumed to be shared knowledge and therefore Given information.

To summarise, **endophoric** reference points inwardly to the language of the discourse and is a cohesive device because it creates links between the textual parts of the discourse. **Exophoric** reference points outwardly to the discourse situation and is not a (textual) cohesive device. **Endophoric** reference utilises a limited number of lexical forms, mainly personal and demonstrative pronouns. **Exophoric** reference utilises many other linguistics forms, such as nouns phrases, to reference things in the context of the discourse.

Endophoric reference: anaphora and cataphora

There are two types endophoric reference:

- **Anaphoric** (pointing backwards)
- **Cataphoric** (pointing forwards).

Anaphoric reference (or anaphora) is the most common. For example, the use of 'she' and 'her' in example 1 and 'it' in example 2 are anaphora because the pronouns point backwards to something already mentioned in the discourse (known as the antecedent). Cataphoric reference (or cataphora) is less common than anaphora and is where the referent of a pronoun comes after the pronoun in the discourse. For example, in example 3 (which is taken from the spoken section of the BNC), the pronoun 'she' refers forward to 'my mother'.

3

She was a good provider, my mother was.

A summary of the different types of reference we have discussed so far can be found in Figure 3.1

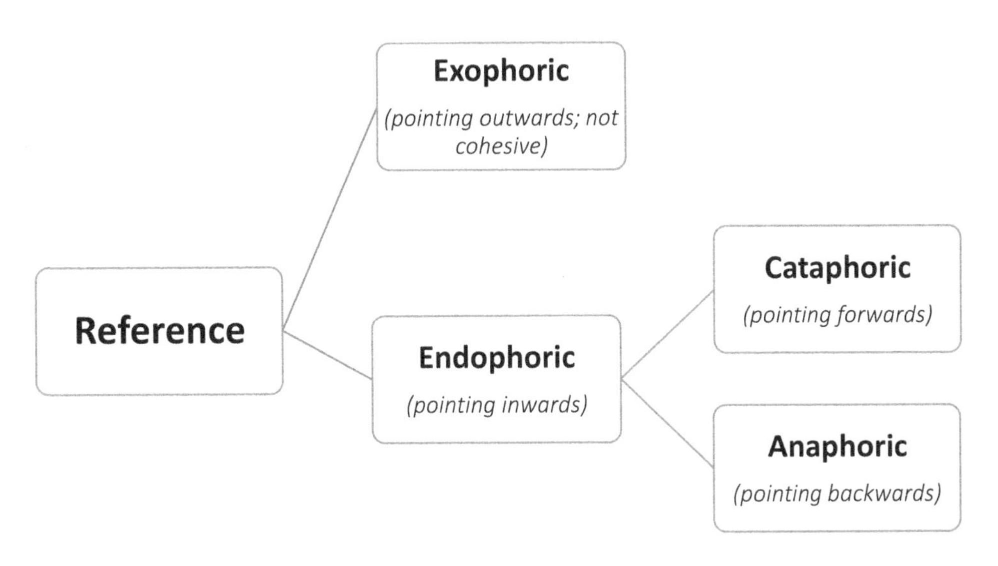

Figure 3.1 Summary of reference

Personal, demonstrative, and comparative reference

We have seen so far that reference is a cohesive device when pronouns and other reference items point forwards or backwards within the discourse to things already introduced or that are about to be introduced. Halliday and Hasan (1976) describe three types of cohesive reference: personal, demonstrative, and comparative. An inventory of the lexical items used for each type of reference are as follows.

(i)	**Personal reference**	
	pronoun	'he', 'she', 'it', 'they' 'him', 'her', 'them'
	Possessive determiner	'his', hers', 'its', 'their', 'theirs'
(ii)	**Demonstrative references**	
	Pronoun/determiner	'this'/'that', 'these'/'those'
	Adverb	'here'/'there', 'now'/'then'
	Determiner	'the'
(iii)	**Comparative reference**	
	determiner	'more', 'less', 'another', etc.
	adjective	'similar', 'different', etc.
	adverb	'similarly', 'likewise', etc

Personal reference

This type of reference employs personal pronouns and determiners to create cohesive links between the reference item and the thing being referenced, which can be animate, inanimate, or abstract. We encountered personal reference in example 1 where the pronoun 'she' and the possessive determiner 'her' referred anaphorically to 'Veronica'. The different pronouns refer to the same entity, Veronica, so they are **co-referential**.

Demonstrative reference

With demonstrative reference, the reference items are demonstrative pronouns and adverbs of space and time that typically mark proximity or distance. In other words, they have a pointing function, known as **deixis**. For instance, in example 4, 'this' makes anaphoric reference to 'support'. Like personal reference, demonstrative reference is co-referential because the reference item and the thing it references both identify the same, real-world thing, which in the case of 4 is financial support offered by the UK Government (emphasis added).

4

> Find out what support is available in England to help increase your income. <u>This</u> includes the Cost of Living Payment, Universal Credit and Carer's Allowance.
>
> GOV.UK, Cost of living support

Halliday and Hasan (1976) include markers of spatial and temporal deixis ('here', 'there', 'now', 'then') because in some circumstances, these can be used cohesively. According to Halliday and Hasan (1976: 75) 'then' has the meaning "'at the time just referred to'" and 'now' "'this state of affairs having come about'".

The referential use of 'then' as a marker of temporal deixis is demonstrated in example 5 (emphasis added).

5

> [CMC] became one of the first IT companies to spot the prospects for software services exports to the US and in 1991 made probably the first cross-border acquisition by an Indian IT company . . . By **then** it was already a Rs 100 crore company.
>
> CNBC18.com, 04/04/2022

In 5, 'then' (highlighted) refers back to '1991' – the time just referred to.

Halliday and Hasan (1976) also include 'the' in the list of demonstratives. We saw in the previous chapter how the definite article 'the' can indicate that information in a discourse is Given. This function is also cohesive because it indicates that "the item in question is specific and identifiable; that somewhere the information necessary for identifying it is recoverable." (Halliday and Hasan 1976: 71). If the definite article is cohesive then the information is recoverable from the discourse, which means 'the' is used **anaphorically**. Thompson (2013: 218) usefully sums up the meaning of anaphoric 'the' as, "you know the one I mean [. . .] because I've already mentioned it". For example, the noun phrase, 'the opportunity', in example 1 (*Windrush Review*), anaphorically refers back to 'work at The University of the West Indies'. Therefore, the item 'the opportunity' is, to use Halliday and Hasan's words, "specific and identifiable" and "the information necessary for identifying it is recoverable" from the discourse.

Comparative reference

Another form of reference is comparative reference, which involves lexical items that set up a relation of contrast or similarity between the reference word(s) and something already mentioned in the discourse. For instance, in example 6, which is taken from the *British Medical Journal*, that 'adenocarcinoma is **more** common' references back to another type of carcinoma mentioned at the start of the sentence.

6

> Oesophageal squamous cell carcinoma is the predominant subtype of oesophageal cancer in Asian populations, occurring in 90% of patients, whereas adenocarcinoma is **more** common in North America and western Europe.
>
> *BMJ* 2022; 377: e068714, 19/04/2022

Comparative reference therefore assumes that something has already been mentioned in the discourse against which the thing currently being talked about is being compared.

Activity 3.1 Personal, demonstrative, and comparative reference

Consider the following examples. Identify the cohesive reference, say whether it is personal, demonstrative, or comparative.

(a) Kim Kardashian has broken the internet for the thousandth time in her life after a video of her reacting to Kanye West staring at Rihanna has captured everyone's attention.

Cosmopolitan.com UK, 29/06/2018

(b) [ESTATE AGENTS] are excited to bring to the market a much sought after, spacious three-bedroom detached house situated within the charming village of Logierait. This is an excellent opportunity which will appeal to a broad range of potential buyers.

Rightmove, 08/02/2022

(c) Adverse events related to treatment resulted in death in nine of 327 (3%) patients in the sintilimab-chemotherapy group and six of 332 (2%) patients in the placebo-chemotherapy group (tables S10 and S12). The rates of adverse events were similar when we grouped patients by chemotherapy regimen.

BMJ 2022; 377: e068714, 19/04/2022

Our answers are at the end of the chapter.

Ellipsis and substitution

Substitution and ellipsis refer to different ways in which parts of the discourse can be omitted from the discourse because they can be recovered or presumed from the co-text. As we noted in the previous chapter, information that can be omitted because it is recoverable is Given.

Ellipsis

With ellipsis, the text producer leaves gaps (i.e. omits words) which the receiver must 'fill in' using their knowledge of the preceding discourse or contextual information. Ellipsis can be found in questions and answers, where answers are often elliptical. Consider the following constructed examples.

7

(i) A Did the donkey eat the carrot?
B Yes [the donkey ate the carrot].

(ii) A Did the donkey eat the apple?
B No, [the donkey did not eat the apple, it ate] the carrot.
(iii) A What did the donkey eat?
B [the donkey ate] a carrot.
(iv) A I like carrots. Do you [like carrots]?
B Yes. [I do like carrots]

In each example the words in square brackets are the possible missing words and these are recoverable from the preceding discourse (i.e. the question).

Substitution

Substitution is where a part of the discourse is substituted with a 'gap filler' which can be an adverb, pronoun, or determiner. Bloor and Bloor (2013) suggest a three-way classification of substitution: nominal, verbal, and clausal. Nominal substitution is where nouns or noun phrases are substituted by lexical items such as 'one', 'ones', 'same', 'some', and 'any'. Various possibilities for this are demonstrated in the following made-up examples (substitute word underlined; substituted words in square brackets).

8
(i) I really like carrots. Can I have some? [carrots]
(ii) I really like carrots. Chantenay are my favourite ones. [carrots]
(iii) I really like carrots. Do you have any? [carrots]
(iv) You're having carrots? I'll have the same. [carrots]

Sometimes the Predicator is substituted for a form of the verb 'do' (typically, but not always, accompanied by 'it' or 'that'). When this happens, often the Object is also substituted with a demonstrative pronoun ('that'). This is shown in the following examples (substitute word underlined; substituted words in square brackets).

9
(i) A: Your donkey ate all my carrots!
B: My donkey would never do that! [eat your carrots]
(ii) A: So, your donkey likes carrots.
B: Oh, it does. [likes carrots]

In 9(i) 'do that' acts as a substitute for Predicator and direct Object, 'eat your carrots', while in 9(ii) 'does' substitutes for Predicator and direct Object 'likes carrots'.

Some lexical items such as 'so' and 'not' can substitute for Subject, Predicator, and Object (or longer stretches of discourse). The following made-up examples demonstrate this (substitute word underlined; substituted words in square brackets).

10

(i) A Did the donkey eat the carrot?
B Yes, I think so. [the donkey did eat the carrot]

(ii) A Did the donkey eat the carrot?
B I think not. [the donkey did not eat the carrot]

In 10(i), 'so' substitutes for 'the donkey did eat the carrot', while in 10(ii) 'not' is the negative equivalent and substitutes for 'the donkey did not eat the carrot'. In both cases, Subject, Predicator, and Object are substituted by a single word.

Activity 3.2 Substitution

Look at the following extracts and identify the substitution and explain what has been substituted with what.

(a) Is Katrina pregnant? Fans seem to think so.

Daily Times, Lahore, 18/08/2022

(b) JG: Now in 'Men in Black II' you show off the board in a different way, it's where you have the Michael Jackson cameo. How did you get him to do that?

(Question posed to director of *Men in Black II*, Barry Sonnenfeld by *Insider* reporter Jason Guerrasio)

Insider, New York, 01/07/2022

(c) He told me he has changed his mind about a child and doesn't want another but loves me and if we end up having one, would just go with it rather than lose me.

www.mumsnet.com, 09/08/2018

Conjunction

Conjunction creates a relationship between clauses, sentences, and longer stretches of text (e.g. paragraphs) by making links between what precedes and/or what follows. In Halliday and Hasan's words, conjunction concerns how "linguistic elements that occur in succession" relate to each other, and how that relationship is created in the discourse (Halliday and Hasan 1976: 227). Conjunctions can be realised by single words like the adverbs 'however', 'actually', and so on, as well as prepositional phrases such as 'as a result of', 'in spite of'. Halliday and Hasan (1976: 228) refer to these types of connectors as **conjunctive adjuncts** because they are doing the job of conjunctions and their clausal function is that of Adjunct. As you might recall from our discussion of the English clause in the previous chapter, an Adjunct is a word or phrase that adds extra information to a clause but is not necessary to make the clause grammatically complete (we will see how that works in example 11 below). Halliday and Hasan (1976) set out four types of conjunction: **temporal, additive, adversative**, and **causal**.

Temporal

Temporal conjunctives signal time and sequencing relations. Consider the following invented example.

11

> I ate lunch. Afterwards, I had a drink

In 11, the adverb 'afterwards' is an example of a **temporal conjunctive adjunct.** It is an Adjunct because the clause 'I had a drink' is grammatical on its own and does not require the adverbial 'afterwards' to complete it, and it is conjunctive because it creates a time (temporal) relation between 'I ate lunch' and 'I had a drink'. Without 'afterwards', there is no explicit relation between the two events and no temporal sequencing, so 'afterwards' is a "cohesive agent" (Halliday and Hasan 1976: 229). Its presence in the sentence presupposes the presence of something happening earlier in the discourse. If someone were to simply say, "Afterwards, I had a drink.", then it is likely that the hearer would ask, "After what?"

As well as signalling the sequencing of events described by the discourse, temporal conjunction can also relate to progression in the "communication process", which means the sequence in which elements of a discussion, explanation, or description are presented (Halliday and Hasan 1976: 263). This sort of cohesive sequencing is achieved by adverbs such as 'first'/'firstly', 'second'/'secondly (etc.), 'next', 'then', 'finally', and is prevalent, for example, in academic and management reports. For instance, consider the following extract from a report prepared by the US government National Centre for Biotechnology and Information (NCBI):

12

> In our analysis, we have attempted to mitigate this limitation [autonomy] in a number of ways. **First**, our central analysis was based on an agnostic approach to trAE inclusion [. . .] **Second**, subanalyses were performed to address potential sources of bias within each investigator's AE reporting pattern [. . .] **Finally**, [. . .] we performed a subanalysis of laboratory values for the most predictive trAE in our cohort . . .
>
> https://www.ncbi.nlm.nih.gov/pmc/articles/PMC6066474, 25/07/2019

Also encompassed in temporal conjunction and related to the internal sequencing of the discourse is what Halliday and Hasan label '**here and now**' relations and **summary**. 'Here and now' uses lexis to refer inwardly to the discourse, while summary expresses the culmination of, for instance, the discussion, argument, description, or explanation in the discourse (Halliday and Hasan 1976: 264). For example (emphasis added):

13

> The essential idea <u>at this point</u> in our discussion is that, from an ontological viewpoint, there is no sharp line between a "significant" and a "nonsignificant" difference;
>
> *American Psychologist*, 1989, 44(10): 1277

14

> <u>To sum up</u>, the study presents important implications for predicting user engagement in digital platforms and the social information signaling these platforms can adopt.
>
> *Behaviour & Information Technology*, 21/07/2022
> doi: 10.1080/0144929X.2022.2101024

In example 13, 'at this point' realises 'here and now' relations by referring internally to the discussion in hand and presupposes previous elements of the same discussion. In 14, 'to sum up' realises summary relations and presupposes the full extent of the description of the research presented in the paper.

Additive

Additive conjunctions express that there is more in addition to what has gone before and is realised by, for example, 'and', 'also', 'further', 'what is more', 'moreover', 'additionally'. Additive also includes **alternative** relations (e.g. 'or', 'alternatively'), **comparative** (e.g. 'likewise', 'similarly', 'by contrast', 'conversely') and **appositive** (e.g. 'that is', 'in other words', 'for instance'). The short extract from the trade magazine *Grocer* in example 15, which reports on the experiences of a 'secret shopper', shows the additive function of 'moreover' (emphasised) and forms a connection between examples of messiness in the shop and low stock levels, all of which connect back to a lack of staff.

15

> The lack of staff resulted in a messy shop floor - there were several unmanned shopping and restocking trolleys throughout the store. . . . <u>Moreover</u>, the

food counters were nearly depleted of options and five of our required items were out of stock.

Grocer, 16, 04/12/2021

Adversative

The adversative conjunctive signals a relationship of "'contrary to expectation'" (Halliday and Hasan 1976: 253) and contrast, and includes 'yet', 'but', 'however', 'nevertheless', and 'though'. For example, 'nevertheless' in the extract from a *Times of India* article about Bollywood actor Aahana Kumra suggests that grabbing headlines is contrary to expectations and in contrast to not being a 'star kid' (emphasis added).

16

[. . .] soon she realised why things will not change for her so easily as she is not a star kid. **Nevertheless**, she surely knows how to grab headlines [. . .]

Times of India, indiatimes.com, 23/01/2022

Included in the adversative category are **corrective** relations which are realised by, for example, 'instead', 'rather', 'I mean', and **dismissive** relations which dismiss what has gone before and can be realised by 'anyhow', 'whatever', 'in any case'. The following examples, taken from the record of UK Parliament (*Hansard*), helps to show how corrective and dismissive adversative conjunctives operate (emphasis added).

17

Tim Farron: [. . .] he [the Prime Minister] says nothing about outdoor education, which is an industry of vast importance to us in the lakes and dales, and of great value to young people right across the country. There are 15,000 people employed in the sector; **at least**, there were, but some 6,000 have now lost their jobs.

Hansard, Volume 689, 22/02/2021

18

Mr Dunne: [. . .] will my right hon. Friend consider offering occupiers of listed premises in town centres [. . .] a VAT exemption on repairs and maintenance of those premises [. . .]?

Mr Hammond: [. . .] under EU law, we cannot introduce a reduced rate of VAT that is limited to repairs, maintenance and renovation of listed buildings. **In any case**, VAT incurred on their

> properties by VAT-registered businesses may be recoverable from Her Majesty's Revenue and Customs, [. . .].
>
> *Hansard*, Volume 660, 21/05/2019

In 17, the conjunctive 'at least' makes a correction to what was said immediately prior to it, and so according to Halliday and Hasan (1976: 25) expresses "'as against what has just been said'". In 18, the conjunctive 'in any case' relates back to the request for a VAT (value added tax) exemption made by Mr Dunne and, as a preface to stating that VAT can be claimed back, serves to dismiss the request as pointless.

Causal

Halliday and Hasan (1976) suggest that some causal conjunctives realise general causal cohesive relations (e.g. 'so', 'thus', 'therefore', and 'consequently'), while others identify the specific relations of **reason** (e.g. 'for that reason'); **result** (e.g. 'as a result') and **purpose** (e.g. 'for that purpose'). For example, in the following extract from an academic journal article, 'for that purpose' creates an explicit purpose relation between using 'a novel Bayesian approach' and examining 'the effects of monetary policy' (emphasis added).

19

> We examine the effects of monetary policy on income inequality in Japan. For that purpose, we use a novel Bayesian approach that jointly estimates the Gini coefficient from grouped income data and the dynamics of macroeconomic quantities.
>
> *Empirical Economics*, 62(5), May 2022

Coordinating conjunctions

Coordinating conjunctions are lexical items (such as 'and', 'but', 'or') that are typically used to join together (co-ordinate) words, phrases and clauses (e.g. 'the donkey and the carrot'). When used in this way, these conjunctions are not cohesive devices. However, if they are used at the start of a sentence this can be cohesive. Consider the following abridged example from the US government web pages (emphasis added):

20

> In January 2021, Americans had very few tools to protect against COVID-19, and the tools we did have were in limited supply. Over the last year, together, with states, localities, and public and private partners, the Administration has mobilized an unprecedented, whole-of-society effort to give Americans the tools they need to protect themselves.

> The Administration has put vaccines at the center of our COVID-19 response because vaccines are the best tool we have to prevent hospitalization and death. [. . .].
>
> The Administration has also expedited the development, manufacturing, and procurement of COVID-19 treatments, building a diverse medicine cabinet filled with more treatments now than at any point in the pandemic. [. . .]
>
> The nation's testing supply has increased dramatically. We now have free testing sites at 21,500 locations around the country. [. . .].
>
> **And** the U.S. government has successfully put equity at the heart of a nationwide public health response. Hispanic, Black, and Asian adults are now vaccinated at the same rates as White adults. This is the result of an all-of-society effort that got America to where it is today [. . .].
>
> The White House, *National COVID-19 Preparedness Plan*, March 2022

The extract is part of an extended text that sets out the U.S. Government's plan for Covid-19 under Joe Biden. In this part of the text, the Biden Administration is stating what they have done already to protect the country against Covid. This extends over a series of paragraphs, the beginnings of which we have included above. The first sentence in the final paragraph of the extract starts with 'And'. The use of 'and' is conjunctive because it connects the point made in the final paragraph with those that preceded it. It is also cohesive because, as Halliday and Hasan (1976: 227) explain, lexical items that are "conjunctive" create cohesion "indirectly" by presupposing "the presence of other components in the discourse". The use of 'and' in example 20 therefore presupposes that at least one other related point has been made in the text which this sentence/paragraph is adding to. Starting the sentence with 'and' also provides a finality to what is ostensibly a list of the "tools" that have been "given" to Americans to protect themselves. It is the final element and the metaphorical 'cherry on the top' stating as it does that everything has been "mobilized" with "equity".

Conjunction summary

To summarise, the four main types of conjunction along with an abridged overview of subtypes are presented in Table 3.1[2] with examples of the conjunctives (words and phrases) that realise cohesion. It is worth noting that the categories of conjunction are not agreed (on this point, see Thompson 2013: 226) and the list of conjunctives is not exhaustive, potentially open-ended, and a word or phrase can belong to more than one category.

Table 3.1 Categories and subtypes of conjunction based on the hierarchy presented in Halliday and Hasan (1976: 244)

Types/subtypes	Examples
Temporal	*just then, soon, meanwhile, afterwards*
– sequential	*then, next, after that, firstly, previously, finally, lastly*
– here and now	*here, at this point, now*
– summary	*to sum up, in summary, in short*
Additive	*and, also, moreover, furthermore, in addition*
– alternative	*or, or else, alternatively*
– appositive	*that is, I mean, for instance, for example*
– comparative	*likewise, similarly, in the same way, by contrast, conversely*
Adversative	*but, yet, however, though, nevertheless*
– contrastive	*in fact, actually, as a matter of fact, at the same time*
– correcting	*instead, rather*
– dismissive	*in any case, anyway, anyhow*
Causal	*so, then, therefore, because, consequently*
– reason	*for this reason, it follows*
– result	*as a result, from this*
– purpose	*for this purpose, to this end*

Activity 3.3 Conjunctive cohesion

Consider the following short extracts from news reports. Do they contain any cohesive conjunctions? If so, where and what type(s)?

(a) Rapper and businessman Cassper Nyovest [. . .] no longer feels safe following the brutal murder of his friend and amapiano pioneer DJ Sumbody. As a result, the Destiny hitmaker has decided to beef up security, according to Zimoja.

https://www.myzimbabwe.co.zw, 13/02/2023

(b) In Los Angeles County alone [. . .] one in every five people has tested positive for the virus. On January 11, the county hit a grim milestone: 30,000 recorded COVID-19 deaths. Meanwhile, vaccines are being rolled out at a snail's pace and frontline workers are overwhelmed.

The Jerusalem Post (online), 14/01/2021

Our answers are at the end of the chapter.

Reiteration (lexical cohesion)

Reiteration refers to the use of semantically related lexis in the discourse to create **lexical cohesion**. Reiteration is reference to the same entity or idea by the

repetition of a lexical item, or the use of other semantically connected lexis via **synonymy, antonymy, hyponymy, meronymy** and **collocation**. These aspects of reiteration are as follows.

- **Repetition** is the recurrence of a lexical item in a discourse including morphological variants (e.g. eat, eaten, eat, ate).
- **Synonymy** describes a semantic relation of similar or equivalent meaning (e.g. magic/sorcery; little/small).
- **Antonymy** describes a complementary (or opposite) relationship between lexical items (e.g. little/large; clever/stupid).
- **Hyponymy** refers to 'kind of' relationships (e.g. a carrot is a kind of vegetable), and 'specific-to-general'/'general-to-specific' relationships (e.g. carrot is a specific kind of vegetable; vegetable is a more general term than carrot). Hyponymy incorporates the related notions of superordination and subordination. For example, 'carrot' is a specific member of the set 'vegetable', and so it has a hyponymic relationship to 'vegetable', where 'vegetable' is the superordinate, and 'carrot' is the subordinate. Also included in hyponymy is the idea of "general nouns" (Halliday and Hasan 1976: 275), such as 'stuff' and 'thing', which can be seen as general superordinate categories. For example, the general noun 'thing' can be seen as a broad superordinate category that includes a vast range of other types of things such as, for example, food. Food is a less general category that includes, for example, vegetable, which is a superordinate category that includes carrot.
- **Meronymy** extends the notion of reiteration and lexical cohesion to include 'part of'/'has a' lexical relations. For example, an apple has a core and pips; core and pips are parts of an apple.
- **Collocation** is the tendency for some words to co-occur with certain others. For example, in the UK the word 'fish' has a strong tendency to co-occur with 'chips' (partly due to the tendency in the non-textual world for actual chips to co-occur with battered cod or haddock on a plate). We look at collocation again in Chapters 5 and 11.

Let's consider reiteration in some of its forms and how it creates lexical cohesion by looking at a UK Government press release on Covid-19 (all emphases added).

21

> **Young** coronavirus (COVID-19) **patients** have told their stories of battling the virus and suffering long-term debilitating effects as part of a new film encouraging people to get their vaccines.
> The video features several **patients** who experienced serious symptoms of COVID-19 or developed long COVID, as well as the doctors and frontline staff who treated them, to warn of the dangers of the virus for those who are not vaccinated. It is narrated by A&E doctor, Dr Emeka Okorocha.

> It comes as **people aged** 16 to 17 in England are offered a **COVID-19** vaccine by today (Monday 23 August), meeting the government's target. More than 360,000 have already been vaccinated and letters and texts were sent last week to the remaining **people** inviting them to book an appointment with their GP or visit their nearest walk-in centre.
> All at-risk **people aged** 12 to 15 in England have also been invited for a vaccination and **young people** are encouraged to take up the offer as soon as possible to build vital protection before returning to school in September.
> The latest figures show that hospitals are seeing a rise in unvaccinated **young** adults admitted with **COVID-19**. A fifth of **COVID-19** hospital admissions in England are **aged** 18 to 34–4 times higher than the peak in the winter of 2020.
>
> Press release, UK Department of Health and Social Care, 23/08/2021

The extract contains numerous examples of lexical cohesion. For example, there is repetition of 'COVID-19', 'young', 'people', and 'aged' (all highlighted in bold), and word forms that share the same stem ('vaccine'/'vaccines'/'vac cination'/'vaccinated'/'unvaccinated'; 'offered'/'offer'; 'admitted'/'admissions') (all underlined). The lexical items 'film' and 'video' have a relationship of synonymy, as do the ages ranges '16 to 17'/'12 to 15' and the phrase 'young people' and '18 to 34' and 'young adult' (outlined in boxes). There is also a rela tionship of synonymy between 'coronavirus' and COVID-19, and 'long-term debilitating effects' and 'long COVID'. The press release that the extract is taken from concerns public health and medicine and there are several lexical items relating to this semantic domain. For example, there is mention of 'doctors', 'frontline staff' (presumably nurses, support workers, and porters), 'A&E doctor' and 'GP' which are semantically related hyponymically as these are all kinds of health worker. Similarly, 'hospitals', 'walk in centre' are kinds of institutions providing healthcare (we might also include 'GP' if we see that lexical item referencing a whole practice rather than an individual). There is also a meronymic relationship between 'hospitals' and 'patients' and 'A&E' because hospitals have patients, and Accident and Emergency departments are part of a hospital. We can also see a collocational relationship (i.e. a tendency to co-occur) between 'doctor' and 'patients'; 'doctor', 'patients', and 'treated'; and 'hospital' and 'admissions'. These and other lexical relations in the text are summarised below.

Repetition	'COVID-19', 'young', 'people', 'aged', 'patients', 'offer'/'offered', 'invited'/'inviting', 'vaccine'/'vaccines'/'vaccinated'/'unvaccina ted'
Synonyms	'COVID-19'/'coronavirus'/'the virus'; 'film'/'video'; 'long-term debilitating effects'/'long-COVID'; 'young people'/'16 to 17' and '12 to 15'; 'young adults'/'18 to 34'.

Hyponymy	'Doctors' and 'frontline staff' are kinds of health workers; 'hospitals' and 'walk in centres' are kinds of healthcare institutions.
Meronymy	'Hospitals' have 'patients' and 'A&E' depts. 'Hospitals' also have 'doctors' and 'frontline staff'.
Collocation	'doctors' and 'patients' and 'treated'; 'GP' and 'appointment'; 'hospital' and 'appointment'; 'hospital' and 'patients'; 'hospital' and 'admissions'; 'hospitals' and 'admitted'.

The short extract from the government press release is rich with lexical cohesion. We can also see how the cohesive device of reference interacts with the reiteration. For example, the first mention of the new film uses the indefinite article ('**a** new film'); the next mention uses a different, semantically connected term, 'video', but we are guided to understand that the same entity is being referenced by the definite article (e.g. '**the** video') (our emphasis). Similarly, 'the virus' is used to reference 'coronavirus' and 'COVID-19' and the use of the definite article (along with the semantically connected word) guides us to understand that this noun phrase is referring to something that has already been introduced in the text.

Activity 3.4 Collocation

Let's play a little word association game. When you encounter each word below, write down the first word that comes into your mind:

Night
Knife
Hat
Tea
Smoke

Whatever you have written down is likely to be what often collocates (or co-occurs) with the words in the list. For example, 'Night' often collocates with 'Day'. Collocations can offer insight into what a speaker deems culturally or socially prominent for them. For instance, we offered this list to some family members and one of our relatives who is a new mum came up with 'light' (night light). Can you guess why?

Conclusion

In this chapter we have summarised Halliday and Hasan's (1976) important framework for cohesion which involves reference, ellipsis/substitution, conjunction, and reiteration. As we have seen, cohesion in discourse is achieved via numerous lexical means, and Halliday and Hasan's framework systematically sets out the various linguistic possibilities. There is an interplay between Theme and Rheme, Given and New, cohesion and English grammar. The choices made at the syntactic and lexical levels influence thematic organisation, information structure and the way the text coheres. Thematic patterns coincide with referential and lexical cohesion; similarly, Given information can be elided as well as having referential connections. Themes and information form sequences in texts and this sequencing is supported by cohesion. In the next chapter we will develop the notion of sequencing by discovering more about the sequences that occur in spoken interactions.

Further reading

For clear and accessible introductions to coherence and cohesion, and Systemic Functional Linguistics more generally, see Thompson (2013) and Bloor and Bloor (2013)

Answers to activities

Activity 3.1 Personal, demonstrative, and comparative reference

Identify the cohesive reference and say whether it is personal, demonstrative or comparative.

(a) Kim Kardashian has broken the internet for the thousandth time in <u>her</u> life after a video of <u>her</u> reacting to Kanye West staring at Rihanna has captured everyone's attention.

Cosmopolitan.com UK, 29/06/2018

Personal reference: the possessive pronoun 'her' (used twice) refers *anaphorically* to the proper noun (the antecedent) 'Kim Kardashian'. The noun and the possessive pronoun are *co-referential* because they both refer to the same person in the real world.

(b) [ESTATE AGENTS] are excited to bring to the market a much sought after, spacious three-bedroom detached house situated within the charming village of Logierait. <u>This</u> is an excellent opportunity which will appeal to a broad range of potential buyers.

Rightmove, 08/02/2022

Demonstrative reference: at the start of the second sentence, 'this' refers *anaphorically* to the house mentioned in the previous sentence (and perhaps to the fact that it is for sale).

(c) Adverse events related to treatment resulted in death in nine of 327 (3%) patients in the sintilimab-chemotherapy group and six of 332 (2%) patients in the placebo-chemotherapy group (tables S10 and S12). The rates of adverse events were **similar** when we grouped patients by chemotherapy regimen.

BMJ 2022; 377: e068714, 19/04/2022

Comparative reference: 'similar' forms a *comparative relationship* between rates of adverse events when patients were grouped by chemotherapy regimen and adverse events under different circumstances.

Activity 3.2 Substitution

Identify the substitution and explain what has been substituted with what.

(a) Is Katrina pregnant? Fans seem to think **so**.

'So' substitutes for 'Katrina is pregnant'.

(b) Now in 'Men in Black II' you show off the board in a different way, it's where you have the Michael Jackson cameo. How did you get him to do **that**?

The pronoun 'that' substitutes for (something like) 'cameo in the movie'.

(c) He told me he has changed his mind about a child and doesn't want **another** but loves me and if we end up having **one**, would just go with **it** rather than lose me.

The pronouns 'another' and 'one' are used to substitute for 'a child'. The pronoun 'it' refers back to 'having one'.

Activity 3.3 Conjunctive cohesion

(a) Rapper and businessman Cassper Nyovest [. . .] no longer feels safe following the brutal murder of his friend and amapiano pioneer DJ Sumbody. **As a result**, the Destiny hitmaker has decided to beef up security, according to Zimoja.

https://www.myzimbabwe.co.zw, 13/02/2023

There is a *causal relation* of *result* that is realised by 'as a result', and this creates a cohesive causal link between Nyovest not feeling safe and him beefing up security.

(b) In Los Angeles County alone [. . .] one in every five people has tested positive for the virus. On January 11, the county hit a grim milestone: 30,000 recorded COVID-19 deaths. **Meanwhile**, vaccines are being rolled out at a snail's pace and frontline workers are overwhelmed.

The Jerusalem Post (online), 14/01/2021

Temporal conjunction is realised by 'meanwhile' which presupposes that other events have been described in the discourse that are happening at the same time as vaccines being rolled out, etc.

Activity 3.4 Collocation

Here are the answers from our small sample of respondents:

Night – Day
Knife – Crime
Hat – Stand/Coat
Tea – Coffee
Smoke – Fire

'Night' is linked to 'day' because they are antonyms. 'Knife' collocates with 'crime' which attests to the prevalence of knife crime in the recent press (January 2023) in our small sample group's region. 'Hat' collocates with 'stand' which could be said to be a compound term 'hat-stand', but other respondents in our sample said 'coat'. We wondered what they might say if we asked them in summer! 'Hat' and 'coat' are both subordinates of the superordinate term 'clothes', and so are cohesively linked along those lines. 'Tea' and 'coffee' are collocated along the same cohesive relationship as 'hat' and 'coat' in that the relationship is member of a set ('hot drinks'). 'Smoke' and 'fire' collocate via a causal relationship, in that smoke indicates the presence of fire and fire causes smoke to form. There is, after all, no smoke without fire.

Notes

1 This independent review authored by Wendy Williams, the title of which presupposes (some might say erroneously) that lessons were learned, is licensed under the terms of the Open Government Licence v3.0, which can be viewed at: nationalarchives.gov.uk/doc/open-government-licence/version/3

2 Halliday and Matthiessen (2014) describe an expanded hierarchical classification of cohesion, which has three basic categories: *elaborating*, *extending*, and *enhancing*. These expand out to nine further subtypes (of which *additive*, *adversative*, *causal*, and *temporal* are just four), and these expand further to more than 20 sub-subtypes.

References

Bloor and Bloor (2013) *The functional analysis of English: A Hallidayan approach*. London: Routledge.

Halliday, M. A. K and Hasan, R. (1976) *Cohesion in English*. London: Longman.

Halliday, M. A. K. and Matthiessen, C. (2014) *An introduction to functional grammar* (4th edition). London: Routledge.

Thompson, G. (2013). *Introducing functional grammar*. London: Routledge.

4 Analysing spoken discourse

Introduction

In this chapter we continue our exploration of discourse by looking at spoken interactions. The analysis of spoken discourse is concerned with examining how utterances between conversation participants are connected, structured, and organised. Analysts attempt to find regularities in the function and sequencing of utterances and explain how these regularities systematise conversation and contribute to meaning making within discourse communities. Using approaches from Conversation Analysis (CA), developed in the 1970s by Harvey Sacks, Emanuel Schegloff, and Gail Jefferson (see, for example, Sacks et al. 1974) and the Birmingham School of spoken Discourse Analysis (see, for example, Sinclair and Coulthard 1975), this chapter explains how to analyse spoken discourse.

Analysis of spoken discourse involves looking at the meanings of the words used (semantics), the order in which they occur (syntax), the way in which they are uttered (intonation), their position within the discourse (co-textual sequencing), and the situation in which they are uttered (context). We also need to understand what function the words are performing (the pragmatic force) in the context they are uttered. This is because when we speak, we are doing things with words; we are performing social actions (Schegloff 2007: 2) or verbal acts (Sinclair and Coulthard 1975) such as requesting information, issuing a directive, or making an offer. Therefore, as we will see in this chapter, looking at the function of an utterance in a conversation is an important part of analysing spoken discourse.

How spoken discourse is analysed

The analysis of spoken discourse centres on making observations about the way real (rather than invented or scripted), naturally occurring spoken interactions unfold dynamically between participants as they react and respond to each other. Such analysis requires data collection, which involves creating:

(i) audio recordings of dialogue (once permission has been obtained; we deal with the ethics of data collection in Chapter 12); and
(ii) written representations of the spoken interactions in the form of detailed **transcriptions**.

DOI: 10.4324/9781003351207-4

Transcriptions of spoken discourse aim to record in as much detail as possible not only **what** is said but also **how** it is said. This means that the phonological features associated with spoken discourse (e.g. loudness, intonation, stress, pauses) are represented graphologically in the written record. Transcriptions also identify different speakers involved in the conversation to show **who** said what. All these features are important for discovering patterns in spoken dialogue and exploring how meaning is communicated.

Transcriptions can also use orthographic means to represent the pronunciation of words (e.g. 'whadja won' instead of 'what do you want'). Our observation is that this convention is applied rather inconsistently and unsystematically across transcriptions (on this point, see Walker 2013: 471), and apparently ignores the existence of the International Phonetic Alphabet (IPA). The extent to which pronunciation is represented in the transcription will depend on the analyst. Our approach in this chapter is to restrict such orthographic representations to where they are absolutely necessary; for example, elided syllables are not transcribed (e.g. 'because' is transcribed as 'cause' if the first syllable is not said). Whatever conventions are adopted, they need to be applied consistently throughout.

Data used in this chapter

Notice that transcribing a spoken interaction is both analytical and interpretative. When viewing a transcription prepared by another person, you are viewing their 'take' on the spoken dialogue using whatever transcribing conventions they use. Therefore, where possible, it is important that analysing spoken dialogue should include listening to the audio (or audio-visual) recordings as well as scrutinising the written transcript. For that reason, throughout this chapter, we will be basing our discussion on data obtained from the Santa Barbara Corpus of Spoken American English (**SBCSAE**) (Du Bois et al. 2000–2005) and the spoken section of the British National Corpus (**BNC**). We use these corpora because they are well documented, freely available online, and include the audio recordings that the transcribed data is derived from (see the end of this chapter for details). This means that readers can listen to the original conversations themselves, which can be extremely helpful for understanding the transcriptions and how the conversations proceed. We base our transcriptions on those from these corpora, but we have used different transcribing conventions for some prosodic features. We will introduce the conventions as we go along and present a summary at the end of this chapter.

Spoken Interactions

When we talk, we do not produce words in a continual stream. Instead, as analysts have long since recognised, our words form smaller, meaningful units (see, for example, Crystal 1979). As Szczepek Reed (2010: 354) puts it, "speakers produce talk on a chunk-by-chunk basis". In written discourse we achieve 'chunking' graphologically using, for example, punctuation marks which help to divide the discourse and the information it contains into meaningful units such as clauses, sentences, and paragraphs. In spoken discourse, however, full stops, commas, etc. are not possible (although, see Activity 4.1). Instead, spoken discourse contains numerous other important phonological features including pauses, 'uhms' and 'ahs', and variation in voice pitch. It is these phonological means that help divide the speech into units of meaning and contribute to meaning making and without them, some meaning is lost. To illustrate this, read through example 1, which is a transcription of the words used in a spoken conversation between two friends obtained from the SBCSAE. We have omitted most punctuation (apostrophes are included) because when we are speaking, we do not use full-stops (periods), commas and so on. Following Jefferson (2004), we have used uppercase letters to mark proper nouns and the start of a turn (i.e. the initial letter of first word is capitalised). Look at the words from the conversation and consider whether there are any places where you are not sure what meaning is being communicated (turns are numbered).

1

1. ALINA:	Remember Tyke lives next door to Mom
2. LENORE:	Yeah
3. ALINA:	Okay two weeks ago I'm watching tv and David Horowitz is going to have this former car radio thief on
4. LENORE:	It's her boyfriend
5. ALINA:	Yeah her ex-boyfriend Mike he's the one that stole (name)'s radio
6. LENORE:	How do you know
7. ALINA:	Well cause well he he was a cocaine addict

(SBC006, Cuz, Santa Barbara Corpus)

Note: The name of person whose radio was stolen is unclear in the recording and has been replaced with (name) in the transcription.

It is likely that when you read example 1, there are places where you intuitively want to place punctuation to indicate, for instance, where you think a question is being asked, where a sentence ends, or where there is a pause. There might be places, however, where you cannot determine, for example, whether an utterance is a question or a statement. This is because your intuitions are based solely on the words that the speakers produced, their arrangement in the transcription, and your knowledge of English grammar. However, when engaged in spoken conversation, participants also create (and interpret) meaning using phonic (and other[1]) resources such as pitch, loudness, word duration, pauses, and speed of delivery. Therefore, unless you listen to the recording of this conversation, you are missing out on numerous phonic signals that combine with the words and syntax to help create meaning (Selting 2010: 6; see also Crystal 1979: 5). The phonological means we employ to help create meaning in spoken discourse are usually referred to as **prosody**, or **prosodic** features. In the next section we will examine how prosody helps in meaning making in spoken discourse.

Activity 4.1 Punctuation in spoken discourse

Back in the day, Victor Borge famously created a comedy sketch using the idea of sound effects to indicate punctuation in texts he read from. His comedy act was not too far from reality, because in spoken discourse we do use sound features to convey meaning in the same way orthographic conventions do so in written discourse.

To find out what used to pass as comedy, search for Victor Borge on YouTube, or follow this QR code.

QR 4.1 Victor Borge sketch

As you read on through the sections on prosody in this chapter, consider Borge's sketch from a linguistic perspective and what (if any) problems there might be with the central premise of his comedy.

Prosody in spoken discourse

Over these next two sections we will introduce two important prosodic features: pauses and intonation. We will illustrate our discussion using the extract in example 1.

Pauses

Pauses are the short but noticeable silences that occur during spoken interactions as a result of speakers hesitating, thinking about what to say next, and breathing. When examining spoken data, analysts time pauses to the nearest tenth of a second and transcribe them within the turn in which they occur using a system of symbols (see below). Pauses that occur in between turns (i.e. after one person finishes speaking and before another person starts) are marked on a separate line of the transcription because it is not clear who the pause "belongs to" (Du Bois et al. 1992). According to Stenström (1994: 7), pauses can also be non-silent or filled with voiced sounds such as 'um' or 'erm'. Additionally, pauses can also include audible inhalation or exhalation (which means they are filled with breathy sounds). The following pause categories and transcription codes are based on those developed by Jefferson (2004), Du Bois et al. (1992), and Stenström (1994).

Short pause – 0.2 seconds or less	(.)
Medium pause – 0.3–0.6 seconds	(. .)

Long pause – 0.7 seconds or over (e.g. 1.2 seconds)	(1.2)
Short filled pause	(um)
Longer filled pause (one or more colons lengthen pause)	(u:m)
Audible inhale	(H)
Audible exhale	(Hx)

Pauses can be used by speakers to break their speech into units, and this can help to make meaning. To illustrate, let us now return to example 1 (labelled 1a below) where we can see the same conversation between Alina and Lenore, but this time with pauses marked using the coding conventions set out above.

1a

1.ALINA: Remember Tyke (. .) lives next door to Mom
(1.8)
2. LENORE: Yeah
(. .)
3. ALINA: Okay (. .)(H)(. .) two weeks ago I'm watching tv (. .) and David Horowitz is going to have this former car (. . .) radio thief on (. . .)
4. LENORE: it's her boyfriend
5. ALINA: (H) (.) Yeah her ex-boyfriend (. .) Mike (. . .) he's the one that stole (name)'s radio
(2.2)
6. LENORE: How do you know
7. ALINA: (H) Well (. . .) cause well (. .) he (. .) he was a cocaine addict

The transcription now shows that the spoken dialogue involves pauses of different lengths, some with audible inhalation. The addition of pauses to the transcription helps to indicate how the spoken discourse is divided into units. This is particularly clear in Alina's first turn, where the pause divides the turn into two meaningful units: (i) 'Remember Tyke' and (ii) 'lives next door to Mom'. We can also notice at this point that each of these units have a different discourse function; we will return to the functional analysis of units later in the chapter.

Activity 4.2 Pause relocation

Try saying Alina's first turn, but this time with a pause after 'remember':

Remember (.) Tyke lives next door to Mom

What effect, if any, does this have on the information chunking and potential meaning of the turn?

We give our answer at the end of the chapter.

Pauses can perform a similar role to the punctuation we find in written discourse by dividing up the talk into meaningful units. While there is not a one-to-one relationship between pauses and meaningful units of information, pauses are a good place to start in the transcription process, once the words have been transcribed. Another crucial prosodic feature in creating meaning in spoken discourse is intonation.

Intonation

According to Daniel Jones, an early pioneer in speech science, intonation is "the variations which take place in the pitch of the voice in connected speech" (Jones 1960). Intonation, then, refers to the way in which speakers change their voice pitch (or 'tone') during spoken interaction. Intonation can rise, fall, rise and fall (rise-fall), and fall and rise (fall-rise). These changes can occur across syllables, single words or groups of words and create what are known as **pitch contours** (Carr 2012: 107), and each contour helps to communicate meaning beyond the words uttered. Some linguists suggest that intonation can indicate, for example, attitude to information (doubt or certainty), emotions (happiness, sadness, boredom, annoyance), and empathy (friendliness, hostility to hearer). While there is no universal agreement on this, there is some consensus that changes in pitch can indicate whether the utterance is complete or more information is to follow. For instance, it is generally accepted that a fall in a pitch can indicate that a person is finishing what they are saying and is sometimes referred to as a **terminal intonation contour**. On the other hand, a rise in pitch can signal incompleteness and is referred to a **non-terminal intonation contour**. To illustrate these general tendencies, try recording yourself saying the following out loud:

> Events will take place in London Paris Washington and Sydney

Now, listen back to your recording. Think about where the intonation changes in your voice as you say the words. Our hope is that you will find that your voice pitch rises on all items in the short list of cities apart from the last one, where your voice pitch falls. Rising intonation signals that there are more items to follow and falling intonation signals that the list is complete.

One way in which intonation can be indicated in transcriptions, and the method we use in this chapter, is by placing arrows either before the word or within the word where the pitch movement occurs[2] (see, for example, Carr 2012). For instance, if we return to our list of cities, the intonation can be shown in the following way:

> Events will take place in Lon↗don Pa↗ris Washing↗ton and Syd↘ney

The upward arrows indicates that 'London', 'Paris', and 'Washington' are said with rising intonation, while 'Sydney' is said with a downward pitch movement which starts on the final syllable. Other documented pitch movements include the fall-rise (indicated by ↘↗), the rise-fall (indicated by ↗↘), and level tone (indicated by →). These five pitch movements are sometimes referred to as **tones** and their transcription symbols are summarised in Table 4.1.

Table 4.1 Pitch movements and symbols

Pitch Movement	Arrows
rise	↗
Fall	↘
rise-fall	↗↘
fall-rise	↘↗
Level	→

Intonation and syntax work together to create meaning, where **falling tone** is typically used for statements, commands, and wh-questions (Carr 2012: 121–122), and a **rising tone** is used for yes/no questions, to turn statements into questions, and non-final clauses. For example:

(i) Statement:	He asked you to ↘leave
(ii) Command:	Get out of my ↘house
(iii) Wh-question:	When are you ↘leaving
(iv) Yes-no question:	Are you leaving ↗now
(v) statement as questions	You are leaving ↗now
(vi) Non-final clause:	He promised to ↘↗leave . . . . (but he ↘didn't)

These intonation patterns are what <u>tend</u> to happen in spoken discourse and are <u>not</u> hard and fast rules. Different intonation is possible, and any of the above may be said with different intonation contours, which may communicate different meaning. For example, commands can become polite offers if said with a rising tone and yes-no questions said with a falling tone can give information rather than seek it, for example:

> Have some ↗cake (i.e. would you like some cake?)
> Would you like to ↘leave (i.e. do that again and you're leaving!)

Even with the possible variations in tone contours, in spoken discourse the following general pattern is recognised:

- rising tones indicate more is to come or information is being sought;
- falling tones indicate finality or information is being given.

Intonation therefore plays an important role in how we create meaning in spoken discourse not least because it can be instrumental in letting our interlocutor know whether we are coming to the end of what we are saying or continuing. Together, pauses and intonation help to divide up spoken discourse into units of information and meaning. Let us now look at some examples of intonation at work in spoken discourse by considering again the conversation between Alina and Lenore. In Example 1b, below, we return to the transcription but this time with symbols added to indicate intonation.

1b
1.ALINA: Remember ↗Tyke (. .) lives next door to ↗Mom
(1.8)
2. LENORE: ↗↘Yeah
(. . .)
3. ALINA: ↘Okay (. .)(H)(. .) two weeks ago I'm watching ↘↗TV (. .) and David Horowitz is going to have this former →car (. . .) radio thief ↗on
(. . .)
4. LENORE: it's her ↗boyfriend
5. ALINA: (H) (. .) ↗↘Yeah=her ex-boy↘friend (. .) ↘Mike (. . .)
he's the one that stole (name)'s ↘radio
(2.2)
6. LENORE: How do you ↘know
7. ALINA: (H) ↗↘Well (. . .) cause ↘well (. .) →he (. .) he was a cocaine ↘addict

In turn 1, we can see that rising intonation makes it clear that the first unit is a request for information and is intended as a question. The second unit also ends with rising intonation and, although it is giving information to Lenore, it is connected to the initial request for information by the intonation.

In turn 4, Lenore makes a statement, but the rising intonation on 'boyfriend' suggests that she is seeking clarification and not stating a fact. This appears to be how Alina interprets Lenore's utterance because she responds with an affirmative 'yeah' as though it were indeed a yes-no question.

The rise-fall intonation on 'yeah' at the start of turn 5 suggests that it is a separate unit of information from that which follows – 'her ex-boyfriend' – which has its own intonation contour. Note the lack of pause between 'yeah' and 'her'. When two units of information have no pause between them, this is known as **latching**, and the convention is to use an equal sign (=) to mark where this happens. Latching (i.e. not pausing) is one method of indicating that the turn is not over and that the current speaker is going to continue.

Other prosodic features

There are, of course, other prosodic features associated with spoken discourse that we do not have space to discuss in this chapter. These include the loudness or quietness of the spoken words relative to the surrounding talk, the lengthening of words, and the speed of delivery. The transcription conventions for these features are shown in Table 4.4 at the end of the chapter. Some of these features will be useful for tackling Activity 4.3.

Activity 4.3 Okay

Key and Peele (2015), two male comedians, perform a sketch in which they acted as two female characters, let's call them Speaker 1 and Speaker 2 (find the clip on YouTube; top tip – search for 'key and peele okay' or follow the QR code below).

QR 4.2 Key and Peele 'Okay' sketch

In the sketch, speaker 1 begins by berating her unfaithful boyfriend, going through all the things she will do to him for cheating on her and what she will do if he dares to cheat on her again. As the conversation continues Speaker 1 moves the metaphoric goalposts a little each time so that she relents a little more on how much she will tolerate from her cheating boyfriend. For example, she says that her man gets just one chance . . . and then after that, he gets one more. She goes on to say that she won't let him cheat in the house . . . but then says he can, just not when she's at home. And so on. All the way through, Speaker 2 responds to each conversational turn with only one word: 'Okay'. Speaker 2's meaning, though, varies widely and this is achieved through different prosody.

Try to transcribe the different 'okay' responses from Speaker 2. How does prosody generate different meanings of the same word?

Our answers are at the end of the chapter.

Syntax

Our knowledge of how words and phrases are conventionally arranged (syntax) also plays a part in our understanding of what counts as a meaningful unit of information. Often, when we speak, we do not use complete grammatical sentences. However, the notion of syntactic completion is important for identifying what is a meaningful piece of information.

For instance, in example 1, Alina's first turn contains two grammatically incomplete units: 'Remember Tyke' and 'lives next door to Mom'. Although 'Remember Tyke' is syntactically complete as an imperative, the rising intonation on 'Tyke' means that it is intended as a question. As such, it is incomplete because it lacks an auxiliary verb and Subject at the start of the clause (e.g. **Do you** remember Tyke?). Knowledge of English grammar alongside the contextual situation (Alina is directing the question at Lenore) means that the auxiliary verb and Subject are not essential for understanding and can be elided. With 'lives next door to Mom', some sort of grammatical Subject is missing, but we can still make sense of that utterance and interpret it as a meaningful unit of language. It is possible, therefore, to make sense of these utterances and understand them as complete and meaningful, even though they are grammatically incomplete. However, consider how you would interpret Alina's opening if she had said the following:

> Do you re↗member (. .) she lives next door ↗to

The question 'do you remember?' invites the hearer to remember something but is incomplete because the 'something' cannot be retrieved from the context or from the prior discourse (because Alina's turn is an opening). The question therefore has an empty slot that cannot be filled by the hearer, and would probably results in a response such as 'remember what?' The second question, 'she lives next door to?' is grammatically incomplete and only makes sense if it is seen as a request for information ('she lives next door to *who*?'). However, 'she' has no antecedent (see Chapter 3), so the hearer is likely to be left wondering 'who is she?' In both cases, is not possible for us to complete these two questions because their incompleteness is not just a matter of grammar. It is probably possible to think of a situation where, if the essential information was **Given** (see Chapter 3) then these questions could make sense. Notice, then, that the position of an utterance within the conversation is also key to making and understanding meaning.

Activity 4.4 Try saying this at home

Can you say the following sentence in two different ways to communicate two different meanings?

> Precisely at that point I called a taxi.

Think about what resources you use to change the meaning of the sentence.
Using the codes we introduced above to show pauses and intonation, transcribe the different ways of saying the sentence.

We give our answer at the end of the chapter.

Turns, turn taking, and turn transition

An obvious observation about the transcription in example 1 that we have not discussed so far is that it is divided into **turns**. This reflects the fact that the actual real-life conversation proceeded in that way – the two participants took turns to talk with Alina speaking first followed by Lenore, and so on. That the participants took turns to talk might seem a rather banal remark, but research into spoken discourse has found that turn taking and its organisation is of fundamental importance in spoken interaction (Schegloff 2007: 1). In this section we will deal with the notion of turns and turn taking.

Turns

Simply put, turns consist of words and meaningful sounds (such as 'mmm'). A turn can be defined as everything uttered by one speaker before another speaker starts to speak (Stenström 1994: 4). As discourse analysts, it is an important task to separate a transcription of a conversation into turns, which we can achieve by noticing when different speakers are speaking. This can be tricky when there are more than two people involved in a conversation, and analysts must become very good listeners. Additionally, the boundaries between turns can become blurred when, for example, the talk of conversational participants overlaps. Turns can vary greatly in size from one word (or meaningful sound such as 'mmm') upwards, with the context of the conversation (e.g. job interview, casual conversation, classroom interaction) influencing the length of speaker's turns (as well as content and function). For example, it is likely in a job interview that many of the turns produced by the interviewer will be short and aim to elicit information from the interviewee, while many of the turns produced by interviewee will be comparatively long because they will aim to provide as much relevant information as possible to demonstrate aptitude and suitability for the vacancy.

Turn taking

Turn taking is, according to Clayman (2013: 150), "an elementary form of social behaviour" because "interactants must act not as independent agents but in close coordination with one another". What Clayman is getting at is that turns are not pre-determined by the participants before the conversation begins; turns are established dynamically by the participants as the conversation progresses and so participants must cooperate to create a dialogue. Participants take it in turns to contribute to the conversation and tend to talk one at a time. If more than one person does speak at the same time, then this usually happens very briefly with overlaps occurring in predictable places (a point we will return to later in the chapter).

Turn transition

The ground-breaking work of Sacks et al. (1974) revealed that when people take turns at talking, they signal that a potential end to the turn is approaching, and their interlocutor uses those signals to anticipate the completion of a turn.

They also suggested that there is a tacit understanding that when someone is speaking, they hold the floor and that transfer to another speaker only occurs at specific places. Turn taking is therefore managed by conversational participants, who intuitively recognise when a turn is coming to an end and when there is the possibility of a transition to another speaker (Schegloff 2007: 5). Sacks et al. (1974: 703) introduced the term **Transition-Relevance Place (TRP)** for the point in an interaction where another speaker may take a turn and thus, the floor. A TRP and therefore the possible end of a turn can be signalled by syntactic completion and prosodically via intonation and pauses. Typically, a rising or falling intonation contour on a potentially final word or syllable in a syntactic unit can indicate a possible place for a transition between speakers.

Let's consider how TRPs work by returning to Alina's first turn in example 1 (labelled 1c below). We can see that there are two possible TRPs each at the end of an information unit. Both end in rising intonation indicating that these are places where Lenore could take the floor. The pauses strengthen the possibility of these being TRPs. Transition occurs at the second TRP when Lenore takes the floor (in turn 2) and answers the question. Lenore's response has falling intonation contour suggesting it is complete and completion is reinforced by the pause that follows. At that point, there is a transition back to Alina. In turn 3, Alina's first information unit ends in a falling tone but is followed by an audible intake of breath (after 'Okay'). Such inhales can indicate that the speaker has not finished speaking and that there is more to come. Indeed, Alina does have more to say, and Lenore, who stays quiet, correctly does not see this as a relevant place to take the floor.

1c
1. ALINA: Remember ↗Tyke (.) lives next door to ↗Mom
(1.8)
2. LENORE: ↗↘Yeah
(. .)
3. ALINA: ↘Okay (.)(H)(.) two weeks ago I'm watching ↘↗TV (.) and David Horowitz is going to have this former →car (. .) radio thief ↗on
(. .)
4. LENORE: it's her ↗boyfriend
5. ALINA: (H) (.) ↗↘Yeah=her ex-boy↘friend (.) ↘Mike (. .)
he's the one that stole (name)'s ↘radio
(2.2)
6. LENORE: How do you ↘know
7. ALINA: (H) ↗↘Well (. .) cause ↘well (.) →he (.) he was a cocaine ↘addict

Note that turn 3 ends in rising intonation and is followed by a pause. This suggests that a question is being asked or a response sought and places an obligation on the hearer to answer (perhaps through politeness – see Chapter 5), which creates a TRP. Indeed, Alina seems to be handing the floor to Lenore here. The actions we perform when we speak (questioning, answering, informing, directing, and so on) are therefore also important for understanding turn transitions and sequences in conversations. We return to the idea of performing speech acts in the next section.

To summarise, turns are all the words spoken by one person before another person takes over (Stenström 1994: 4). A turn ends when the person stops (or is stopped from) talking and someone else starts (although, we will see exceptions to this general idea later in the chapter). So long as we can recognise that one person has stopped talking and another person has started then we can work out where one turn ends and another begins. Within turns, speakers create units of meaning using a combination of words, syntax, and prosody. The hearer in a conversation knows when a point is approaching where taking the floor might be appropriate or when it is their turn to talk; the speaker signals (syntactically and prosodically) that a turn might be ending, or a point is approaching where a transition is relevant. Conversational participants therefore use what they hear to ascertain relevant points for taking a turn to talk.

Functional analysis of turns

So far, our analysis of spoken dialogue has considered how the prosodic and syntactic features of talk play a part in creating meaning. We now consider the function of what people say in a turn because when people speak, they perform actions with their words. For instance, we saw that in Alina's first turn (in 1c above) she performs the action of asking a question. The importance of considering what actions talk performs is noted by Schegloff (2007: 2), and the analytical framework for spoken discourse developed by Sinclair and Coulthard (1975; see also Coulthard 1992) incorporates the idea of talk as action whereby conversations proceed through **predictable** sequences of **Acts**.

Acts and actions

The notion of Acts is derived from the work of Austin (1979) and Searle (1976, 1979) who developed research on 'speech acts'. These refer to what we are *doing* with language when we use it in certain ways and in certain contexts. Speech acts are effectively actions that we perform, directly or indirectly, using words. They include, for example, apologizing, promising, denying, offering, thanking, and threatening. Sinclair and Coulthard (1975) use 'acts' in a similar way to Austin and Searle, but their Acts[3] form part of a grammar of spoken discourse. The number and type of Acts are potentially open-ended. Both Francis and Hunston (1992) and Stenström (1994) provide extensive lists that agree in general on the different classes of Acts but differ in terms of labels and number. Table 4.2 provides a sample of Francis and Hunston (1992) and Stenström's (1994) classifications. Following Stenström (1994), Acts are enclosed in angle brackets.

Table 4.2 Selected list of Acts after Francis and Hunston (1992) and Stenström (1994)

Act	Gloss
<greet> / <part>	'hello'/'goodbye'
<reply-greet> / <reply-part>	Respond to <greet> / <part>; e.g. echoic 'hello' / 'goodbye'
<offer>	Offer somebody something
<request>	Request permission or ask someone to do something
<accept>	Accept <offer> or <suggest>; grant or agree to <request>
<reject>	Turn down <offer>; deny or refuse <request>
<thank>	Express thanks/gratitude
<question>	Request information: wh-question, yes/no-question
<answer>	Respond to <question> providing informative answer.
<inform>	Provide information
<suggest>	Suggest an idea
<acknowledge>	Let the other person know 'message received'; acknowledge <thank> or <apology>
<apology>	Say you are sorry
<summon>	Attract someone's attention (e.g. say 'excuse me' or use the person's name)
<reply-summon>	Respond to <summon>
<evaluate>	Provide an evaluation or judgement

Acts are verbal actions within turns and indicate what the person is doing by uttering words with a particular prosody. Let's return to the first two turns of the conversation between Alina and Lenore. These are repeated below but this time we have labelled the Acts in both turns using categories from Table 4.2.

1d
1. ALINA: Remember ↗Tyke (.) <question>
lives next door to ↗Mom <inform>
(1.8)
2. LENORE: ↗↘Yeah <answer>

Simply put, this is a question-and-answer sequence: Alina asks a question and Lenore provides an answer. However, in turn 1, Alina performs two Acts, which coincide with the two speech units that are separated by a pause and end with rising intonation. The first functions as a yes/no-question which requests confirmation where either 'yes' or 'no' is an appropriate response. The second functions to inform Lenore (presumably to prompt her memory) even though it is said with rising intonation like a question. In turn two, Lenore gives an appropriate response to Alina's information request by providing confirmation.

In example 1d, it is not difficult to decide what Act is being performed. But it is not always so clear cut. Searle's work (1976) on speech acts offers the following to help identify what Act is taking place and what effects it generates:

1. **Locutionary act:** the words and prosodic features (i.e. the locution) used by the speaker.
2. **Illocutionary force:** the intention of the speaker by uttering the locution.
3. **Perlocutionary effect:** the effects of the locution on the hearer intended by the speaker.

Let's consider the three terms above in relation to the conversation between Alina and Lenore. In turn 1, Alina utters words in a particular way (locutionary act) which we judge to have the intended illocutionary force of requesting confirmation from Lenore, with the intended outcome of receiving the requested information. This appears to be the way Lenore interprets Alina's locution, since she provides the sought-for confirmation. We therefore judge Lenore's locution to have the illocutionary force of an informative response. Thus, Alina's request for confirmation has the desired perlocutionary effect.

Form and function

There is no one-to-one fit between the words uttered (the locution) and the Act they perform since (i) different words can perform the same function, and (ii) the same words can be used for different functions. A crucial factor in how an utterance functions is how and where it is uttered within the discourse and in what context (physical/social situation). For example, consider the following made-up example.

2

(a)	(b)
A: Here's your pie.	A: Here's your pie.
B: Thank you.	*(B eats pie)*
A: You're welcome.	A: You're welcome.

In scenario 2(a), the 'thank you' said by B offers thanks to A for the pie. The Act of thanking could have been achieved by any number of different forms such as 'cheers', 'nice one', or 'sound'. The utterance 'you're welcome' in 2(a) functions to <acknowledge> the thanks. In scenario 2(b), however, A does not offer any thanks and, consequently, 'you're welcome' has a different function. Instead of being a polite acknowledgement, it is sarcastic and functions to <evaluate> or pass judgement on the lack of thanks and implies something like 'I want you to know that thanks were expected but not received and that did not go unnoticed' (readers may have their own, equally valid, thoughts on the Act and the implied meaning). Part of the reason why 'you're welcome' functions as a polite acknowledgement in 2(a) is because it follows a <thank> Act. Similarly, part of the reason why 'you're welcome' cannot be a polite acknowledgement in 2(b) is because no thanks have been offered.

Therefore, what happens immediately prior to an utterance affects its meaning, and one utterance can raise expectations about or predict what the next utterance will be (in terms of function). A statement of fact functions as a response to a request for information if it follows a request for information, 'yes' only grants permission if it follows a permission request, and a question can be observed to be recognised and understood as a question when it is followed by an answer of some nature (Wilkinson and Kitzinger 2017: 75). The sequential position of an utterance in a conversation is therefore crucial to assessing its function (see Schegloff 1968: 1083; Stivers 2013: 192). So too are social norms and expectations.

Activity 4.5 'I'd like a pie, please'

Consider the following (made-up) situations where 'I'd like a pie' is uttered. Does the statement have a different function depending on the situation and discourse position it occurs in?

At home
A: What do you want to eat?
B: I'd like a pie please.

At the bakery
A: I'd like a pie, please.
B: Certainly. Here you are.

Now, consider the possible different discourse functions of the following: 'hello', 'excuse me'. Think of situations where the different functions might occur.

We give our answers at the end of the chapter.

Sequencing

Spoken discourse happens in sequences. Functional elements of dialogue are ordered in specific ways and influence what happens around those elements. For example, asking a question raises the expectation of an informative response. If the expectation is not realised (i.e. the response is absent) then this is marked and goes against expectations (Stivers 2013). In this section we will examine just some of the possible sequences in spoken discourse identified by scholars.

Adjacency pairs

The notion of **adjacency pairs** was introduced by Schegloff and Sacks (1973) and describes the close sequencing of two turns where the second turn is related to the first. More precisely, though, it is the sequencing of the Acts performed in turns that better describe adjacency pairs: one type of Act is closely followed by another particular and predictable type. For example, a <question> is usually followed by an <answer> and this forms a pair where the <question> is the First Pair Part (FPP) and the <answer> is the Second Pair Part (SPP). The idea is that the FPP predicts the SPP, so when a speaker asks a question, it usually means that the next utterance will contain an answer (although, as we will see, there are exceptions to this). There are other Acts that can be involved in adjacency pair sequences some of which are shown in Table 4.3.

Table 4.3 Examples of Acts that can form adjacency pairs

FPP	SPP
<greet>	<reply-greet>
<offer>	<accept> / <reject>
<request>	<accept> / <reject>
<summon>	<reply-summon>

Let's look at an example, this time from the spoken section of the BNC. In extract 3, the context is that a mother is interacting with two children who are doing different activities; her focus is on just one child when the other child speaks.

3

1. CHILD:	↘↗Mu:::m	<summon>
2. MOTHER:	Hell↗o:	<reply-summon>

(BNC spoken section, file KBW)

In turn 1, the child attracts the mother's attention. This is an example of a <summon>/<reply-summon> sequence where turn 1 is the FPP and turn 2 the SPP. Turns 1 and 2 contain one Act each. The child's locution has the force of summoning or attracting her attention. The mother responds to the <summon> with 'hello'. Notice that the position in the sequence and the preceding Act (along with the rising intonation) helps to determine that 'hello' is not functioning as a greeting in this case.

Support Acts

In example 3, the turns contain just one Act each and they form a neat pair, with one Act following immediately after the other. However, you do not need to look at very many spoken data to see that this is not always what happens. Our Alina and Lenore example is a case in point. In example 1d above, we saw that the sequence involves a recognisable <question> and <answer> pair. However, we also saw that, along with the <question> Act, Alina's first turn contains an <inform> Act. This expands the sequence. The <question> is of primary importance in the sequence – it takes the lead. Without the <question> there would be no sequence (imagine if Alina had started with 'lives next door to mom'). The <inform> has a supporting role; it assists in Alina's conversational goal of getting an informative response by offering relevant information to help Lenore answer. The sequence in 1d therefore involves a pair of Acts: a **primary** Act crucial for creating a sequence, and a **secondary** Act that helps to achieve the conversational goal (for more on primary and secondary Acts, see Stenström 1994: chapter 2).

Sequence expansion

Sequences in conversation can be more complex than so far described. For example, one or more adjacency pairs can be embedded within the initial pair sequence in what is known as **insert expansion**. For example, a request for information might be followed by another request seeking clarification (Schegloff 1972: 76–79) which is answered before the original request is answered. We can see how this works in example 4, which shows more of the conversation between the mother and child we met in example 3.

4

1. CHILD:	↘↗Mu:::m	<summon>
2. MOTHER:	Hell↗o:	<reply-summon>
3. CHILD:	Could you get me from the ↘shelf (.) the black felt ↘pen	<request FPP^{1}>
4. MOTHER:	Which ↘shelf	<question FPP^{2}>
5. CHILD:	The big one with all the (unclear) on ↘top (.) there's some ↘colours (.) there isn't black (. .) felt ↘pen	<answer SPP^{2}>
6. MOTHER:	↘Right (. .) I'll see what I can →do.	<accept SPP^{1}>

(BNC spoken section, file KBW)

As we established above, the first two turns involve a <summon> and a <reply-summon>. Following that, in turn 3, the child makes a <request> – they want their mother to do something. This forms the FPP of an adjacency pair. The SPP, however, is in turn 6 when the mother agrees to the <request> with an <accept>. In between this not-so-adjacent adjacency pair is an **insertion sequence** which is itself an adjacency pair. Its purpose is to establish more information about the question and its insertion suspends the SPP sought in turn 1. Once the mother gets the information she needs, then she agrees to the <request>. It is, of course, possible for more sequences to be inserted in between the initial question and the final answer. For example, the mother could ask the child to say 'please' (which would be a <request>), and only when the 'please' was forthcoming would she issue the SPP for the child's original <request>.

Sequence Coupling

As we saw with our Alina and Lenore example above, turns can contain more than one Act; Alina elicited information from Lenore by issuing a <question> and an <inform> Act. It is also possible for the Acts in one turn to conclude one sequence and start another. In extract 5, obtained from the BNC, we can see in turn 1, Heidi's second Act is a <request> for permission ('please may I . . .') and constitutes a FPP in a <request>/<accept> adjacency pair. In turn 2, Vicki performs an <accept> by giving permission (with 'Mhm') and so provides a SPP to conclude that sequence. Vicki's turn contains a second Act which is a <request> ('Would you like to . . .') which initiates another sequence. Notice that the <request> is in the form of a question which seeks information about what Heidi would 'like'. This is an indirect way of saying 'get it yourself' and is therefore requesting action (we discuss indirect ways of asking for things in Chapter 6). In turn 3 Heidi's 'Mhm' functions as an <accept> and completes the sequence with an acceptable SPP.

5

1. HEIDI:	Excuse me ↘mum (. .)	<summon>
	↑please may I have some ↓more	<request>
2. VICKI:	↘↗Mhm (. .)	<accept>
	Would you like to help yourself ↘love	<request>
3. HEIDI:	↘↗Mhm	<accept>

(BNC spoken section, file KC3)

Pairs with three parts

Conversational sequences can have more than two parts. For example, consider example 6 from the Santa Barbara Spoken Corpus.

6

[Door opens and closes; Karen enters room]

1. KAREN:	Hi ↘sweetie	<greet>
2. SCOTT:	(. .) ↘Hey	<greet-reply>
3. KAREN:	Sweetie ↘frumptious	<acknowledge>

(SBC034, What Time is it Now?)

In 6, Karen's first turn contains the Act of <greet>, where she says 'Hi' to her partner on her return home from work. Scott's turn contains a <greet-reply>

where he responds to the <greet> with 'Hey'. In the third turn, Karen continues the greeting with an <acknowledge> which continues the greeting with a further term of endearment. In Conversation Analysis, this added extra is known as **post expansion** of the adjacency pair. As <greet>/<reply-greet> conventionally form an adjacency pair, the first two Acts are predictable, but the third Act is not. The FPP is expected given the situation (arriving home) and predicts the SPP; it would be unusual if the <reply-greet> were not present. However, if Karen's extra acknowledgement were absent, this would not be marked.

There are situations, though, where post expansion of a sequence might be expected and the lack of it marked. For example, if you are providing important information (such as bank card details) following a <request>, then the lack confirmation might lead you to wonder if the information was received. Similarly, the lack of thanks following a <grant> of permission might not go unnoticed. The point is, though, that while these third parts might be desired, their predictability (or otherwise) rests on the circumstances of the exchange. For instance, Sinclair and Coulthard (1975) found that in teacher–pupil interactions, where teachers ask questions to test pupil knowledge, some sort of confirmation of the correctness (or otherwise) of the answer is required by the teacher and is predictable in that context.

Activity 4.6 Adjacency pears

Consider the following two extracts taken from the spoken section of the BNC. Both examples contain pears, but can you see any adjacency pairs or any other sequences? For each turn, say what Acts are being performed and mark FPPs and SPPs.

(i)

1. CHRISTOPHER Why do you always have pears mummy?
2. DOROTHY Cos I just fancy them at the moment.

(BNC spoken section, file BNC KBW)

(ii)

1. SIMON What can I take? (. .)
2. SANDRA Well you were going to take a satsuma and some Quavers weren't you?
3. SIMON Yeah.
4. SANDRA We haven't got a satsuma, what about a pear, packet of Quavers and a pear?
(. .) Do you like pears or
5. SIMON Yeah.

(BNC spoken section, file BNC KDW)

We give our answers at the end of the chapter.

Preferred/dis-preferred responses

The initiating Act of an adjacency pair can often present different response options. For example, an <offer> can be accepted or rejected. The different alternatives are valued differently and are known as preferred and dis-preferred responses. Whether a response is either preferred or dis-preferred is not motivated psychologically by the interlocutors – i.e. not what the people involved in the conversation prefer, which will differ from conversation to conversation. Rather a preferred response is one that will enable the accomplishment of the *action* that the sequence of turns is aiming to achieve, while the alternative is dis-preferred (Schegloff 2007: 59). For example, if we assume that a successful offer is one that results in the giving of whatever is being offered, then the acceptance of an offer is preferred over a rejection since this enables the completion of the action. Dis-preferred responses tend to be more linguistically complex because they often involve giving reasons for the response, which can necessitate a longer turn than a preferred response. (In Chapter 7 we will see that dis-preferred responses also link to politeness.)

Backchannels

When we are involved in spoken dialogue, participants expect some sort of audible oral feedback from the other, no matter how minimal. Try keeping silent next time you are on the phone and see how long it takes for the other person to say something along the lines of 'Are you still there?'. Such feedback during spoken conversations is known as backchannelling and is crucial for keeping the conversation going. Backchannels inform the speaker that their interlocutors are still involved in the conversation and include noises such as 'ah', 'oh', 'mmm', laughter, and words such as 'yes', 'sure', 'really'. Consider the following example from the SBCSAE.

7

1. FRED:	last night I got into a hassle with James ↘Bo:yd (. .) (H) I'm in the ↗cafeteria [and I] took a break (.) that was just a ↑LITTLE BIT↑ too long ↘man (.) you ↘know
2. RICHARD:	[yeah]

(SBC047, On the Lot)

Note: The up arrow (↑)indicates a step up in pitch. We have marked a step up across words by enclosing the words with up arrows (↑this is all higher pitch↑).

Example 7 demonstrates that backchannels can overlap with an ongoing turn. In the example, Fred is telling Richard about his shift in the factory, and his turn is continuous from 'last night' to 'you know'. Our transcription aims to show that Richard saying 'yeah' overlaps with Fred saying, 'and I' by enclosing the overlapping words in square brackets.

Overlapping talk

Sidnel (2010: 52) notes that there is a widespread view that people in conversation interrupt and talk over one another. However, evidence from recorded and transcribed data shows that this is not the case. Instead, overlapping talk tends only to occur at Transition Relevance Places (see above) when one speaker's turn could be coming to an end. At that point, the other speaker might start talking a fraction of a second before the previous turn ends, as they sense the other person is finishing (Sidnel 2010: 52). Such overlaps are thought to help the conversation advance because they indicate that speakers are taking notice of and responding to what the other is saying (Sidnel 2010: 53). In example 8, Richard's contribution in turn 3 overlaps with Fred's talk, but is supportive because it shows Richard pre-empts what Fred is about to say and joins in with the 'telling', which demonstrates Richard's engagement with Fred's story.

8

1. FRED:	(H) and then he comes into the ↘cafeteria (H) and I thought he was coming in to chase everybody ↘away
2. RICHARD:	[He was after you].
3. FRED:	[(H) But he's] coming after me.

(SBC047, On the Lot)

Note: Overlapping talk is indicated by square brackets.

The overlap occurs at a possible TRP because Fred's first turn is syntactically complete and ends with a fall in pitch (a terminal intonation contour).

However, speakers can also talk over each other to retain ownership of the conversational turn and control the conversation, but such incidents are marked and noticeable. Interruptions are different from overlaps because (i) they tend not to occur at Transition Relevance Places and (ii) rather than helping the conversation proceed they can stop conversational actions progressing and signal that the speaker is declining to participate.

Summary of transcription conventions

Analysing spoken discourse relies on accurately transcribing the spoken data in a way that records the features that are important for meaning making. The following are just some of the transcription codes used in CA. Many of the symbols in the table were originally developed by Gail Jefferson (see Jefferson 2004) and have become the default notation used by analysts. The idea is that the system provides details of vocal production of spoken utterances. The overview in Table 4.4 is based on a combination of Jefferson (2004) and the Discourse Transcription System in Du Bois et al. (1992, 1993).

Table 4.4 Summary of transcription symbols

Pauses between words and utterances		
(.)	dot in round brackets	Small pause, 0.2 seconds or less
(. .)	Two dots in round brackets	Medium pause 0.3–0.6 seconds
(0.0)	numbers in round brackets	Timed pause 0.7 seconds and over
let's go==okay	equal signs	Latching. No pause between turns or between information units within a turn.
Let's [go] [okay]	Single left and right square brackets	Start and end of overlapping speech
Characteristics of speech production		
wor–	dash/hyphen	Cut-off
wo:rdwo:::rd	Colon	Prolonged vowel or consonant sound. Multiple colons indicate longer sound
word	Underlining	Emphasis or stress
WORD	underlining + upper case	Loud talk relative to the surrounding talk
°word°	degree sign (shortcut – Alt 248)	Quiet talk relative to the surrounding talk
<word>	Left/right angle brackets	Talk slowing down
>word<	Right/left angle brackets	Talk speeding up
(H)	Uppercase H in brackets	Inbreath (more hs for longer duration)
(Hx)	Uppercase H lowercase x in brackets	Outbreath (more hs for longer duration)
w(h)ord	bracketed h (or hs) within a word	Breathiness while talking – usually laughter within the word
↗	Upward diagonal arrow (short cut – 2197 followed by Alt x)	Rising tone
↘	Downward diagonal arrow (short cut – 2198 followed by Alt x)	Falling tone
↗↘	Upward and downward diagonal arrow	Rise-fall
↘↗	Downward and upward diagonal arrow	Fall-rise
→	Level arrow (shortcut – 2192 followed by Alt x)	Level tone
↑	Up arrow (2191 Alt x)	Step up in pitch
↓	Down arrow (2194 Alt x)	Step down in pitch
Transcriber notes		
( )	Empty brackets	inaudible/unintelligible word
(word)	Bracketed word	uncertain word
((sneeze)) ((leaves room))	Double brackets	comments or descriptions of non-verbal activity or sounds that are not accounted for by other symbols

Conclusion

In Chapters 2 and 3, we explored written discourse and examined how information structure and meaning making is a matter of graphology and syntax. In this chapter, we have examined how in spoken discourse it is a matter of phonology and syntax (Brown and Yule 1983). What we have discussed covers only some of the many features of spoken discourse. Its dynamic nature means that there are lots of methods at our disposal for making meaning, many of which are constantly evolving and adapting to social and interpersonal needs. These methods incorporate lexis, semantics, syntax, pragmatics, and prosody, as well as turn taking and sequencing. The dynamic nature of spoken discourse also means that interlocutors must pay attention to linguistic and non-linguistic elements in interactions. These non-linguistic factors can include hierarchical relationships concerning power and social distance, as well as cultural differences and social expectations (see Chapter 7). In subsequent chapters, we will look in more detail at this interplay between linguistic and extra-linguistic phenomena.

Further reading

For an excellent practical guide to intonation with a companion website which includes many useful audio files, see Collins et al. (2019). There are numerous introductions to CA; for example, Sidnel (2010) offers a comprehensive introduction that covers the key elements of CA in an approachable and accessible style. Stenström (1994) provides an accessible guide to analysing spoken discourse that combines the ideas from CA and from the Birmingham School (Sinclair and Coulthard 1975).

Resources

Santa Barbara Corpus of Spoken American English (SBCSAE) contains approximately 250,000 words of spoken American English from a variety of different situations, including face-to-face family chats, telephone conversations, and business meetings. Sound files can be found at www.talkbank.org in the 'Conversation Banks' under 'CABank'.

QR 4.3 SBCSAE link
(https://www.linguistics.ucsb.edu/research/santa-barbara-corpus)

BNC corpus of spoken and written English contains 100 million words of spoken and written British English from the early 1990s: 10 million words spoken data; 90 million written.

QR 4.4 BNC link
(http://www.natcorp.ox.ac.uk/)

QR 4.5 Web-based interface link (http://corpora.lancs.ac.uk/BNCweb/index.html)

Follow QR 4.5 for details of a web-based interface to the BNC, including how to sign up to use the corpus for free.

Answers to activities

Activity 4.1 Punctuation in spoken discourse

We asked you think about whether there were any issues with the basic premise of Borge's comedy routine, in which he reads out loud from a book and indicates the punction in the writing with sounds effects. However, as this chapter explains, we already do that in a way using pauses and intonation, so no additional sound effects are really needed.

Activity 4.2 Pause relocation

The effect of a pause after 'remember' creates an imperative structure whereby Alina instructs (or commands) Lenore to remember, and then provides the details of what must be remembered. We could also see this as Alina telling Lenore something (that Tyke lives next door to mum) rather forcibly.

Activity 4.3 Okay

Key and Peele's 'Okay' sketch shows how one lexical item can, through prosodic manipulation, communicate a variety of diverse attitudes towards Speaker A's propositions. For example, Speaker B begins by pitching her 'Okay' in a higher tone (↑Okay↑) which could be said to signal support when she acknowledges her interlocutor's decision not to take any more crap from her cheating boyfriend. Later, when A concedes that she will take some crap, but not all of it, B's 'Okay' is pronounced as a drawled 'Oka:::::y' with the vowel sound [**eɪ**] lengthened considerably. There is some overlap as the sketch progresses, but as B starts to question A's approach to her boyfriend's cheating, her 'Okay' changes from long to short until she finally interrupts exclaiming '↗O (.)↘KAY!' with her two hands up as if to stop her friend from speaking further. She has, at this point, clearly had – and heard – enough. Then the cheating boyfriend walks in looking all buff and with a smile that would melt an ice cream on the spot and she's all like 'Oka:: ↗y'. As speaker A acknowledges, her girl 'been speaking words of wisdom all night'.

Activity 4.4 Try saying this at home

The two ways we had in mind to break the utterance into two units in different places are:

> ↘Precisely (.) at that point (.) I called a taxi
> Precisely at that ↘point (.) I called a taxi

The difference is whether 'precisely' acts on its own as an agreement response or modifies 'at that point'.

Activity 4.5 'I'd like a pie, please'

At home
A: What do you want to eat? [request for information/offer: I will get you something to eat]
B: I'd like a pie please. [informative response/acceptance of offer: get me a pie!]

The inference that an offer has been made might be cancelled if A says something like 'then you'd better go to the bakery and buy one'.

At the bakery
A: I'd like a pie, please [request for action: sell me a pie!]
B: Certainly. Here you are. [acknowledgement of request + appropriate action]

'hello' can function as a greeting and as a way to attract someone's attention.
'excuse me' can be used to attract attention, request action (move!) and apologise.

Activity 4.6 Adjacency pears

(i)

1. CHRISTOPHER	Why do you always have pears ↗mummy	<question>	FPP
2. DOROTHY	Cos I just fancy them at the ↘moment.	<answer>	SPP

<question> / <answer> adjacency pair.

(ii)

1	SIMON	What can I ↗take (. .)	<question>	FPP^{1}
2	SANDRA	Well you were going to take a satsuma and some Quavers weren't ↘you	<question>	FPP^{2}
3	SIMON	↗↘Yeah	<answer>	SPP^{2}
4	SANDRA	We haven't got a ↘satsuma (.)	<inform>	
		what about a ↘pear = packet of Quavers and a ↘pear	<suggest>	SPP^{1} FPP^{3}
5	SIMON	mmm	<accept>	SPP^{3}
6	SANDRA	(.) Do you ↗like ↘pears ↘though	<question>	FPP^{4}
7	SIMON	↘↗Yeah	<answer>	SPP^{4}

<question> / <answer> adjacency pair with <question> / <answer> insertion sequence.

Note: <inform> in turn 4 provides a follow-up to the FPP^{2} and SPP^{2} and frames the response to the initial <question> in turn 1. The response in SPP^{1} is a <suggest> which both closes the first sequence and initiates another. Simon's 'mmm' seems to <accept> the <suggest> which closes that sequence.

Notes

1 There are also visual clues, such as gaze and gesture, that we don't have space to explore in this book.
2 An alternative method – adopted by DuBois et al. (1993) – is to use backslash (\), forward slash (/) and underscore (_).
3 Act has an initial capital letter to show its status as a technical term within Sinclair and Coulthard's (1975) discourse grammar.

References

Austin, J. L. (1979) 'Performative utterances'. In J. O. Urmson and G. J. Warnock (eds), *Philosophical Papers* (3rd edition), pp. 233–252. Oxford: Oxford University Press.

Brown, G. and Yule, G. (1983) *Discourse analysis*. Cambridge: Cambridge University Press.

Carr, P. (2012) *English phonetics and phonology: An introduction*. Oxford: John Wiley & Sons.

Clayman, S. E. (2013) 'Turn-constructional units and the transition-relevance place'. In J. Sidnell and T. Stivers (eds), *The handbook of conversation analysis*, pp. 150–166. Oxford: Wiley-Blackwell.

Collins, B., Mees, I. M., and Carley, P. (2019) *Practical phonetics and phonology: A resource book for students*. London: Routledge.

Coulthard, M. (ed.) (1992) *Advances in spoken discourse analysis*. London: Routledge.

Crystal, D. (1979) 'Neglected grammatical factors in conversational English'. In Sidney Greenbaum et al. (eds), *Studies in English linguistics for Randolph Quirk*, pp. 153–166. London: Longman.

Du Bois, J. W., Cumming, S., Schuetze-Coburn, S., and Paolino, D. (eds) (1992) *Discourse transcription. Santa Barbara Papers in Linguistics 4*. Santa Barbara: University of California, Department of Linguistics.

Du Bois, J. W., Schuetze-Coburn, S., Cumming, S., and Paolino, D. (1993) Outline of discourse transcription. In Jane A. Edwards and Martin D. Lampert (eds), *Talking data: Transcription and coding in discourse research,* pp. 45–89. Hillsdale, NJ: Lawrence Erlbaum.

Du Bois, J. W., Chafe, W. L., Meyer, C., Thompson, S. A., Englebretson, R., and Martey, N. (2000–2005) *Santa Barbara corpus of spoken American English, Parts 1–4*. Philadelphia, PA: Linguistic Data Consortium.

Francis, G. and Hunston, S. (1992) 'Analysing everyday conversation'. In M. Coulthard (ed.), *Advances in spoken discourse analysis*, pp. 123–161. London: Routledge.

Jefferson, G. (2004) 'Glossary of transcript symbols with an introduction'. In G. H. Lerner (ed.), *Conversation analysis: Studies from the first generation*, pp. 13–31. Amsterdam: John Benjamins.

Jones, D. (1960) *An outline of English phonetics* (9th edition). Cambridge: Heffer.

Key, K. M. and Peele, J. (2015) 'OK'. *Uncensored*. Series 5, Episode 6. Comedy Central.

Sacks, H., Schegloff, E. A., and Jefferson, G. (1974) 'A simplest systematics for the organisation of turn-taking for conversation'. *Language*, 50, 696–735.

Schegloff, E. A. (1968) 'Sequencing in conversational openings'. *American Anthropologist*, 70, 1075–1095.

Schegloff, E. A. (1972) 'Notes on a conversational practice: formulating place'. In D. N. Sudnow (ed.), *Studies in social interaction*, pp. 75–119. New York: Free Press.

Schegloff, E. (2007) *Sequence organisation in interaction: A primer in conversation analysis*. Cambridge: Cambridge University Press

Schegloff, E. and Sacks, H. (1973) 'Opening and closings'. *Semiotica*, 8(4), 289–327.

Searle, J. (1976) 'A classification of illocutionary acts'. *Language in Society*, 5(1), 1–23.

Searle, J. (1979) *Expression and meaning. Studies in the theory of speech acts.* Cambridge: Cambridge University Press.

Selting, M. (2000) 'The construction of units in conversational talk'. *Language in Society*, 29(1), 477–517.

Selting, M. (2010) 'Prosody in interaction: State of the art'. In D. Barth-Weingarten, E. Reber, and M. Selting (eds), *Prosody in interaction*, pp. 3–40. Studies in Discourse and Grammar, vol. 23. Amsterdam: John Benjamins,.

Sidnel, J. (2010) *Conversation analysis: An introduction.* London: John Wiley and Sons.

Sinclair, J. and Coulthard, M. (1975) *Towards an analysis of discourse.* Oxford: Oxford University Press.

Stenström, A-B. (1994) *An introduction to spoken interaction.* London: Longman.

Stivers, T. (2013) 'Sequence organisation'. In J. Sidnell and T. Stivers (eds), *The handbook of conversation analysis*, pp. 191–209. Oxford: Wiley-Blackwell.

Szczepek Reed, B. (2010) 'Intonation phrases in natural conversation: A participants' category?' In D. Barth-Weingarten, E. Reber, and M. Selting (eds), *Prosody in interaction*, pp. 191–212. Studies in Discourse and Grammar, vol. 23. Amsterdam: John Benjamins.

Walker, G. (2013) 'Phonetics and prosody in conversation'. In J. Sidnell and T. Stivers (eds), *The handbook of conversation analysis*, pp. 455–473. Oxford: Wiley Blackwell.

Wilkinson, S. and Kitzinger, C. (2017) 'Conversation analysis'. In C. Willig and W. Stainton Rogers (eds), *The SAGE handbook of qualitative research in psychology*, pp. 74–92. London: Sage Publications.

5 Analysing meaning in discourse

Introduction

Over this and the next chapter we are going to explore how we communicate **meaning** through language. Our exploration will cover topics that are typically associated with the linguistic subdisciplines of **semantics** and **pragmatics**, where the former is usually glossed as **the study of meaning of words and sentences** and the latter the study of **meaning in context**. The pragmatic meaning of an utterance might vary from context to context, so is unstable and depends on its environment to make meaning. The semantic meaning is more stable and tends to be tied to linguistic form and co-text rather than contextual factors. Meaning is derived from several semantic and pragmatic factors in combination, some of which we introduced in Chapter 1. This chapter begins by outlining different types of meaning before going on to discuss **entailment** and **presupposition**.

What do we mean by meaning?

The notion of meaning is far from simple, and the idea of semantic and pragmatic meaning recognises that understanding what a piece of language means concerns not just what is encoded by the language itself (the words and their order), but other factors such as the social situation in which the language occurs. Dictionaries can give us a range of meanings that a word is typically used to signify, but we only know a word's meaning once it is used in a specific context. Back in 1923, Ogden and Richards explored the idea that words had a variety of different meanings and suggested 22 possible types of meaning. Leech (1981) proposes a wholly more manageable seven, namely conceptual (or denotative), connotative, affective, collocative, reflective, social, and thematic. The basic idea of Leech's framework is that a word (or piece of language) has a conceptual meaning (i.e. it denotes something) but also carries with it various associations (connotative, affective, collocative, reflective, and social). It may also carry with it, as we saw in Chapter 2, thematic meaning depending on where the word (or piece of language) occurs in the clause. The meanings in Leech's framework are

DOI: 10.4324/9781003351207-5

summarised in Table 5.1 and over the rest of this section we will consider six of Leech's seven in more detail below (thematic meaning is not discussed here because we dealt with that in Chapter 2).

Table 5.1 Leech's seven meaning types (after Leech 1981: 23)

Meaning type		Gloss
Conceptual		Denotative or 'dictionary' meaning
	Connotative	Experiential meaning relating to the signified concept
	Affective	Feelings and attitudes of speaker/writer
Associations	Social	Meaning to do with social circumstances
	Reflective	Meaning transfer from other senses of same expression
	Collocative	Meaning transfer from co-occurring words
Thematic		Organisation of the message (see Chapter 2)

Conceptual meaning

What do you do if you want to know what a word means? Probably, you look it up in a dictionary. This gives us a word's **conceptual** meaning. At the heart of conceptual meaning is the study of 'signs' (known as **semiotics**). In short, language is comprised of **signs**; which are words together with their meanings. All linguistic signs, therefore, must have a label and a concept to have meaning, as we will now explain.

Signifier, signified, and referent

Think of a word and you will automatically think of what the word means. The word together with its meaning constitutes a **sign**. If you have no meaning for a word, the word is simply a '**signifier**' with no '**signified**' concept (yet). Let's consider the word 'chair' and what it means (see Figure 5.1).

Figure 5.1 This is a chair

When you were very young you probably learnt how to read using books with sentences very similar to the one in Figure 5.1 with a matching picture. The word 'c-h-a-i-r' is an arbitrary collection of letters in a particular order (if written), or an arbitrary collection of sounds in a particular order (if spoken), that English writers and speakers use to signify the concept 'chair'. The collection of letters is arbitrary because there is nothing inherently 'chair-y' about the word 'chair'. Furthermore, in languages other than English, different combinations of letters signify the same concept of 'chair', for example, chaise, sedia, cathaoir, stoel, oche, kiti, and tuoli (see Table 5.2). The combination of the word (or the sounds we make when we say the word) with the concept it signifies constitute the 'sign' (Saussure 1983). As well as the sign, there are, of course, the real-world entities or things (physical chairs) to which the sign refers, and these are known as the referent. These real-world entities, or referents, will share a set of qualities that make them chairs (e.g. a surface to place your backside, something to support your back). To summarise:

- The word 'c-h-a-i-r', known in **semiotics** as the **signifier**.
- The concept 'chair', known as the **signified**.
- The **sign** is the totality of the signifier and the signified.
- The sign 'chair' can refer to real-world entities/things.
- The real-world 'chair' is the **referent**.

The signifier and signified are mental constructs, that is, they are conceptual. So, the sign itself is conceptual. The referent is a real-world example of the thing or concept signified by the signifier. The **sign** for 'chair' (as in Figure 5.1 above) will have at least as many different **signifiers** as there are languages, as Table 5.2 demonstrates.

Table 5.2 Some signifiers for 'chair'

Signifier	Language
Stoel	Dutch
Kurasee	Hindi
Scaun	Romanian
Cathaoir	Irish
Kerusi	Malay
Sandalye	Turkish
Stól	Icelandic
Cadira	Catalan
Kursi	Somali
Chaise	French

Of course, what constitutes a 'chair' in the real world, in this case 'a piece of furniture used for sitting on', may differ depending on where you are in the world. Indeed, there may well be as many kinds of chairs as there are words for 'chair', but there will be some essential features that make the different chairs, chairs. The point is that the word–concept (signifier–signified) relationship is arbitrary. This is the case for most words in any language; the exception is onomatopoeic words which are **iconic** in that they acoustically resemble the concepts they represent.

So how do we know that 'c-h-a-i-r' means 'chair' in English? The answer is convention. This is the word conventionally used to mean 'chair'. Amazingly, we have learnt these conventional referential relationships for thousands upon thousands of words. This is what it means to have **linguistic competence**. Moreover, we can use them and combine them with other words to make meaningful utterances. This is evidence of our **linguistic performance**. We even know words for things for which there are no real-world referents. If we were to ask you 'Have you ever seen a unicorn?' you will reply negatively (we hope) but would have no trouble thinking of the signified concept (a horse-like creature with a single horn in the middle of its forehead) triggered by our use of the signifier 'u-n-i-c-o-r-n'. Similarly, if we ask you about 'love', you will know what we mean even though you could not point to the concept or real-world referent in the same way you can point to a real-life chair.

Meaning is not simply about signifiers and what is signified, however. Take a word like 'apartment', that, according to the *Oxford English Dictionary* (OED), has the following conceptual meaning (i.e. what it denotes):

> a flat, typically one that is well appointed or used for holidays.

So, presumably 'flat' means the same thing? Not quite. The OED cites the meaning of 'flat' as follows.

> A set of rooms forming an individual residence, typically on one floor and within a larger building containing a number of such residences.

So, when do we use 'flat' and when do we use 'apartment'? What is the difference between a 'flat' and an 'apartment'?[1] The answer lies partly in social attitudes as well as associations that the word carries with it, and this is what we discuss over the rest of this section in relation to Leech's other types of meaning.

Connotative meaning

In addition to conceptual meaning (those dictionary definitions we just talked about) meaning is also achieved through association. This is how **connotative** meaning comes about. According to Leech (1981: 12), connotative meaning is "the communicative value an expression has by virtue of what it *refers* to, over and above its [denotative] content" and is derived from the "'real world' experience one associates with an expression" (Leech 1981: 13). For example, the word 'mother' could be said to connote 'nurturer' or 'carer', but this is not part of the denotative meaning of 'mother'; rather they are further qualities that we expect 'mother' to have. Therefore, conceptual (denotative) meaning of concepts can be elaborated upon and imbued with connotative meanings that derive from our own knowledge of them in the real world. The differences between 'flat' and 'apartment' might well depend on our accumulated perceptions of the concepts gleaned from our social experiences as well as our conceptual or denotative understanding of them. For example, if the environments in which we encounter 'apartment' consistently show more positive realisations of the concept than 'flat', then we might tend to consider 'apartment' as connoting something more socially attractive, possibly luxurious.

What the flat/apartment example demonstrates is that linguistic expressions (phrases or lexical items) trigger access to what is known as encyclopaedic knowledge, which includes knowledge of denotation (dictionary knowledge) as well as a large range of other knowledge (see Evans 2019: 367, 387). When we think of a signified entity, we often think of the most common or prototypical example of that signified entity. A prototypical example of either a 'flat' or 'apartment' might be 'a self-contained housing unit that occupies part of a building'. However, the connotations of 'apartment' may well differ from that of 'flat'. Where we grew up (in the north of Ireland and England), 'apartment' had more positive connotations than 'flat' because the former was associated with a more affluent, professional socioeconomic community, whereas the latter was typically associated with a lower socioeconomic community.

The history of a word (its **etymology**) can also help explain why some words have more positive connotations than others. Historically, Latinate lexis carries more social prestige than Germanic terms[2] and so it may not surprise you to note that 'apartment' is Latinate and 'flat' is Germanic. Note, though, because connotative meanings (connotations) emerge over time, they are "relatively unstable", "indeterminate", and "open-ended" (Leech 1981: 13).

Affective meaning

Affective meaning relates to the attitude of the text producer towards what is being talked about and can be expressed denotatively or connotatively (Leech 1981: 15). Think about the differences between referring to your neighbour's canine friend as a 'dog' or a 'mutt', or referring to a person as being 'discerning' or 'picky'. Whichever we choose can say something about what we think of those characteristics or the people who exhibit them. Similarly, terms like 'expat', 'migrant', 'asylum seeker', and 'refugee' can say a lot about a speaker's/writer's ideological positioning (see Chapter 8 for more on this idea). Whatever the topic, the lexical choices we make indicates something about our feelings or attitudes towards that topic. Of course, it is not just the content of the discourse about which we have affective responses – our choices can also reflect our attitudes towards interlocutors, too. As we saw in Chapter 1, we might use more standard forms when addressing someone with whom we are unfamiliar, e.g. 'Please would you mind lowering the volume of your music?', whereas we might tell our flatmate to 'Turn that racket down' (we develop this example in Chapter 7).

Social meaning

This type of meaning is to do with the "social circumstances" (Leech 1981: 14) associated with certain words or expressions. Social circumstances include **dialectal** differences which relate to geographical location (regional or global). For instance, in the north of England, in some regions a pathway between buildings is referred to as a 'snicket' while in others a 'ginnel'. In other (global) locations, the word 'alley' or 'alleyway' is used. Other social circumstances include interpersonal relationships (social relationships), discipline/domain (e.g. law, medicine, football), social activity (e.g. lecture, consultation, sports commentary), and time period (e.g. 18th century). Words and expressions may also carry with them associations to do with formality, where some words can sound official, while others are colloquial or slang (e.g. 'dwelling', 'house', 'pad', 'crib'). Additionally, some may carry associations of social status (or class) (e.g. 'grub', 'luncheon'). Any or all these different types of social meaning may be carried by a word at the same time. Test your understanding of social meaning by trying Activity 5.1.

Activity 5.1 Social meaning and synonyms

Consider what social (and other) associations are carried by these sets of (near) synonyms.

'wee', 'small', 'diminutive',
'flat', 'apartment', 'condominium'
'lunch', 'dinner', 'tea', 'luncheon'
'tradie', 'tradesman', 'tradesperson', 'navvy'

We give our answers at the end of the chapter.

Reflected meaning

Many words and expressions have more than one conceptual meaning, and it is the context of use and the surrounding co-text that enable us to tell which concept is being evoked. Sometimes, though, some words and expressions, regardless of the context and co-text, carry with them associations from their other conceptual meanings. Leech (1981: 16) suggests that this is most striking with taboo words such as, for example, 'erection' and 'ejaculation' where their sexual associations "rub-off" (as Leech puts it) onto their other senses. Similar reflective associations might also be invoked by 'rub-off', especially when in close proximity to the words 'erection' and 'ejaculation' (or maybe it's just us). The notion of associations transferring from nearby words leads us on to the idea of collocation and Leech's next type of meaning.

Collocative meaning

Collocation is a term used to reflect the relationship of co-occurrence between words. Therefore, collocative meaning is influenced by the company a word normally keeps. The idea is that a word can become associated with other words it frequently co-occurs with and acquire or take on some of their meaning. Leech uses the example of 'pretty' and 'handsome' (1981: 17) which, at the time of publication of Leech's book, tended to co-occur with females and males respectively. Both words might be said to mean the same thing, and so are synonyms, but, like our 'flat'/ 'apartment' pair, their use demonstrates why no synonym is truly equivalent in actual use. The words each carry (different) extra meaning that results from their collocational partners or habits. In the case of 'handsome' and 'pretty', they are gendered. Handsome has a collocative meaning of 'maleness', while pretty carries the collocative meaning of 'femaleness'. While these collocational tendencies probably seem intuitively sound, we can test our intuitions empirically by looking at real discourse data. One way to do this would be to read through lots of texts, looking for the words 'handsome' and 'pretty' and assessing whether they describe male or female subjects. This method might take some time.

An alternative means for those with less free time on their hands, and one that we explore in Chapter 11, is to use a large collection of text data known as a **corpus** and search through that using specially designed computer tools. For example, the British National Corpus (BNC) is a 100-million-word corpus of spoken and written British English from various genres compiled in the 1990s (we met the BNC in Chapter 4). The corpus is freely available online via a web interface which allows for searches of the corpus data. The web interface will also automatically calculate the collocates of a word – i.e. show us the collocational tendencies of a word we are interested in. So, we can use the corpus to assess the maleness of 'handsome' by looking at the frequent collocates of the word in the corpus.

The word 'handsome' occurs in the BNC 1,577 times and among its most frequent collocates are 'man' (which collocates with 'handsome' 132 times), 'he' (131 times), and 'his' (102). Other, less frequent, collocates include 'her' (45), 'she' (41), and 'woman' (23). These results begin to indicate that 'handsome' has a tendency to co-occur with words denoting males rather than females which helps to explain its collocative meaning of 'maleness'. Searching for 'pretty' in the same corpus offers contrasting results. The word 'pretty' when used as an adjective occurs 2,613 times in the corpus and its most frequent collocates include 'she' (209 times), 'girl' (122), 'her' (107), 'woman' (56), 'girls' (48). The only male collocate in the list is 'boy'. These collocation tendencies in the BNC data help to show why 'pretty' has a collocation meaning of 'femaleness'.

Have a look at Activity 5.2 below for more on collocation. We return to the concept of collocation in Chapter 11 when we discuss corpus linguistics.

Activity 5.2 Collocation

Consider the words below. Do you perceive them as negative? Positive? Neither negative nor positive? Reflect on your own attitudes to the concepts to which the words refer. Why might you hold those attitudes? What do you think has informed them? Can you think of a context of use in which these words might appear?

Commit
Juvenile
Happen
Cause

You can test the collocations of these words and phrases using the British National Corpus 'search' function.

(The additional online support materials on the book's web page provide instructions.)

We now develop our discussion of meaning in discourse by taking a closer look at how co-text and context build on or shape meaning. Following that, we discuss the logical meanings that words carry when used in sentences that trigger presuppositions, which are meanings that are not explicitly stated but rather implied or assumed.

Working out meaning in discourse: co-text and context

Knowing what a word or phrase 'means' in discourse depends on two primary things:

(i) its co-text
(ii) its context

By 'co-text' we mean the linguistic company the word keeps in the text, so the other words that occur around the word in the utterance. Look at the following sentence and consider what concept is signified by 'chair':

> Ivan sat on the chair

There are other meanings of 'chair', including a person who calls or hosts a meeting. It is reasonable to assume, though, that the 'chair' that Ivan 'sat' on is a piece of furniture designed for doing just that (as in Figure 5.1), and this assumption is largely down to co-text. Importantly, the verb 'sit' relates to the conventional function of chairs as furniture and seeing that word in close proximity to 'chair' is likely to trigger the 'chair as furniture' concept. Because of its co-text, then, you would know that the meaning of 'chair' is not a person who hosts and manages a meeting (unless you attend some very strange meetings). In short, even though we might know the different conceptual meanings of the word 'chair', we can only tell which concept is being signified once we see 'chair' in its co-textual environment.

We must also consider the **context** or situation of the utterance. If we are in a meeting and the host has not yet arrived and someone asks 'Where is the chair?', we would reasonably assume them to be referring to the person who hosts the meeting and not a piece of furniture. This is because the situation determines that 'chairpersons' be present at meetings and the semantic understanding of 'chair' as meaning 'chairperson' is triggered by the question ('where is the chair') in conjunction with the lack of a host of the meeting. This is contextual-specific knowledge which means we need to know something about how meetings are organised, what roles people play, and what is appropriate or necessary for a meeting to take place. We are helped to the correct sense of 'chair' by the co-text as well. The definite article 'the' signifies a very specific 'chair', and therefore, unless there is a chair in the sense of 'a piece of furniture' that everyone expects should be in the meeting but is not, the meaning of 'chair' as chairperson will be easily – and correctly – reached.

The role of contextual knowledge in meaning making is the focus of 'pragmatics', which we deal with in more detail in Chapter 6. Nonetheless, as the example above shows, pragmatics and semantics are interlinked.

Activity 5.3 What's in a word?

The words we choose to refer to concepts can have profound effects, some ideological (see Jeffries 2010: Chapter 1). Back in 2019, the UK was involved in negotiations to leave the European Union (EU). During the negotiations, Labour MP Hilary Benn (a member of the official opposition party) introduced the European Union (Withdrawal) (No. 2) Act. The Act became law in September 2019 and stipulated that the Prime Minister had until 19 October 2019 to either make a deal with the EU and get it agreed in Parliament or get MPs to approve a no-deal exit from the EU (known as 'Brexit').

In a heated debate in the House of Commons on 25 September 2019, the Prime Minister at the time, Boris Johnson, repeatedly referred to the Act as 'the Surrender Act'.

Johnson: The truth is that a majority of Opposition Members are opposed not to the so-called no deal; this Parliament does not want Brexit to happen at all. Many of those who voted for the surrender Act a few weeks ago said then that their intention was to stop a no-deal Brexit.

(*Hansard*, Volume 664, 25/09/2019)

He also used the terms 'capitulation Act' and 'humiliation Act'. The repeated use of the word 'surrender' caused uproar in the House and generated a lot of criticism of Johnson. Using your knowledge of conceptual and associative meaning, suggest why the word 'surrender' was so inflammatory.

We will now move onto **entailment** and **presupposition**, which are areas of meaning that for some are semantic, while for others pragmatic. The distinction, if there is one, lies partly in whether entailment and presupposition are discourse phenomena or non-contextual. The standard position on entailment and presupposition taken by semanticists (summarised by Saeed 1996) aims to explain the information that we can derive from an utterance or sentence based on our language knowledge (i.e. our linguistic competence).

Entailment

In this section, we introduce entailment and briefly show how it can be used in the analysis of discourse. We owe much of our discussion here to Saeed (1996), which would be useful further reading for anyone wishing to find out more about this topic.

Entailments are, according to some (see for example Kroeger 2018), a type of meaning-based inference, whereby we make inferences based on meaning relations presented in the text and not on context external to the text. Entailment can be summarised as:

> The truth of one utterance guarantees the truth of another utterance.

Consider the following statements.

1

(a) Rob is younger than his sister, Kim.
(b) Kim is older than her brother, Rob.

There is a relationship between the statements whereby the truth of statement 1(a) guarantees the truth of statement 1(b). That means, if (a) is true then (b) must also be true. We can say, then, that (a) entails (b). Entailment is symbolised by the logical symbol ⊨ (also known as the 'double turnstile'): 1(a) ⊨ 1(b).

Conversely, if statement (a) is false (i.e. Rob is not younger than Kim), then entailment (b) must also false (i.e. Kim is not older than Rob). Furthermore, if (b) is false, then it follows that statement (a) cannot be true. Saeed (1996: 95) states the relationships involved with entailments as follows:

> A sentence **p** entails a sentence **q** when the truth of the first sentence (**p**) guarantees the truth of the second sentence (**q**), and the falsity of the second sentence (**q**) guarantees the falsity of the first sentence (**p**)

Saeed's definition can be summarised as 'if **p** is true then **q** is true/if **q** is false then **p** is false'.

We can work out the entailment in 1(a) through the comparative relationship between Rob and Kim that is signalled by the comparative adjective 'younger'. The entailment is therefore a logical conclusion that we can draw from the statements derived from their linguistic composition and the meaning relations they encode. We use our knowledge of the meaning of lexical items and their relationship with other lexical items within the discourse. We do not need to know anything about Rob and Kim (such as who they are); the entailment depends on the comparative relationship set up in the statement containing a comparative adjective. Other comparative adjectives also trigger entailments (e.g. 'smaller', 'heavier', 'richer').

Let's consider another example of entailment.

2

(a) Next door's cat killed a mouse in my garden.
(b) The mouse is dead.

Statement 2(a) entails statement 2(b): 2(a) ⊨ 2(b)

The entailment is derived from the relationship between 'kill', the action, and 'dead', the state resulting from the action. We know that if 2(a) is true then 2(b) must also be true. Therefore, the logical conclusion we draw from 2(a) is 2(b). Put another way, 2(b) is the logical consequence of 2(a). However, if 2(b) is not true (i.e. the mouse is alive), then 2(a) cannot be true (i.e. the cat did not kill the mouse).

Entailments are also involved in hyponymic relationships. As we saw in Chapter 3, hyponyms involve generic-specific relations (see Leech 1981: 135–7). For example, 'animal' is a generic group within which there are numerous types including 'cat' and 'mouse'. To see how that works with entailment, consider the following phrase (which, at the time of writing, is a controversial hashtag on social media).

3

(a) All men are trash.
(b) ⊨ Bob, who is a man, is trash.

Statement 3(a) entails 3(b) because 3(a) makes a generic, hyponymic statement that applies to any group member. The logical consequence of the generic statement is that since Bob is a man, he is part of the generic group and so is trash. We can present this entailment in the following way.

All Xs are Ys
A is an example of X
Therefore, A is Y

In a similar way, where a specific group member is specified in a statement, then a generic entailment can be derived. For example, in 4(a) a specific type of animal is identified from which we can derive a generic entailment.

4

(a) Next door's cat shat in my garden.
(b) ⊨An animal shat in my garden.

If 4(a) is true, then it entails statement (b) because cats are a type of animal. The reverse, however, does not hold:

5

(a) An animal shat in my garden
(b) *Next door's cat shat in my garden

The truth of (a) does not guarantee the truth of (b). The hyponymic relationship between animals and cats does not logically entail that if an animal shat in your garden, then it was a cat, because many species belong to the generic group 'animal' any of which might have paid your garden a visit (within reason).

Saeed (1996) also suggests that entailment can account for synonymy, as the following examples illustrate:

6

(a^1)Rob has an older sister.
$\models$(b^2) Rob has an older female sibling

and

(c^1) Rob lied about his age.
$\models$(d^2) Rob did not tell the truth about his age.

In the examples in 6, the statements (a^1) and (c^1) entail synonymous statements, where 'sister' and 'female sibling' are synonymous, as are 'lied' and 'not tell the truth'.

Activity 5.4 Pinning the entailment on the Prime Minister

Consider this following short extract from the UK Westminster Parliament. The utterance is made by Boris Johnson during Prime Minister's Questions on 20/01/2021 (when Boris was having a go at being Prime Minister of the UK).

> I think it is very important that the Prime Minister of the UK has the best possible relationship with the President of the United States – that is part of the job description, as I think all sensible Opposition Members would acknowledge.
>
> *Hansard* HC, Volume 687, column 958, 20/01/2021)

Work out the entailment in the statement and explain how the entailment works.

We provide an answer at the end of the chapter.

Presupposition

Presuppositions are to do with information that is contained in discourse but is not stated explicitly; instead, it is assumed. There are two types of presupposition – existential and logical – which are triggered in discourse by certain words and structures. Presuppositions are different from entailments because whereas entailments are logical consequences (i.e. if p is true then q must also be true) presuppositions are background assumptions or things that need to be taken for granted for an utterance to be true.

Existential presuppositions

These are presuppositions derived from definite noun phrases, which are noun phrases with a determiner that is either the definite article, 'the', or a demonstrative or possessive pronoun (e.g. '**the** coast', '**that** cat', '**her** car', '**his** coat', '**our** nation'). Recall that definiteness also indicates Given information (see Chapter 2), and there is a connection between what is Given and what is presupposed. Existential presupposition is fundamental to the way in which communication works because, if we want to talk about the world, we often need to make some assumptions about what exists in the world. Imagine trying to forecast the weather without making some assumptions about the geography of a country – what is the north and the south and so forth. Consider this example from the UK Met Office website.

7

> Outlook for Monday to Wednesday: Unsettled, rather mild and windy with rain at times, heavy in **the** west. Colder for **the** north with some hill snow. Gales in **the** south, and later in **the** north [our emphases].

The words in bold signal information that is necessarily presupposed to make the forecast possible, and readers are likely to accept the information without objection. Labels like 'the north' and 'the south' can be contentious, though, and can become political. With political motivation in mind, here are two examples, both taken from press releases about immigration policy produced by the UK Home Office during the Conservative and Liberal Democrat coalition government in 2012.

8

> To play a full part in British life, family migrants must be able to integrate – that means they must speak **our language** and pay their way . . .
>
> UK Home Office, 11/06/2012
> https://tinyurl.com/46mh7wcr)

9

> Settlement in the UK is a privilege. We are sweeping aside **the idea that everyone who comes here to work can settle**
>
> (UK Home Office, 29/01/2012
> https://tinyurl.com/ypftnbv9)

Extract 8 presupposes that 'our language' is a single language in the UK. Of course, some language communities within the UK (where there are a few native languages including Welsh, Gaelic, and Irish) might disagree with that, or at least ask, who does 'our' refer to?

The comment in 9 presupposes that an idea exists (in bold). The whole noun phrase and its contents are presupposed, which include the following.

- the idea (which implies a belief held by some people because ideas do not just exist in the ether);
- people come to the UK to work;
- people who come to the UK can settle.

The noun phrase packages up these ideas and takes these things for granted (see Jeffries 2010: Chapter 1).

Logical presupposition

Logical presuppositions are the assumptions that we can draw from the meaning of some words and phrases. These sorts of presupposition can be triggered lexically and syntactically.

Lexical triggers

Logical presuppositions can be triggered by some **change of state** verbs (e.g. 'stop', 'start', 'return', 'continue', 'resign', 'finish'). We met a change of state verb earlier in example 2: 'next door's cat killed a mouse in my garden'. The verb 'kill' is a change of state verb whereby something that was living becomes dead. We said that there was an entailment – that if the statement is true that the mouse has been killed then it must also be true that the mouse is dead. 'Kill' also carries with it a presupposition; it presupposes an earlier state – if the mouse has been killed, then it must have been alive before it was killed. Killing something presupposes that the something was alive before it was killed and entails that the something becomes dead.

Some **iterative** adverbs, adjectives and verbs (e.g. 'again', 'rewrite', 'final') can also presuppose earlier activities or states. Consider the following examples (the convention is to use >> to mean 'presupposes'):

10

(i) She rewrote history
>> history was already written
(ii) For the last time, shut up
>> the polite request has been made before
(ii) He lied again
>> he has lied before

Consider now the following tweet below posted on Twitter on 28 December 2021 by the Association of Flight Attendants (AFA), which contains logical presuppositions (highlighted).

11

> "There are two significant caveats in the guidance that recognize concerns raised by our union. CDC recommends **reducing** quarantine to 5 days only if asymptomatic and with **continued** mask wearing for an **additional** 5 days." Read our full statement: [statement included].
>
> (AFA-CWA @afa_cwa (2021), our emphases)

The verb 'reducing' presupposes (in this context) the existence of a quarantine period that is longer than the five days; 'continued' presupposes that wearing face masks is already happening; and 'additional' presupposes that there is already a specified time period in place.

Another group of lexical triggers for logical presuppositions are what are known as **factive verbs.** These are a small group of verbs in English that presuppose the Complement to be true. These include 'understand', 'knew', 'realise', and 'regret'. The above tweet in (11) includes the clause 'recognize concerns raised', where 'recognize' presupposes the existence of the concerns raised. Extract 12 below, which is taken from the *State of the Union Address* given by George W. Bush on 28 January 2003, provides another example.

12

> The British Government have learned that Saddam Hussein recently sought significant quantities of uranium from Africa.

Bush's use of the factive verb 'learned' presupposes the truth of the content of the subordinate clause and leaves no room for Saddam Hussein's actions to be mere possibility.[3] Lexical triggers therefore introduce relationships between what is asserted linguistically and what underlying assumptions we need to accept as being true for the asserted information to make sense.

Syntactic triggers

Presuppositions can be triggered **syntactically** by cleft and pseudo-cleft structures (we introduced these in Chapter 2). In each of the examples below, >> outlines the presupposition.

13

(a) It was his cat that annoyed me.
(b) What annoyed me was his cat.
>> something annoyed me.

14

(a) It wasn't me who walked mud into the carpet.
(b) What I did not do was walk mud on the carpet.
>> someone walked mud into the carpet.[4]

Presuppositions can be triggered by comparative structures (in each example >> denotes the presupposition).

15

(a) He was as ugly as next-door's cat.
>> next-door's cat is ugly.

16

(a) She was as corrupt as a politician.
>> politicians are corrupt.

In each case, the basis of the comparison is the aspect that is presupposed.

Testing presuppositions

Presuppositions are said to survive negation, meaning that they persist even when the statement that creates them is negated; for example:

17

(a) It was his cat that annoyed me.
>> I was annoyed.
(b) It wasn't his cat that annoyed me.
>> I was annoyed.

Example 17 shows that we can negate the statement by adding a negative particle to 'was' and the presupposition that 'I was annoyed' (along with the existential presupposition that the cat exists) remain intact, thanks to the cleft structure which presupposes *something* 'annoyed me'.

Presupposition and propositions

Presuppositions are not attached to propositions but the forms and syntactic structures that realise a proposition. A **proposition** is the basic meaning that we can distil from a sentence or utterance. Consider the following.

(i) The cat sat on the mat.
(ii) The mat is what the cat sat on.
(iii) It was the mat that the cat sat on.
(iv) It was the cat that sat on the mat.
(v) The mat was sat on by the cat.

Even though the sentences are grammatically different they involve the same two entities, 'cat' and 'mat', and the same action, 'sit'. The proposition of the sentence is derived from the relationship between the two entities. So, no matter which way the sentence is structured, the proposition remains the same.

Now consider the following two sentences.

18

(a) It was the cat that annoyed the dog.
(b) It was the dog that the cat annoyed.

In both sentences, there are the same two entities – the dog and the cat – and there is the same relationship between them – the cat annoys the dog. Therefore, in both sentences, the proposition is the same. However, as we established above, with cleft structures, it is the content of the subordinate clause (the cleft clause) that is presupposed. So, 18(a) and 18(b) above have different presuppositions, as we show in 19 below.

19

(a) It was the cat that annoyed the dog.
>> the dog was annoyed
(b) It was the dog that the cat annoyed.
>> the cat annoyed something or someone

Presuppositions in discourse

Presuppositions can be important in some discourses. For example, within the context of courtroom cross examinations or police interviews, lawyers and police officers can ask questions that contain presuppositions that introduce assumptions into the record that the witness or suspect must actively contest. Sidnel (2020) notes that presuppositions in questions used during such questioning can prove difficult for the witness (or suspects) to disagree with or challenge. According to Ehrlich and Sidnell (2006), the potential problem for witnesses on the stand in court is that the rules of courtroom interactions may not permit them to confront the presupposition; instead, they must simply answer the question that carries the presupposition. Presuppositions in questions can also be seen in political discourse. This is true of the question-and-answer exchanges routine within the UK parliament. For example, each of the questions below asked in the House of Commons introduce a presupposition.

20

(a) When will the Prime Minister stop ducking responsibility, do the right thing and reverse her kamikaze Budget, which is causing so much pain?

(Keir Starmer (Labour)
Engagements, Volume 720, 12/10/2022)

(b) Can the Chancellor tell us at what point in his predecessor's so-called plan for growth did he realise that it was a recipe for economic disaster?

(Peter Grant (Scottish National Party)
Economic Stability, Volume 722, 15/11/2022)

(c) When will the Prime Minister start standing up for what is right . . . ?

(Anna McMorrin (Labour)
Leaving the European Union, Volume 653, 21/01/2019)

In 20(a) the lexical trigger 'stop' presupposes that the Prime Minister (on that day it was Liz Truss) was, in fact, 'ducking responsibility'. In (b), the factive verb 'realise' presupposes that the content of the clause that follows is a fact, that the 'plan for growth' was a 'recipe for economic disaster'. The primary thrust of the question is to ask whether the Chancellor realised something while the 'something' (contained in the subordinate clause) is taken for granted. In (c), the lexical trigger 'start' presupposes that the Prime Minister (Theresa May at that point) was not already standing up for what is right. In each example, the presupposition introduces an assumption into the debate that is potentially damaging to the addressee.

Activity 5.5 Presuppositions and the negation test

The following sentence is taken from a news story that appeared in an online police community chat forum in October 2011. See if you can identify the presupposition(s) and what triggers it/them. Try negating the trigger(s) – does the presupposition remain intact or is it cancelled?

An HIV positive couple are alleged to have attacked police officers after refusing to stop having sex in a public swimming pool.

Police Community, 24/10/2011
https://tinyurl.com/3ym2cyfd)

We give our answer at the end of the chapter.

Presupposition and entailment

The line between presupposition and entailment is contested and not categorical. Some people concede that there is no such thing as logical presuppositions but rather these are types of entailment (Leech 1981: 286–287). Indeed, when tackling discourse (rather than isolated examples) it is sometimes difficult to separate out presupposition from entailment. It is important to not become encumbered by categories of meaning phenomena because categories are inevitably leaky. As discourse analysts, we should use such categories and their descriptions as starting points for discourse analysis. Any analysis of discourse should describe where meanings lie and how they can be accounted for rather than simply assigning labels to parts of a discourse. For us entailment is what we can logically conclude from a statement (e.g. if your football team did not win, then we can conclude that they lost or drew) while presupposition is what must be assumed to be in place for the statement to hold true or make sense (e.g. if your football team lost *again*, then we have to assume that they have lost before for the statement to make sense).

Conclusion

This chapter has shown how meaning operates in a number of different ways. Meaning is derived from forms (e.g. lexis) and from grammar (e.g. cleft structures). Meaning can be polysemous and is often deducible from context, e.g. 'chair' as referring to 'piece of furniture for sitting' or 'person who hosts a meeting'. The relationship between words and things is arbitrary, but often follows linguistic conventions. Meaning is explicit or denotative, but it is often connotative, which is to say, implicit (we talk about implicatures in the next chapter). Interpreting meaning relies on our knowledge of language but also on our knowledge of the world and how it works. Encyclopaedic knowledge is built up over time and we draw on this to make meanings from others' utterances. Meaning is also social – we use what we know about social and cultural conventions to determine what people mean when the form of their utterances does not reflect their intended meanings (such as when we ask a question but mean it as a request). In the next chapter we explore pragmatic meaning and consider the complex relationship between context and meaning potential. Chapter 7 develops pragmatic concepts further by considering why and how we 'do' certain types of meaning.

Further reading

If you are interested in developing Activity 5.1 on collocational meaning, specifically its core concept, 'semantic prosody', see Louw (1993), Hunston (2007), and Morely and Partington (2007). For a general introduction on types of semantics and other types of meaning, see Saeed (1996) and Leech (1981). For more presupposition triggers, see Levinson (1983: 181–184). If you want to learn more about presupposition in critical stylistics, see Jeffries (2010).

Answers to activities

Activity 5.1 Social meaning and synonyms

'wee', 'small', 'diminutive' – 'diminutive' has formal or official associations, 'small' is conventional, 'wee' is colloquial and associated with Scotland and Ireland.

'lunch', 'dinner', 'tea', 'luncheon' – whether a noon-time meal is referred to as 'lunch' or 'dinner' has regional and class associations; the same is true for whether 'dinner' or 'tea' is used to refer to an evening meal. So, it is what the word refers to that communicates social meaning and not the word in isolation. However, 'luncheon' has associations with upper social class regardless of what meal it refers to.

'tradie', 'tradesman', 'tradesperson', 'navvy' – 'tradie' is used in Australia to refer to a tradesperson; 'tradesman' carries with it association of gender stereotypes; 'tradesperson' is more woke; 'navvy' is a labourer, but it is outdated and so has association related to time period.

Activity 5.2 Collocation

The words in the list tend to be perceived negatively, but not always. This intuition can be supported by corpus evidence, such as from the BNC corpus of spoken and written English. Here are the words with some frequent collocates from the BNC (we discuss collocates in corpora further in Chapter 11).

Commit – often collocates with negative things such as 'crime'.
Juvenile – frequent collocates include 'delinquency', 'crime', 'offenders'. However, in some contexts, such as zoology and horticulture, 'juvenile' is used simply to refer to an age group (e.g. juvenile elephants are between five and ten years old) and does not hold negative connotations. Therefore, context of use can affect the connotations a word carries.
Happen – 'accidents' and 'disasters' happen, but then so do 'miracles' (but not overnight), so sometimes the evidence for collocational meaning is not clear cut.
Cause – frequent collocates include 'problems', 'damage', 'death', concern', 'trouble'.

Activity 5.3 What's in a word?

The conceptual/denotative meaning of 'surrender' is quite negative since it conventionally refers to 'giving up' and submitting to an opponent. The word brings with it connotations of war, and therefore being on the losing side.

By using the word, Johnson signalled his attitude towards the Act, indicating that it effectively handed power to the European Union. This attitude contrasts with MPs who supported the Act who suggested that it protected the UK from leaving the European Union without a deal.

In the debate that followed Johnson's use of 'surrender', many MPs criticised its use. Their discussion of it involved other words that appeared to be triggered by 'surrender', notably 'betrayal', and 'traitors'.

Rachel Reeves: We have a Prime Minister who has broken the law and uses dangerous language of betrayal and surrender, which sows division and worse in the communities we all serve.
(*Hansard*, Volume 664, 25/09/2019)

Tracy Brabin: We are hearing from the Prime Minister words such as the "humiliation" Act, the "surrender" Act, and the "capitulation" Act. All of these words suggest that we, because we disagree with him, are traitors, that we are not patriots, but nothing could be further from the truth.
(*Hansard*, Volume 664, 25/09/2019)

That 'surrender' suggests betrayal and traitorousness seems to indicate further connotative meaning relating to experiential knowledge. So, as 'mother' connotes 'nurture', 'surrender' appears to connote 'traitor' and 'betrayal'.

Another possible reason why 'surrender' was used by Johnson, and why it was so effective in creating controversy is that (both intuitively and according to the BNC) a frequent collocate is 'unconditional'. This potentially carries over meaning (collocational meaning) of a complete loss of power and sovereignty, which is of course what Johnson was hoping to communicate, regardless of whether it was a true reflection of reality.

You can read the full debate on the Hansard website: https://hansard.parliament.uk

Activity 5.4 Pinning the entailment on the Prime Minister

I think it is very important that the Prime Minister of the UK has the best possible relationship with the President of the United States – that is part of the job description, as I think all sensible Opposition Members would acknowledge.

The underlined section includes an entailment. The entailment is similar to our 'all men are trash' example. The statement entails that any member of the opposition party who is sensible acknowledges Y. Boris Johnson is saying that:

All Xs [where X is 'sensible Opposition member'] would acknowledge Y
Person Z is an X
Therefore, Z acknowledges Y

The logical consequence of the entailment is that if you are a member of the opposition party but you don't acknowledge Y, then you are not sensible.

Activity 5.5 Presuppositions and the negation test

The presuppositions are fronted by >>

an HIV positive couple are alleged to have attacked police officers after refusing to stop having sex in a public swimming pool.

>> the couple were having sex in a swimming pool
>> the couple had been asked to stop

Negating the *propositions* leaves the presuppositions intact:
An HIV positive couple are alleged to have attacked police officers after **NOT** refusing to stop having sex in a public swimming pool.

>> the couple were having sex in a swimming pool
>> the couple had been asked to stop

Notes

1 About £75,000, at time of writing.
2 The 'Inkhorn' controversy in the early 16th century started a bit of a row about borrowed words for which native words already existed. The borrowings were considered to have more prestige than their antecedents because most came from scientific writings or classical literature (and so connoted high learning and consequently, prestige). Think of it as a kind of sociolinguistics snobbery.
3 It became apparent, however, over the years following the speech that the British intelligence – which was part of the justification of invading Iraq in 2003 – was incorrect.
4 An implicature – that the speaker is accused of doing *something* – is likely to be generated here through a flout of the maxim of Quantity via the negated particle 'not'.

References

Bush, G. W. (2003) *State of the Union Address*. Office of the Press Secretary. The White House. Accessed 18 June 2021. https://georgewbush-whitehouse.archives.gov/news/releases/2003/01/20030128-19.html 2003

Ehrlich, S. and Sidnell, J. (2006) '"I think that's not an assumption you ought to make": Challenging presuppositions in inquiry testimony'. *Language in Society*, 35(5): 655–676. doi: 10.1017/S0047404506060313

Electronic Immigration Network (2012) 'UKBA: Automatic settlement for skilled workers to end'. Press release. 20 February. Accessed 3 January 2023. https://www.ein.org.uk/news/ukba-automatic-settlement-skilled-workers-end

Evans, V. (2019) *Cognitive linguistics: A complete guide* (2nd edition). Edinburgh: Edinburgh University Press.

Home Office (2012) 'Radical immigration changes to reform family visas and prevent abuse of human rights'. Press release, UK Government. Accessed 11 December 2022. https://www.gov.uk/government/news/radical-immigration-changes-to-reform-family-visas-and-prevent-abuse-of-human-rights

Hunston, S. (2007) 'Semantic prosody revisited'. *International Journal of Corpus Linguistics*, 12(2): 249–268.

Jeffries, L. (2010) *Critical stylistics: The power of language*. London: Palgrave.

Kroeger, P. (2018) *Analyzing meaning: An introduction to semantics and pragmatics*. Berlin: Language Science Press.

Leech, G. (1981) *Semantics: The study of meaning* (2nd edition). Harmondsworth: Penguin Books.

Levinson, S. C. (1983) *Pragmatics*. Cambridge: Cambridge University Press

Louw, B. (1993) 'Irony in the text or insincerity in the writer? The diagnostic potential of semantic prosodies'. In M. Baker, G. Francis, and E. Tognini Bonelli (eds), *Text and technology: In honour of John Sinclair*, pp. 157–176. Amsterdam: John Benjamins.

Morely, J. and Partington, A. (2007) 'A few frequently asked questions about semantic – or evaluative – prosody'. *International Journal of Corpus Linguistics*, 14(2): 139–158.

Ogden, C. K., and Richards, I. A. (1923) *The meaning of meaning: A study of the influence of thought and of the science of symbolism*. New York: Harcourt Brace Jovanovich.

Saeed, J. I. (1996) *Semantics*. Oxford: Wiley-Blackwell.

Saussure, Ferdinand de (1983) [1916] *Course in general linguistics* (trans. Roy Harris). London: Duckworth.

Sidnell, J. (2020) 'Presupposition and entailment'. In J. Stanlaw (ed.), *The international encyclopedia of linguistic anthropology*. doi: 10.1002/9781118786093.iela0325

6 Meaning and context

Introduction

This chapter deals with what is traditionally known as **pragmatics** which, like semantics, is concerned with meaning. However, whereas semantics relates to the relationship between linguistic form and meaning (i.e. dictionary or **denotative** meaning), pragmatics deals with the function of utterances which involves taking into account the context within which linguistic forms are produced (we introduced 'context' in Chapter 1). In this way, pragmatics is concerned not so much with 'meaning' as with '**meaning potential**' (Allwood 2003). As we progress through this chapter, we will explore context and meaning potential in discourse, and we will consider linguistic choices made by language producers and the ways in which receivers use them in discourse to make meanings.

What is pragmatics?

Imagine that you borrow your friend's phone and then accidentally drop and break it. Your generous but slightly upset friend might say, 'I could KILL you'. The context of situation, however, makes it clear that this utterance is not to be taken literally because friends tend not to kill each other over minor breakages. The semantic meaning, therefore, is not the intended one. The pragmatic meaning can be ascertained quite quickly as an expression of annoyance at the broken phone even though the words 'I am very annoyed' are nowhere to be found in the utterance. Contrast this with the same utterance being said in a thriller movie by a kidnapper. The chances are that the literal meaning prevails, which we can determine based on the context of the utterance: the situation of a kidnapping, our background knowledge (see previous chapters) of the things kidnappers usually do, the fact that we are watching a thriller in which we expect bad things to happen, and so on.

Thus, context is relevant for the **producer** (speaker or writer) and the **receiver** (the hearer or reader) of the language: the receiver must make meaning from the language produced by the producer in any given situation, and the producer is

DOI: 10.4324/9781003351207-6

cognisant of the receiver's potential interpretation. This involves what is referred to as **common ground** between producer and receiver, which is shared knowledge and a shared appreciation and understanding of the context in which the language is produced.

Additionally, context accounts for interpersonal relationships, such as the relationship between speakers. For instance, friends are socially close, share common interests and, so, tend not to want to kill each other over accidental damage to their possessions. On the other hand, social distance and different goals or purposes between kidnapper and hostage put them at odds with each other, interpersonally speaking. Finally, context includes the utterance in its wider linguistic environment, or **co-text** (see Chapter 1). This allows meaning to be derived from what is said around it. To offer an example of co-text, consider the following utterance taken from the BBC World News headlines on 13 January 2021:

> 'Trump impeachment: Several Republicans to join Democrats in House vote'

The word 'house' has a few meanings. Here are just some:

Noun

1. a family dwelling
2. a legislative assembly

Verb

3. to put something back in its place
4. to provide accommodation

Adjective

5. to assign a quality to a head noun, e.g. a type of music ('house music').

The grammatical structure of the sentence means the word 'House' is functioning as an adjective because it pre-modifies the noun 'vote' as in sense 5 above. Because 'House' appears here in a sentence about political matters and is surrounded by political lexis ('impeachment', 'Republicans', 'Democrats', 'vote') we interpret it as meaning 2 above, 'legislative assembly'. The graphological form of the word (its initial letter is capitalised) may also lead us to this interpretation, but our common-ground knowledge of headlines means that capitalisation is common and cannot be relied upon as the only indicator of meaning 2.

Context summary

As we discussed in Chapter 1, contextual factors (and the contextual assumptions associated with each of them) have a bearing on the discourse situation, and include the following.

- Physical space: where the discourse is happening (the immediate location of the utterance), e.g. a classroom, a bus queue, a restaurant, a street.
- Social situation: the people involved and the interpersonal relationship between speaker and addressee, e.g. a teacher and student, two work colleagues, a mother and child, two strangers, two friends, a kidnapper and a hostage.
- Real-world knowledge: what the speaker and addressee know about the world and the way the world works including shared cultural, ideological, and habitual knowledge, e.g. people typically don't kill each other when they break stuff; in some cultures assertiveness is considered rude, whereas in others, it's empowering.
- Textual context: the way in which the discourse is happening. This includes the co-text (i.e. the text around the utterance), which can be grammatical or sentential, or structural, e.g. the sequencing of 'turns' in conversations.

Activity 6.1 depicts a language event that aims to help exemplify the concepts just introduced.

Activity 6.1 'Did you keep the receipt?'

Figure 6.1 'Did you keep the receipt?'

Imagine a situation where someone gives a friend or relative the rather fetching jumper pictured in Figure 6.1 as a gift. On opening the gift, the recipient asks the giver 'Did you keep the receipt?'

If we consider only the utterance's semantic value, we have an interrogative form which has as its goal the acquisition of information about the whereabouts of the store receipt.

But what do you think the recipient REALLY means? Or, what is the recipient aiming to (i) communicate and (ii) not communicate to the gift giver? What is being pragmatically communicated? What do you need to know of the context (of gift giving; of interpersonal relationships, of cultural habits, etc.) in order to 'get' the speaker's intended meaning? Consider other possible ways in which the receiver could have responded. Think about these questions before reading on.

Implicature

In the gift-giving scenario in Activity 6.1, you have probably worked out that the intended meaning is that the recipient does not like the jumper and is asking for the receipt so they can exchange it. The receiver could have said simply, 'I don't like it'. This is truthful, to the point, and communicates exactly the amount of information needed to convey the speaker's intended meaning. Yet this (or something similar) has not been explicitly uttered. Instead 'did you keep the receipt' is all we have to go on. Therefore, arriving at the correct or intended meaning depends on the hearer doing a bit of inferencing work. In this section we explore how and why inferences are reached in discourse through the highly influential work of Paul Grice (1975) and his ideas about conversational cooperation and implicature.

Cooperative principle

Grice's work appreciated that as communicators we want to communicate something meaningful. Therefore, it is expected that we are cooperative conversationalists and that our interlocutors (i.e. our conversational partners) are also being cooperative when they interact with us. This is part of what makes us social beings. Grice (1975: 45) suggested a Co-operative Principle (CP) which states:

> Make your conversational contribution such as is required, at the stage at which it occurs, by the accepted purpose or direction of the talk exchange in which you are engaged.

Now, if we take Grice's CP rather literally, our Christmas jumper example does not really appear to be the most efficient way to communicate our dislike of the jumper. Instead, it goes 'around the houses' a little bit, indirectly expressing the intended meaning. But Grice is not commanding us to be completely transparent in our utterances, nor is he saying 'get to the point' in every exchange.

We are not, after all, robots without feelings. The general idea with the CP is that conversation can be approached directly and indirectly to different degrees, but typically, conversational interactants intend their meanings to be picked up regardless of the level of transparency they adopt. To that end, conversation tends to consist of connected contributions that are:

> characteristically, **to some degree at least**, cooperative efforts; and each participant recognizes in them, to some extent, a common purpose or set of purposes, or at least a mutually accepted direction.
>
> (Grice 1975: 45, our emphasis)

So, even if the "common purpose" or "mutually accepted direction" of a conversation is to get out of wearing that Christmas jumper, which, at the same time, may insult our gift giver, we must cooperate (conversationally in the Gricean sense) to make and understand meaning in our discourse exchange. Therefore, while we might not be cooperating in the everyday sense of the word because we are arguing or disagreeing or potentially insulting one another, we are still cooperating conversationally so that our interlocutor knows what we are doing is arguing or disagreeing, insulting, and so on. We are communicating these things in a way so that it is mutually understood.

Grice's Co-operative Principle aims to explain how utterances can communicate meaning that is additional to or different from the semantic meaning of the words uttered. In Grice's explanation, he separates out what we *say* from what we *mean;* he reserves 'say' to indicate "something close to" the "conventional meaning" (1975: 45) (i.e. semantic meaning), and 'mean' for what is implied, suggested, or hinted at by the utterance. Grice suggests the verb **implicate** for the action of generating meaning beyond what is said and the noun **implicature** for these implicated meanings. Speakers implicate or generate implicatures by not adhering to basic expectations that underpin the Co-operative Principle, as we will now explain.

Maxims

Within the CP Grice tentatively introduces some key principles of conversational cooperation that he calls **maxims** of which there are four types. They are **Quantity**, **Quality**, **Relation**, and **Manner** (Grice uses upper-case initial letters for these maxim types). The general idea is that we observe these maxims for optimum transparency and efficiency. So, as cooperative participants in an interaction, there is an expectation that we will not say too much or too little (maxim of Quantity), that we will be honest (maxim of Quality), stick to the point (maxim of Relation), and be coherent and unambiguous (maxim of Manner).

We set the maxims out below, quoting directly from Grice (1975: 45–46), and follow them with examples.

The maxim of Quantity refers to "the quantity of information to be provided" so that speakers should:

1. "Make your contribution as informative as is required (for the current purposes of the exchange)."
2. "Do not make your contribution more informative than is required."

The maxim of Quality refers to the truthfulness of the contributions so that speakers should "try to make your contribution one that is true" and incorporates two sub-maxims:

i "Do not say what you believe to be false."
ii "Do not say that for which you lack adequate evidence."

The maxim of Relation states simply:

1. "be relevant".

The maxim of Manner relates to not what is said but how it is said so that speakers should "be perspicuous" (i.e. be clear and easy to understand!) and:

i "Avoid obscurity of expression."
ii "Avoid ambiguity."
iii "Be brief (avoid unnecessary prolixity)."
iv "Be orderly."

As with the Co-operative Principle, even though the maxims are phrased as imperatives they are not directives or rules. Instead, they are conceived as a set of conventional expectations we have when we engage in conversation (e.g. we expect our interlocutors to avoid being vague or ambiguous). The idea is that if a conversational turn does not fulfil these expectations (i.e. does not observe the maxims) we might be prompted or "compelled" (Potts 2015: 185) to search for an alternative **implicated** meaning because we assume the person is still co-operating conversationally but for some reason is not observing the maxims at the level of what is said.

Flouting maxims

This leads us to examine why interlocutors would not observe maxims. Grice's maxims are often exploited, perhaps to be polite or because it would not be appropriate in some situations to be direct (we discuss politeness in Chapter 7). When a speaker 'blatantly' fails to adhere to a maxim and is being cooperative in doing so, then this is known as **flouting** a maxim. When flouting, the speaker wants the hearer to notice that a maxim has not been observed and intends for the hearer to derive an alternative meaning (an implicature) from this flout.

This alternative meaning is not explicitly encoded in the language uttered but is implicated by the flout. In other words, the implicated meaning cannot be traced to the form of the utterance. Also, because there is an expectation that the speaker is observing the cooperative principle, the hearer assumes that the speaker's flout is meaningful and not simply a ploy to derail the conversation just to be mischievous. Given all these assumptions, the hearer therefore needs to work out how what was said by the speaker is a meaningful turn within the ongoing interaction. To do this, the hearer must infer what the speaker is implicating by the utterance.

Before going on to look at how Grice's CP can help with the analysis of real discourse, we will work through each of the maxims and demonstrate how flouting might work using made-up examples. Each example centres on the hypothetical scenario where an adult hearer is asked whether they have seen the animated Disney film, *Frozen*.

Flouting the maxims of Quantity

maxim (1) – be as informative as required:

A: Have you seen *Frozen*?
B: I might have. *[meaning that they have but they are embarrassed to admit it]*

maxim (2) – do not be more informative that required:

A: Have you seen *Frozen*?
B: Yes, I saw it on March 8th, March 19th, March 24th, March 29th, April 2nd, April, and I think I also saw it last week. *[Meaning that they have seen it a lot.*[1]*]*

Flouting the maxims of Quality.

Recall that this category has one super maxim ('Try to make your contribution one that is true'), which is qualified by two submaxims. Our examples deal with the submaxims:

Submaxim (i) – do not say what you believe to be false:

A: Have you seen *Frozen*?
B: Only about a gazillion times. *[Meaning that they have seen it a lot]*

Submaxim (ii) – do not say what you lack evidence for:

A: I can't believe you haven't seen *Frozen*.
B: There are literally thousands of people who haven't seen *Frozen*. *[Meaning – believe it! It's not a big deal!]*

Our made-up examples aim to show how the two submaxims of Quality differ. The flout of submaxim (i) is definitely not true because (a) gazillion is not an actual number and (b) if gazillion were a number it would be potentially so huge that it would not be possible to see the film that number of times (based on average life expectancies and typical length of films, the most you could expect to watch a film of 90 minutes, assuming non-stop watching from birth to death, is around 430,000 times, give or take a thousand[2]).

The second example is different because there is a good chance that there are many people around the world that have not seen the film; it sounds reasonable and might be true. Person B, who utters the statement, might not believe it to be false and they might suspect it is true. However, without some sort of survey, the statement lacks evidence. It is fairly common to say things that lack evidence. We refer you to the previous sentence as an example of that sort of thing. The key with Gricean implicature is that the statements that lack evidence need to be made so as to exploit the Quality submaxim, and therefore communicate an implicature. With our made-up example, B implies that A needs to recognise that there are plenty of people in the world with better things to do than watch feature-length cartoons.

Flouting the maxim of Relation

The category of relation has just one maxim: be relevant.

A: Do you want to go and see Frozen?
B: I'm 55 years old. *[Meaning: No, I don't want to see Frozen – why would I? I'm a grown-up!]*

Flouting the category of manner

Grice sets out one supermaxim (be perspicuous!) and four further submaxims for this category (and says that there might be more). The submaxims describe various ways in which one might observe the supermaxim.

A: [talking to a person of interest in the presence of young sibling/related child] Please indicate the extent to which you would find it agreeable to accompany me to the kinematograph this postmeridian to partake in ocular and aural stimulation via F-R-O-Z-E-N. *[Meaning: I don't want the young child to understand my utterance]*
B: I am laundering my cranial follicular protein filaments. *[Meaning: I don't want to go with you.]*

In the example above, A is asking B on a date to the cinema to see the film *Frozen*. In our rather contrived scenario, A is blatantly not observing the category of Manner and flouting the supermaxim by not being clear and easy to understand. The idea is that while A wants B to understand that an invitation is being issued, A does not want the small child, who is also present and within hearing distance, to understand the utterance and to think that the invitation includes them. A therefore communicates the invitation to B but in such a way that an implicature is also generated: that A wants B to know that the child is not meant to understand and is not invited. A therefore exploits the maxim of Manner by flouting it. Our view is that submaxim (i), avoid obscurity of expression, is most pertinent here because:

- issuing an invitation in the form of an imperative when a more straightforward and clear way would be to use an interrogative (e.g. 'Shall we go to the cinema?');
- the imperative is in fact a request for information relating to B's emotional response to an invitation, which is not the clearest way in which to offer an invitation;
- embedding the content of the request within a noun phrase (which starts with 'the extent') again reduces the clarity of the utterance;
- using Latin phrases (postmeridian), rarely used variants of words (kinematograph), and technical terminology (ocular and aural) are more obscure than the more common alternatives;
- and spelling out *Frozen* is less clear than simply saying the word.

It is important to note that a single utterance can flout more than one maxim. In the above example, the invitation is longwinded, so speaker A also flouts submaxim (iii) of Manner by not avoiding prolixity. Note that this submaxim (be brief – avoid unnecessary prolixity) seems closely connected to the category of Quantity. However, while the Quantity category focuses on what information is communicated, the Manner category focuses on how it is communicated. So, submaxim (iii) of Manner reminds us that while the right amount of information is provided (not too much; not too little) more words than necessary might be used to convey that information.

To summarise, to flout a maxim is cooperative because it requires the hearer to know that the speaker's non-fulfilment of maxims is being done for a reason that they want the hearer to 'pick up' (see below for further examples). The box below consolidates some of the ideas above.

Doing implicature in a post-football match press conference

Football press conferences can be very entertaining discourse situations, especially for those interested in pragmatic implicature. On 19 February 2020 Jose Mourinho, then manager of the English football club Tottenham Hotspur (Spurs), was interviewed at a press conference following his team's 0–1 defeat to Leipzig at the former's home ground. You can watch the interview by following QR code 6.1 (and we re-visit this press conference in Chapter 7).

QR 6.1 Jose Mourinho post-match interview

The extract opens with a forced choice question "Was it Spurs that were bad or [. . .] Leipzig [. . .] good?" where neither option casts Spurs in positive light. Mourinho answers the question with a yes-no question, "You think we were bad?" and throws the first choice in the initial question ('bad') back to the reporter. The reporter's response "Well, the result says you lost at home" flouts the **maxim of Relation** (by not answering the question with either 'yes' or 'no') and **Quantity** (by saying more than is required: either 'yes' or 'no'). These flouts give rise to the **implicature** that losing at home means that the team is 'bad'. The discourse context (a post-match conference) means that those in the interaction will share some common ground knowledge: that away wins are more impressive than home wins; that this is reflected in the points awarded in deciding the winner in tie-breaking situations[3] and conversely, that, psychological factors such as an advantage gained from increased home supporters and familiar surroundings mean that winning should be easier for the home team.

With this shared background or common ground information, it's pretty clear that the implicature will be picked up. The assumption has to be that conversational cooperation is the communicative goal here, unless there are overriding reasons to suggest otherwise – in which case it wouldn't be a flout and there would be no implicature. Mourinho interprets the Relation flout ("Well, the result says you lost at home") as a hedged insult: that Spurs were bad and that they should have won because they would have had the easier time of it given that they played at their home ground. When Mourinho leaves the press conference, as he walks away, he shouts "Great question, mate". This is an ironic side-swipe at the reporter and is a flout of the **maxim of Quality** as Mourinho does not mean what he says. The reporter retorts "Great answer", which may well generate a similar implicature because it's not clear whether he is being ironic. If he is, then he, too, flouts the Quality maxim and in doing so distances himself from the harm done by Mourinho's side-swipe. Or maybe he simply misses the implicature.

Violating maxims and opting out

Sometimes speakers do not observe the maxims, for example, for interpersonal reasons such as politeness (see Chapter 7) or institutional constraints on what information can be shared, and so on. Grice (1975: 49) sets out some ways in which the maxims may not be fulfilled. These include (a) violating a maxim and (b) opting out of the CP. Both jeopardise the CP but in slightly different ways.

Violate

A conversational participant may "quietly and unostentatiously" not fulfil a maxim. Grice notes that "in some cases" this is "liable to mislead" the other participant. So, a lie would be a violation of the Quality Maxim. In violating a maxim, a speaker is being intentionally uncooperative, in which case such unostentatious violations are not relevant to what is communicated. However, as Jeffries and McIntyre note, violations of the Quality maxim are 'notoriously difficult to spot in real life data, for the simple reason that an effective violation of this maxim is one that is not noticeable' (2010: 107).

An example of a violation

On 28 May 2022, the Champions League final, a high-profile football match, was held at the Stade de France in Paris. The match was between Liverpool and Real Madrid. The policing of the match was a shambles and the Liverpool fans were held back by police where they patiently waited in very dangerous circumstances for over two hours at the entrance to the ground. According to French news reports, French Interior Minister Gerald Darmanin falsely claimed that "massive, industrial-scale and organised fraud in fake tickets" was to blame for the scenes at and around Stade de France, claiming further that 30,000 to 40,000 Liverpool fans arrived at the stadium either "without tickets or with counterfeited tickets". This was a lie intended to mislead the public and deflect attention away from the shambolic actions of UEFA and the French police. The violation of the Quality maxim was later 'found out', which led to a hedged retort from a parliamentary member. Responding to Darmanin's **violation** to a general audience, MP Manuel Bompard flouted the Manner maxim: "When you make a mistake – and mistakes happen – the best thing is to acknowledge your error, not to invent fake figures to try to hide it" (France24 2022). Bompard here flouts the Manner maxim by being ambiguous in using what appears to be generic 'you/your'. By flouting the Manner maxim, and referring to nobody specifically, the hearer can easily pick up the implicature that the pronouns refer specifically to Darmanin. (See also Activity 5.4 in Chapter 5.)

Explicitly opt out

Opting out is when a conversation participant makes it clear in some way or another that they will not or cannot be cooperative. Grice's example is "*I cannot say more; my lips are sealed.*" Common phrases such as 'no comment' also fall into this category. In opting out, a speaker is jeopardising the CP, but doing so 'on record', which is to say they explicitly state that they will opt out. Opting out can be a conversational strategy to avoid committing to a proposal or suggestion (think of political figures who refuse to be drawn on topics). On the other hand, opting out can be a noble or genuine attempt to respect contextual constraints, such as when business decisions are forbidden from being discussed, or there are legal implications to saying more.

Infringement of maxims

Thomas (1995) suggests that another way in which maxims are not fulfilled that is not mentioned by Grice[4] is by **infringement**. Thomas uses infringement for when a speaker breaks a maxim because her/his performance is impaired in some way. The following is Thomas's definition:

> A speaker who, with no intention of generating an implicature and with no intention of deceiving, fails to observe a maxim is said to 'infringe' the maxim. In other words, the non-observance stems from imperfect linguistic performance rather than from any desire on the part of the speakers to generate a conversational implicature. This type of non-observance could occur because the speaker has an imperfect command of the language (a young child or a foreign learner), because the speaker's performance is impaired in some way (nervousness, drunkenness, excitement), because of some cognitive impairment, or simply because the speaker is constitutionally incapable of speaking clearly, to the point, etc.
>
> (Thomas 1995: 74)

Neurodivergent people can often infringe maxims in interactions. In one study (Losh and Capps 2006), children with Autism Spectrum Disorder were asked to respond to the question: "Tell me about a time when you felt embarrassed". In one instance, a boy (ten years old) gave the rather under-specific response: "Usually . . . when I say things." (Losh and Capps 2006: 814). Here, the child infringed the Quantity maxim by saying too little and not making their contribution as informative as required. In another study, Losh and Gordon (2014) found that autistic participants tended to produced off-topic and irrelevant remarks, departed from main story themes, and produced less coherent stories. These studies demonstrate that while participants' contributions were intended to be cooperative, their responses appeared to be inadvertently uncooperative at times.

One literary example of maxim infringement can be found in the interactions of Mark Haddon's character-narrator in *The Curious Incident of the Dog in the Night-Time*. Christopher, the narrator, presents as an Autistic person which leads him to (at times) unintentionally infringe conversational maxims. In Haddon's novel, Christopher's social capabilities are markedly different from neurotypical people, so, on the one hand he infringes maxims, while on the other hand he rigidly adheres to them in ways that make him seem robotic or aloof. The following exchange between Christopher and his neighbour, Mrs Alexander, who is trying to befriend him, demonstrates this when she asks why he disappeared a few days earlier while she was inside the house getting some biscuits for them to share out in the garden (we have added speaker turns for ease of reference):

Mrs A.: What happened to you the other day?
CB: Which day?
Mrs A.: I came out and you'd gone. I had to eat all the biscuits myself
CB: I went away
Mrs A.: I gathered that

(Haddon 2004: 69)

When Christopher tells Mrs Alexander 'I went away' he is observing the Quality maxim, but conversational conventions mean that Mrs Alexander wants to know more than the obvious 'truth' of him leaving (as she has established that much already). Therefore, Christopher's response offers less information than is required to be cooperative. Yet, as Christopher is not intending to communicate anything other than the literal truth his response is not a Quantity flout – he has no desire to raise an implicated meaning in his response (such as 'I don't want to talk right now'). Thus, he has infringed rather than intentionally flouted the Quantity maxim. (for more on Haddon's use of infringement to characterise Christopher, see Semino 2014).

Doing implicatures in real discourse: memes

In this section, we will focus on digital communication. As noted above, an implicature is generated when maxims are flouted. The hearer is encouraged to arrive at a meaning through inference. This occurs in all types of interactions and so Grice's ideas can be applied to more contemporaneous discourse, such as electronic messaging. In social messaging apps, like Instagram, WhatsApp, and Facebook, discourses are often multimodal in the sense that words combine with images in meaning making. The success of communication depends on shared or 'common ground' knowledge or values. Memes and 'stickers' used in messaging apps are examples of multimodal discourse and combine topical, culturally specific images with words in novel ways to implicate meanings. Because memes tend to employ indirectness, they require greater cognitive processing similar to other indirect utterances (Shibata et al. 2011; van Ackeren et al. 2012), and this extra effort may help develop or reinforce interpersonal relationships between interlocutors. Memes are cooperative 'utterances' in the same way that conversational utterances are cooperative because both rely on shared common ground knowledge. Indeed, memes exploit common ground-ness and their use can even strengthen the interpersonal relationship between sender and addressee. This is partly because memes typically employ humour, which reflects well on the sender's character because humour 'tickles' the addressee (Simpson 2001). Additionally, the addressee invests greater processing effort to interpret the meme's indirect message and is rewarded for that, usually by 'getting' the humour. As such, memes can reinforce in-group membership. In other words, if the implicature generated through the meme is successfully decoded, the sender and receiver are jointly successful in terms of meaning making on the one hand, and sharing (and getting) the humour of it on the other. The interpersonal relationship can become stronger as a result (O'Boyle 2021).

Context, culture, and implicature

Memes often use cultural figures to reinforce in-group membership or "groupness" (Brubaker and Cooper 2000). For example, O'Boyle's (2021) study of a "neighbourhood drinking group" called "the Man Shed" discusses how a small community of residents communicated using Donald Trump memes during the early part of the Covid pandemic in 2020. The study acknowledges the social function of such discourse. O'Boyle concludes that the phatic function of communication "play[s] an important though inconspicuous role in relationship maintenance" (2021: 460).

While Donald Trump is a globally recognised cultural figure in the real world, fictional characters can be equally thematised in social messaging exchanges. One such figure, a cartoon sponge, with which many Gen Z young adults (people born between 1997 and 2012; see Dimock 2019) may be familiar.[5] The meme below in Figure 6.2 uses a character we have called Absorbent Andy to represent the meme. It shows him wearily getting out of his chair with the text 'Ight Imma head out' added. The lexis is African American vernacular: 'ight' is a clipped form of 'Right' or 'Alright' and 'imma' is a contraction of 'I am going to'. Let's assume the meaning in the original context is literal (Absorbent Andy gets up and goes out). In the meme version, the intended meaning is non-literal (or literal AND non-literal).

When used non-literally, users flout the maxim of Quality because the literal interpretation (of physically exiting) is not the intended meaning. Rather, the 'leaving' is metaphorical – 'I'm exiting this situation' (in a polite, playful, awkward, or embarrassing way). Second, the co-text, that is, the text produced by the speaker that accompanies the meme, is needed to correctly decode the intended meaning. For example, one social media user employs the meme in reference to

Figure 6.2 An artist's representation of the 'Imma head out' meme featuring Absorbent Andy

an absent dad (Figure 6.3), where child abandonment is euphemistically encoded as a temporary 'heading out'.

This particular version of the meme (6.3) flouts the maxim of Quantity, because the 'out' is insufficient information. In fact, it is an example of a **scalar implicature**, which means that implicated meaning is informative to a degree on a conceptual scale ('scalar') ranging from weakly informative to strongly

Figure 6.3 The absent dad variant

informative. The use of 'out' introduces a range of different kinds of 'out' that have greater 'communicative strength' (Potts 2015: 18) (e.g. out to the shop, out for the rest of the person's life). The father in Figure 6.3 is both literally out (he has indeed left the room) but also at the same time figuratively out for the remainder of the child's life. The British comedian Micky Flanagan immortalises this scalar meaning when he talks about going 'out' (for a beer without the intention of staying out), rather than 'out-out' (a more intentional, planned night 'out'). In the meme example above, the 'out' is semantically true (and so adheres to the maxim of Quality), but is not as true as it could be because it does not specify where on the scale of 'out' the dad sits (which appears to be 'out for the whole person's life').

Another adaptation of the 'Imma head out' meme has relevance for a subset of Gen Z interlocutors: fans of the American singer Halsey (Figure 6.4). The Halsey version of the meme says 'Ight, Imma head to the Badlands'. *Badlands* is a Halsey album that, according to some listeners (personal communication), invokes melancholy, sadness, or simply reflection. Used this way, the meme means 'I'm exiting this situation to be sad/reflect'. Decoding it relies on the receiver making the intertextual connection (to *Badlands*), interpreting it as a flout of the Quality maxim (for there is no such physical place as 'Badlands'), and then picking up the implicature that the sender is in a particularly pensive mood. Once the meme has gained cultural prominence, its appropriation becomes meaningful, too. The 'out' becomes a kind of 'time out' for quiet reflection or introspection. Of course, the addition of the wig and outfit in Figure 6.4 helps steer the reader to the meaning of 'Badlands', although we are not quite sure what Halsey would make of her doppelganger's aesthetic!

The meme can be used in lots of situational contexts, such as the university classroom (Figure 6.5). This is one that we, as teachers, are rather familiar

ight, imma head to the badlands

Figure 6.4 The Halsey variant

Professor: "Attendance isn't requ-"
Half the class:
ight, imma head out

Figure 6.5 The student variant

with. In this version, the accompanying text presents the teacher's utterance 'Attendance isn't required', but the final word is cut off (the rhetorical term for this is *aposiopesis*) by the 'half the class' getting up to leave. The humour is partly derived from the novel way that the meme has been appropriated, and partly from the contextual familiarity that the target social group (students) has with the collective common ground information invoked by the teacher's announcement (that half the students leave). The student meme generates an implicature that if a class is not compulsory a lot of students will not attend; it is by picking up the implicature that the humour is successfully carried. Here, the 'out' is literal.

As can be seen from these examples, memes and their various permutations require cooperation from sender and addressee. The implicatures memes generate depend on a shared understanding of context (e.g. university) and they incorporate sociocultural themes or events (e.g. music genres, cartoons). The payoffs from working out their intended meanings can build or reinforce social group membership and strengthen interpersonal relationships.

Conclusion

In this chapter, we have discussed the cooperative principle and the maxims to which speakers orientate their contributions. We showed how speakers often flout these maxims to generate implicatures so that what they say is not often what they mean. Shared knowledge and expectations of cooperation lead hearers to deduce implicatures when it appears that maxims have been flouted. Flouts often occur for particular reasons, namely social politeness (see Chapter 7), irony, or for humorous purposes. Grice's CP relates to real-life conversations, but the principle governs all kinds of discourse, such as print ads, political poster campaigns, government warnings, interpersonal app messaging, memes, and so on. Indeed, Grice alludes to the ubiquity of the CP across a range of discourse situations in one of his examples which involves a reference given by a teacher, person (A), about a former philosophy student, Mr X. The reference goes like this: "Dear Sir. Mr. X's command of English is excellent, and his attendance at tutorials has been regular. Yours.etc." (Grice 1975: 52). Grice states that:

> ['A'] cannot be opting out, since if he wished to be uncooperative, why write at all? He cannot be unable, through ignorance, to say more since the man is his pupil; moreover, he knows that more information than this is wanted. He must, therefore, be wishing to impart information that he is reluctant to write down. This supposition is tenable only if he thinks Mr. X is no good at philosophy. This, then, is what he is implicating.
>
> (Grice 1975: 52)

Maybe the next time you ask for a reference, you might want to read not only what is there, but what is not there!

The language used in any discourse situation, whether written, spoken, or multimodal, conveys a particular semantic or conventional meaning that is tied to the forms in the utterance. Yet as we have seen, pragmatic meaning is conveyed through and around the language used. It is conveyed by the speaker but with the hearer in mind, as implicatures must be capable of being picked up by the hearer to function successfully. Pragmatic meaning, then, is a kind of joint effort (hence 'cooperation') because when the speaker implicates meaning the implicature is not tied to the forms of the sentence. As Grice (1981: 185) notes: "It is important that what is conversationally implicated is not to be thought as part of the meaning of the expressions that are used to get over [carry or communicate] the implication."

This means that if a speaker wishes to generate a specific implicature, whether it's to communicate their dislike of a gifted Christmas jumper or emphasise their indignation on an issue, there are several strategies at their disposal for doing so. Speakers can either flout a maxim or they can opt out. The situation and wider context (which includes interpersonal relationships, mode of communication and so on) will determine which route they take. It is also important to note that while different utterances might implicate the same meaning they might also generate different pragmatic, social, political, and cultural effects. Context, in all cases, is crucial.

Further reading

The sociolinguistic objectives in interpersonal interactions assume an element of cooperation between interlocutors as Grice sets out in his seminal work.

However, Grice's approach is not the endpoint of such discussions. Some scholars have developed a robust and nuanced approach to implicature and pragmatics more generally by focusing on one of Grice's maxims, the maxim of Relation. This forms the basis for the development of Relevance Theory, which has as its central tenet that a speaker's contribution to conversation carries 'a presumption of optimal relevance' (Wilson 2016). Robyn Carston notes the usefulness of Relevance Theory over the Gricean model when she says that "Relevance-based pragmatics stands a better chance of providing a psychologically sound explanation of utterance interpretation, since it is grounded in a theory of how we process and represent information in general" (1995: 213). Sperber and Wilson (1986), Clark (2013), and Scott et al. (2019) offer accessible and insightful studies using Relevance Theory.

For more on scalar implicatures, see Zondervan (2010) and Potts (2015). Additionally, Noveck (2001) explores the relationship between logical and pragmatic reasoning when children and adults encounter scalar implicatures.

Notes

1 Give us a break. It's been a long few years in lockdowns and isolation.
2 See note 1.
3 Until the 2021–2022 European Football season, if a two-legged tie was drawn between team A and team B, and team A scored the most away goals, then team A would be deemed the winner. So, if team A drew 1–1 at home and 2–2 away, they would go through to the next round on away goals.
4 Grice does use the term 'infringement', albeit in a different way, to subsume flouting, clashes, and explicit opting out.
5 We cannot include the original character here due to copyright, so Eve Canning produced a generic sponge-shaped character that we have called 'Absorbent Andy'.

References

Allwood, J. (2003) 'Meaning Potential and Context. Some consequences for the analysis of variation in meaning'. In H. Cuyckens, R. Dirven, and J. Taylor (eds), *Cognitive approaches to lexical semantics*, pp. 29–65. Berlin: Mouton de Gruyter.

BBC World News (2021) 'Trump impeachment: Several Republicans to join Democrats in House vote'. 13 January. Accessed 2 June 2022. https://www.bbc.com/news/world-us-canada-55642101

Brubaker, R., and Cooper, F. (2000) 'Beyond "identity"', *Theory and Society*, 29(1): 1–47.

Carston, R. (1995) Quantity maxims and generalised implicature. *Lingua*, 96(4): 213–244.

Clark, B. (2013) *Relevance theory*. Cambridge: Cambridge University Press.

Dimock, M. (2019) 'Defining generations: Where Millennials end and Generation Z begins'. Pew Research Center, 17 January. Accessed 4 July 2023. https://www.pewresearch.org/short-reads/2019/01/17/where-millennials-end-and-generation-z-begins.

France24 (2022) 'Champions League final "could have been better organised", French interior minister tells Senate'. 1 June. Accessed 13 February 2023. https://www.france24.com/en/france/20220601-macron-backs-darmanin-wants-full-transparency-on-champions-league-chaos

Grice, H. P. (1975) 'Logic and conversation'. In P. Cole and J. Morgan (eds), *Syntax and semantics vol. 3*, pp. 41–58. New York: Academic Press.

Grice, H. P. (1981) 'Presupposition and conversational implicature'. In P. Cole (ed.), *Radical pragmatics*, pp. 183–98. New York: Academic Press.

Haddon, M. (2004) *The Curious Incident of the Dog in the Night-Time*. Harmondsworth: Penguin.

Halsey (2015) *Badlands* [album]. Astralwerks.

Jeffries, L. and McIntyre, D. (2010) *Stylistics*. Cambridge: Cambridge University Press.

Leech, G. N. (2014) *The pragmatics of politeness*. Oxford Studies in Sociolinguistics. Oxford: Oxford University Press.

Losh, M. and Capps, L. (2006) 'Understanding of emotional experience in autism: Insights from the personal accounts of high-functioning children with autism'. *Developmental Psychology*, 42(5): 809.

Losh, M. and Gordon, P. C. (2014) 'Quantifying narrative ability in autism spectrum disorder: A computational linguistic analysis of narrative coherence', *Journal of Autism and Developmental Disorders*, 44(12): 3016–3025.

Noveck, I. A. (2001) 'When children are more logical than adults: Experimental investigations of scalar implicature'. *Cognition*, 78(2), 165–188.

O'Boyle (2021) 'WhatsAppening Donald: The social uses of Trump memes'. *European Journal of Cultural Studies* 25(2): 458–462.

Potts, C. (2015) 'Presupposition and implicature'. In S. Lappin and C. Fox (eds), *The handbook of contemporary semantic theory* (2nd edition), pp. 168–202. Hoboken, NJ: John Wiley and Sons Inc.

Scott, K., Clark, B., and Carston, R. (eds) (2019) *Relevance, pragmatics, and interpretation: Essays in honour of Deirdre Wilson*. Cambridge: Cambridge University Press.

Semino, E. (2014) 'Language, mind and autism in Mark Haddon's The Curious Incident of the Dog in the Night-Time'. In M. Fludernik and D. Jacob (eds), *Linguistics and Literary Studies/Linguistik und Literaturwissenschaft*, pp. 279–304. Berlin: Mouton de Gruyter.

Shibata, M., Abe, J. I., Itoh, H., Shimada, K., and Umeda, S. (2011) 'Neural processing associated with comprehension of an indirect reply during a scenario reading task'. *Neuropsychologia*, 49: 3542–3550. doi: 10.1016/j.neuropsychologia.2011.09.006

Simpson, P. (2001) '"Reason" and "tickle" as pragmatic constructs in the discourse of advertising'. *Journal of Pragmatics*, 33(4): 589–607.

Sperber, D. and Wilson, D. (1986) *Relevance: Communication and cognition*. Oxford: Blackwell Press.

Thomas, J. (1995) *Meaning in interaction: An introduction to pragmatics*. London: Longman.

van Ackeren, M. J., Casasanto, D., Bekkering, H., Hagoort, P., and Rueschemeyer, S. A. (2012) 'Pragmatics in action: Indirect requests engage theory of mind areas and the cortical motor network'. *Journal of Cognitive Neuroscience*, 24: 2237–2247. doi: 10.1162/jocn_a_00274

Wilson, D. (2016) 'Relevance theory'. In Y. Huang (ed.), *Oxford handbook of pragmatics*. Oxford: Oxford University Press.

Zondervan, A. (2010) *Scalar implications or focus: An experimental approach*. Amsterdam: Netherlands Graduate School of Linguistics.

7 Politeness

Introduction

In the previous chapter we considered the importance of context and the ways in which the relationship between producer and receiver influence how the 'message' is communicated. We showed how meanings are often not traceable to the semantic content alone. We established that, as creative users of language, we adapt linguistic structures so that our utterances can carry meanings that are either direct or indirect. We discussed Grice's Co-operative Principle, which accounts for utterances that are direct (and generally adhere to conversational maxims) and those that are indirect (typically by flouting maxims). It is by flouting maxims that we create implicatures which communicate something different than what we actually say. We also looked at the ways in which discourse makes use of shared sociocultural knowledge to generate and interpret implicatures and showed, with reference to memes, that shared knowledge is often specific to a particular social group or discourse community.

In this chapter, we present a pragmatic framework that explains one of the reasons why we use and invest so much cognitive effort in creating and interpreting implicatures in everyday interactions. The framework we introduce offers a range of pragmatic strategies that attend to linguistic meaning in its social, cultural, personal, and professional contexts. It is the framework of **politeness**, first introduced by Brown and Levinson in the 1970s and developed in the 1980s and beyond.

Politeness in a non-linguistic sense is already familiar to you – it is those little markers of good manners, like saying 'thank you', that help endear you to one another, not least by showing that you appreciate what you do for each other. The pragmatic framework of politeness focuses on a wider range of phenomena than good manners and attends to their 'payoffs' in social interactions. According to Leech: "politeness is concerned with avoiding discord and fostering concord, only insofar as these are manifested through communication, especially through what meanings are expressed or implicated" (Leech 2014: 88).

Leech sees politeness as having a social motivation and a psychological one. The social motivation is to maintain "concord" and avoid "discord", while

DOI: 10.4324/9781003351207-7

the psychological goal is to avoid damage to self-image (yours and your interlocutor's). Let's start with an example. Imagine you are working from home and your roommate is playing their music a bit too loud for you to concentrate on your work. You want to say something that effectively communicates your wish for them to turn down their music, but telling them to turn it down imposes upon them because you are making demands on their freedom to do as they wish. At the same time, you risk offending them by suggesting that you do not share their desire to listen to loud music. So, there is a tension between achieving your goals but managing the imposition to maintain social concord with your roommate. There are a number of ways you can achieve your goal linguistically, using language. Arguably, the more direct you are, the clearer your message will be and the less cognitive effort your roommate will need to process your utterance, so directness is more economical. Theoretically, then, if you want someone to turn down their music you can formulate a short, direct utterance that communicates your intended message in the most economical way:

(1) turn down your music[1]

Being concise and direct in (1) means your message is economical and clear. After all, you are adhering to Grice's conversational maxims (see Chapter 6) – you are being concise and to the point so observe the Quantity maxim; you are being truthful and so uphold the Quality maxim; your utterance is relevant to the situation, so you adhere to the maxim of Relation; and you are unambiguous and have avoided perspicuity, thus adhering to the Manner maxim. In short, you are observing the **cooperative principle** in the most direct way. So far, your utterance appears to satisfy the 'effective' part of your wish to communicate. However, in uttering (1) you are perhaps less likely to achieve the outcome you desire. This is because you risk potential discord, not just by the making the imposition, but by the way you do it, in this case using an **imperative** structure. Devoid of context, this utterance is essentially an order or command, which assumes a relationship where you have more power than your roommate, (and this might be something your roommate objects to or resents). So, while you have communicated your wishes, you have done so in a way that has causes discord rather than maintains concord. From this simple example, we can see that language is not simply a medium for imparting information from one person to another in order to get things done. Language is also instrumental in building and maintaining relationships. It is – and requires – negotiation. This leads us to adjust our linguistic choices according to the kinds of interpersonal relationships we have or wish to create with our interlocutors and the contexts in which we use language. We make language choices that are mindful of the other person as well as ourselves. This idea that our language choices are influenced by social factors was discussed at length by Erving Goffman, who introduced the influential notion of **face** (Goffman 1967).

In the following sections we discuss face and the contiguous concept, **face-work**, before dealing with how face is addressed and redressed through the phenomenon of politeness.

Face

Face is a sociological concept that has great significance for discourse analysts as it attends to the way language users acknowledge and respect cultural conventions and handle empathy, power relationships, and self-presentation in communication. First introduced by Goffman, whose work was based on earlier traditional notions of politeness in East Asian cultures, the concept of face is: "the positive social value a person effectively claims for himself [sic] by the line others assume he [sic] has taken during a particular contact" (Goffman 1967: 5).

Following Goffman (1967), Brown and Levinson developed 'politeness theory' and used face metonymically (see Chapter 8) to stand for the whole person, their reputation and character. Much of our social communication is done cognisant of each other's face. Politeness is essentially face-work; when we 'do' politeness, we are doing face-work.

To unpack this a little, **face** is the "public self-image" (Brown and Levinson 1987: 61) that a person wishes to project and protect in everyday interactions. This means we do not want to 'lose face', nor do we wish to threaten our addressee's face by what we say to them. We like to be thought of as decent humans who make good choices in life and we want our discourse to reflect this. Therefore, if the 'line' (to use Goffman's word – think 'stance' or 'approach') someone takes in an interaction threatens our positive self-image, that tends to bother us. And, equally, we generally take pains to ensure that the 'line' we take does not threaten the face of others so as not to bother them. In this way, we demonstrate empathy, show that we are aware of socially appropriate linguistic behaviour, and that what we say and how we say it respects and preserves our interpersonal relationships.

Face threats and face-work

In Brown and Levinson's politeness theory, there are two types of face: **positive face** and **negative face**. When we talk about **positive face**, we are referring to a person's positive public self-image, the right for them to have their opinions valued, their ideas appreciated, their choices respected, and so on. For example, saying 'I really like your music' considers the positive face of your interlocuter because it praises their choices. On the other hand, when we talk about **negative face**, we are talking about the right to be free from impositions. Asking your roommate to lower their music imposes on their right to feel unimpeded, and hence, disregards their negative face-wants. Brown and Levinson define positive and negative face as follows.

positive face:	"the want of every member that his [*sic*] wants be desirable to at least some others'"
negative face:	"the want of every 'competent adult member' that his [*sic*] actions be unimpeded by others"
	(Brown and Levinson 1987: 62)

Any language event that causes a risk to face is called a **face-threatening act** or FTA for short. Impositions are considered **face-threatening acts** to negative face because they place the hearer (H) under an obligation to do something, even if H does not feel obliged (and even if they do not do it). In the example above, the roommate may feel obliged to lower the volume of the music which impedes them from listening to their music as they want, and it makes them do something they would not have otherwise done. On the other hand, an FTA to positive face is any threat to a person's public self-image – saying 'I really don't like your music' is a threat to positive face because it undermines the hearer and their life-choices, desires, and so on.

The 'positive' and 'negative' terminology is unfortunate because the words already have commonplace meanings that suggest they are diametrically opposed. However, in the politeness framework we have to suspend our common ground understanding of the terms because in the theory positive and negative are not oppositional, where one is 'good' and the other is 'bad', but rather each addresses different wants that a person may be perceived to favour. Those wants (face-wants) are that our positive self-image is preserved and respected (positive face) and that we don't feel imposed upon in respect of our time, energy, or resources (negative face). Of course, there are many times in our lives when we simply *have* to impose on others. In doing so, we potentially threaten their negative face. Or, we have to say something or do something that will likely cause them to feel aggrieved or disappointed or hurt and so on, which potentially threatens their positive face. Doing politeness, then, is about balancing the risks to face with the demands our FTAs invariably carry, and then finding an appropriate strategy or strategies to minimise that risk. In politeness terminology, to minimise the threat is to **mitigate** it or **redress** it with a **politeness strategy** or **strategies.**

There are many strategies for doing face-work and previous scholars (for example, Brown and Levinson) have separated strategies into the categories 'positive politeness strategies' and 'negative politeness strategies'. However, we find this distinction might be a little misleading because it could imply that certain politeness strategies are directed exclusively to one face or the other (i.e. 'positive politeness strategies' can only be employed to anoint positive face). In reality, politeness strategies can be employed to redress FTAs to positive *or* negative face. So, rather than differentiate between them as 'positive politeness strategies' and 'negative politeness strategies' we refer to them collectively as '**politeness strategies**' – but it's important to know to which face they are oriented! Therefore, we will use terms like 'politeness strategy oriented to positive face' or 'politeness strategy oriented to negative face'. There is, of course, plenty of overlap in that some strategies can mitigate threats to either face, and more than one strategy can be employed in an utterance. We present many of them in the table below (and you can probably add your own strategies to these). It is important to point out at this stage that different cultures will do politeness differently and we return to this point later. In this section we will explore how politeness strategies work in discourse.

Table 7.1 Some politeness strategies

Politeness Strategy	Examples 1
Acknowledge the imposition (*includes 'indicate reluctance'*)	'I know this is a lot to ask but . . .' 'I wouldn't usually ask you this but . . .'
Hedges	'**Could** you, **er**, close the window **maybe**?'
Be pessimistic	'You **wouldn't just** close the window?'
Be optimistic	'**You'll close** the window, right?'
Minimise the imposition	'Does anyone have a **tiny little bit** of milk I could use for my coffee?'
Apologise	'**I am so sorry** to have to ask you, but . . .'
Ask forgiveness	'**Forgive me** for being blunt but that outfit needs its own therapist'
Joke	'You must've been born in a hospital with swinging doors!' *(Sending humorous memes also falls into this category)*
Use conventional indirectness	'**Could** you pass me the salt?'
Use deference (i) *Honorifics*	'**Dr Canning**, I'd like to make an appointment'
Use deference (ii) *humble self*	'I won't be able to work this out by myself – could you help?'
Impersonalise *(Includes 'state the FTA as a general rule')*	'It would be great if the table could be set for dinner' 'Students must return books' 'Books must be returned' 'Smoking is not allowed here''No smoking'
Provide overwhelming reasons	'Well, this morning, my alarm clock failed to go off three times, then I had a headache when I woke up, then my dog ate my homework, then my granny got sick, so could I have your homework to copy for class?

Politeness Strategy	Examples 1
Seek agreement/avoid disagreement	S1. 'You been at the library?' S2. 'Well, I gotta go there tomorrow, but today I was at the lab'
Use in-group markers *(includes code-switching and dialectal forms)*	'Hey **mate**, we are next in line' 'Spill the tea, **sis**' 'OMG are you ***sleggin**?' (*this means 'joking' or 'winding me up' in Belfast English)
Claim common ground	'You like Grimes?[2] Me too!'
Exaggerate	'You're the **best** friend **EVER**!'
Understate	'I **may** have written **a little tome**' *(imagine it was said by Stephen Hawking about his bestselling book)*
Irony	S1: 'Dude, I broke your phone' S2: 'Well, **aren't you the bright spark?**'
Use tautologies *(note the overlap here with avoid disagreement)*	S1: 'This coronavirus is a real bummer and I'm so sick of staying in' S2: '**It is what it is**'
Use rhetorical questions	S1: '**How many times do I have to invite you here before you actually come?**' S2: 'I know, sorry, I should make more effort'
Compliment	'You have a **lovely** home/hairdo/family/work ethic . . .'

Activity 7.1 Politeness in real discourse

Examples of real discourse have been provided below with context. Example (A) is written email communication from an academic in a British university to all staff inviting participants to respond to a survey for their research project. The second (B) is a spoken exchange taken from the Santa Barbara Corpus of Spoken American English (see Chapter 4) between a bank employee and the president of the bank in Illinois, USA. The participants are Jim, who is the president, and Joe, who is the employee. Joe is taking minutes for the meeting. Example (C) is from the UK version of *The X-Factor* (Cowell 2013), a television talent show in which singers audition in front of four celebrity judges for a place in the competition. In the exchange, the judges are Louis Walsh (music producer), Gary Barlow (from the successful British group *Take That*), Nicole Scherzinger (from *The Pussycat Dolls*), and Simon Cowell (music producer). The auditionees, Liddia and Ryan, are, in spite of their enthusiasm and energy, not terribly good at singing.

Can you spot any potential FTAs? And to which face? Are any strategies used to mitigate the FTAs? What are they? We offer some possible answers at the end of the chapter.

(A) The academic email

Happy St. Patricks Day! Sorry for cross posting (or if you have already completed) but I wanted to send out a reminder for the [redacted] Questionnaire.

Responses have been amazing so far and I am having a final push for participant collection. I would ask anyone who plays sports (either competitively or for fun) and is over the age of 18 to take 5-minutes to complete my PhD questionnaire.

Please find the link below:

[redacted]

This study has been approved by the University Ethical Approval system at [university name redacted].

Many thanks

(B) The bank meeting

JIM: I got a couple things here, [. . .], just to kind of bring us up to speed, Matt has tentatively accepted our offer for employment, but since he's going to be a dual employee, th- you really don't need to put this in the minutes.

JOE: Okay.

(C) The X-Factor audition

The context for this example is that *X-Factor* judges Gary Barlow and Louis Walsh rate an audition by Liddia and Ryan poorly. Walsh calls them both 'deluded', and Gary Barlow tells them that they haven't got a voice between them. To watch the audition and commentary, scan the QR code. The relevant segment begins at 26:23 minutes.

QR 7.1 Liddia and Ryan's *X-Factor* audition

Using politeness strategies to mitigate face-threatening acts

So how do we 'do' politeness? If we return to our music-loving roommate, our desire to have the music volume lowered means that we have to do an FTA. Activity 7.2 asks you to have a go at identifying some of the strategies that might serve to reduce the threat to face in the utterances (a)–(f).

Activity 7.2 Mitigation strategies

If we wanted our roommate to turn down their music, we could choose a number of ways of getting our intended result. Let's imagine a sort of *Groundhog Day* scenario where we do the FTA six times in six different ways. In each scenario we utter one of the options set out below ((a) to (f)), all of which are oriented to face to varying degrees. Refer back to the politeness strategies in Table 7.1 and see if any are employed in (a) to (f). Which utterances might work best? Which might not work well at all? Can you think of a reason why (f) is a strategy? We give some possible answers throughout the remainder of the chapter.

(a) Turn your music down
(b) I can see how much you're enjoying your music so I hate to have to ask if you wouldn't mind lowering the volume a little?
(c) It's nice music, but a bit loud, so please could you lower it?
(d) I can't really concentrate on my work
(e) Wow, you kinda like your music loud, huh?
(f) Ed fucking Sheeran[3] at 400 decibels – who hurt you?

Even though all the utterances desire the same outcome, only (a), (b), and (c) make the intention explicit (but with varying degrees of directness). We need to dig a bit deeper to get to the intended meaning in (d), (e), and (f) as they flout maxims and so are risk averse in their approach to the FTA (yes, even (f) could be considered risk averse to **negative face** – not so much to **positive face**!). Yet because they generate implicatures they are also risky in terms of whether or not the implicatures get 'picked up' by the hearer, meaning that the speaker's intended meaning must be inferred by the hearer because it is not explicitly conveyed. For instance, (e) and (f) could be so indirect that the implicit request is lost on the hearer.

According to Brown and Levinson, when approaching an FTA, there are a number of options open to us. We can do the FTA:

1 on-record (directly, or 'baldly')
2 off-record (indirectly)

Or we can choose not to do the FTA and

3 opt out (say nothing in order to avoid the FTA)[4]

Once a speaker decides what approach to take (i.e. do the FTA on-record, off-record, or opt out), they can then select from a number of redressive strategies that are oriented to the hearer's positive or negative face (or both). Figure 7.1 shows these approaches and roughly plots their level of explicitness (on the left of the diagram) and how they are executed strategically (on the right).

Whether speakers deliver the FTA on-record or off-record they can choose to 'soften' the FTA with redressive action by choosing a strategy or strategies that work to minimise threats to face. We will consider each of our scenarios in (a) to (f) in turn, but first, we present them in their corresponding positions in the model in Figure 7.2 below.

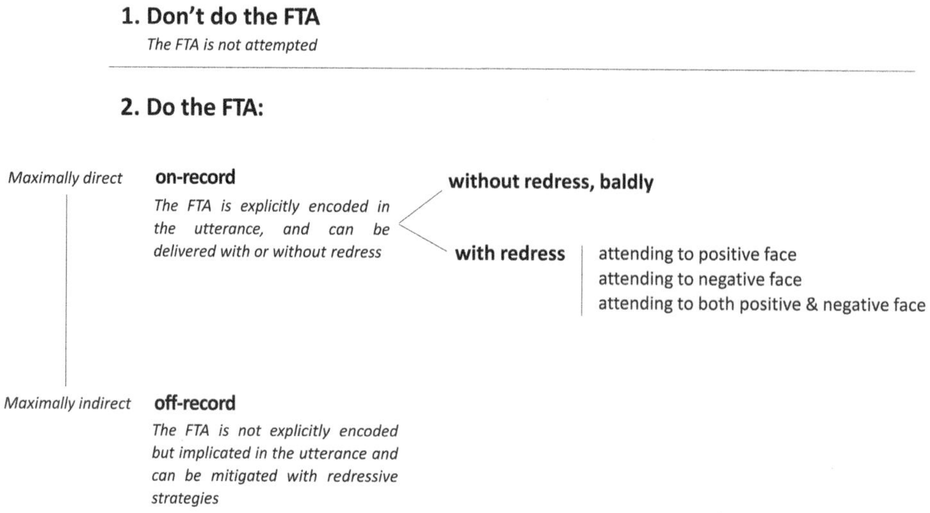

1. Don't do the FTA

The FTA is not attempted

2. Do the FTA:

Maximally direct **on-record**
The FTA is explicitly encoded in the utterance, and can be delivered with or without redress

without redress, baldly

with redress
attending to positive face
attending to negative face
attending to both positive & negative face

Maximally indirect **off-record**
The FTA is not explicitly encoded but implicated in the utterance and can be mitigated with redressive strategies

Figure 7.1 Approaches to FTAs

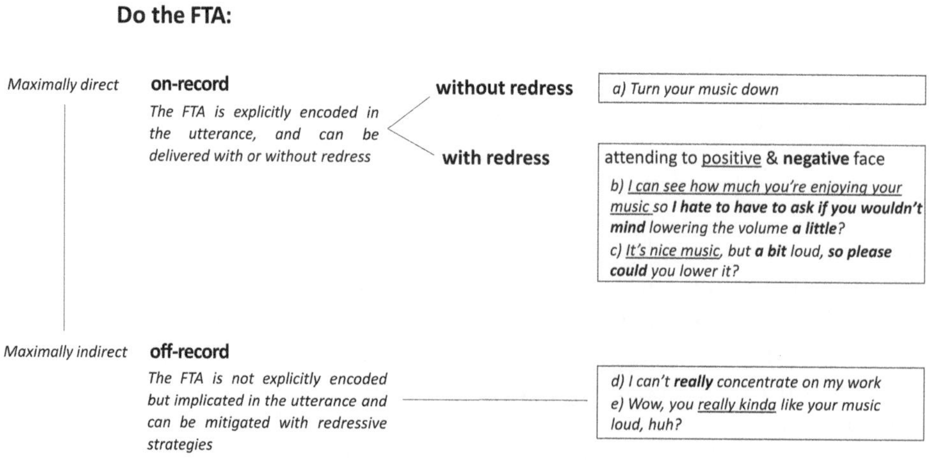

Do the FTA:

Maximally direct **on-record**
The FTA is explicitly encoded in the utterance, and can be delivered with or without redress

without redress
a) Turn your music down

with redress
attending to positive & **negative** face
b) I can see how much you're enjoying your music so ***I hate to have to ask if you wouldn't mind*** *lowering the volume* ***a little****?*
c) It's nice music, but ***a bit*** *loud,* ***so please could*** *you lower it?*

Maximally indirect **off-record**
The FTA is not explicitly encoded but implicated in the utterance and can be mitigated with redressive strategies

d) I can't ***really*** *concentrate on my work*
e) Wow, you really kinda like your music loud, huh?

Figure 7.2 Doing the FTA 'turn your music down'

On-record FTAs

We start with the on-record utterances first. Any politeness strategy mentioned will appear in italics. Utterance (a) is maximally direct because it gets to the point. By being maximally direct, however, it constitutes an FTA to the positive and negative faces of the hearer. Consequently, the FTA is done 'baldly'. It is also on-record because the words used directly correspond to the intended meaning: grammatically it is an imperative, and desired action is explicitly encoded (we will see later in the chapter that orders and requests can be made using a range of grammatical forms).

Utterance (b), which is less direct than (a), mitigates the imposition by using a few **politeness strategies** (italicised here and throughout the chapter). First, the speaker *acknowledges the value* of the music to the roommate ('I can see how much . . .'). In this way the utterance "anoints" (Brown and Levinson 1987) the positive face of the roommate by 'buttering them up' before hitting them with the imposition (Figure 7.2). So, the speaker attends to both positive and negative face. To use Brown and Levinson's terms, the speaker is able to "pay back in face whatever [they] potentially [take] away by the FTA" (1987: 71). Utterance (b) is doing other work – it *acknowledges the imposition* the speaker is making to the hearer ('I hate to have to ask . . .'), which foregrounds the risk to their own positive face in asking. This is likely to predispose the hearer to respond positively as a proportionate 'return' for the risk the speaker takes in asking. Additionally, it presents the request in a *pessimistic* way, thus not demanding or even expecting compliance ('if you wouldn't mind . . .') which, even though this is only a "token bow" to the negative face-wants of the hearer it still gives them an out (Brown and Levinson 1987: 70–71). Finally, it *lessens the imposition* with 'lowering the volume *a little*' foregrounding the fact that what the speaker is asking is small and so refusing would seem unreasonable.

Similarly, utterance (c) encodes a small imposition through 'a bit' and butters up the hearer by complimenting their music choice. Also, the choice of verb 'could', as opposed to 'would', is indirect because even though it's intended as a request to turn the music down, grammatically it asks the hearer about their ability to do so. In this way we can see that both positive and negative face are attended to and therefore both politeness strategies are used together.

In these ways (from (a) to (c)), the speaker orients their utterances to the hearer's **face-wants** through a range of different politeness strategies while still remaining on-record about their communicative intentions (to get the music turned down). In summary then, speakers can show that they are attending to the negative face of hearers by using politeness strategies such as *acknowledge* or *lessen the imposition*, and *be pessimistic*. In addition, speakers can anoint the positive face of hearers by *acknowledging the value* (of the loudness of the music) and by *complimenting* the hearer, which helps to soften the blow of the imposition.

Off-record strategies

Utterances (d), (e), and (f) are off-record because the form of the utterance does not semantically or syntactically correspond to a particular request/demand to lower the volume of the music. The intended meanings need to be picked up by H through implicature. Going 'off-record' is a politeness strategy in itself. But even off-record utterances can carry some risk to face. Here are (d) to (f) again:

(d) I can't really concentrate on my work
(e) Wow, you kinda like your music loud, huh?
(f) Ed fucking Sheeran at 400 decibels – who hurt you?

Utterance (d) does not explicitly state but rather implicates the intended meaning by *offering a reason* from which H must infer relevance in the context. As such, it flouts the maxim of Relation. The reason given shifts the focus to the speaker's incapacities rather than the hearer's actions. This is a form of *deference* as the speaker is *humbling themselves*. Utterance (d) uses additional strategies, namely *hedging* with 'really'. Think of 'hedging' rather literally as a way of softening the hard edges of your driveway – it is the same for language. Hedges are elements of language that are used pragmatically, even though they may well have semantic meaning. That is, their presence is doing interpersonal work in helping take the edge off the parts that we feel may cause a bit of a threat/damage to the addressee. Some hedges include the **adverbials** 'just', 'only', and 'really'. In utterance (d), 'really' weakens the proposition making it less face-threatening. The hedge offers only partial commitment to the verb 'concentrate' so the roommate may feel less responsible for the distraction their music caused than if no hedge was used.

Utterance (e) is a comment about the other person's likes, so once again does not address the goal of the speaker, making it an off-record utterance. It uses the *hedge* 'kinda' which softens the off-record FTA and offers only partial commitment to the verb 'like'. It also *employs a tag question* ('huh?') which nudges the force of a grammatical assertion towards a less face-threatening interrogative structure, yet with no onus on H to reply.

Finally, you'll notice that utterance (f) is not in Figure 7.2. We will address it separately here so as not to complicate the diagram above. Utterance (f) is clearly off-record because it does not contain any request or order to lower the music. As such, it flouts a number of maxims. It flouts the Relation maxim in asking 'who hurt you?' which does not appear to be linked to the preceding clause. Additionally, it does not explicitly link to the speaker's intention to get the roommate to lower the volume. The utterance also flouts the Manner maxim (avoid prolixity) by not being brief ('at 400 decibels' versus 'loudly') and the Quality maxim by asserting '400 decibels' (clearly an exaggeration). Yet, the indirect request – essentially a threat to *negative* face[5] – is delivered in such a way that it also carries with it a threat to *positive* face (that the choice of Ed Sheeran is a poor one[6]). It appears to go against the general idea of politeness which is to maintain social harmony and avoid social discord. In fact, it's possible to read it as confrontational. So why include it here in a discussion of politeness? The answer is in the interpersonal relationship between the two interlocutors. Given that they are roommates, this confrontational utterance is an example of "banter" (Leech 1983), a kind of 'mock impoliteness' which is done as a marker of solidarity and intimacy (let's face it, you'd not get away with that utterance to a stranger on the train). We say a bit more about impoliteness in the section on further reading at the end of this chapter.

The humble hedge

Brown and Levinson devote quite a bit of space to hedges in their discussion of the politeness framework. We met some hedges in the examples above, and other hedging strategies include the use of minimising or diminutive adjectives such as 'little' (or 'wee' if you come from Ireland or Scotland), 'tiny', and so on. Recall the jumper example we discussed in Chapter 6. Let's return temporarily to Christmas Jumper-gate in utterance (1) and mitigate it in (1a) with adverbial hedges:

(1) 'I don't like this jumper'
(1a) 'I **just** don't **really think** I like this jumper'

Here, hedging with 'just' puts some distance between the speaker ('I') and the 'not liking', both syntactically by positioning the grammatical Subject further away from the verb and figuratively by downplaying the imposition. Notice how this offers a little bit of protection to the speaker's own positive face as well as the addressee's positive face because they are minimising the not liking by using an adverb of degree ('just'). In some cases, adverbs like 'really' and 'just' tend to offer more interpersonal social value than semantic value, as in our example. By downgrading the 'don't like' to 'don't **think** . . . like' the speaker reduces the commitment to the not liking and consequently the force of the FTA. The latter is an example of using a lexical verb ('think') modally to hedge a speaker's commitment to a face-threatening proposition, which in turn, reduces the face threat of the proposition for both parties.

Impositions come in many forms, and even something low-stakes like asking to borrow a book from a friend or asking a roommate to lower their music can constitute an imposition. We impose on people all the time. Just take today, for instance; how many times have you used communication in ways that amount to an imposition? (We did it in the last sentence – we asked you to think about your communication and we mitigated that imposition with 'just'). Did you try to get a flatmate to give you 'a wee taste' of milk for your coffee? Did you message a friend or family member to ask for a lift 'just up to the shop'? Have you emailed a teacher to ask for 'a little more' clarity on a scheduling issue or 'only' one more day for that deadline? Or did you ask to borrow your friend's phone 'for a quick sec'? In our classes, our students frequently email us saying 'I have a small question', regardless of the size of their question. Whatever you have tried to procure, chances are that you adapted your way of asking depending on who you were asking and what you were asking for, and we would be willing to bet that you used a wee hedge at some point.

Non-linguistic considerations

In the politeness framework language operates in conjunction with **sociological variables**. This means that when we approach an FTA, we need to consider a few sociological factors in weighing up what is, for the specific encounter, the most effective and socially appropriate option to take. Brown and Levinson note three factors that should be considered when approaching an FTA. They are as follows.

the **social distance** between the interlocutors (abbreviated to D for 'distance'. Genius, eh?)
the **relative power** of the interlocutors (P)
the **ranking** (or **scale**) of the imposition (R)

These can be explained using the six scenarios featuring our noisy roommate. In that example, the relationship between the speaker and hearer will influence the choices the speaker makes when approaching the FTA. We consider the issue of power (P) first.

Power (P)

If interlocutors are good friends, some of the on-record utterances may be less threatening to face, or the FTAs are mitigated by social factors. This is because the friendship puts them on equal footing and means that neither one has **power** (P) over the other. To use the terms outlined in Brown and Levinson's model (1987: 77), being on an equal footing means that the speaker cannot impose their own plans at the expense of the hearer's. Compare this with a situation where there is a disproportionate **power** relationship between the two interlocutors, such as when someone is giving you a lift in their car and they are blasting the car radio. In that situation the driver has more power (they own the car, they drive the car, they are doing you a favour) and the asymmetrical power balance means it's more face-threatening to tell the driver to lower the music than to tell your roommate (all other things being equal).

Social distance (D)

Linked to power (P), distance (D) concerns the nature and degree of the social relationship that exists between speaker and hearer. Brown and Levinson define social distance as being related to 'frequency' of interactions. This is premised on the argument that the greater the frequency of interactions you have with someone, the less distant you are from them interpersonally. It follows then, that the less social distance there is, the more freedom speakers will have in tackling an FTA. For example, good friends, family members, and couples are generally able to approach an FTA with less risk to face than those with greater social distance because the familiarity places the relationship on a more secure (and equal) footing. For instance, your mother might be able to tell you that your outfit would look better in the bin, but a sales assistant in a shop is not likely to be so on-record because the interpersonal relationship is more distant (and arguably calls for more politeness). Of course, you could argue that your mother's FTA to your positive face is more damaging *because* of the close relationship (and that the sales assistant's FTA is less damaging because the distance between you means that it won't have repercussions for your future relationship). You could also argue that the sales assistant simply wants the sale, in which case this might be an instance of what we might call covert motivation! Perhaps in such situations mothers rank higher on the power variable than shop assistants. Maybe this wasn't such a great example, but it does show the complex interpersonal work our language choices have. In our roommate example, there is likely to be less social distance (D) (because roommates frequently interact) and equal power (P). The important point that Brown and Levinson make is that social distance is only one key factor that must be considered in conjunction with the other two; so, if power was equal and the imposition was small, the social distance would be the only variable in play and speakers modify their approaches to FTAs accordingly. The example they offer is as follows.

i) Excuse me, would you by any chance have the time?
ii) Got the time, mate?

According to Brown and Levinson (1987: 80) utterance (i) contains more strategies and would be used when the interlocutors are distant, and (ii) is more likely to feature where they are socially 'close'.

Social distance is dynamic and can change over time (even over a very short space of time). For example, you may start the semester addressing your new teacher with 'Dear professor', but a few weeks in as social distance shrinks you might change to show less deference, e.g. 'Dear Brian', 'Hi Brian', but probably not 'S'up B-Dawg'. On the other hand, even though social distance is less in this situation, the power factor might mean that you retain honorifics (e.g. terms of deference such as 'Dr/Prof.') for the whole semester.

It is important to note, however, that cultural differences give different weight to the three variables. For example, Gu's work (1992) on Chinese politeness demonstrates that social distance is reflected in address forms; only speakers considered socially close to their hearers will use first names as terms of address, whereas surnames are considered the default "non-kin public address term" (Gu 1992: 250). It is not just in naming that politeness strategies vary in different cultural contexts. Yangmeishan and Wencheng (2019) show that in Chinese culture, where familial relationships are highly valued, family members are not typically thanked for small favours. Indeed, they show that making explicit expressions of gratitude to close family members is akin to 'socio-pragmatic failure'. Explicit expressions of gratitude are reserved for non-kin or socially distant interlocutors.

Ranking of imposition (R)

Finally, the nature of an FTA itself can be gauged on a **rank scale** of imposition, which answers the question how imposing is the imposition? This is culturally dependent. What is meant here is that the FTA is gauged as **weighty** by the degree to which it "interferes with an agent's wants of self-determination or of approval" in that culture (Brown and Levinson 1987: 77). Translating this to a request to a roommate to lower their music, the risk to face is proportionately low in terms of its impediment on the hearer's freedom to act as they wish. (A high impediment would be if you were asking them to never play their music again). Therefore, all other things being equal, going on-record is an appropriate strategy because it carries less risk than if one or other factors were not equal. Indeed, for sincerity to prevail, redressive action for any FTA would need to be proportionate to the **weightiness** of the FTA; too much redress, as in (g), runs the risk of sounding sarcastic, too little (h) and it sounds rude.

(g) I'm so sorry, I can't believe I have to ask you this, especially since we've been friends for years now, and it's only because I cannot really concentrate on my work which has to be in for tomorrow morning or I'll fail my course and nobody wants that to happen and certainly not you, as you are so supportive of me, but could you possibly turn down your wee music honey?
(h) Lower that.

A short analysis of a football press conference

To close this chapter on politeness, we re-visit the extract from the previous chapter on the exchange between Jose Mourinho and a journalist at a press conference following Mourinho's team's defeat. In Chapter 6 we considered the conversational implicatures in the exchange; in this section we consider politeness and show how the variables of power (P), social distance (D), and ranking (R) intersect in a real discourse situation. Our analysis explores the context-dependent nature of these variables and the importance of social roles. We will examine how different values in D, P, and R can ameliorate the risk to the speaker's positive face when the speaker issues on-record FTAs.

Recall that the exchange between Jose Mourinho, the then manager of Tottenham Hotspur (Spurs), and the reporter occurred during a press conference which took place on 19 February 2020, following his team's home defeat to Leipzig. The QR code links to the interview segment.

QR 7.2 Jose Mourinho interview

Football press conferences are arenas where powerful figures (such as players and managers) are interviewed by the press (who also have power) in front of a wide television audience. This presents a contradiction as the manager is, to some degree, at the mercy of the journalist asking the questions. There is also a cultural expectation in post-match press conferences that the journalist will ask questions and that the manager will answer them. Power (P) is at play, then, particularly when the journalist asks questions that offend the manager or that imply negative capability (and so are highly ranked (R) FTAs). What happens in our example could be construed as a tug-of-war over power (P) precipitated by an FTA to Mourinho's negative face that is ranked highly (R), compounded by the social distance (D) between the two, which is likely to also be high. The reporter poses a question ("Was it Spurs that were bad or Leipzig that were good?") that presents an either/or scenario, leaving Mourinho little option for a way out. Therefore, the reporter imposes on Mourinho, threatening his negative face (his desire to be not imposed upon) in the first instance by trying to get Mourinho to commit to one of two (restricted) options, that the opposing team was "good" or that Mourinho's team was "bad". Neither option is complimentary towards Mourinho's team because neither evaluate their performance positively. The reporter's question therefore also threatens Mourinho's positive face because it suggests that his team was either 'bad" or not as good as the opposition, which attacks the way his team played and thus his competency as a manager. Instead of answering the question, Mourinho repeats it and sends it back to the reporter seeking clarification: "You think we were bad?" However, Mourinho's question focuses on the first of the two options originally offered by the reporter (which is more direct than the reporter's utterance) and obligates the reporter to provide a yes/no response. This could be perceived as an FTA to the reporter's negative face due to the obligation to commit to a response. Yet Mourinho still offers the reporter a way out of committing to the proposition that Spurs were "bad" as the latter can reply with 'no'.

In his reply to Mourinho, the reporter avoids the preferred response (polar questions require 'yes' or 'no') choosing instead to respond with "Well, the result says you lost at home". This is indirect because it answers the question via an implicature (that we explained in the previous chapter) and commits an FTA to Mourinho's positive face **off-record**. As we discussed in Chapter 6, the response flouts the **maxim of Relation** and **Quantity** giving rise to the **implicature** that losing at home means that the team is "bad". Additionally, the response is mitigated with a *hedge*, "well" which is a type of discourse marker that signals justification is being offered for the implicature by prefacing what the hearer, Mourinho, may not want to hear (Owen 1981; Jucker 1993). In Lakoff's terms (1973: 458), 'well' implies "a complex-answer" to a question and, according to Jucker, is used "in cases in which respondents know that they are not giving directly the information the questioner has requested" (Jucker 1993: 440) as is the case here. The journalist attempts to preserve his own positive face by avoiding taking personal responsibility for the 'saying' himself. Instead, he *impersonalises* the contentious claim by deferring to an inanimate agent, "the result". As *impersonalisation* is a politeness strategy, the reporter mitigates the FTA. This allows him to put distance between him (the reporter) and the perceived insult to Mourinho.

Mourinho uses his power as a prolific manager to opt out when he says he is "not going to answer". It also allows him to assert baldly and **on-record** that he "does not like" the question and thinks it is "out of order", thus issuing an **FTA** to the reporter's **positive face**. Notice though, that he tells the reporter that it is his "question" that is out of order and not the reporter himself who is out of order. It could be that Mourinho is still attempting to maintain social concord with an interlocutor who has, by all accounts, relatively high (P). As Mourinho gets up to leave the press conference he appears to **anoint** the reporter's **positive face** by issuing a *compliment* ("Great question") and using an *in-group marker* ("mate"), but this may have been done ironically (the non-verbal communication will help in discerning this) and is actually an FTA to the reporter's positive face (it flouts the maxim of **Quality** as Mourinho means the opposite of what he has said). The exchange culminates in an excellent side-swipe by the reporter who regains some of his damaged face by replying with the echoic retort, "Great answer" which also anoints Mourinho's positive face if it is a genuine compliment, but it's more likely that it is meant ironically (via a Quality flout) and so threatens rather than anoints Mourinho's positive face.

Conclusion

Politeness is one of the primary reasons that we choose to communicate meanings indirectly. When doing politeness, we employ a range of politeness strategies that mitigate potentially face-threatening acts. These strategies can be used to mitigate threats to negative face, for example when imposing on a hearer's time, energy, or resources. They are also used to "anoint" the positive face of our hearer, for example, when we acknowledge their right to be liked, respected, and valued. In attending to the "face-wants" of others, we are subtly protecting our own positive face. The context of the interaction will often determine whether we go on- or off-record in our utterances. Additionally, the context will determine what, if any strategies are used, and how many are appropriate. Power, social distance, and the weightiness of the FTA (P, D, R) all dynamically interact in helping us to make a plethora of communicative decisions in every single interaction.

Further reading

In the discussion above about the music-loving roommate, we talked about how utterance (f) exhibits impoliteness in that it appeared to invite discord as it resembled an insult and as such an FTA to positive face. To read more on impoliteness, banter, and mock impoliteness, see Leech (1983, 2014), Culpeper (1996), and Bousfield (2008). For more on how cultural differences influence politeness, see Gu (1992).

Answers to activities

Activity 7.1 Politeness in real discourse

(A) The academic's email

Happy St. Patricks Day! Sorry for cross posting (or if you have already completed) but I wanted to send out a reminder for the Sporting Superstitions Questionnaire.

Responses have been amazing so far and I am having a final push for participant collection. I would ask anyone who plays sports (either competitively or for fun) and is over the age of 18 to take 5-minutes to complete my PhD questionnaire.

Please find the link below:

[redacted]

This study has been approved by the University Ethical Approval system at [University name redacted].

Many thanks

The email's objective is to invite staff to take part in a survey. This effectively **imposes** on the recipients' freedom to act, and as such, constitutes an FTA to **negative face**. As responding to the survey is not a requirement, the sender must appeal to the addressee to secure their participation or predispose them to participate. Thus, the sender begins with a greeting – one that sends good wishes for "St. Patrick's Day" (17 March). The sender then *acknowledges the imposition*, i.e. the potential drain on the receiver's workload for having to read the email (perhaps more than once), "Sorry for cross posting (or if you have already completed)". This is mitigated first by issuing an *apology* and then by *offering reasons* for the message, "but I wanted . . .". Before asking for participation, the sender softens the imposition by issuing a *compliment*, describing the responses to date as "amazing". This anoints the positive face of the receiver. The FTA to **negative face** is mitigated further through *depersonalisation*, in which the action required from the receiver is first characterised as noun rather than a verb: "a final push for participant collection". The nominal group "participant collection" is presented as a phenomenon and does not need an Actor, grammatically speaking. This mitigates the role of the sender. Moreover, the sender's role is as a Carrier in a Relational process of having (see Chapter 9), "I am having a final push . . ." rather than a Material process of doing (contrast this with 'I am pushing you for . . .'). The asking is *hedged* with the modal "would", which softens the force of the request and is *depersonalised* somewhat with "anyone" rather than the more direct 'you'. Finally, *deference* to a higher authority via the university's ethics committee offers a nod to the legitimacy of the survey, which would have relevance for the receiver, and which shows goodwill.

(B) The bank meeting

> JIM: I got a couple things here, [. . .], just to kind of bring us up to speed, Matt has tentatively accepted our offer for employment, but since he's going to be a dual employee, th- you really don't need to put this in the minutes.
>
> JOE: Okay.

Jim, the president, and therefore the hierarchically powerful (P) interactant, imposes upon Joe, the employee, by asking him not to include something in the minutes. As minute-taker, Joe would ordinarily decide what goes into the minutes and what doesn't, and so should be free to make those administrative decisions himself. Jim imposes his will on Joe. This constitutes an FTA to **negative face**. However, the imposition is ranked as low (R) because power is unequal (P) (because Jim is more senior, he has more freedom to impose on employees). Even so, Jim *hedges* his FTA by using *hedging* terms like "really" in "you **really** don't need to put this in the minutes". By framing the imposition as something that Joe doesn't "need" to do Jim demonstrates that he is cognisant of Joe's negative face-wants. Presented like this, Jim appears to be considerate, which mitigates the imposition on Joe who is effectively being told what to do (or rather, what not to do). Brown and Levinson offer this formula for 'calculating' the weightiness of an FTA, where W=weightiness, x=FTA and (S, H)= speaker, hearer:

$$Wx = D\ (S, H) + P\ (H, S) + Rx$$

In our example of Jim and Joe, we can put it like this:

W(you **really** don't need to put this in the minutes') = D (Jim, Joe) + P (Jim, Joe) + R 'you **really** don't need to put this in the minutes'

$$Wx = >D + >P + <Rx$$

(C) The *X-Factor* audition

The first FTA is to the auditionees, Liddia and Ryan. It is a criticism of their performance and so is oriented to **positive face**. The judge, Gary Barlow, delivers it with "you haven't got a voice between you. You couldn't get a gig in an empty pub". This is harsh, yet his position as judge and the reputation of the show as the source of some acerbic insults to wannabe performers means that the FTA is perhaps not uncharacteristic nor uncommon, and so not as impactful within the culture of TV talent shows. This could be why it is not heavily mitigated. He does say "There's nothing to critique here", which provides *reasons* for his negative review. He finishes with another mitigating approach, this time a *hedge* in "There's **just** no" before he is interrupted. While Barlow focuses his critique on their singing ability, Louis Walsh goes further and insults their character, "You are the two most deluded people I have heard all day". This is a rather bald FTA to positive face and constitutes 'impoliteness' (see further reading). More unusually, the contestant, Ryan, hits back at Louis with an FTA to his positive face, "You wouldn't know what talent was . . .". The power differential between them makes this more threatening than Louis's FTA. While judge Nicole exchanges some banter with them, Gary urges her to decide "is it a 'no' . . .", which constitutes an FTA to her negative face. He poses it as a *question* rather than an imperative, and so mitigates it a little. He also offers *reasons* for his FTA "We're waiting . . . ". At this point, Ryan interjects telling Gary "There is no need to be rude". This is an FTA to Gary's positive face. Ryan mitigates it with a *tag question* "is there?" which effectively *seeks agreement*. Ryan then utters a series of FTAs to Gary's positive face, ironically by saying what he will not say "'cos I'm not that rude". In uttering the latter, Ryan is effectively able to absolve himself from insulting Gary, which he does indirectly, and at the same time preserves his own positive face "but I'm not going to [say all that] 'cos I'm not that rude". The cat is well out of the bag, however. Which, ironically, is what their singing sounds like.

Notes

1 'Please' is not a requirement. But it will probably increase the likelihood of getting the outcome you want.
2 Grimes is a Canadian musician, singer, and producer.
3 Ed Sheeran is a British singer popular for his catchy ballads. If by some twist of fate Ed Sheeran chances upon this chapter we would like it known that our example does not reflect our views on his musical career. We also think 'Bad Habits' is a banger.
4 This is not always a 'way out' of an FTA as there is some communicative force in saying nothing, contrary to Keith Whitley (or Ronan Keating depending on your age), who claims 'you say it best when you say nothing at all'. https://www.youtube.com/watch?v=xNU7iIdw7Ss
5 We say 'essentially' because this utterance does seek to have the music-loving roommate turn down the volume (so constitutes an off-record imposition). Additionally, it does not

avoid discord, but actively courts it ('who hurt you'?) and so, in certain contexts could be read as an FTA to positive face.

6 Again, sorry Ed and Ed fans. Although, to be honest, one of us is still salty over 'Galway Girl'.

References

Bousfield, D. (2008) *Impoliteness in interaction* (Vol. 167). Amsterdam: John Benjamins.

Brown, P. and Levinson, S. C. (1987) *Politeness: Some universals in language usage* (Vol. 4). Cambridge: Cambridge University Press.

Cowell, S. (2013) *The X-Factor*. Series 10. Syco Entertainment Thames. FremantleMedia.

Culpeper, J. (1996) 'Towards an anatomy of impoliteness'. *Journal of pragmatics*, 25(3): 349–367.

Goffman, E. (1967) *Interaction ritual: Essays on face-to-face interaction*. Chicago: Aldine.

Gu, Y. (1992) 'Politeness, pragmatics and culture'. *Foreign Language Teaching and Research*, 4: 10–17.

Jucker, A. H. (1993) 'The discourse marker well: A relevance-theoretical account'. *Journal of Pragmatics*, 19(5): 435–452.

Lakoff, R. (1973) 'Questionable answers and answerable questions'. In B. B. Kachru, R. B. Lees, Y. Malkiel, A. Pietrangeli, and S. Saporta (eds), *Issues in linguistics: Papers in honor of Henry and Rente Kahane*, pp. 453–467. Urbana, IL: University of Illinois Press.

Leech, G. (1983) *Principles of pragmatics*. London: Longman.

Leech, G. N. (2014) *The pragmatics of politeness*. Oxford Studies in Sociolinguistics. Oxford: Oxford University Press.

Owen, M. (1981) 'Conversational units and the use of "well . . ."'. In P. Werth (ed.), *Conversation and discourse*, pp. 99–116. London: Croom Helm.

Yangmeishan, Z. H. O. U., and Wencheng, G. A. O. (2019) 'Socio-pragmatic failure of Chinese non-English majors in intercultural communication'. *Sino–US English Teaching*, 16(5): 209–215.

8 Metaphorical meanings in discourse

Metaphor and metonymy

Introduction

In Chapter 5 we explored semantics and different types of meanings. In this chapter, we continue our exploration of meaning but this time we look at **figurative** or non-literal meaning. Focusing on **metaphor** and **metonymy**, we outline key theories about figurative meanings including Conceptual Metaphor Theory (CMT), and we align with existing scholarship that posits that metaphors and metonymies are not simply textual phenomena but conceptual phenomena too. Throughout the chapter we use examples from a range of discourse contexts, including political commentary, TV sitcoms, song lyrics, and everyday expressions. We explore how figurative language can prompt us to think about things (e.g. people, events, activities) in different ways and how this might impact on our social and cultural understandings of such things.

What is a metaphor?

'Metaphor' derives from the Greek 'meta+pherein' meaning 'over' + 'to carry', which becomes 'to carry over' or 'transfer'. So, in a metaphor, something is 'carried over' or 'transferred'. But what is transferred and why? And what is the outcome of the transfer? These are questions we also need to address in order to answer our main question: 'what is a metaphor'. Most dictionary definitions refer to 'metaphor' as an 'expression' (also Black 1955: 275) in which one thing is expressed to describe or 'substitute' for another unrelated thing. At its simplest, this is what a metaphor is and does. It 'transfers' one meaning or sense of something to another. But metaphor is not simply an 'expression' that operates on a linguistic level, although linguistic expressions trigger metaphors. As we shall see, metaphors also operate on a conceptual level because they invite us to think about one thing in terms of another. Writing in 1936, I. A. Richards says this about metaphor:

> In the simplest formulation, when we use a metaphor we have two thoughts of different things active together and supported by a single word, or phrase, whose meaning is a resultant of their interaction.
>
> (Richards 1936: 93)

DOI: 10.4324/9781003351207-8

Richards's view of metaphor is the basis for the cognitive view that we present in this chapter – metaphor as an 'interaction' between two 'ideas' or, in current terms, 'concepts' and 'conceptual domains'. However, already we are dealing with two terms that need explanation: **concept** and **conceptual domain.**

Starting with 'concept', recall that in Chapter 5, we talked about semantics and the nature of signs. We used the example of a 'chair' as being a sign by virtue of it having both a linguistic expression (the word 'c-h-a-i-r') and a mental construct (our own mental image of a 'chair'). The latter is a **concept** in that it is an image or idea conceived in our minds regardless of whether it exists in the world. The sign, then, is the totality of these two things; it comprises both a word and concept (and if we throw a real chair into the mix we get a third part, the 'referent'). When we use a metaphor, we are using two mental constructs or **concepts** across which we transfer meaning(s). Which brings us to 'domain'. Studies of metaphor often use the term **conceptual domain** to account for concepts at different sides of the transference. A conceptual domain involves a broader set of meanings or ideas. So, for example, the concept 'chair' sits within a conceptual domain that includes other closely related concepts such as legs, back, seat, and 'to be sat on'. So, a domain is a complex of related concepts and meanings; they are networks of conceptual knowledge and they are activated by lexical items (Langacker 2008: 47). With a metaphor, a concept from one domain (the **target**) is talked about in terms of concepts from another domain (the **source**) The result is that attributes associated with one domain are 'carried across' or mapped on to the other. So now we have a third term that needs some clarification: **mapping.**

When a person encounters a lexical item being used metaphorically (like 'virus' in 'computer virus') they draw parallels between it (virus) and the concept to which it likely targets (a piece of digital code that can be destructive to digital files and software).[1] Thus, the **source domain** is used to understand or reconceive the **target domain**. Properties are selected from the source domain (invited by the lexical term that triggered the metaphor) and applied to the target, generating a more accessible, nuanced, or novel way of understanding the target. By 'parallels' we mean properties that could conceivably or plausibly apply to both domains, and thus interact. Figure 8.1 shows the relationship between source and target in a metaphor.

Often metaphors are used where a non-metaphorical expression could be used. For example, a classmate with three essays to produce in one week may tell you they are 'drowning in work' when they could have said something like 'I am really overworked'. But metaphor is not simply a process of substitution. Therefore, the use of the metaphor 'drowning' must generate some additional meaning to justify the hearer putting in the processing effort to work it out. The effect, then, of using a metaphor can be to amplify or enrich the interpretation of the target domain over and above what can be achieved by a non-metaphoric expression. These additional or enriched interpretations are not discernible from the more literal option of 'I've got too much work'. The metaphor then, gives a fuller picture of the state of the speaker.

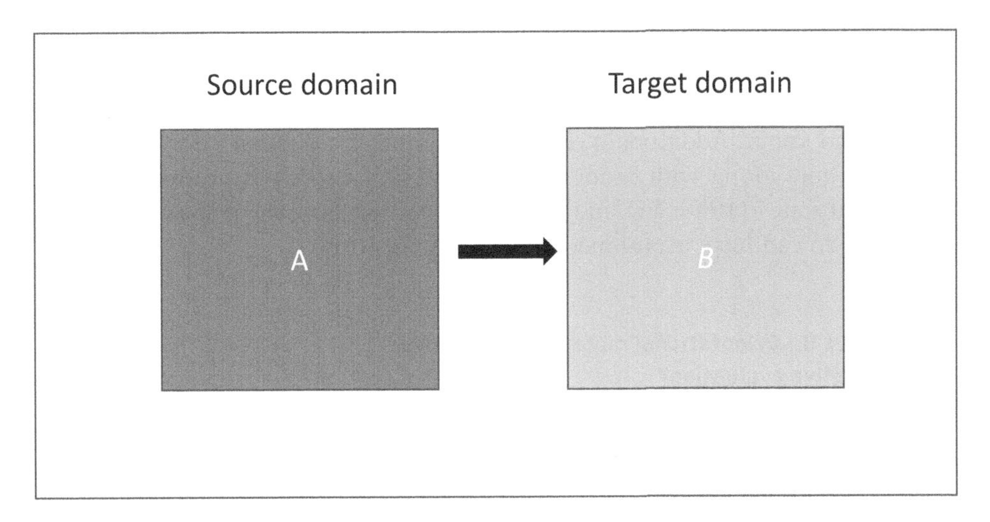

Figure 8.1 Metaphorical relationship between source and target domains

The conceptual basis of metaphors

Often, we have recourse to metaphors when we struggle to communicate an abstract phenomenon. Mental health, for instance, is difficult to discuss literally. We frequently talk about our mood being 'up' or 'down' to signify when we are happy or sad. In other words, we invoke one conceptual domain 'orientation' (up/down) to refer to another ('mood'). There are many expressions that draw on the concept of orientation in relation to mental health (e.g. 'I'm really *low*'), but, of course, we cannot literally have a raised or lowered mood. The metaphors in the italicized comments below relate to declining mental health; the first from a celebrity fitness personality, Joe Wicks, describing the effect of a Covid lockdown and the second from guidance issued by the UK National Health Service (NHS) during the same period (emphases added).

(i) It's okay to be upset and *feel down* right now [. . .] I don't have anxiety or depression, but right now I feel *so low*, and *so down*.

(*Guardian*, 5 January 2021)

(ii) At times like these, it can be easy to *fall into* unhealthy patterns of behaviour that end up making you feel worse.

(NHS website, https://www.nhs.uk/every-mind-matters/coronavirus/mental-wellbeing-while-staying-at-home)

Unsurprisingly, such metaphors are called **orientational** metaphors. They are expressed more broadly as GOOD IS UP and BAD IS DOWN which points to their **conceptual** origin from which various metaphorical expressions such as 'I'm feeling a bit *down* today' are derived.[2] The basis for orientation metaphors like GOOD IS UP and BAD IS DOWN is, according to Lakoff and Johnson, physical: when we are sick, we are usually physically lying down, when we are well, we are up and about. Additionally, Lakoff and Johnson note that "drooping posture typically goes along with sadness and depression, erect posture with a positive emotional state" (1980: 15). In this way, we can see how the physical positioning of up/down can have useful metaphorical applications.

Activity 8.1 Orientational metaphors - positive or negative evaluation?

Read the following extract from an article by Stewart Lee in the *Guardian* newspaper on 10 July 2022 and try to identify the orientational metaphor – how is it lexically expressed? The piece was written a few days after ex-British prime minister, Boris Johnson, had resigned following a spate of controversies. Lee writes:

> Johnson's premiership, a mindless rotting meat zombie held together with the Sellotape™® of lies and the sticky excretions of his own spaff-faucet, began a sudden and dramatic slide into the ocean on Wednesday, like an arctic ice shelf made entirely of frozen shit.
>
> (Lee 2022)

You might also want to consider the co-text – how might you interpret the orientational metaphor in light of its appearance alongside so many other pejorative words?

The experiential basis of metaphors

As we can see from the orientational metaphors discussed above, metaphors can derive from experiential phenomena. If we take an abstract concept such as 'love' as a target domain, we can see that many 'love' metaphors are based on physical sensations and sensory experiences of, for example, temperature (e.g. 'the relationship is *heating* up'), hunger ('*starved* of love'), thirst ('I can't *quench* this desire'), pain ('I'm *aching* to see you'), light ('you *light up* my life'), and sound ('my heart *sings* when I am with you'). Others are based on connections between experiences (Lakoff and Johnson 1980; Grady 1997).

For example, we can feel the heat emanating from another person when we are physically close to them and, usually, we to choose to be physically close only to those we care about. We can therefore connect physical proximity with warmth, both of which we might also connect with affection. Consequently, we might understand the concept of affection via the conceptual metaphors AFFECTION IS CLOSENESS, and AFFECTION IS WARMTH (Grady 1997; see also Duffy and Feist forthcoming, 2023). We can also connect other emotional states with heat via our experience. For example, we know that we can get hot when we are stressed, embarrassed or angry and it is known that physiological effects (raised body surface temperature and increased heart rate) are triggered by a release of hormones in the body when we experience certain emotions. Such physiological experiences can explain conceptual metaphors such as LOVE IS HEAT (see, for example, Goatly 2007) and ANGER IS HEAT (see Lakoff 1987; Kövecses 1986, 1990). These conceptual metaphors (in small capitals) are also known as **primary metaphors** (Grady 1997) and these can be realised linguistically via a vast array of metaphorical expressions (words that trigger metaphors are sometimes called 'lexical metaphors'), as the above examples have shown. In fact, many metaphorical expressions can draw on the same source domain. Conversely, the same source domain can be used to metaphorically understand a range of different target concepts. Consider the following metaphorical utterance:

(iii) 'I see what you mean'

The concept 'seeing' in (iii) is a sensory one – perception – that is not literally true when it applies to 'mean'. We cannot, after all, 'see' what someone 'means' when they say or do something because meaning does not have physical form; we can only *understand* what someone 'means'. Thus, 'see' is a metaphor in utterance (iii). So how do we get from the realm of invisible cognition to being able to 'see' meaning? It is useful to regard metaphors as operating on a generic level and a specific one. Conceptual metaphors operate at this generic level, and lexical metaphors are their specific instantiations (the relationship is structurally similar to that of genus to species).[3] In fact, several lexical metaphors might stem from one conceptual metaphor and so share the same "underlying organisation" (Simpson 2014: 43). You might have encountered expressions like '*look* at things from where I'm standing' or 'he's got his *blinkers* on when it comes to promotion', or 'I *smell* a rat', and so on ('rat' is also metaphorical!). All of these expressions systematically construe cognition as something to do with 'seeing' or 'smelling' – in other words, 'sensing'. They are all **conceptually** linked to sensing. The conceptual metaphor, then, that captures these corresponding metaphoric expressions is COGNITION IS SENSING. In this way such "conventional ways of talking" about knowledge as something we can *sense* "presuppose a metaphor we are hardly ever conscious of" (Lakoff and Johnson 1980: 5). The specific lexical metaphors from this conceptual one derive from an overarching source-to-target mapping. In Grady's terminology, this hierarchical relationship of governance from the primary (generic) level is the source of a "basic mapping" that is "lacking in detail" (Grady 1997: 33). The lexical (specific) metaphors provide the detail by putting meat on the bones, as it were.

There are, though, different levels of *conceptual* generality when discussing conceptual metaphors. Readers could, if they wanted, take the level of abstraction to its most general (the 'bones' we refer to above) or to a lesser level (somewhere closer to the 'meat') when analysing metaphoric mappings. In the diagrams and analyses that follow we will use 'CONCEPTUAL' to refer to the most general level and 'conceptual' to signal less general mappings. This is because it can be useful to group conceptual metaphors into categories on different levels of abstraction. We show this in Figure 8.2.

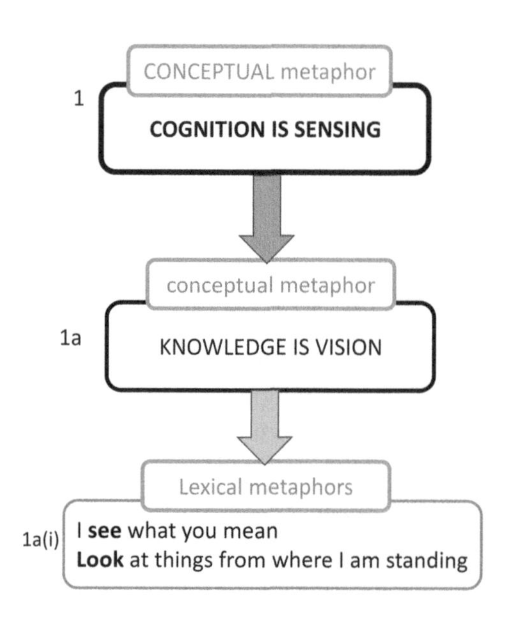

Figure 8.2 Mapping between conceptual and lexical metaphors

In Figure 8.2, we have tried to make knowledge visible! We show an overarching CONCEPTUAL metaphor, which is rather abstract, leading down to a less general mapping that is still conceptual, and then finally down further to lexical metaphoric expressions. The CONCEPTUAL level is 'COGNITION IS SENSING'. The level below it (labelled 'conceptual' in lower-case letters) refines the CONCEPTUAL metaphor somewhat and groups the lexical metaphors below it together. The bottom two levels derive from the top and share its underlying structure.

In Figure 8.3 we show two different but related mapping trajectories at the conceptual level and the lexical metaphors that can result. First, (1a), KNOWLEDGE IS LIGHT, and second, (1b) KNOWLEDGE IS VISION.[4] You will see that (1a) and (1b) are governed by the CONCEPTUAL metaphor above it.

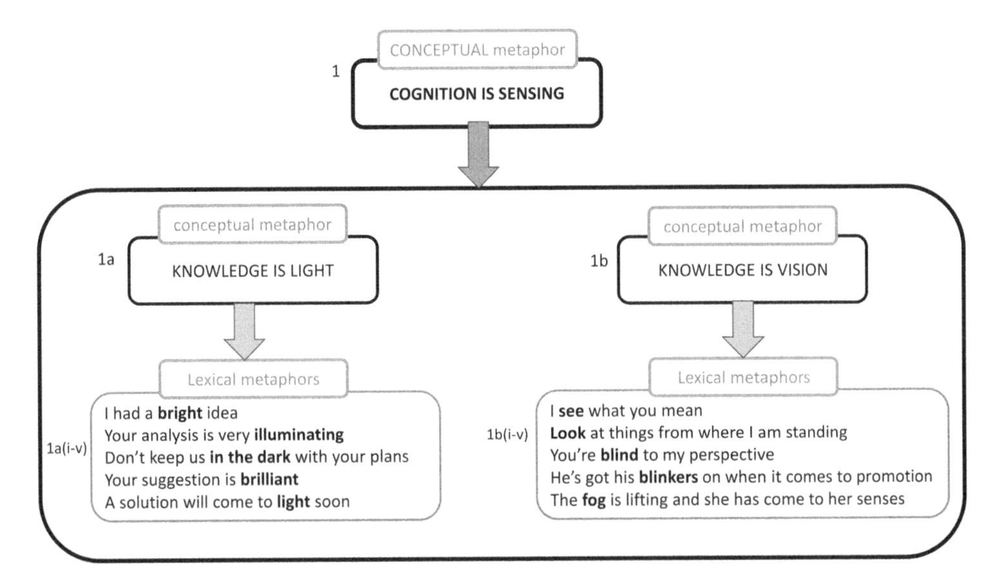

Figure 8.3 The different levels of metaphor production for 'KNOWLEDGE IS LIGHT' and 'KNOWLEDGE IS VISION'

In terms of doing discourse analysis, noting different levels of abstraction allows us to draw together patterns in metaphor use. It also helps show how metaphors are conceptual and not simply linguistic phenomena. Indeed, this is the basis of Lakoff and Johnson's Conceptual Metaphor Theory (CMT) (1980) which takes as its central premise that we *think* metaphorically (e.g. we think about mental health as being 'up' or 'down').

Activity 8.2 Metaphor in literary fiction

Below is a text example from a short story by Haruki Murakami (1994). Which words in the short extract are being used metaphorically? Can you identify the generic CONCEPTUAL metaphor from which the lexical metaphors derive?

"potentiality knocks on the door of my heart"

Novel metaphors

Some metaphors are so entrenched in language that their meanings are accepted almost instinctively. The lexical metaphor 'enlightenment' is one such example. Knowledge as something 'illuminating' is so conceptually embedded and accepted that we no longer consciously perceive of it as metaphoric. In fact, if you asked someone to spot the metaphoric content in this noun phrase 'the path to enlightenment' they might offer 'path' first (from the LIFE IS A JOURNEY conceptual metaphor). However, some metaphoric mappings have less obvious connections between source and target. Consider the metaphor in (iv) below. You might find it unusual.

(iv) The shop was **hiving** with people

In this example, the word that acts as the lexical trigger for a metaphorical interpretation and entry point to the metaphoric source domain is 'hiving'. Before reading further, reflect on (iv) and note your responses to it. What meaning do you think it is targeting?

Activity 8.3 Real examples of the 'hiving' metaphor

Let's look more closely at the 'hiving' metaphor. Below are some real examples of speakers using the metaphor (emphasis added) in online customer reviews (a, b, e) and news articles (c, d):

(a) "Discovered Muriel's Restaurant after visiting the Natural History Museum and heading for the tube back to our hotel. The place was **hiving** with people which is always a good sign."

(Tripadvisor reviewer from Ballygally, north of Ireland, 21 April 2015 https://tinyurl.com/3ya39ur5)

(b) "Good atmosphere – you can sit at tables, counter or bar. Lavery's in general is buzzing currently. I watched a game on TV there recently and the place was **hiving**. Two thumbs up for The Woodworkers."

(Tripadvisor reviewer from Belfast, north of Ireland, 16 August 2015 https://tinyurl.com/4c2aents)

(c) "The first thing that was on our agenda was people's safety," said Mr Rainey [chairperson of the centre hosting the event]. "We don't want to be seen to be jumping to conclusions. To me, I thought the place was **hiving** with security staff on Saturday night."

(BBC NI News, 6 November 2013 https://tinyurl.com/2p885ua5)

(d) "'I remember driving up – we'd obviously have been there a couple of hours before the game – and even on the outskirts of the town, the place was **hiving**. The crowds were unbelievable,' remembers Strain."

(*Belfast Telegraph*, 25 April 2020)

(e) "the number of people in the spa impacted the quality of our stay. After check in, we put or robes on and went down to the spa – and it was **hiving** with people."

(Tripadvisor reviewer from Belfast, Northern Ireland, 8 April 2019 https://tinyurl.com/bder3euu)

What, if any, common denominators characterise these examples? What might they tell you about the relationship between discourse communities and certain metaphors? How might the use of this particular source domain evaluate the activity it targets?

We provide answers at the end of the chapter.

Analysing the 'hiving' metaphor

Let's take a closer look at the 'hiving metaphor. In it, the lexical trigger for the metaphor is 'hiving' because shops (and shoppers) do not literally 'hive'. So, a non-literal meaning must be invoked in order to make the utterance make sense. The mapping might go something like what we present in Figure 8.4.

In Figure 8.4, there are two domains: the source domain is 'hiving', which is to say, the word 'hiving' triggers a metaphor that evokes the status of the shop as having properties or characteristics of beehives (let's call this 'hive-ness'). They include 'physical space' (1), 'contains bees' (2), are 'densely populated' (3), are sites of 'purposeful activity' (4) making honey, and so on. The target domain is the shop's (very busy) status, and it has properties of its own – for the sake of consistency, we'll call these 'shop-busyness'. To make sense of the utterance then, we select and map properties from the source domain to the target domain. Which ones we map depend on which appear to be the most contextually relevant and may depend on our cultural background (Lakoff and Johnson 1980: 142–144). There could be variation, then, in what we map from the source domain to the target and how we conceive of both domains; as Steen and Gibbs point out:

> such variation between people in a community may have important effects on their experience of specific linguistic expressions as conventional or new, easy or difficult, appropriate or inappropriate, and so on, and may influence people's production and comprehension of specific linguistic expressions in concomitantly varying ways.
>
> (1999: 3)

Returning to our source domain, we map some of the 'hive-ness' characteristics onto the target domain of 'shop-ness'. The presence of the source domain 'hiving' compels us to project a "set of associated implications" (Black 1979: 28),

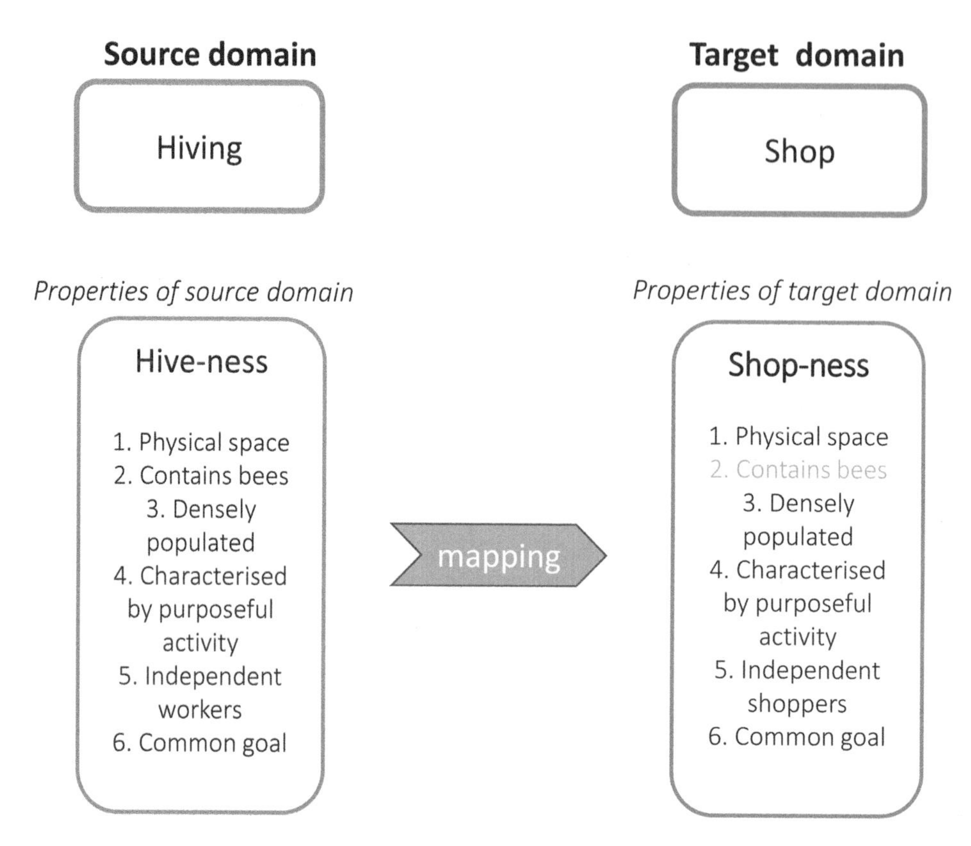

Figure 8.4 Metaphoric mapping for 'hiving'

that are capable of being asserted of the source domain. In other words, we map characteristics of 'hive-ness' on to the target 'shop-ness' to generate an understanding of the target domain that has a contextually meaningful parallel with the concept 'hive' (otherwise, why use the metaphor?).

Making sense of metaphors sometimes requires extra cognitive work on the hearer's behalf because the intended meaning of a metaphor is not that which is literally stated. In other words, when we say the shop was 'hiving' our knowledge of shops helps us understand that they do not tend to be densely populated by bees working to produce honey. To make sense of the utterance we must 'pick up' the metaphor's implicated content which arise from what Black calls a "system of relationships" between source and target domains (Figure 8.4) and construes as an "*implicative* complex" (1979: 28, our emphasis) that demands uptake from a hearer.

This leads us to ask the following questions: If metaphors demand interpretation, then what properties from the 'system of relationships' do we map? And why? And what can these mappings do to our knowledge of each of the domains (source and target)?

What do we map and why?

For the 'shop' to be 'hiving' we assume it to share a property exhibited (prototypically) by hives, namely that the shop is uncharacteristically, even frenetically busy. In fact, this is a more precise rendering of our target domain:

> **Source:** 'hiving'
> **Target:** 'the shop is uncharacteristically, even frenetically (threateningly?) busy'

It is important to note, as Lakoff and Johnson do, that "metaphorical structuring [. . .] is partial, not total. If it were total, one concept would actually *be* the other, not merely be understood in terms of it" (1980: 13). This means that there are things we do not map, for example, the second property in Figure 8.4, 'contains bees', because it would not make much sense to say that shops contain bees. We do map some of the properties of bees, though (e.g. that they are densely populating the hive). This is only one of several properties of hives (Figure 8.4). The metaphor prompts us to perceive shared (or potentially shareable) characteristics between the two domains which we map from source to target domain.

Earlier we suggested that commonplace knowledge of either or both domains in a metaphor differs according to cultural and personal experience (real or imagined!) of them. If you were badly stung by a bee or bees as a child and grew up being afraid of bees and hives then you might map this fear from the source domain 'hiving' to the target domain 'shop' and interpret the metaphor as conveying a fearful or potentially dangerous or threatening shopping environment. It might lead you to view shopping as a fearful activity even if you had not considered this before. In this way, the metaphor can lead you to see the world in a certain way; it has "the power to create a new reality" (Lakoff and Johnson 1980: 145). The converse of this is also true – if you despise shopping even before encountering the metaphor then you may be primed to pick out properties from the source domain that convey a negative view of shops and shoppers. Alternatively, if you are a bee-lover this property may not transfer across in the metaphorical mapping. The point is that your interpretation of a metaphor will be shaped by and through your own personal experience, and this uptake can shape or re-shape how you view the target/source domain.

Novel metaphors in song lyrics

Aristotle believed that the mastery of metaphor was "a sign of genius" because, according to him, "a good metaphor implies an intuitive perception of the similarity in dissimilars" (2008: 1459a 3–8). But what does it mean to have a 'good' metaphor? (for more on this, see Black 1977; Giora et al. 2004; Littlemore et al. 2014). It depends. It might mean that the metaphor does a good job of communicating the desired mapping. However, there is a particular kind of metaphor that

Aristotle may have in mind here – the 'creative' or 'novel' type, often found in literary fiction. Aristotle's view is partly responsible for the rather narrow view that metaphors are only literary devices (as opposed to conceptual, everyday tools).

Let's start with Aristotle's claim. If we assume by 'good' he meant 'novel', his point appears to be that the 'genius' of creating a novel metaphor derives from your ability to introduce a rather unusual way of seeing one thing – the target domain – in terms of something else – the source domain – for which a connection is not so obvious. Such metaphors self-consciously draw attention to themselves. Novel mappings can be found in many discourse situations including fiction (as noted above) and song lyrics.

For example, Alanis Morissette sings about "transparent dangling carrots" (Morissette and Ballard 1998) and Twenty One Pilots have a song called 'Neon Gravestones' (Twenty One Pilots 2018) in which the gravestones "call" for the "bones" of the speaker. Let's assume that the target concepts in these examples are 'motivation' and 'death' respectively. These metaphors help us to look upon the target in a fresh way. For example, we interpret 'transparent dangling carrots' as a reference to the speaker's motivation for which the primary conceptual metaphor is EMOTIONAL STATES ARE OBJECTS. This comes from the practice of dangling a carrot in front of a donkey to motivate it to walk. As the donkey never really gets the carrot, there is often a negative connotation to such 'dangling carrots', but whether this is carried over in Morissette's song is anyone's guess. The metaphor is embellished with the addition of 'transparent', implying that the speaker is not able to visibly perceive the metaphoric carrot, so the motivation is difficult to pin down or the motivation was false or meaningless. When Twenty One Pilots sing of 'neon gravestones' that 'call', the lyric invokes an OBJECTS ARE ANIMATE ENTITIES metaphor by humanising a gravestone that is capable of 'calling'. That the gravestone is 'neon' leads the hearer to interpret it as having the property 'attractive' or 'welcoming' (on the basis that neon signs tend to attract visitors to events or locations). This is incongruous because gravestones are not 'clubs' that people are motivated to join or enter. Indeed, in our interpretation of the song, we read it as an appeal to those considering suicide to resist the 'call' of 'neon' gravestones. In cases of novel metaphors[5] like these, the 'accepted commonplaces' are passed over in favour of what Black calls "specially constructed systems of implications" resulting in "made to measure" mappings (1955: 290).

Before reading on, have a look at Activity 8.4.

Activity 8.4 Making meanings through metaphoric mappings

Consider the meaning of the following line from rapper Akala's song, 'Shakespeare' (Akala 2007).

"keep spittin' ya darts, mine is javelins"

Before reading further, can you identify the source and target domains in Akala's song lyric example? What properties do you think might be mappable? What meaning or meaning potential might these mapped properties give rise to? Cognisant of Black's interactionist view of metaphor, do the mappings lead you to view the source or/and target differently in light of the metaphor's context? How so?

Perhaps your answers to the first question in Activity 8.4 yielded something similar to the following.

Source domain: Sharp objects
Target domain: Rap
The conceptual metaphor that governs these lexical metaphoric expressions is WORDS ARE OBJECTS.

Regarding the second question, some of the following associated implications may get mapped.

- sharp objects are gradable on several scales that include weight, size, reach
- "javelins" generates a potential for damage to a stimulus (it would be less damaging to get hurt by a dart than a javelin!)
- superiority (darts are inferior instruments to javelins if what you want to do is throw them a great distance)

The mapping encourages us to understand the quality of rap in a gradable manner in the same way that the relationship between darts and javelins is scalable/gradable. By this, we can conclude that Akala's rap is more impactful, because it is sharper, and has a greater reach or scope than his contemporaries' rap. Notice that the comparison generated by the metaphor introduces this scale as one of the implicatures that we derive from the metaphor's use. We may also import the associated implication that 'sharpness' carries in other metaphors such as 'sharp wit' (good), 'sharp tongue' (bad, but depending on whether you're on the receiving end or not), 'sharp dresser', and so on. We may be encouraged to view rap in new ways as a result of the mappings. This new way of seeing can refresh or disrupt our perception of the target domain. It can challenge us to see the target domain in a new way (sometimes forever!).

Extended metaphors

Sometimes, metaphors are creatively expanded or 'extended'. This means that once a source domain has been invoked, other properties of that source domain come into play in lexical metaphoric expressions that help to elucidate the target concept. We offer an example in the following activity. Have a look and try to work out what is happening metaphorically before reading further.

Activity 8.5 Extended metaphors

In the American medical comedy TV show *Scrubs* (Callahan and Kerns 2004), the character Dr Perry Cox, who is known for his acerbic wit (his discourse offers many fine examples of 'spittin' javelins'), participates in an exchange with his psychology colleague, Dr Molly Clock, in which both employ the same metaphor in different ways in a short exchange about types of people. Whereas Clock claims that people are not "pure evil", she concedes that some have a "hard outer shell". An exchange follows whereby Cox and Clock conceptualise human personality types as being "nougaty" or having "creamy centres", before Cox concludes the exchange with the retort that people are mostly "bastard-coated bastards with a bastard filling". You can scan QR code 8.1 to watch the clip (from 5:55 mins).

QR 8.1 Comedic effect from extended metaphor

There are different concepts at play in their exchange – can you tell whether there is a primary conceptual metaphor at work, and if so, what is it?

So, what is going on in the example from Activity 8.5? First, Molly attempts to elucidate the target domain "personality type" through a 'container' source domain using a conceptual metaphor PEOPLE ARE CONTAINERS (see Lakoff and Johnson 1980 for a full description of this type of primary/conceptual metaphor). Molly introduces a metaphoric interpretation through the lexical terms "hard outer shell" and "creamy centre". These are examples of lexical metaphors. If you guessed a primary conceptual metaphor, did you get 'CONTAINER'? The 'container' (of sorts) turns out to be chocolate. The two properties "hard outer shell' and "creamy centre" are likely to be from the same source domain, so that "hard shell" does not, for example, refer to a turtle. This is because the presence of two lexical metaphors from the same conceptual domain ('shell' and 'creamy centre' are both properties of chocolates) are more likely than two lexical metaphors from two different conceptual domains assuming that both are being cooperative. Therefore, "shell" and "creamy centre" prime the hearer to interpret a confectionery link rather than a reptilian one. Then, Molly **extends** the chocolate container metaphor by introducing new conceptual elements of the chocolate source domain, e.g. "nougaty". So now we have "creamy centre" pitched against "nougaty centre" in a kind cline of hardness that concretises 'evil' and 'good' personality types. This is a common conceptual cline in which 'soft' is 'good' and 'hard' is bad/difficult/stubborn and so on. It is fairly conventionalised in lexical metaphors such as 'you're such a *softie*, and 'don't be too *hard* on them'.[6] Dr Cox initially negates Molly's chocolate metaphor but then merges it with his own creative metaphoric source domain of "bastards" producing a mixed metaphor so that people can be said to be "bastard-coated" and have "bastard filling". Of course, he is not trying to say that people are chocolates either, but he *is* capturing the same metaphoric mapping of people as confectionery 'containers' where their "shell" and "filling" are more novel because both are . . . well . . . 'bastard'. In Dr Cox's view of people, they are not simply 'bastards' in the nominal sense, but also in the biological or corporeal sense being comprised of 'bastard' parts filled with 'bastard' centres. In this way, Cox's mixed metaphor "selects, emphasizes [. . .] and organizes features of the [target domain] by *implying* statements about it that normally apply to the [source domain]" (Black 1955: 291–292, emphasis in original). Of course, it is also rather amusing which is really more the point.

Activity 8.6 Metaphorical extension and elaboration in BBC TV's *Dragon's Den*

Dragon's Den, a BBC reality series that broadcasts entrepreneurial pitches to an audience of wealthy, shrewd investor 'dragons', incorporates a host of metaphoric puns in its narration of each of the entrepreneurial pitches. The show's presenter, Evan Davis, provides the voice-over narration to the goings-on in the 'den'. After reading about metaphorical extension, see if you can match the investment-seeking pitches to the groups of metaphors Davis invokes in his corresponding comments from episode 13 in series 18 (*Dragon's Den* 2021). Then identify the lexical metaphors and see if you can link any of them to an overarching conceptual metaphor. Do you see any metaphorical patterns between the pitches and the lexical metaphors?

You can watch the episode by scanning QR code 8.2 (if you can access BBC iPlayer).

QR 8.2 Match the metaphor group to the entrepreneurial pitch

The pitches:
Pitch 1: A 'Rev-off' device to turn a regular push bike into an e-bike
Pitch 2: An optometrist duo pitch a screen that limits blue light exposure from digital devices.
Pitch 3: An entrepreneur is selling trees to offset the carbon footprint via an app
Pitch 4: A busy mum who is a teacher is pitching her 'family-themed' fruit preserves
Pitch 5: Comedian, Darren, is pitching his idea for a 'dog poo' lifter.

Metaphor group A
"Will he scoop up an investment?"
". . . find out if there's any brass where there's muck"
". . . [his pitch] is anything but a walk in the park"
"[the product] falls foul"

Metaphor group B
"[Will she] be the toast of the den?"

"[As a teacher and mum] she is spread pretty thin"
"stuck into questions"
"a ready-made partnership"
"sweeten a potential deal"
"sticky situation"
"sweet success"
"pump up the jam business"

Metaphor group C
"[The duo] have their sights set on two particular dragons"
"catch the eye of the dragons they're about to go face-to-face with"
"[Will they] green light a deal for the blue light duo?"
"see eye-to-eye"

Metaphor group D
"stumps up any cash"
"dig deeper into the [business idea]"
"Will his digging unearth a valuation?"
"the sapling business"
"get to the root [of the finances]"
"[He] has his investment dreams felled"

Metaphor group E
"back in the saddle [. . .] like riding a bike"
"gives entrepreneurs a rough ride"
"a smooth ride so far"
"hit a stump in the road"
"put the skids on their pitch"
"[The idea] was a non-starter"

Metaphors in political discourse

The use of some metaphors can promote a particular worldview in the mappings they generate. This is because metaphors can have ideological outcomes. Their use in some contexts can lead hearers to reconceive of the target domain in ways that reinforce existing or establish new social and cultural stereotypes. For example, in the UK, refugees are often discriminated against and negatively presented in public discourse through metaphors that present their arrival as a negative phenomenon. Such metaphors may convey the speaker's attitude or stance towards the target domain. The following comment by David Cameron, then Prime Minister of Britain, incorporates a metaphoric mapping linking refugees to insects and reveals ideologically – and culturally – damaging comparisons.

> 'You have got a **swarm** of people coming across the Mediterranean, seeking a better life . . .'
>
> (Elgot and Taylor 2015)

Cameron came in for quite a bit of criticism for this comment about refugees entering Britain, and rightly so. The metaphorical use of 'swarm' was the issue for many, as this "dehumanis[ed] desperate men, women and children" seeking refuge in the UK (Lisa Doyle, quoted in Elgot and Taylor 2015). The metaphor is the linguistic manifestation of a conceptual metaphor, PEOPLE ARE INSECTS. The source domain 'swarm' triggers associated implications, namely visions of insects invading a physical space. These largely pejorative connotations (see Leech's meaning types in Chapter 5) are mapped across to the target domain so that refugees are reconfigured linguistically and conceptually as parasitic insects. To be more specific, insects in 'swarms' tend to do damage to crops, gardens, and so on (if you've ever had to deal with vine weevil wreaking havoc on your agapanthus you'll see the point here), so the parasitic implications can extend to refugees. Indeed, Cameron more or less made this point a year earlier when writing about his changes to the UK's immigration policy (Cameron 2014) in which he fuelled the 'swarming' metaphor by saying "most new jobs used to go to foreign workers".[7] The implication that refugees *take* jobs from UK residents is an erroneous, yet popular belief in the UK. The implicated comparison of refugees to insects incorporates – and makes it easier to accept – this metaphorically construed 'invasion' that extends beyond the land itself into the economy, parasitically eating up jobs that sustain the inhabitants of that country. This in turn can change how we look at 'swarms' of insects, even just by foregrounding some of their properties over others.

The metaphor has become popularised to the point that the novelty has worn off. This is insidious because it naturalises the pejorative discourse about refugees by making the comparison part of the "background" information (Simpson 2014: 96) we hold about refugees. Indeed, the metaphor that posits a mapping between insects and refugees has often been **extended** as the following show (our emphasis in bold italic).

(a) President Trump in a tweet claimed that Democrats "want illegal immigrants, no matter how bad they may be, to pour into and ***infest*** our country"
(Twitter, 19 June 2018)

(b) Rima and her children joined the stream of refugees on what has become known as the ***"ant road"***, from Turkey to Western Europe.
(*Guardian*, 19 December 2015; see Mujagić and Berberović 2019 for other examples)

(c) Meanwhile, migrants continue to ***crawl*** into the country.
(Hart 2021; see also for other examples)

These metaphors incorporate corresponding properties of the source domain, such as manner of movement ('crawl'), density ('swarm'), and so on, and lexicalises them to develop the primary conceptual metaphor. But they also make it easier to map properties that may not be intended by the metaphor producer such as 'disease' (see Charteris-Black (2006) for more on the DISEASE metaphor), or parasitic behaviours (such as feeding off British economy by taking jobs).

Amnesty International (2020) reported on the growing concern over "dangerous" language choices when referring to refugees and quotes the United Nations High Commissioner for Refugees as saying that "this type of language stigmatizes refugees, migrants and other people on the move, that gives legitimacy to a discourse of racism, hatred, and xenophobia". Such metaphors invariably stigmatise refugees, legitimises racism, and perpetuates xenophobia. Of course, it is not the metaphor itself that does this, but the metaphor producer(s), and to some degree, the metaphor-hearers can be complicit in this process if, upon making the connection, they choose to commit to the implicit mapping and accept it as a valid one.[8]

Activity 8.7 Making meanings through metaphors

What follows is a short exercise to test whether metaphors help us understand concepts in a particular way when influenced by a metaphoric source. Make a list of five totally random nouns or noun phrases that contain 'concrete' concepts. Ask a friend or classmate to make a list of five abstract concepts. Now swap your lists with each other. Compare the lists side by side. The list of concrete nouns is the source domain list and the list of abstract nouns is your target domain list. Now try to map the source on to the target to create a metaphor that reconstrues the target according to the source. What properties do you map? Why? How do these mappings steer your understanding of the target? Does your mapping generate a positive or pejorative position towards the target?

Now try to flesh out your metaphoric mapping by offering a context or situation in which the mapping 'works'. One of us did this exercise with our students and you can see some of the creative mappings they came up with at the end of this chapter. Can you see how some students **extended** the metaphor?

These are the lists that we each came up with.

Abstract nouns		**Concrete nouns**
hope		sea urchin
power	is a	campsite
truth		orange
patience		tree
evil		canal

Now to create some context! Let's just take one as an example: HOPE IS A SEA URCHIN. This could derive from a conceptual metaphor EMOTION IS A LIVING BEING. We aren't too familiar with sea urchins but working with what we *do* know, we might say that the property 'rare' characterises sea urchins (relatively speaking) because they are only found in certain waters and at certain depths, so hope can often feel like it's 'rare' or out of reach; we have to *dive deep* to get it. Sea urchins are prickly, so we may map the fact that we cannot hold hope easily in our hands or that hope is elusive in a more general sense (note how it is almost impossible to make the mapping without recourse to other metaphors). We might even conclude that the metaphor producer is feeling hope*less*. This affirms the point made earlier that metaphors can say something of the producer's view of the world.

Metonymy

Metonymy is connected to metaphor in that metonymic structures are also mappings and are used non-literally (-ish). In a metonymy, like metaphor, something stands for something else. The difference is that in a metonymy, the mapping is not across two separate conceptual domains (as it is in metaphor), but rather, resides within a single (target) domain accessed through a trigger term that acts as a **vehicle** to the metonymic interpretation.

Within-domain mapping

The relationship in a metonymic mapping is within the same domain and so we use slightly different terms for the two parts of a metonymy. Instead of 'source' and 'target' the conventional terms are 'vehicle' and 'target'. Because metonymic mappings are based on a 'stands for' relationship, they are typically between a part of a thing and its whole (part-to-whole). Some examples include producer for thing produced, cause for effect, type for token, and so on. The relationship also works in reverse so there are 'effect for cause' mappings and so on. Like metaphors, these mappings operate at a generic **primary** level with lexically **specific** instantiations and applications. The following sentences contain specific metonymies. The metonymic vehicle is in bold type and it carries (hence 'vehicle') the metonymic relationship:

a) Have you seen the recent **Tarantino**? ([film] producer for [film] produced)
b) Why are **Iceland** going back to the polls? (country for the people of the country)
c) Don't be such a **Karen** (a member of a set for characteristics of all members in that set)
d) **The bump** won't let me eat spicy food any more (sign of pregnancy for the state of pregnancy)

The metonymic relationship is in parentheses after each example so that 'Tarantino', a movie producer, is used to stand for the movie he has produced, and so on. In terms of the primary mapping, example a) is CREATOR FOR CREATION, (see Quintilian 1921); in b) the primary mapping is PLACE FOR PEOPLE; in c) it is TYPE FOR TOKEN; whereas in d) it is EFFECT FOR CAUSE. Note also, that these metonymies only work if the cultural reference is known to the interactants, so you'd need to know who Quentin Tarantino is in order to understand that his film is metonymically invoked in a), and so on. This emphasises the point we made earlier that context is really important for making sense of metonymic and metaphoric mappings.

Metonymy or metaphor?

Grady (1997) offers a useful test for distinguishing between metaphor and metonymy – the 'is like' test. In a metaphor the 'is like' test usually works in presenting the source domain as being *'like'* the target, for example:

'The shop was **hiving**' > The shop *is like* a hive.

However, in metonymy, the 'is like' test makes no sense, for example:

'Why are **Iceland** going back to the polls?' > *Iceland *is like* people
('Iceland' stands for the people who live in Iceland)

Ubiquity of metonyms

Metonymies are as ubiquitous as metaphors. We use them every day. Let's take a particular type of communication to illustrate this. Emojis are essentially metonymic signs that invoke a characteristic of a concept or domain to represent or substitute for the whole concept or domain. In some cultures, champagne is considered a common element in celebrations. Imagine, then, you sent the following message in Figure 8.5 to your friend or colleague after they finished a particularly difficult book chapter:

yay, you finished your chapter! 🍾

Figure 8.5 WhatsApp message

The little champagne bottle conveys the meaning of 'celebration' by invoking a key or salient element of celebration – champagne – through the metonymic mapping SYMBOL FOR THING SYMBOLISED. Therefore, following Simpson (2014), we can say that metonymy takes a "salient characteristic from a single domain" and "upgrades" it to "represent that domain as a whole" (45). Whatever text producers choose to 'upgrade' from the target domain is often contextually dependent. For example, if you were in a hospital and overheard a doctor say to the ward staff officer, 'I need to go and prep bed four', you probably would not think they were off to tidy up the bedding and fluff the pillows, but rather, that they were about to administer some pre-surgical drugs to the person *occupying* bed four. While this might sound a bit impersonal to say the least, the issue is that it is a contextually derived metonymy because it takes the salient characteristic *for the participants* (i.e. the fourth bed in a ward) to stand for the entirety of the domain (the patient in bed four).[9] To use Forceville's term, it has 'relevance' as well as salience (2002). It also provides an economical (if impersonal) way of signalling the target domain in a busy place with a high turnover of people like a hospital ward. Therefore, the staff choose a characteristic that best captures the target domain in the most efficient way *for them*. The same metonymy may not work so well in a different context. Imagine you share a bedroom with your sister who has overslept and is at risk of missing her commute to work. You probably wouldn't offer to go and 'wake up bed two'. There is no justifiable contextual reason for referring to your sister in this way, because you know her name, there is probably not a regular stream of people arriving and leaving your house, and you probably don't have to spend every morning going round your family members and waking them up one by one (and if you did, you'd probably use their names).

Metonymy and worldview

Metonymies, like metaphors, can shed some light on the text producer's worldview. To give an example, in her collaboration on the song 'Girls like you' with Maroon 5, the artist Cardi B sings about wanting, among other things, a 'white horse' and 'carats' (Maroon 5 featuring Cardi B 2018).[10] The 'carats' is a reference to diamonds through a UNIT OF MEASUREMENT FOR THING MEASURED metonymy. Her invocation of this specific characteristic can tell us something of how she (her singing persona) views diamonds. In this metonymy, diamonds could be referenced by any of their characteristic or salient 'parts': 'sparkler' (EFFECT FOR CAUSE), 'knuckle-buster' (EFFECT FOR CAUSE), and many more besides. Cardi B's reference to them as 'carats' encourages us to consider their material worth over and above their aesthetic value as diamonds are valued in marketable or fiscal terms on the basis of their carat weight.

'Karenymy'

Some metonymies are pejorative – not because they are inherently 'negative' but because their use in particular contexts and by particular speakers makes them so. This is perhaps less noticeable (and so more insidious) when their use has become systemic. One example of this is the now common, if rather pejorative metonymy 'Karen', which is used throughout social media to refer to middle-class white women who complain a lot, usually to assert privilege – a TOKEN FOR TYPE mapping in which the name or 'token' represents or stands for all women of a particular type. Of course, this information needs to be accommodated by a hearer in order for the metonymy to work![11] Like metaphors, metonymies can be extended. For instance, there is a 'Karen' haircut, 'a coronavirus Karen' (she refuses to wear masks, is anti-vax), and so on. Indeed, the Karen metonymy is so pervasive now that it has caused problems for actual Karens, as the following tweets from a UK supermarket's account show:

> Sainsbury's: 'We won't be challenging customers without a mask when they enter or when they are in store since they may have a reason not to wear a mask. Karen'
>
> C.G. (Twitter user): Highly offensive putting Karen at the end . . . stick it'
>
> Sainsbury's: Hi [C], sorry for the confusion. Karen is the name of the colleague who responded to the query. Andy'
>
> (Sainsbury's, Twitter, 23 July 2020)

Metaphors and metonymies

As we said at the beginning of this chapter, metaphors and metonymies are ubiquitous phenomena. Often, they give rise to meanings by working together. The final examples in this chapter explore this interrelationship through novel utterances that generate metaphor/metonymy combinations.

A 'moo' point

In the American TV sitcom *Friends,* the character Joey Tribbiani is known for his rather one-dimensional way of looking at the world. One notable instance occurs in series 7, episode 8, which you can see by scanning QR code 8.3.

QR 8.3 A 'moo point' metonymy

In a conversation with the character Rachel, in which they are discussing strategies on how to woo a man she likes, Joey advises that if this man isn't interested in Rachel then all of "this" is a "moo point" (Lin and Bright 2000). Joey 'explains' himself by latching on to the metonymic element 'moo' (SOUND OF ENTITY FOR WHOLE ENTITY) as representing a whole cow by further claiming that the opinion of the man "is like a cow's opinion" which, as he puts it, "doesn't matter". Therefore, the "moo point" metaphor derives from a metonymy which you can test using the 'is like' test: 'A moo (Vehicle) is like a cow (Target)'.

But this does not make sense. Instead, we can say that the sound of a cow – the 'moo' – is substituting conceptually for the whole of the animal. So, when Joey invokes the sound of the cow through the vehicle term, 'moo', he is intending his hearer, Rachel, to understand the 'moo' as ***standing for*** the cow itself. He inadvertently invokes a mapping chain that moves from metonymy to metaphor in the following ways: a metonymy (SOUND OF ENTITY FOR WHOLE ENTITY) is the source domain in a metaphoric mapping in which the target is the notion of irrelevance ('it doesn't matter'). So, the metaphor (incorporating the metonymy) would be something like IRRELEVANCE IS A COW. The conceptual metaphor then, would be STATES ARE LIVING ENTITIES (see Figure 8.6). Presumably, Joey's utterance makes sense if it's premised on a belief that the opinion of a cow is insignificant and has no bearing on human relationships.

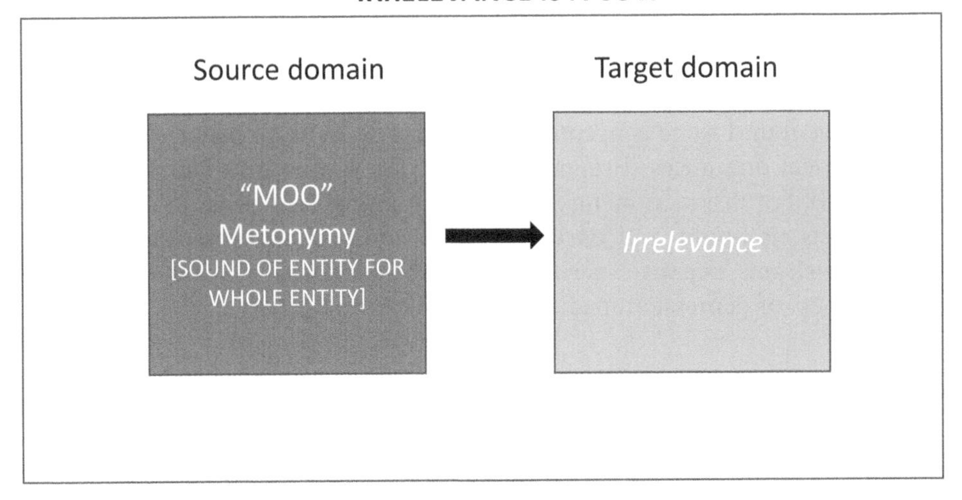

Figure 8.6 The 'moo point' metaphor/metonymy

You'll see that the meaning is not directly traceable to the grammatical or lexical elements but resides in an implicature (so implicitly traceable, in a sense). This is the case for all metaphors (remember that metaphors are not literally true and so flout Grice's Quality maxim).

Conclusion

This chapter has shown how metaphors and metonymies are not simply figures of speech that show a text producer's linguistic skill or 'genius' but rather are systematised ways of seeing the world, the entities that inhabit it, and the goings-on that occur within it. It also shows how both tropes rely on *implicated* unstated meanings in order to make sense so that in some ways they call upon the hearer to actively participate in seeing the world the way the metaphor or metonymy frames it. We have also shown how metaphors can develop through *extension* to form whole discourses about communities, events, behaviours, and so on. And we have demonstrated how much we rely on metaphors in everyday language and thinking, too, and that contrary to Aristotle's claim, they are not only the product of creative genius (or we are ALL creative geniuses!) To employ another well-wrought metaphor, the following chapter *moves away* from the content of discourse to examine discourse structure. More specifically, it considers the how experience is represented in discourse.

Further reading

Metaphors are often employed to make sense of abstract concepts. One such study is Duffy and Feist's work which examines the concept of 'time' in a book-length study, *Time, Metaphor, and Language: A Cognitive Science Perspective* (2023). In terms of the rhetorical value of conceptual metaphors, approaches to CMT have found some conceptual metaphors to be more persuasive than non-metaphorical utterances (Brugman et al. 2019; Sopory and Dillard 2002; van Stee 2018). For instance, metaphorically presenting depression in terms of 'ups' and 'downs' or 'bright' and 'dark' periods, in comparison to non-metaphorically as 'positive' and 'negative' periods, has been shown to increase the perceived effectiveness of depression medications (Keefer et al. 2014).

Answers to activities

Activity 8.1 Orientational metaphors – positive or negative evaluation?

> Johnson's premiership, a mindless rotting meat zombie held together with the Sellotape™® of lies and the sticky excretions of his own spaff-faucet, began a sudden and dramatic **slide into** the ocean on Wednesday, like an arctic ice shelf made entirely of frozen shit.
>
> (Lee 2022)

It's fair to say that, while not the most interesting part of the utterance, this negative comment has an orientational metaphor as part of the main verb phrase, signalled by bold type, 'a sudden and dramatic **slide into** the ocean'. Sliding into the ocean (as opposed to 'slide up') suggests a BAD IS DOWN metaphor. Therefore, we are encouraged to read this as a negative comment on Johnson's premiership.

Of course, the co-text makes this abundantly clear. We are told the premiership (or the man?) is a 'mindless rotting meat zombie' (this conflates several metaphors, one of being without sense ('mindless') and another connoting decay ('rotting') and a contiguous concept, death ('zombie'). The 'sticky excretions' links cohesively (see Chapter 3) to 'spaff' (a colloquial term for 'semen' or 'ejaculation') and 'shit'.

Activity 8.2 Metaphor in literary fiction

'Potentiality' is the Subject in a clause in which it is said to 'knock' on something. Therefore, the phenomenon ('potentiality') is animated by virtue of being able to 'knock'. This triggers a conceptual metaphor, ABSTRACTIONS ARE ANIMATE OBJECTS. The grammatical Object, 'the door of my heart' is also metaphoric as there is no literal door on a heart. So, perhaps the speaker is conceiving of the heart as a space that houses emotions (such as love) through the metaphor THE HEART IS A CONTAINER. In metaphoric terms, the act of knocking acts as a source domain for the target concept of desiring access (to the speaker's emotions). Overall, the speaker's meaning in uttering 'potentiality knocks on the door of my heart' appears to be something like 'this meeting is an opportunity for love'. But Murakami's metaphoric version is arguably much more poetic!

Activity 8.3 Real examples of the 'hiving' metaphor

Example (a) is from the Tripadvisor website and is part of a review of a restaurant in London. The reviewer notes they are from Ballygally in the north of Ireland. Example (b) is also from Tripadvisor and the Belfast author is reviewing a bar called the Woodworker Tap House. Example (c) is from a BBC news report into overcrowding at an event in Fintona, in the north of Ireland, in 2013, in which people attending a music event were crushed and injured in the premises. Example (d) is from a regional newspaper, the *Belfast Telegraph*, and reports on the excitement remembered at a 1990 football match in which local side Portadown won their first league title. You will see that the interpretation of 'hiving' is largely positive (a, b, d) and example (c) may be perceived as negative or neutral. Example (e) is negative as it laments the fact that too many people were at the spa when the author wished to use it.

All the authors are from the north of Ireland and therefore speakers of Hiberno-English. A simple online search using the phrase 'place was hiving', or 'room was hiving' generates a very limited set of results, all of them Hiberno-English speakers. This is interesting for sociolinguistic understandings of metaphors as regionally specific! You might want to think of any metaphors you use in your own speech community that could be used to identify that particular speech community.

Activity 8.6 Metaphorical extension and elaboration in BBC TV's Dragon's Den

Metaphor group E is from Pitch 1: A 'Rev-off' device to turn a regular push bike into an e-bike

Metaphor group C is from Pitch 2: An optometrist duo pitch a screen that limits blue light exposure from digital devices.

Metaphor group D is from Pitch 3: An entrepreneur is selling trees to offset the carbon footprint via an app

Metaphor group B is from Pitch 4: A busy mum who is a teacher is pitching her 'family-themed' fruit preserves

Metaphor group A is from Pitch 5: Comedian, Darren, is pitching his idea for a 'dog poo' lifter.

Activity 8.7 Making meanings through metaphors

Abstract noun	Concrete noun	Mapping (as presented by students from University College Utrecht, Netherlands)
Terror	Pancake	TERROR IS A PANCAKE It [pancake] is heavy and sticky. And just like the pancakes that form a sort of tower, so do the terror and the problems when they start accumulating. The syrup that overflows on top is just like the thoughts that you can't get out of, it is sticky and stays on you; it feels like it cannot be taken off even after you clean your hands with kitchen paper.
Love	Boat	LOVE IS A BOAT Love is a boat, rocks from side to side with strong waves. It may sink, it may stay afloat, but it's constantly moving. It can carry you.
Love	Soup	LOVE IS SOUP Love is soup, can warm you up from the inside, keep you happy and warm when you're cold, can also burn you and leave you scarred.
Future	Wheel	FUTURE IS A WHEEL Always in motion and it goes forward. The wheel is the first invention, so it also reflects the past.
Language	Room	LANGUAGE IS A ROOM Language is like a room. You can decorate it as you want, it takes various shapes and forms, it is a space of possibility, but you have to work within the space.

Notes

1 We refer to linguistic expressions of metaphors as **lexical metaphors**.
2 This way of representing the conceptual nature of metaphors using small capitals and an 'X is Y' formulation, as we have here, stems from Lakoff and Johnson (1980). It shows, as Kövecses puts it, that "the particular wording does not occur in language as such, but it underlies *conceptually* all the metaphorical expressions" that derive from the capitalized metaphoric 'X is Y' structure (2010: 4, our emphasis).
3 Grady (1997) calls the conceptual or generic metaphor a 'primary' here but there are a range of terms for such metaphors. Some widely used terms include 'root metaphors' (Pepper 1935; Brown 1977; Goatly 1997), 'primary systems' (Black 1955), and 'principal metaphors' (Brown 1977). Having so many terms doesn't really help, though. We have opted to go with 'primary' as stated in the chapter.
4 Reconceiving of 'knowledge' as something we can *see* is a culturally entrenched metaphor, particularly in religious discourse (Canning 2012).
5 The reference to 'gravestones' invokes a metonymy in which the *place-marker* for the dead (gravestone) stands for the *state* of being dead (LOCATION FOR STATE). We deal with metaphor/metonymy combinations later.
6 Also note that 'hard' is used to denote 'toughness' as in 'Oooo, you're hard', said to Akala after he spits some javelins.
7 This was an unsubstantiated claim for which Cameron was rebuked. If you can bear to read the British tabloid press you will find many examples of this metaphor.
8 Arguably hearers are oriented to make the connection, but not to accept it
9 Note how the metaphor test helps you see that it is a metonymy (*a bed is like a person). Asterisks are used to show that the utterance does not work.
10 We don't think Cardi B is referring literally to 'a white horse and a carriage' and she didn't answer our email to confirm.
11 Perhaps the case of Caren Z. Turner offers one example of a real-life 'Karen' (if social media is anything to go by). Turner was a Port Authority Commissioner who arrived at the scene of a traffic violation where two Port Authority officers had pulled over her child and some friends. Turner used her senior role to try to get the officer who stopped her child and their friends to drop the violation. He didn't. Here is the link to the clip of the incident: https://www.youtube.com/watch?v=Goj-1stJpoA

References

Akala (2007) 'Shakespeare' [song]. *Comedy, tragedy, history* [album]. Freedom Lasso. Illa State Records.

Amnesty International (2020) 'Why the language we use to talk about refugees matters'. Accessed 10 July 2023. https://www.amnesty.org/en/latest/news/2020/03/why-the-language-we-use-to-talk-about-refugees-matters

Aristotle (2008) *Poetics* (trans. S. H. Butcher). Accessed 6 January 2022. https://www.gutenberg.org/files/1974/1974-h/1974-h.htm#link2H_4_0003

Black, M. (1977) 'More about metaphor'. *Dialectica*, 31(3–4): 431–457.

Black, Max (1955) 'Metaphor'. *Proceedings of the Aristotelian Society*, 55(1): 273–294.

Black, Max (1979) 'More about metaphor'. In A. Ortony (ed.), *Metaphor and Thought*. Cambridge: Cambridge University Press.

Brown, R. H. (1977) *A poetics of sociology: Towards a logic of discovery for the human sciences*. Cambridge: Cambridge University Press.

Brugman, B. C., Burgers, C., and Vis, B. (2019) 'Metaphorical framing in political discourse through words vs. concepts: A meta-analysis'. *Language and Cognition*, 11(1): 41–65.

Callahan, B. (Writer) and Kerns, J. (Director) (2004) 'My common enemy'. *Scrubs,* series 4, episode 7. ABC Studios.

Cameron, D. (2014) 'We're building an immigration system that puts Britain first'. *The Telegraph,* 28 July. Accessed 6 July 2023. https://www.telegraph.co.uk/news/uknews/immigration/10995875/David-Cameron-Were-building-an-immigration-system-that-puts-Britain-first.html

Canning, P. (2012) *Style in the Renaissance: Language and ideology in early modern England*. London and New York: Continuum.

Charteris-Black, J. (2006) 'Britain as a container: Immigration metaphors in the 2005 election campaign'. *Discourse & Society*, 17(5): 563–581.

Dragon's Den (2021) Season 18, episode 13. BBC Studios Factual Entertainment Productions.

Duffy, S. and Feist, M. I. (forthcoming, 2023) *Time, metaphor, and language: A cognitive science perspective*. Cambridge: Cambridge University Press.

Elgot, J. and Taylor, M. (2015) 'Calais crisis: Cameron condemned for "dehumanising" description of migrants'. *Guardian*, 30 July. Accessed 6 July 2023. https://www.theguardian.com/uk-news/2015/jul/30/david-cameron-migrant-swarm-language-condemned

Forceville, C. (2002) 'Further thoughts on delimiting pictorial metaphor'. *Theoria et Historia Scientiarum*, 6(1): 213–227.

Giora, R., Fein, O., Kronrod, A., Elnatan, I., Shuval, N., and Zur, A. (2004) 'Weapons of mass distraction: Optimal innovation and pleasure ratings'. *Metaphor and Symbol*, 19(2): 115–141.

Goatly, A. (1997) *The language of metaphors*. New York: Routledge.

Goatly, A. (2007) *Washing the brain: Metaphor and hidden ideology*. Amsterdam: John Benjamins.

Grady, J. E. (1997) *Foundations of meaning: Primary metaphors and primary scenes*. Berkeley: University of California.

Hart, C. (2021) 'Animals vs. armies: Resistance to extreme metaphors in anti-immigration discourse'. *Journal of Language and Politics*, 20(2): 226–253.

Keefer, L. A., Landau, M. J., Sullivan, D., and Rothschild, Z. K. (2014) 'Embodied metaphor and abstract problem solving: Testing a metaphoric fit hypothesis in the health domain'. *Journal of Experimental Social Psychology*, 55: 12–20.

Kövecses, Z. (1986) *Metaphors anger, pride, and love: A lexical approach to the structure of concepts*. Philadelphia, PA: John Benjamins.

Kövecses, Z. (1990) *Emotion concepts*. New York: Springer-Verlag.

Kövecses, Z. (2010) *Metaphor: A practical introduction* (2nd edition). Oxford: Oxford University Press.

Lakoff, G. (1987) *Women, fire, and dangerous things: What categories reveal about the mind*. Chicago: University of Chicago Press.

Lakoff, G. and Johnson, M. (1980) *Metaphors we live by*. Chicago: University of Chicago Press.

Langacker, R. W. (2008) *Cognitive grammar: A basic introduction*. Oxford: Oxford University Press.

Lee, Stewart (2022) 'I'm not answering my phone, in case it's No 10 offering me a job'. *Guardian*, 10 July. Accessed 28 July 2022. https://www.theguardian.com/commentisfree/2022/jul/10/boris-johnson-out-corruption-tory-mps-resignation.

Lin, P. (Writer) and, Bright, K. (Director) (2000) 'The One where Chandler doesn't like dogs'. *Friends*, Series 7, episode 8. Bright/Kauffman/Crane Productions, in association with Warner Bros. Television. Accessed 30 January 2023: http://www.friends-tv.org/epguide.html#seventh

Littlemore, J., Krennmayr, T., Turner, J., and Turner, S. (2014) 'An investigation into metaphor use at different levels of second language writing'. *Applied Linguistics*, 35(2): 117–144.

Maroon 5 featuring Cardi B (2018) 'Girls like you' [song]. *Red Pill Blues* [album]. Cirkut and Jason Evigan.

Morissette, A. and Ballard, G. (1998) 'Thank U' [song]. *Supposed Former Infatuation Junkie* [album]. Maverick Records.

Mujagić, M. and Berberović, S. (2019) 'The immigrants are animals metaphor as a deliberate metaphor in British and Bosnian-Herzegovinian media'. *Explorations in English Language and Linguistics*, 7(1): 22–51.

Murakami, H. (1994) 'On seeing the 100% perfect girl one beautiful April morning'. In Murakami, *The Elephant Vanishes*. London: Vintage.

NJ.com (2018) 'Complete 1-hour video: Port Authority commissioner confronts police during N.J. traffic stop'. 26 April. Accessed 10 July 2023. https://www.youtube.com/watch?v=Goj-1stJpoA

Pepper, S. C. (1935) 'The root of metaphor theory of metaphysics'. *Journal of Philosophy*, 32(14): 365–374.

Quintilian (1921) *Institutio Oratoria*. Vol. III, Book 8, Ch. 6. Loeb Classical Library. New York: G. P. Putnam's Sons.

Richards, I. A. (1936). *The Philosophy of Rhetoric*. New York: Oxford University Press.

Simpson, P. (2014) *Stylistics. A resource book for students*. New York: Routledge.

Sopory, P. and Dillard, J. P. (2002) Figurative language and persuasion. In J. Price Dillard and M. Pfau (eds), *The persuasion handbook: Developments in theory and practice*, pp. 407–426. London: Sage Publications.

Steen, G. J. and Gibbs Jr, R. W. (eds) (1999) *Metaphor in cognitive linguistics: Selected papers from the 5th international cognitive linguistics conference, Amsterdam, 1997* (Vol. 175). Amsterdam: John Benjamins.

Twenty One Pilots (2018) 'Neon Gravestones' [song]. *Trench* [album]. Fueled by Ramen.

van Stee, S. K. (2018) 'Meta-analysis of the persuasive effects of metaphorical vs. literal messages'. *Communication Studies*, 69(5), 545–566.

9 Representing experience in discourse

Introduction

In previous chapters, we looked at the pragmatics of discourse in different contexts. In this chapter, we examine the discursive goings-on in one particular institutional setting, that of forensic police reporting. Over the course of the chapter, we will present a model of transitivity as a methodological tool for the analysis of clause structures in police reports and show how the same actions and events can be rendered or construed in different ways in discourse. This is because clauses can contain constituents that refer to agents who 'do' actions, as well as affected entities who are acted upon. As we saw in Chapter 2, clauses typically contain a grammatical Subject and a Predicator (verb) (but see below), so 'I ran' is a clause, whereas 'I ran because I was afraid' is a clause complex containing two clauses: a main clause ('I ran') and a subordinate clause ('because I was afraid'). So, a simple clause like 'I threw a stone at the window' contains an agent, 'I', an entity acted upon 'a stone' an action, 'threw', and a circumstance that elaborates upon the aforementioned constituents 'at the window'. To bring these grammatical functions and their clausal arrangements to life, we offer a little crime pastiche in Activity 9.1 and ask you to imagine that you witnessed it. Then we ask you to think about all the different ways you might produce a narrative of the crime (as a witness) and to consider some of the semantic and pragmatic meanings of those different ways of saying.

Activity 9.1 Rendering experience in language

The pastiche

You are out for a walk and you witness a person run up to an elderly lady, push her over, grab her handbag and run off in the opposite direction. You call the police for help knowing that the bag-grabbing lady-pusher has committed a crime and that the elderly lady may need your help as a witness if she chooses to pursue justice. The police call-taker is the first person to whom you tell your story of the crime you just witnessed.

DOI: 10.4324/9781003351207-9

Telling and retelling

Give an account of this event to a friend and record it on your phone. Have them re-tell it back to you and record that, too. How did you each tell it? What was left out in the telling? How did you phrase the goings-on?

Now, imagine that you will tell your story of the crime again when you give a formal witness statement to the police. And again, when you tell it to your friends and family. This amounts to a lot of re-tellings. How might you phrase each one? What words might you choose? Why? Are you more specific with certain details to the police than with your friends? Do you focus on different elements of the story depending on whom you tell it to? Why? What are they? What elements are consistent across all the tellings?

Different ways of telling

To address some of the questions from Activity 9.1 we offer a sample 'telling'.

Let's say the first telling of your story is to the police emergency number and it goes like this (turns are numbered for reference).

1 Call-taker: Police, what's the emergency?
2 Witness: Hi, I've just seen a man push over an old lady and steal her bag.
3 Call-taker: Okay, is the lady hurt?
4 Witness: I don't think she's badly hurt but I'm not sure.
5 Call-taker: Okay, what's your location?
6 Witness: I'm at the junction of Anytown Road and Sometown Way, beside the town hall at the traffic lights
7 Call-taker: Right, I'm sending someone now, they should be with you in around 6 minutes. Is the attacker still on the scene?
8 Witness: No he ran off down Anytown Road with the bag.
9 Call-taker: Okay, thank you, an officer should be with you very soon.

You have just given the first (admittedly brief) 'telling' of the **at-issue event** (a more neutral term for 'crime' at the investigative stage) to the police call-taker. You will give another to police officers in person when they arrive on the scene and, following that, a third telling in your formal witness statement. This third retelling of your story will become evidence for any future prosecution case. It is important to capture this retelling thoroughly, carefully, and in a timely manner (to limit misremembering or gaps in recall) so let's pretend you do it the following day at the police station.

During the interaction between you and the police officer who writes up your statement, you are probed about the colour of the victim's handbag.

After a bit of discussion about it, you conclude, tentatively, that you 'think it might have been red', putting stress on the underlined word to emphasise the lack of certainty. The officer distils this information into the following on your statement:

'I believe the handbag was red'.

This could be interpreted as having a greater commitment to the certainty of the assertion (known as epistemic modality) than your spoken version (the latter contained the modal verbs 'think' and 'might' which have been removed in the officer's version). When the statement is finished, you read over it and sign it to verify its content. Three months later you are asked to be a witness in court for the case as the perpetrator has been caught and charged with theft and assault. In an adversarial court system, your statement is challenged by the perpetrator's legal team who cross-examine you about the bag's colour. You repeat your uncertain stance in the courtroom saying 'I'm not sure what colour it was'. The defence points out this anomaly between 'I am not sure' vs 'I believe'. Yet to you, these phrases amount to the same thing – you don't really remember the colour for certain. There is now doubt over the veracity of your version of events which undermines your evidence. The prosecution case falls apart and our bag-grabbing lady-pushing perpetrator walks free.

What we can learn from this invented case is that you as a witness are, essentially, reduced to your word on that statement. One of the key features of witness statements (and indeed, police reports), is that they are narratives about who or what did what to whom or what. Knowing this information is necessary because to produce a coherent story of a crime (the at-issue event), who is doing what and to whom, needs to be clear and unambiguous. While SPOCA identifies clausal components, transitivity tells us more about what they are doing and their relationship to each other. Let's take our bag-grabbing perpetrator again and show the different constituents and their roles within the story in the second turn of the made-up phone call with the police call-taker.

Hi, I've just seen a man push over an old lady and steal her bag

I [participant]
've just seen [action]
a man [doer]
push [action]
over [circumstance]
an old lady [affected participant]
and steal [action]
her bag [affected entity]

Laying it out like this shows who or what did what to whom or what (the roles performed by each grammatical unit are in square brackets). For instance, the first action reported is one of 'seeing' followed by 'push' and 'steal'. It's clear who the agent of the action of 'push' is ('a man'), and so on. We return to these constituents later as they will define the functional roles outlined in the clauses in our story. These roles will be the focus of the transitivity analysis later.

Activity 9.2 SPOCA spotting

Recall that in Chapter 2 we introduced a SPOCA (Subject, Predicator, Object, Complement, and Adjunct) analysis of the clause. This analysis identifies the clausal function of words and phrases in clauses. Now we want to consider a complementary analysis that identifies what clausal constituents are doing in the reality that the clause renders. This reality can be presented in any number of different ways – for instance, the way the reality is identified (e.g. using nouns and adjectives), the actions performed in that reality (e.g. verbs) and positions in time and space (e.g. prepositions, adverbs). Identify the SPOCA elements of the retelling above in the following sentence.

Hi, I've just seen a man push over an old lady and steal her bag

We give our answer at the end of the chapter

Another way of telling

We now want to introduce another way of telling the same story that obscures some of these story constituents/roles (we have numbered the sentences for reference). What kinds of questions might this new version generate? What roles are missing? How does this compare with your version in Activity 9.1?

> (1) On my way home there was a robbery. (2) An elderly woman's bag was stolen and she was pushed over. (3) I called the cops.

Nominalisation

You may have noticed that our bag-grabbing lady-pusher is missing from this version. His role has been backgrounded linguistically through a process called **nominalisation** that is, turning an action into a thing, i.e. 'robbed' (a verb) becomes a noun, 'robbery'. Consequently, the text producer presents the doing as something that 'is' – it simply exists. A good place to find nominalisations is in journalistic discourse, where the convention is to anchor news stories on headlines that encapsulate an action or series of actions into a single noun phrase. For example, read the following BBC news headline (28 December 2022).

> Murder arrests over Birmingham nightclub stabbing
>
> (BBC News 2022)

The act of murdering appears here as a modifier 'murder' for 'arrests' which is a noun derived from a verb 'to arrest'. The stabbing of a young man is presented here as a noun (a gerund – see Chapter 2), 'stabbing'. Such grammatical conversions may be due to discourse constraints on headline text – often, the body copy that follows makes the agency more explicit (e.g. "Two men have been arrested on suspicion of murdering a man who was stabbed to death on a nightclub dancefloor in Birmingham", BBC News 2022).

As well as the generic constraints and conventions of news stories, police officers often use nominalisations as a way of distancing themselves from reported or unverified actions. This could be a conscious attempt to present a neutral institutional stance. For example, compare the use of the verb form 'allege' in 'Victim *alleges* that suspect did X' against its nominalised counterpart 'There was an *allegation* of X'. In the former, the victim is the source of 'allege' which may imply that they are not believed or there is a lack of evidence from the victim, whereas no agent can be derived from the nominalised form 'allegation' and so no overt stance is taken towards the victim. Police also use nominalisations in the categorization of crimes. For example, an act of violence committed by someone towards another person is categorised as an 'assault' (Calligan 2000) and by doing so, the implicit grammatical transitive structure of 'X assaulted Y' is packaged neatly into a noun 'assault' which obscures not only the perpetrator of the 'assault' but also the victim as Figure 9.1 shows.

Depending on the context, nominalising actions can have the effect of 'glossing over' or eliding who did what to whom for ideological reasons as we later show.

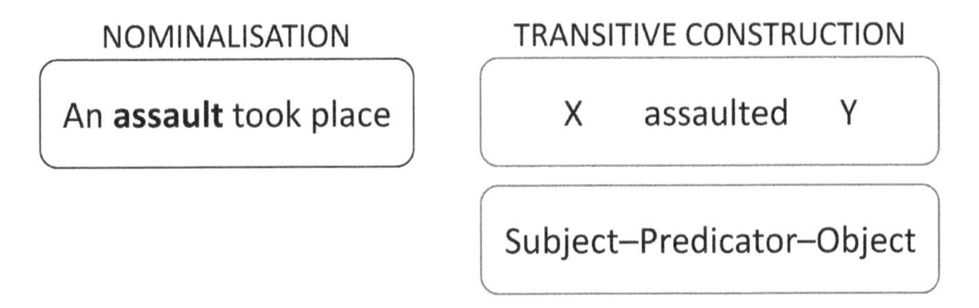

Figure 9.1 Nominalisation vs clause

Passives

Let's return to the last retelling of our robbery story. Here it is again for reference:

> (1) On my way home there was a robbery. (2) An elderly woman's bag was stolen and she was pushed over. (3) I called the cops.

In the first sentence the 'action' (stealing the bag) has been rendered as a noun, 'robbery', doing away with both agent and affected entity. In the second sentence, which contains two coordinated clauses, the victim's bag, and then the victim ('she') are made the Theme (see Chapter 2) so the reader's focus is steered towards the affected person upon whom the action was performed and not the doer who performed the action. This can be seen in Figure 9.2.

Figure 9.2 Passive constructions

Although the actions themselves are documented ('was stolen', 'was pushed over') we are left asking 'by whom'? This version lacks agency and these omissions must be inferred from the passive constructions – in other words, we know that someone did the robbing and the pushing. Language offers many ways of rendering real world (and fictional) experiences.

There are different types of actions (e.g. physical, mental, being) and the way we present these actions can change how we conceptualise the roles therein, or even the whole story. The transitivity framework offers a very serviceable model for delineating these relationships between roles, specifically agency, actions, and circumstances, and makes patterns across these elements explicit. In high-stakes discourse contexts like policing and prosecuting crimes, such elements comprise evidence and so are relied upon in making sense of – and adjudicating on – who did what to whom.

The transitivity model

Transitivity as a framework for text analysis emerged in the 1970s with Margaret Berry's model (1975) and later developed by Halliday (1994) and Halliday and Matthiessen (2014), among others (see Simpson 1993, 2014, for example). The model is based on the grammatical distinction between transitive and intransitive functions of verbs. That means, rather basically, some verbs can take a grammatical Object (transitive), and some verbs cannot (intransitive) or they can be used transitively and intransitively. Examples of verbs that can be used transitively are 'ate', 'took', 'hit', 'climbed', and 'forgotten'. All these are transitive when they accept a grammatical object (O), as the examples in Figure 9.3 show.

Verbs that are unable to take a direct Object or that do not require one are 'intransitive' and so the actions they encode are not executable on another entity. Examples of verbs used intransitively are 'fell' (as in Figure 9.3) 'laughed' ('they laughed a lot'), and 'came' ('She came back early').

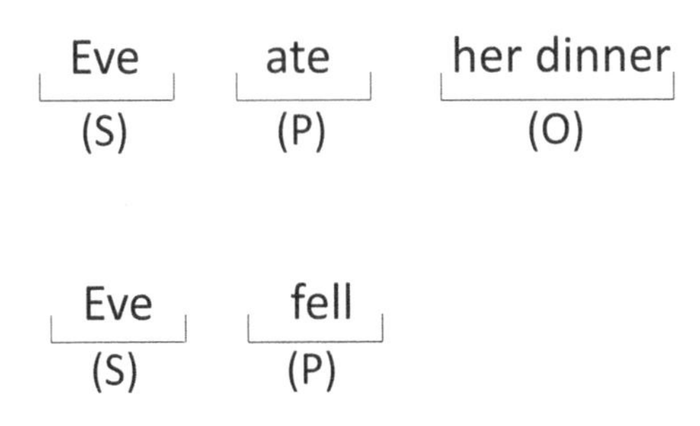

Figure 9.3 Transitive and intransitive verbs

Representing 'inner' and 'outer' experience

The model of transitivity focuses on the clause as a primary unit of analysis (Berry 1975; Halliday and Matthiessen 2014) because it is at this level that goings-on are most basically represented. In clauses, the predicator encodes whatever type of action is taking place, has taken place, or will take place. Therefore, the verb is the central concept in transitivity and is known in the framework as the **process**. There are many kinds of processes that go on in the world. Some processes are considered **outer experiences** because they take place in the world around us, and others are **inner experiences** as they occur in the realm of consciousness or in the person. The other clausal constituents include **participants** who either do or are affected by the action of the verb, and **circumstances** that convey the scope of the goings-on (usually through adverbial or adjective phrases). Processes and their relationships to the other elements of the clause are outlined in the following sections.

Material processes

Material processes are defined by Halliday and Matthiessen as process by which "a quantum of change in the flow of events" results from some "input of energy" (2014: 224). Not very helpful, but in effect, their point is that Material processes capture physical actions that cause change. Mary Ellen Ryder developed this idea further by introducing "parameters" that define "prototypical events" so that the action of Material processes is not limited to causing "change" but also covers "maintaining" a particular state (Ryder 2008). In short, Material processes encode actions or maintain actions that take place in the outer world.

With Material processes, there are two participant roles: the 'doer' of the process and the affected entity. The participant who carries out the process (the 'doer') is referred to as 'Actor', and the affected entity is termed the 'Goal'. In the examples shown in Table 9.1, Actor and Goal roles are filled by 'the perpetrator' and 'the elderly woman' respectively.

Table 9.1 The different Material Processes

Material Process Type				
i	*Material-Intention*	The perpetrator *[Actor]*	robbed	the elderly woman's bag *[Goal]*
ii	*Material-Event*	The crime *[Actor]*	robbed	the elderly woman [of her bag] *[Goal]*
iii	*Material-Supervention*	The elderly woman *[Actor]*	fell	

Material processes can be enacted by human participants ('the perpetrator' in example (i) in Table 9.1). This subtype is known as 'Material-Intention' processes. But there are also options for having non-human entities do the 'acting'. An example is '*the wind* knocked over the bins', where 'the wind' is responsible for the doing, yet is inanimate. In (ii), the Actor is an inanimate participant (specifically it's a noun that has been derived from a verb) which has the effect of distancing the *person* who commits the crime from the act they commit. In such cases of inanimate Actors, the Material process is known more specifically as a 'Material-Event' process. In (iii), the 'elderly woman' is still the affected entity in the little pastiche, but now the process is an involuntary one. This type of Material process is known as 'Material-Supervention'. In other words, the Actor (the elderly woman) is presented as having acted unintentionally, 'fell', without the influence of an external agent. Notice how she is not grammatically positioned as the Goal element in this configuration.

Circumstances

Another element in the transitivity model relates to information around the process and participants that elaborates on the how, where, and when. This information is captured in the part of the clause known as the Adjunct and is thus a deletable component. In transitivity, this constituent is known as the **Circumstance.** In Table 9.1 above the Circumstance in (ii) is in square brackets. In Table 9.2 below we have adapted our examples from Table 9.1 to account for grammatical mood and include optional elements such as the 'Circumstance' (in grey) that provide orientational information or information about the 'how' of the process.

As you can see, there are different linguistic choices being made in all our examples: the lexis and the grammatical structure of the clauses can influence interpretation, particularly in terms of what is considered salient information (see Chapter 2 on Theme and Rheme). They also show the versatility of language and how the relevant constituents can combine to make roles more or less explicit. In Table 9.2, example (i), agency is explicit as is the case with

Table 9.2 Configurations of Material Processes and their clause constituent elements

	Material Process				Circumstances
i	- *in active voice*	The perpetrator *[Actor]*	robbed	the elderly woman's bag *[Goal]*	after much planning
ii	- *in passive voice*	The elderly woman's bag *[Goal]*	was robbed		after much planning
iii	- *using an intransitive verb*	The elderly woman's bag *[Actor]*	disappeared		in broad daylight

all Actor+Process+Goal constructions, which are conveyed in the active voice. In (ii) agency is obscured as the Actor has been excised through the use of the passive voice but can be added if the text producer desires (note that all optional elements are in grey type). In (iii) an intransitive verb form is used (note that, grammatically, you cannot typically 'disappear' something, so the verb cannot conventionally take an Object). The effect of this choice means no external agent is suspected.

Clause elements that are not compulsory, such as the Circumstances, are in grey type. This basically means that text producers can choose to give this information rather than being compelled to do so by grammatical necessity. We can then examine the potential ideological effects of providing the Circumstances in such cases. In Table 9.2 (i) and (ii), the Circumstances offer additional information about intentionality (i.e. that the process was done 'after much planning'), and so we may look on the act with more contempt than we might do if intentionality was not apparent. In other words, including this information may well steer our appraisal of the action as more negative or unacceptable. This may have a bearing on a jury's decision!

A reasonable question to ask at this point is why we need these processes and participants and new terms for concepts that appear to have grammatical labels already – why not just use good old Subject, Predicator, Object, Complement, and Adjunct (SPOCA)? In answer to that question, consider the differences between the grammatical roles of SPO and the transitivity roles of ACTOR-PROCESS-GOAL in the following identical clauses in Figure 9.4.

In these different permutations, the words that fill the grammatical and transitivity slots are defined by where they fall syntactically. However, the syntactic form of the SPO labels tells us nothing about the *functional relationship* between what fills that slot and the other constituents of the clause (i.e. the Predicator and Object). The transitivity configurations, on the other hand, do tell us about these relationships. You can see this in Figure 9.4 where the 'Goal' in the transitivity roles remains consistent across both active and

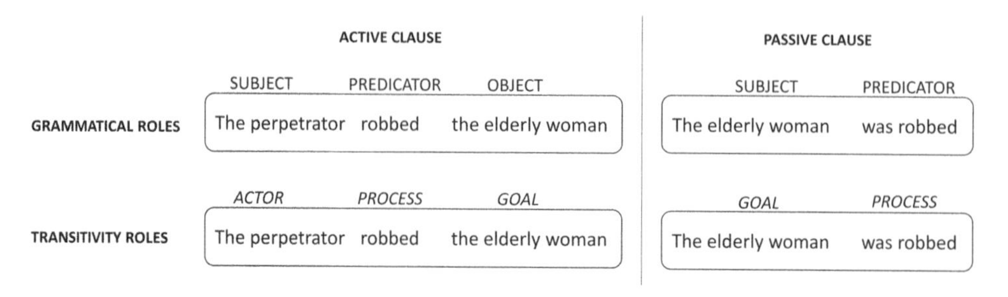

Figure 9.4 Grammatical roles vs Transitivity roles

passive clauses, but yet the role of Subject changes according to whether the clause is active or passive. This means that when we come to analyse a text, we can see more clearly the ideological force or impact of the 'who or what does what to whom' than if we only relied upon an SPO analysis. We take this up later in the chapter.

Mental processes

Mental processes represent 'inner' actions. Halliday acknowledges that different participant roles are required for this type of process. This is because it is not appropriate to assign the (Material) roles of 'Actor' and 'Goal' to entities experiencing a Mental process and the concepts or things mentally experienced as there is no other entity being 'acted' upon. Therefore, the participant roles that better reflect inner experience are known as 'Senser' (the experiencing entity) and the 'Phenomenon' (the thing/concept/feeling experienced). As there are different kinds of Mental experiences, they are subcategorised into three process types, **cognition, reaction,** and **perception.**

(a) Mental processes of *cognition* (e.g. 'think', 'know', 'consider', 'believe')
(b) Mental processes of *reaction* (e.g. 'hate', 'like', 'fear', 'enjoy')
(c) Mental processes of *perception* (e.g. 'see', 'hear', 'taste')

To return to our crime pastiche example, if we were to narrate the story of the robbery, we could conceivably use any of the Mental process types outlined above. We have presented three examples in Table 9.3 below.

Table 9.3 Different formulations of Mental Processes and their constituent elements

	Mental Process				Circumstances
i	*Mental-cognition*	The perpetrator *[Senser]*	devised	a robbery *[Phenomenon]*	after much consideration
ii	*Mental-reaction*	The elderly woman *[Senser]*	felt	threatened *[Phenomenon]*	during her evening walk
iii	*Mental-perception*	The elderly woman *[Senser]*	heard	his approach *[Phenomenon]*	from the left

Clauses (i), (ii), and (iii) are presented here in the active voice, so it is clear who is the Senser and what is being 'sensed'.[1] Unlike Material processes, many Mental processes are unverifiable in that they are experienced in the consciousness of the Senser and so cannot be evidenced easily. In fact, as they are subjective, their role in evidence statements is likely to be infrequent and marked.

Representing states of 'being' and 'having': Existential and Relational Processes

While it is likely that material actions of doing and mental actions of sensing are prototypical 'goings-on', there is another dimension to the experiential realm that we now need to consider. It is the dimension of 'being' and 'having'. Some things are said to simply 'be'; 'Patricia is Irish' is a case in point. Presented as a state of being, the fact of this proposition is taken for granted. We will consider Existential processes first.

Existential processes

Existential processes are those that present happenings as simply existing and often "serve to introduce central participants in the Placement (Setting, Orientation) stage at the beginning of a story" (Halliday and Matthiessen 2014: 308). This is often achieved grammatically by using 'there' as a Subject as in Figure 9.5.

Existential 'there' is often referred to as a 'dummy Subject' which "cannot be queried" (Halliday and Matthiessen 2014: 308). It has the effect of introducing something into a discourse that is accepted unproblematically as existing. We can relate this to our fake crime case. In the clause in Figure 9.5, a 'robbery' is asserted as an existential fact. Nothing is being 'done' explicitly to anyone or anything else. To use the terminology of transitivity, there is only one 'participant', the 'Existent', which in this case is 'a robbery'. Existential processes use a form of the verb 'be', as do many Relational processes, which we now turn to.

DUMMY SUBJECT	PROCESS	EXISTENT
There	was	a robbery

Figure 9.5 Existential process

Relational processes

Relational processes posit a relation between two things. Something is said to 'be' or 'have' something else. The participant roles are 'Carrier' and 'Attribute';

the 'Carrier' is the entity or thing that carries the 'Attribute'. So, in 'the robbery was awful', the Carrier is the 'robbery', and the Attribute is 'awful'. The difference between Relational processes of being/having and Existential processes of existing is that in an Existential process no relationship is established between the Existent (the 'robbery') and anything else, but in Relational processes there is a relationship established (e.g. 'the robbery **was** awful').

There are three types of Relational processes (summarised in Table 9.4):

a) Relational-*Intensive* processes account for 'being' and so are identifiable through the 'be' verb (as main verb) and its variants (e.g. 'been', 'was', 'is', and so on).[2] An example is 'Patricia *is* Irish' which establishes the relation between Patricia and her Irishness.
b) Relational-*Possessive* processes use a form of 'have' as main verb (e.g. has, had, having, and so on) and express relationships of possession (e.g. 'We *had* a short holiday').
c) Relational-*Circumstantial* processes upgrade Circumstances making them an essential element so that they feature as a 'participant'. You will be able to identify them easily enough because they appear 'Circumstance-y' (in that they are usually Prepositional/Adverbial constructions) but they cannot be deleted from the clause without the clause losing its meaning. An example of a Relational-Circumstantial process is 'The rabbits *are in the hutch*'. Try losing the PP phrase 'in the hutch' and just telling your friend 'The rabbits are'. Nope, we don't make sense of that either – unless of course you're having a René Descartes moment. And we've all had one of those.

Table 9.4 Relational Processes

	Relational Process			
i	*Relational-Intensive*	Patricia *[Carrier]*	is	Irish *[Attribute]*
ii	*Relational-Possessive*	We *[Carrier]*	had	a short holiday *[Attribute]*
iii	*Relational-Circumstantial*	The rabbits *[Carrier]*	are	in the hutch *[Attribute]*

We have said above that the verbs 'be' and 'have' operate in Relational processes as main verbs because we want to note the potential confusion between these and other processes that use these verbs as **auxiliaries**. If we return briefly to Material processes, you'll see that they sometimes present the clausal constituents as passives or as past tense forms, both of which make use of the 'be'/ 'have' verbs as auxiliaries. Here are three examples of Material processes that use the 'be' and 'have' verb as auxiliaries (the corresponding transitivity components are in parentheses).

'We | have walked | as far as we could' (Actor | [auxiliary] Process | Circumstance
'Selma | was walking' (Actor | [auxiliary] Process)
'Buster | was walked | by his owner' (Goal | [auxiliary] Process | Actor)

Therefore, a good test of a Relational process is whether the 'be'/'have' verbs are the main verbs: in 'Selma was walking' the 'was' is marking tense rather than 'being'. If the 'be' verb is followed by a main verb, chances are it's not Relational or Existential.

Verbal Processes

These are processes of 'saying' or more accurately, of producing sound. Many entities, both animate and inanimate, can produce sound. In these processes, there is a participant, namely the Sayer (the entity or thing that produces the sound) and the Verbiage (the sounds that are produced). Some verbs that fall into this category: 'shout', 'said', 'moaned', 'groaned', 'whispered', 'creaked', 'yelped', 'claimed', and so on. The constituents of Verbal processes can be seen in Figure 9.6.

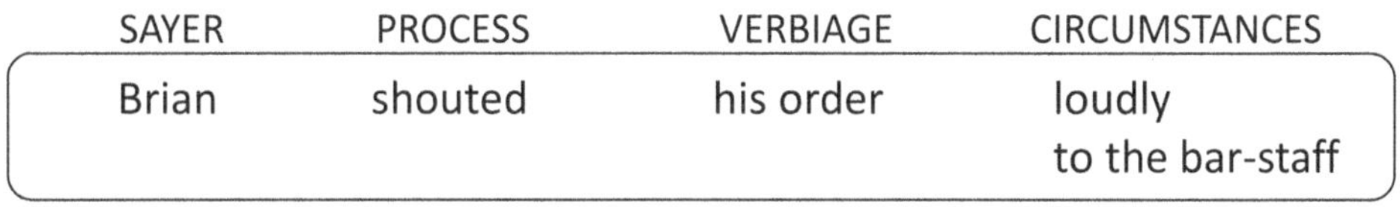

SAYER	PROCESS	VERBIAGE	CIRCUMSTANCES
Brian	shouted	his order	loudly to the bar-staff

Figure 9.6 Verbal process constituents

Table 9.5 summarises the different process types and their constituents.[3]

The discourse situation

Why do we choose to use language like we do? For example, why would we say 'there was a robbery' (an Existential process) as opposed to 'The perpetrator robbed the elderly woman? (a Material process)? Linguistic choices are first and foremost motivated by the discourse situation itself (see for example, Biber and Conrad 2019). For example, you might choose informal, colloquial constructions to tell a friend (e.g. 'He nearly knocked the wind from her!') but more formal language to relate it to a police officer (e.g. 'She was pushed roughly to the ground'). The discourse situation might also determine what you focus on (or omit). For instance, in a judicial setting in which you give your statement to the police, you might foreground different aspects of the story, such as the clothing and build of the suspect, the specific timings, and so on. You may focus less on how you felt (Mental processes) and more objectively

Table 9.5 The transitivity model: Process types and participants

Main Process	Participant roles		Subcategories of main processes	Example clause configurations
Material	*ACTOR*	*GOAL*	**Material-Intention:** contain animate Actors	*Aaron* ***assaulted*** *Brenda*
			Material-Event: contain inanimate Actors	*The chair* ***struck*** *Brenda*
			Material-Supervention: describes involuntary actions	*Brenda* ***fell***
Mental	*SENSER*	*PHENOMENON*	**Mental-Cognition:** e.g. thinking, knowing	*Aaron* ***considered*** *the impact of the assault*
			Mental-Reaction: e.g. hating, liking	*Aaron* ***deplored*** *his violent actions*
			Mental-Perception: e.g. seeing, hearing	*Aaron* ***saw*** *the impact of the assault*
Relational	*CARRIER*	*ATTRIBUTE*	**Relational-Intensive:** e.g. being	*Aaron* ***is*** *an assaulter*
			Relational-Possessive: e.g. having	*Aaron* ***has*** *an assault charge*
			Relational-Circumstantial: e.g. in trouble, over my head	*Aaron* ***was*** *in trouble*
Verbal	*SAYER*	*VERBIAGE*		*Aaron* ***stated*** *he had assaulted Brenda*
Existential		*EXISTENT*		*There* ***was*** *an assault*

on what went on in the 'outer world'. In telling and retelling the same story, a level of variation is expected (Coulthard 2004; Canning 2022, 2023), but it would be reasonable to expect consistency with the key elements – who the participants are and what role(s) they play. But this is not always the case. There are times when obscuring the agency and/or foregrounding (and backgrounding) different clausal components can have particular effects. Applying the framework of transitivity can help us understand how the ways in which text producers choose to present participants and their actions (or not) can prime the reader's judgement. This can have devastating consequences in a high-stakes forensic environment. The next section outlines a case study involving the crime of domestic violence and analyses the police report of the case as it is prepared for prosecutors.

Case study: a case of domestic violence

The following sections relate to information reported in a real police case file. The crime under discussion is classified as 'domestic violence' (sometimes used interchangeably with 'domestic abuse'). Domestic Violence (DV) is defined by the United Nations as "a pattern of behaviour in any relationship that is used to gain or maintain power and control over an intimate partner" (United Nations n.d.). Any abuse inflicted on a person through DV includes "physical, sexual, emotional, economic or psychological actions or threats of actions that influence another person" (United Nations n.d.). In the UK, there is a disproportionately high rate of non-conviction in DV cases with relatively few prosecutions; between March 2019 and March 2020 in England and Wales (excluding Greater Manchester), there were 1,288,018 police-recorded incidents of domestic violence (DV), yet only 61,169 prosecutions (ONS 2020).

In the UK, when police respond to a callout regarding DV, or any report of a crime, there are a number of options at their disposal in dealing with it. They can take administrative action (essentially, do nothing further other than log it), or they can take formal action. In the latter, they can formally interview the suspect if circumstances necessitate it, they can take a witness statement if the witness feels able to give one, and after these documents have been secured they will then file what is called in England and Wales a 'Manual of Guidance' report (MG3) that goes to the Crown Prosecution Service (CPS). The CPS decides whether there is enough evidence to secure a conviction and therefore send the case to court, or whether to 'dispose' of the case in other ways, for example, with a 'simple caution'. Figure 9.7 below (Lynn and Canning 2021) shows the process step by step and accounts for the differing discourse settings within this process.

The culmination of the investigative work of the officer in the case (OIC) is the Manual of Guidance report (MG3) in which the OIC reiterates the 'gist' of the crime using whatever texts have been generated thus far from the witness

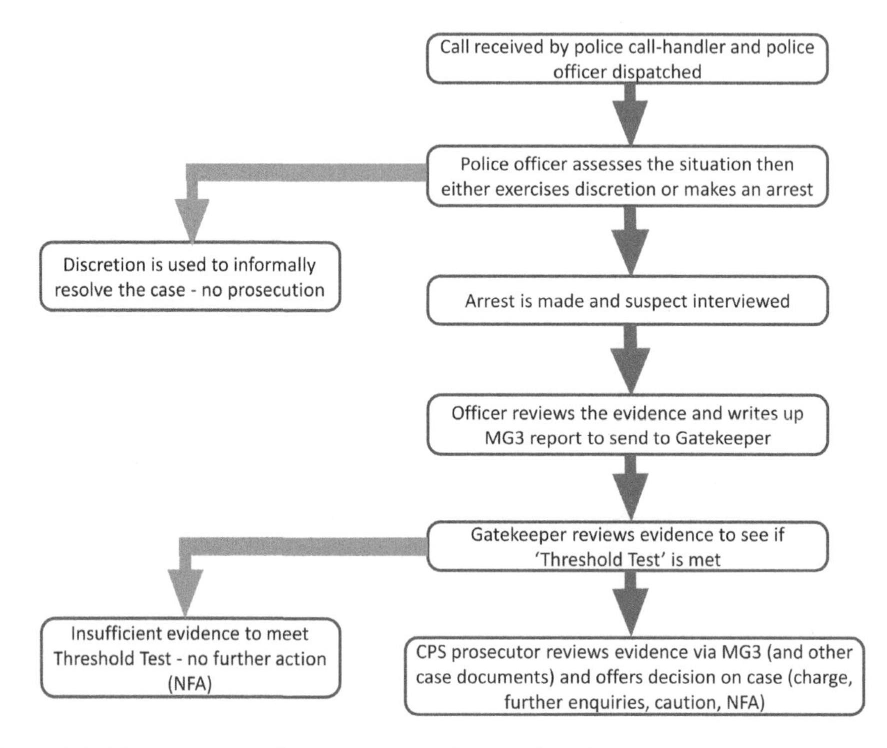

Figure 9.7 The trajectory of a DV case (England and Wales) (Lynn and Canning 2021)

statements, the officer's own notes, and/or the suspect's interview. The MG3 is therefore, by definition, a reformulation of the various (and sometimes clashing) stories that document the crime. In creating this 'gist' the officer can employ many linguistic strategies when making a case for prosecution. For example, they might choose to foreground the victim's injuries and/or the suspect's previous criminal history (if applicable), or to amplify the actions of the suspect by including attitudinal elements in the telling. Conversely, the officer can employ different strategies to not make a case for prosecution, but rather, to dispose of the case by recommending, implicitly or explicitly, a 'simple caution', which is effectively a formal warning. Some ways of doing this could be to obfuscate the action of the crime, to background the victim, background the suspect, or foreground the remorseful state of the suspect. In other words, the officer has the power to steer the case in a particular judicial direction. It is likely, then, that the discursive construction of the police documents can influence the rate of escalation of these cases and ultimately the rate of prosecution. Given the current statistics on the rate of DV convictions in the UK for 2020 was around 6.4 per cent (ONS 2020), examination of this particular type of discourse is crucial and may shed some light on why the conviction rate is so low.

For our analysis, we were fortunate to have rare access to this chain of forensic reporting for a DV case including the OIC's account of the victim's testimony, the full text of the OIC's reformulation of the at-issue event on the MG3 form together with the Gatekeeper's commentary. The case was part of a monthly case load collected from Devon and Cornwall police force in 2010 (Lea and Lynn 2012) as part of an internal investigation into the disparity between regional outcomes of DV cases. We present the case below and ask you to think whether the suspect was convicted.

Activity 9.3 A case of domestic violence (male perpetrator, female victim)

Questions to consider

Do you think the suspect got convicted?
If not, why not? Try to give reasons for your answer.

The case

The case concerns an incident of domestic violence. A male suspect threw a computer at a female, his wife, hitting her on the leg with it. The female victim contacted the police to report the assault and the police attended at their shared home following the callout. When interviewed, the suspect did not deny throwing the computer at his wife.

To convict or not to convict?

Let's think about what we would need to know to work out if the case in Activity 9.3 is likely to result in a conviction. First, we need to understand what the crime actually is. As the charge is 'common assault', we can start with the definition of that in the Criminal Justice Act:

> Any act, which intentionally or recklessly, causes another person to apprehend immediate and unlawful personal violence.
>
> (CJA 1988: Section 39)

In prosecuting a perpetrator for common assault there are a few criteria that must be met in order to meet the evidence threshold. These are known in policing as "points to prove" (Calligan 2000), and for common assault, these are that the perpetrator "unlawfully" and "intentionally" "assaulted another person" (Police National Legal Database 2019: 49 2.1.1). In other words, a clear understanding that the perpetrator did act upon someone in a particular way is needed. Therefore, thinking about our case, the fact that the male suspect threw a computer at the victim while behaving aggressively would suggest that there was enough evidence to secure a conviction or at least escalate the case to court. Let's now see how the transitivity model introduced above sheds light on who does what to whom in a police report, and whether (and how) the report captures – and accurately reflects – the points to prove.

The text below comes from the case that we paraphrased in Activity 9.3. It is an anonymised account of a real DV crime and it was written by the 'officer in the case' (OIC). The witness signed it to verify that she had given the account (the witness did not make a formal statement).

> she said that she had gone into the male's [her husband's] bedroom to see what he was doing and he became aggressive and threw the computer equipment at her. This included a keyboard which had struck the female on the top of her leg.
>
> (OIC notebook)

Analysing the initial crime report

Let's first look at the Material processes presented in the text above, including Actors, Processes, Participants, and Circumstances. These are summarised in Table 9.6.

As can be seen in Table 9.6, there are three Actors: 'she', 'he', and 'a keyboard'. The first Actor is the victim, who is presented as an Actor in a Material process, 'had gone'. There is no Goal affected by her actions. In (ii), the perpetrator is the Actor, but the Goal of the process is not the victim, but 'computer equipment'. In other words, the suspect acts upon an inanimate object. The victim is backgrounded by being placed in a prepositional phrase ('*at* her') and is therefore presented as being a (deletable) Circumstance. The victim is not presented as someone affected by the actions of the perpetrator, but rather as an orientational marker (the trajectory of the throwing). The third Actor is the computer 'keyboard', which is rendered as the entity that performs the assault as it is presented as striking the victim's leg. This presents that action as a Material-Event process. Aside from the Material process 'threw', the only other process in which the suspect engages is a Relational one of 'being' ('he became aggressive'). He is the **Carrier** ('he') of the **Attribute** 'aggressive'. What we can see from the analysis is that the perpetrator – the person accused of doing something – actually did nothing to anyone. The entire report is mediated

Table 9.6 The OIC's account of the witness's story

	Actor	Process	Goal	Circumstance
i	she	had gone *[Material-Intention]*		into the male's bedroom
ii	he	threw *[Material-Intention]*	the computer equipment	at her
iii	a keyboard	struck *[Material-Event]*	the female	on the top of her leg

through a Verbal process of 'said' which presents the information as reported rather than experienced directly by him. By reporting second-hand information the OIC can: 1) neutralise his stance thus presenting himself as impartial; and 2) distance himself from the truth of the reported content without going on record to express doubt (the academic term for this is 'epistemic distance'). In this way, if he is challenged, or if the story is told differently at a later date, the officer can resolve any anomalies by pointing out that he merely wrote what was reported to him.

Analysing the summary report (MG3) of the domestic violence crime

After the officer interviews the suspect (we do not have access to this interview) he achieves a fuller picture of the case. He writes up his summary of the report, the MG3 form (see Figure 9.7 above). This is what the OIC writes ('DP' is 'detained person'):

> She stated her husband (the DP) had thrown a computer keyboard at her which had struck her on the thigh causing injury. He states she came up and he was perhaps a little agitated as he was tired and swung the computer around catching her on the leg.
>
> (MG3 form)

The entire case has now been reduced to two versions of one particular event. If we consider only the Material processes, outlined below in Table 9.7, we can see how the relationships between Actor, Process, and Goal become more abstract as we go down the table.

In any report of a crime, one would reasonably expect Material processes to predominate (it is, after all, a report of 'doing'). Undoubtedly, this report

Table 9.7 Material Processes in the OIC's reformulation of the at-issue event

	Actor	Process	Goal	Circumstance
1	her husband	had thrown *[Material-Intention]*	a computer keyboard	at her
2	[a computer keyboard]	had struck *[Material-Event]*	her	on the thigh
3	She	came *[Material-Intention]*		up
4	[he]	swung *[Material-Intention]*	the computer	around
5	[the computer]	catching *[Material-Event]*	her	on the leg

contains 'doing'. However, what is interesting about these Material processes is who or what fulfils the 'Actor' and 'Goal' roles. The perpetrator is the explicit Actor in only one Material process (of 'throwing') (1) and implicitly in another ('swung') (4). In (1) which is mediated through the victim's perspective, the 'Goal' is the keyboard, not the female victim. She is relegated to the Circumstance ('at her') which maintains the original text as entered into the OIC's notebook. The second Material process ('swung') (4) affects an inanimate 'Goal' ('the computer'). Again, the perpetrator does not act on the victim. The perpetrator can be perceived to have acted intentionally in 'swinging' the computer. However, this choice of a Goal-less process removes culpability; in other words, he cannot be considered to have 'intentionally' struck the victim as he merely swung the keyboard 'around'. The actual assault is presented in (5) through the Material processes 'catching [her on the leg]' and (2) 'struck'. If we consider who carried out these actions, we can see that they are executed by non-human Actors – thus, both are Material-Event processes.

Let's shift our attention now to the Goal element as this captures the entity affected by the actions of the Process. In Table 9.7, there are only two clauses where the female is the affected entity or 'Goal'. In both, the Actor acting upon her is inanimate, 'a computer keyboard' (2) and 'the computer' (5). As stated, in (5) the use of 'catch' implies accidental and thus unintentional contact (contrast with 'struck' in the original). In summary, the OIC presents the victim as the affected entity on two occasions where she has been acted upon, both times by an inanimate object. The perpetrator never does anything to her – when he acts, he does so only upon an inanimate object. In this report, computer keyboards and computers act and go on to cause harm to the victim.

Relational processes in the MG3 account of the crime

It is also worth looking at the Relational processes in the text. Table 9.8 below outlines them.

Relational processes tend to convey states of 'being' or 'having' through the participant roles of 'Carrier' and their relation to an 'Attribute'. Often such attributes are beyond the control of the Carrier. For example, in 'Patricia is Irish' then Irishness is a quality or Attribute that Patricia inherently holds and there is not much agency around the having or not having that Attribute. Of course, that

Table 9.8 Relational processes of 'being' from the OIC's MG3 form

	Carrier	Process	Circumstance	Attribute
6	he	was	perhaps a little	agitated
7	[he]	was		tired

is not true of all Attributes, but 'being' something encodes less agency and intentionality than 'doing' something. The clauses 'he was perhaps a little agitated as he was tired' contain Relational processes, namely 'agitated' and 'tired'. The Attributes are hedged with Circumstantial components, too, 'perhaps' and 'a little' which softens or mitigates the Attribute (see Chapter 7 for discussion of 'hedging'). These clauses precede the action of swinging the computer 'around'. Using these Relational processes to frame the violence can lead to the implicature (see Chapter 6) that the perpetrator's actions were compounded – and even excused – by his tired and agitated state.

Analysing the Gatekeeper's contribution to the case

Finally, the last link in the chain of policing the crime (pre-outcome) is the contribution by the 'Gatekeeper' who reviews the OIC's account before it goes to the Crown Prosecution Service for a charging decision. The Gatekeeper in this case added his contribution to the OIC's account of the crime as follows.

> In interview D/P [detained person] admits that he was tired and agitated and was trying to sleep. An argument develops between himself and his wife resulting in him picking up the computer and swinging it towards his wife. He is suitable for diversion by way of a caution. He has no previous cautions or convictions. PND [Penalty Notice] not possible for a potential domestic.
>
> (Gatekeeper's input to MG3 form)

An interesting feature of this account is its organisation or structure. The full account leads with a Verbal process 'admit', which presents the suspect as playing a facilitative role in the investigation. It's important to point out that an admission of the offence is a necessary precondition for a 'simple caution' (non-prosecutorial and thus non-conviction) outcome. However, what the suspect is 'admitting' to is not the assault, but the Relational processes of being 'tired and agitated'. Notice how the Attributes 'tired' and 'agitated' have greater epistemic certainty in the Gatekeeper's version than in the hedged OIC version. By leading with the Relational processes, the Gatekeeper frames the internal state of the suspect as the lens through which to read his criminal actions. In effect, by making this the Gatekeeper's point of departure it primes the reader to empathise with the suspect. Table 9.9 shows these clausal configurations.

The Relational-Attributive process in (10) 'has no previous cautions or convictions' is used to support the recommendation that the perpetrator should receive a Caution which would dispose of the case in a way that means the suspect does not end up with a criminal record. This recommendation is presented through a Relational process of 'being' ('is suitable') in (Table 9.9), implying that he meets the criteria well.

Table 9.10 presents the Material processes in the Gatekeeper's contribution.

Table 9.9 Relational processes from the gatekeeper's input on the OIC's MG3 report

	Carrier	Process	Attribute	Circumstance
8	he	was	tired and agitated and trying to sleep	perhaps; a little
9	[he]	is	suitable	for diversion by way of a caution
10	He	has	no previous cautions or convictions	
11	PND	[is]	not possible	for a potential domestic

The Gatekeeper backgrounds the victim by relegating her to Circumstantial constituents, 'towards his wife' (Table 9.10). The Gatekeeper then presents the 'argument' as an Actor in a Material-Event process, 'An argument develops'. The DV incident is presented as a direct result ('resulting in') of this 'argument'. None of the preceding texts in this case refer to an 'argument' (noun) or 'argue' (verb), so this **nominalisation** is the first appearance of the term. Taken together, the nominalised 'argument' mitigates the suspect's role in the crime because it doesn't name him as agent and it divides responsibility. This is different from the victim's account in the OIC's notebook in which she is presented as going into his room 'to see what he was doing', which is not the same phenomenon at all as 'an argument'! Framing the assault as preceded by an 'argument' could be read as an attempt to justify the violence through provocation. And we have already encountered an 'excuse' that appears to justify the DV incident in the OIC report ('he was perhaps a little agitated as he was tired'), so the 'argument' frame certainly gives more credence to a narrative that positions the suspect as retaliating to provocation. In terms of what the suspect actually does in the Gatekeeper's text, there are only two Material processes that he engages in, 'picking up' (13) and 'swinging' (14). These two processes do not affect any other human entity. Indeed, there is no reported outcome of the 'swinging' of the computer. The only information offered is its trajectory 'towards his wife',

Table 9.10 Material processes in the gatekeeper's review of the OIC's MG3 report

	Actor	Process	Goal	Circumstance
12	An argument	develops *[Material-Event]*		between himself and his wife
13	him	picking up *[Material-Intention]*	the computer	
14	[him]	swinging *[Material-Intention]*	it [the computer]	towards his wife

another Circumstantial component (14). The object is not presented as having made contact with her in any way. In summary, the Gatekeeper's reformulation not only strikes the act (of common assault) from the formal record but presents the suspect as acting only on a computer. No human participants are affected in any way in this retelling. Unsurprisingly, the case was disposed of out of court with a simple caution.

Conclusion

This chapter has introduced transitivity as a serviceable framework for analysing agency in discourse. Using police crime reports, it shows how discursive constructions of victims and perpetrators can predispose decision makers to out-of-court options by what they choose to report and what they choose not to report in formal crime records. It also shows the utility of transitivity in judicial discourses because it can help identify patterns of reporting that can have very real consequences in the pursuit of justice. A more detailed analysis could determine whether or not such linguistic choices are systemic (i.e. institutional-wide), and whether there is consistency in the presentation of specific roles (e.g. Actor/Goal) or specific transitivity configurations (e.g. Material-Intention vs Material-Supervention; Material vs Relational) that could help explain why some of the many dismissed or early disposed of cases do not proceed through the criminal justice system. The chapter also shows how transitivity can be usefully employed alongside analyses of implicated meanings (see Chapter 6). The following chapter develops Verbal processes by examining how self and others' speech and thought is presented in discourse.

Further reading

A transitivity analysis can elucidate patterns of experience and ideas in a range of discourse contexts. For an accessible introduction, see Bloor and Bloor (2013). One clear example that pre-dates the analysis in this chapter, and which offers a good introduction to the model is Kate Clark's article (1992) on the transitivity patterns in tabloid press reports of sexual violence. Clark exposed a male-centric ideology that underpinned gender-based discrimination that consistently negatively appraised women and, at the same time, deflected blame from their male attackers. Canning's article (2022) looks at further examples of domestic violence crimes using transitivity as an analytical approach. Beyond forensic discourse, transitivity has been applied in literary fiction to demonstrate limited mind style (Burton 1982; Ji and Shen 2004) but see Halliday (1971). For more on nominalisation, see Fowler et al. (1979); Fowler (1991); and Billig (2008).

Answers to activities

Activity 9.2 SPOCA spotting

Identify the SPOCA elements of the retelling in the following sentence.

Hi, I've just seen a man push over an old lady and steal her bag

I = Subject
've [just] seen; push; steal = Predicator
a man; an old lady; her bag = Object
over = Adjunct.
just = Adjunct

Notes

1 Of course, they could also appear in the passive mood ('a robbery was devised'; 'his approach was heard').
2 We don't understand why they are labelled 'intensive'. We like the term 'inherent' or something even remotely connected to the sentiment of 'being', but we will stick with the terminology commonly used in the transitivity model so as not to confuse the issue.
3 In earlier models of transitivity including Halliday's, there is an additional process, 'Behavioural', which exists between Material and Mental processes. They account for typically involuntary processes that the body produces (such as coughing, sleeping, and so forth), but most can fall within Material-Supervention processes enough to problematise the distinction between Behavioural and Material. In fact, our students have often questioned this category and we agree that it makes the model unnecessarily complex. Therefore, we have omitted Behavioural processes from our discussion in this book.

References

BBC News (2022) 'Cody Fisher: Murder arrests over Birmingham nightclub stabbing'. 28 December 2022. Accessed 13 February 2023. https://www.bbc.com/news/uk-england-64108203

Berry, M. (1975) *An introduction to systemic linguistics*. London: Batsford.

Biber, D. and Conrad, S. (2019) *Register, genre, and style*. Cambridge: Cambridge University Press.

Billig, M. (2008) 'The language of critical discourse analysis: The case of nominalization'. *Discourse & Society*, 19(6): 783–800.

Bloor, T. and Bloor, M. (2013). *The functional analysis of English*. London: Routledge.

Burton, D. (1982) 'Through glass darkly: Through dark glasses'. In R. Carter (ed.), *Language and literature: An introductory reader in stylistics*, pp. 194–214. London: George Allen and Unwin.

Calligan, S. (2000) *Points to prove. East Yorkshire: The new police bookshop* (5th edition). Goole, Yorkshire: New Police Bookshop.

Canning, P. (2022) 'Writing up or writing off crimes of domestic violence: A transitivity analysis'. *Language and Law /Linguagem e Direito*, 8(2): 48–69.

Canning, P. (2023) Forensic stylistics'. In M. Burke (ed.), *The Routledge handbook of stylistics* (2nd edition), pp. 521–541. London: Routledge.

CJA (1988) Criminal Justice Act Section 39. Common Assault. Act of the Parliament of the United Kingdom.

Clark, K. (1992) 'The linguistics of blame: representations of women in the Sun reporting of crimes of sexual violence'. In Michael Toolan (ed.), *Language, text and context: Essays in stylistics*, pp. 208–224. London: Routledge.

Coulthard, M. (2004). 'Author identification, idiolect, and linguistic uniqueness'. *Applied Linguistics*, 25(4): 431–447.

Fowler, R. (1991) *Language in the news*. London: Routledge.

Fowler, R., Hodge, B., Kress, G., and Trew, T. (1979) *Language and social control*. London: Routledge.

Halliday, M. (1971) 'Linguistic function and literary style: An enquiry into the language of William Golding's The Inheritors'. In S. Chatman (ed.), *Literary style: A symposium*, pp. 330–368. Oxford: Oxford University Press. (Reprinted in J. Weber (ed.) (1996) *The stylistics reader*, pp. 56–86. London: Edward Arnold.)

Halliday, M. A. K. (1994) *An introduction to functional grammar* (2nd edition). London: Hodder Arnold.

Halliday, M. A. K. and Matthiessen, C. (2014) *An introduction to functional grammar* (4th edition). London: Routledge.

Ji, Y. and Shen, D. (2004) 'Transitivity and mental transformation: Sheila Watson's the double hook'. *Language and Literature*, 13(4): 335–348.

Lea, S. J. and Lynn, N. (2012) 'Dialogic reverberations: Police, domestic abuse, and the discontinuance of cases'. *Journal of Interpersonal Violence*, 27(5): 3091–3114.

Lynn, N. and Canning, P. (2021) 'Additions, omissions, and transformations in institutional "retellings" of domestic violence'. *Language and Law/ Linguagem e Direito*, 8(1): 76–96.

ONS (2020) 'Domestic abuse prevalence and trends, England and Wales: year ending March 2020'. Office for National Statistics. Accessed 10 May 2021. https://www.ons.gov.uk/peoplepopulationandcommunity/crimeandjustice/articles/domesticabuseprevalenceandtrendsenglandandwales/yearending march2020

Police National Legal Database (2019) Accessed 12 November 2021. https://www.pnld.co.uk (subscription required).

Ryder, M. E. (2008) 'Overhauling transitivity'. Conference paper given at annual conference of the Poetics and Linguistics Association (PALA), University of Sheffield, Sheffield.

Simpson, P. (1993) *Language, ideology, and point of view*. London: Routledge.

Simpson, P. (2014) *Stylistics: A resource book for students* (2nd edition). London: Routledge.

United Nations (n.d.) 'What is domestic abuse?' Accessed 7 July 2023. https://www.un.org/en/coronavirus/what-is-domestic-abuse

10 Presenting other people's speech, writing, and thought

Introduction

Have you noticed that when you are in conversation with other people you sometimes tell your conversational partner what someone else said to you in another conversation? We do this a lot in everyday, naturally occurring conversations. This might include, for example, what someone said to us directly (e.g. in another conversation) or what we have overheard being said (e.g. what was said by someone on the TV or in a podcast). We can also tell our interlocutors what other people have written, for example, in a newspaper column, on Twitter, or in a blog. We even tell people what we thought and what other people are thinking. And we can also talk about what we are going to say to another person in the future ('I'm going to tell her I can't work at the weekend').

Similarly, you may have noticed that in news reports (such as those printed in newspapers, published on websites, or broadcast on TV and radio) we are often told what people have said or written elsewhere. Indeed, news reports are often *about* what other people (such as politicians, scientists, and celebrities) have said or written. Other people's discourse (or bits of it) can create news and, consequently, news report can be full of the presentation of other people's words and sometimes even their thoughts.

The phenomenon we are referring to is known as **Discourse Presentation** (DP) and is where we take words (whether spoken or written) and thoughts from (typically) an earlier discourse (e.g. a spoken conversation, a Twitter feed, a web page) and present them in the ongoing discourse. Discourse Presentation, which is also known as **Speech, Writing, or Thought Presentation** (**SW&TP**), recognises that when we communicate, we often draw on and include other discourses (or bits of them, at least) in our own discourses.

Discourse Presentation occurs in many communicative contexts including, for example, prose fiction, academic writing, police statements and news report. As we will discover in this chapter, when presenting the words (and sometimes thoughts) of others, we have several options. Readers will, no doubt, be familiar with the idea of quoting other people, but there are many other ways in which other people's words can be presented. Our discussion will be based on the framework of DP that was originally formulated by Leech and Short (2007) and later developed in the work of Semino and Short (2004) and Short (2012). We

DOI: 10.4324/9781003351207-10

will also draw on the ideas presented in Thompson (1996) which provides an alternative but complementary discussion of discourse presentation. Our exploration of discourse presentation in this chapter will focus mainly on speech and writing. Many of the examples we use are drawn from a large online corpus of news report (see Chapter 11).

What is discourse presentation?

Prototypically, discourse presentation is the presentation of speech, writing or thought from an anterior (earlier) discourse in a posterior (later) discourse. This definition is illustrated by Figure 10.1, which depicts two conversations (labelled 1 and 2). Conversation 1 happens earlier in time and is the **anterior discourse** situation. In this conversation, Jules says to Ginny "What are you still doing here at this time?" Later, Conversation 2 occurs, known as the **posterior discourse** situation. In this conversation, Ginny tells Aled what Jules said. Discourse presentation therefore involves the content (or some part of it) of an earlier discourse being embedded in a later discourse.

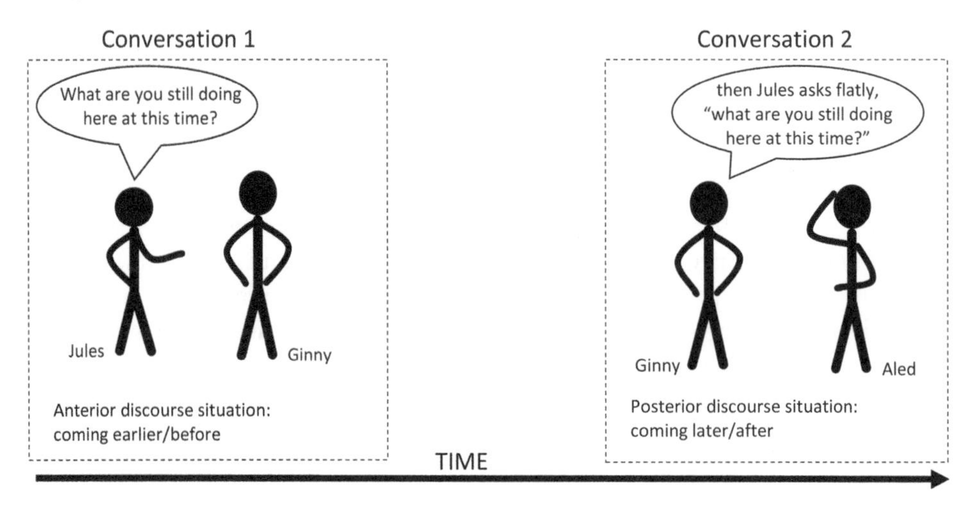

Figure 10.1 The prototypical situation for speech presentation

The example in 10.1 shows just one of a few options open to Ginny for presenting what Jules said. We will discuss the range of options in detail in the next section. The example, which uses what is known as direct speech, exemplifies the different possible elements of discourse presentation (see Thompson 1996: 507). First, there are words that introduce or 'signal' (Thompson 1996) the discourse presentation, and then there are words that reproduce or indicate the content of the original, anterior, discourse. Within the signal, there is language that points to the source of the original discourse ('Jules'), and there is an indication of the speech act performed (see Chapter 4) by the original discourse ('asking'). Finally, there is language that takes an evaluative stance or 'attitude' (Thompson 1996) towards the content of the original discourse, and/or the manner of production, and/or the source ('flatly'). These elements are summarised in Figure 10.2.

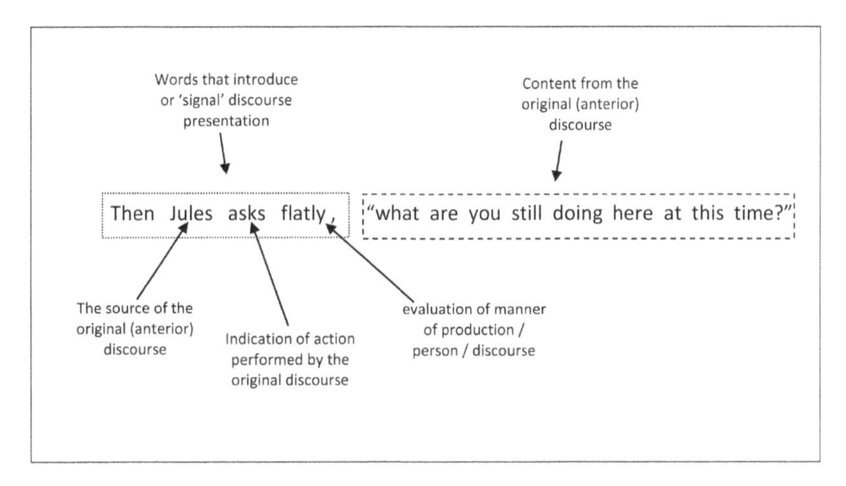

Figure 10.2 Elements of discourse presentation

Following Thompson (1996), when analysing discourse presentation in a text we can use these elements to ask a series of questions about the presentation, as set out below.

1) What language is used to indicate ('signal') the presence of another discourse?
2) What content of the original discourse is presented and how is it presented?
3) What source is attributed to the discourse being presented?
4) Does the language used to present the anterior discourse suggest:

   a. the speech/writing/thought act that was performed by the original discourse; and/or
   b. the manner of production of the original; and/or
   c. the emotive state of the original source.

   If so, how is it/are they indicated?
5) Does the language used to present the anterior discourse suggest that the presenter is taking an evaluative stance ('attitude') toward the original content and/or the source?

The first two questions are about identifying the linguistic forms that indicate discourse presentation is occurring in the text under analysis and, importantly, what content (words and/or ideas) comes from the anterior discourse. Answering these two questions can be tricky and is the crux of the analytical framework we will describe below. The third question deals with whether the source of the original is identified, which can be important when thinking critically about the use of Discourse Presentation to, for example, support claims or arguments (we return to attribution later in the chapter). The fourth and fifth questions deal with the language choices made by the person presenting the original discourse and how these can encode an evaluative attitude toward the content of the discourse and the producer. The language choices relate to how the original discourse is 'signalled', and typically involves verbs and adverbs (but, as we will see in subsequent sections, other forms are possible).

The **speech/writing/thought act** is what the producer of the original discourse is doing with their discourse (e.g. asking a question). The label applied to the act is a matter of interpretation and the choice of the person presenting the discourse. As we saw in Chapter 6, questions (interrogatives) do not always seek information; they can function, for example, as requests for action. The labelling of the speech/writing/thought act therefore depends partly on the structure of the original (e.g. declarative, interrogative, imperative), and the illocutionary force (see Chapter 4). In our example, Ginny chose the verb 'asks' which neutrally labels the interrogative form of original discourse. However, instead of using 'asks', Ginny could have chosen 'demands', which evaluates Jules as having a particular **attitude**: perhaps overbearing and/or assuming discursive power at that point in the conversation. This might lead the hearer to view Jules negatively. As well as attitude towards the person who produced the original discourse, verb choice can express an attitude towards the content of the original discourse (see Thompson 1996: 521–522). For example, the reporting verb 'claim' tends to suggest that the person presenting the discourse is dubious about or is less committed to the propositions contained in the content of the original.

The **manner of production** relates to prosodic features (e.g. loudness, voice quality, speed of production) and is again down to the presenter to decide upon and label using the reporting verb (e.g. 'shouted') and/or a supporting adverb (e.g. 'loudly'). Depending on the choice of verb or adverb, the manner of production can suggest emotive states.

Emotive states can be described by the choice of reporting verb ('sneered') and/or adverb (e.g. 'angrily'). In our made-up example, 'flatly' evaluates the way the words were said and suggests that Jules was either lacking in emotion or being firm. This evaluation is supplied by Ginny, the person presenting the anterior discourse; Jules did not say 'I ask you flatly . . .'. The choice of adverb therefore suggests Ginny's impression of Jules's attitude. It also invites the hearer to share in that evaluation.

As we have seen above, the choice of words used to label the act performed, the manner of production and emotive states can suggest the **attitude** of the original speaker/writer/thinker, and that the presenter is taking an attitude toward the original content and/or the source.

In the following sections, we will consider the elements set out above as we describe the different types of discourse presentation. Readers may wish to refer to these questions as they read on.

Discourse presentation and different voices

For Thompson (1996: 506) discourse presentation is "signalled voices in the text" which includes "any stretch of language where the speaker or writer signals in some way that another voice is entering the text". This definition highlights the idea that the presentation of speech, writing and thought brings other voices into a discourse, and that the different voices are signalled so that the hearer/reader recognises them as belonging to someone (or something) else (although, as we will see, the free indirect categories in the model make other voices difficult to spot). Fairclough (2003: 41) points out that different voices bring with them different points of view and perspectives on the world including, for example, different ideas and opinions (as we saw in Chapter 9).[1] They can introduce information, knowledge, evidence, and arguments to help develop a line of discussion or persuade an interlocutor of the validity of whatever is being reported. Moreover, as we saw in the previous chapter, the inclusion of other voices can also help to preserve impartiality or neutrality towards what is reported. In the following sections, we will explore the notion of different voices in discourses using mainly examples from news report. We will start by describing in more detail the different options for discourse presentation to provide the necessary tools for identifying the presentation of others' discourse.

Report, representation, and presentation

In the version of the framework described in this chapter, the term 'presentation' is used in the category names in preference to 'report' and 'representation', which are both terms that have been used, sometimes interchangeably, in earlier versions of the framework (e.g. Short 1996; Leech and Short 2007). However, Short et al. (2002) and Short (2012: 19) make a distinction between these terms:

- discourse **report** assumes "a match between the lexis, deixis and grammar in the anterior and posterior discourses", when the direct forms are used;
- discourse **representation** "assumes a mismatch";
- discourse **presentation** refers only to the forms used in the posterior discourse and does not necessarily link back to an original, anterior discourse.

To reflect this distinction, in later versions of the framework, the term 'discourse presentation' is used in preference to discourse 'report' or 'representation' (see Short et al. 2002: 336; Short 2012). The advantages of using the term 'presentation' include:

1) it does not make any assumptions about a match or mismatch between what is presented and the original (anterior) discourse. Where there is an anterior discourse that is accessible and available for scrutiny, the discourse analyst can assess whether the discourse presentation in the posterior discourse is representation or report;

2) it makes no prior assumptions about the existence of an anterior discourse, which is the case with hypothetical discourse and that predicted to happen in the future. Also, in fiction there is no anterior discourse because it is all made up.

Therefore, in the model we describe in this chapter, rather than 'R' (for 'representation' or 'report'), which is used with earlier publications, we use 'P' (for 'presentation').

Different types of discourse presentation

There are various ways of presenting other people's words and thoughts from which the person presenting the discourse (the presenter) makes a choice. The choices that are made might be motivated by different reasons, some contextual, others to do with stance and attitude toward the producer of the original (anterior) discourse and/or the discourse itself. In this section, we will describe the different forms discourse presentation can take. The categories we use, which are set out in Table 10.1, are based on those in Short (2012) but with some minor modifications that take into account the work of Thompson (1996).

Table 10.1 shows three parallel clines for speech, writing, and thought that range from direct and (prototypically) faithful rendering of the content of the original (anterior) discourse (e.g. DS), to minimal forms that merely indicate that speech writing or thought occurred (e.g. PS). The direct discourse presentation categories at the top of the table (DS/DW/DT) involve only the supposed original speaker whereas all other categories are a combination, in varying proportions, of the original speaker and the person presenting the discourse.

Table 10.1 Three parallel clines of discourse presentation

Speech presentation		Writing presentation		Thought presentation	
DS	Direct Speech	DW	Direct Writing	DT	Direct Thought
FIS	Free Indirect Speech	FIW	Free Indirect Writing	FIT	Free Indirect Thought
IS	Indirect Speech	IW	Indirect Writing	IT	Indirect Thought
PSA	Presentation of Speech Act	PWA	Presentation of Writing Act	PTA	Presentation of Thought Act
PS	Presentation of Speech	PW	Presentation of Writing	PT	Presentation of Thought

We will start our discussion of the framework by exploring in more detail direct and indirect forms, referring mainly to speech and writing presentation. Each section below will begin with some examples (drawn from various sources), which we will then discuss in terms of their formal attributes and potential effects.

Direct Speech, Writing, and Thought (DS/DW/DT)

(1) "I deeply and bitterly regret that that happened," he [Boris Johnson] said.
(*The Times* and *The Sunday Times* on Twitter, @thetimes. 18/01/2022)

(2) Mr Blair said, "every avenue must be explored".
(*The Report of the Iraq Inquiry* 2016: 37[2])

(3) "The subject offence is extremely serious," she wrote. "At the time of this offence, the accused was on bail in relation to a number of offences."
(ABC Premium News, Sydney, 19/08/2015)

(4) The minibar would not close properly after opening. Never mind, I thought.
(Corpus of London hotel online reviews[3])

(5) "For God's sake," he said, "why did you say that about that girl in Strasbourg for? Didn't you see Frances?"
"No, why should I? If I know an American girl that lives in Strasbourg what the hell is it to Frances?"
"It doesn't make any difference. Any girl. I couldn't go, that would be all."
"Don't be silly."
(*The Sun Also Rises*, Ernest Hemingway, 1926)

Prototypically, direct speech, thought and writing comprises two clauses usually known as a **reporting clause** and the **reported clause**.[4] The reported clause contains the quoted words while the reporting clause signals that someone else's words are being used. Examples (1), (2), and (3) demonstrate that the reporting clause can follow ('he said') or precede the reported clause ('Mr Blair said') or be placed between two reported clauses in **medial** position ('she wrote').

Within the reported clause, verb tense and pronouns are grammatically appropriate to the original (anterior) discourse situation. So, in (1), the pronoun 'I' and the present tense 'regret' are all appropriate for the discourse between Mr Johnson and his addressees. The convention in written texts is for the directly quoted words to be enclosed in quotation marks (inverted commas), although other graphological indicators are also possible such as italics, indentation, and dashes. And, as example (4) demonstrates, quotation marks can be missing altogether. In spoken discourse, gestures (such as air-quotes) or a different voice quality might be used to signal direct presentation (see Halliday and Matthiessen 2014: 447 and Clark and Gerrig 1990: 775–777).

Extract (5) is an example of what is known as **Free** Direct Speech and demonstrates that direct presentation of discourse can be *free* (get it?) of reporting clauses. The example is from Hemingway's (1926) novel, *The Sun Also Rises* and is part of an interaction between the main character and narrator (Jake Barnes) and another character (Robert Cohn). The first reported clause is (conventionally) followed by a reporting clause ('he said'), but subsequent reported clauses are not. Instead, the reader must use the sequencing of the quoted speech to understand that these are alternate turns in the conversation and to work out who says what.

One effect of direct discourse presentation can be, as Short (1996: 293) notes, to bring the original speaker's words (from the anterior discourse) to the foreground. This effect is amplified with Free Direct forms (as demonstrated in example 5), where the presenter is backgrounded by the omission of presenting clauses.

The traditional view of directly quoted discourse is that it presents the exact words (or thoughts) used in the original verbatim. With this view, direct discourse is completely **faithful** to the original. However, the status of direct discourse presentation largely depends on its context. For example, in spoken conversation, if we quote what other people have said there is a tacit understanding between speaker and hearer that any such quotes are likely to be inaccurate because in practice it is very difficult to remember exactly the words that someone used. In these cases, the primary purpose of direct discourse presentation is to help make the story telling more vivid and lively. In other contexts, however, such as news report and academic writing, our expectation is that anything that is quoted directly will be largely faithful to the original. We say 'largely' because even the most accurate quotation of spoken discourse is likely to miss out repeated words, false starts, and other non-fluency features such as *ums* and *ahhs*. Even with print news report, our expectation of faithfulness can change depending on where the quotation occurs. For example, Short (1988) discusses examples of Direct Speech in newspaper headlines that were not actually said by the person they were attributed to. We return to the topic of faithfulness later in this chapter.

Indirect Speech, Writing, and Thought (IS/IW/IT)

(6) Infectious diseases specialists told the Post on Tuesday that symptoms of the Omicron variant emerged quicker.
(*South China Morning Post*, 12/01/2022)

(7) she [Charlotte Newton] thought that he was a soft target and that he would be less likely to call the police because of their secret sexual arrangement.
(*Hull Daily Mail*, Hull [UK], 26/04/2022)

(8) By October 13, Taoiseach Micheál Martin said he did not guarantee that the removal of restrictions on October 22 would proceed as planned
(*Irish Independent*, 01/01/2022)

(9) New Zealand school buildings were generally poorly-ventilated, Kvalsvig said.
(*New Zealand Herald*, 10/01/2022)

(10) Aaron Bell, member for Newcastle-under-Lyme, asked Boris Johnson if he took him for a fool for following rules in the House of Commons on Monday.
(BBC News online, 01/02/2022)

(11) Win promised to campaign for a change in the law and has done so for the nearly 20 years since her husband died.
(*Daily Mail*, London, 03/02/2022)

Unlike direct discourse presentation, where the original discourse is (apparently) quoted faithfully, indirect speech, writing, or thought **paraphrases** the original discourse and presents the meaning carried by the original utterance (the propositional content; see Chapter 5). The presenter is free to choose the words that they think convey the meaning of the original. While some of the original words might be used in IS, there is no guarantee of that so the hearer/reader does not know which words belong to the original discourse and which to the presenter.

Indirect Speech, Writing, and Thought has a two-clause structure, with a reporting clause and reported clause (which expresses the words from the anterior discourse). However, with indirect discourse presentation, the reported clause is subordinate to the reporting clause and does not incorporate quotation marks (because it is not quoting but paraphrasing). The subordination might be marked by the subordinating conjunction 'that' (as in 6 and 7), or it can be omitted (as in 8). Indirect presentation involves shifts in **deixis** (e.g. 'now' becomes 'then', 'here' becomes 'there') and tense and pronouns are changed to be appropriate to the posterior discourse. For example, in (8):

- 'did' is used rather than the 'do' that would be present in the direct rendering ('I do not guarantee . . .');
- 'would' rather than 'will'; and
- 'he' is used instead of 'I'.

There might also be a change in clause type (declarative, imperative, interrogative) where, for example, an interrogative in the original discourse becomes a statement in the posterior discourse. This is the case in example (7) where in the original, anterior discourse, Aaron Bell says:

Does the prime Minister think I'm a fool?

Examples (9)–(11) demonstrate that indirect discourse has other structures. Example (9) shows that, rather than the conventional fronted position, the reporting clause can come after the reported clause (the use of the past tense verb-form 'were' suggests that this is indirect presentation). Examples (10) and (11) demonstrate that other two-clause structures feature in indirect discourse with an if-clause in (10) and a to-infinitive clause in (11) carrying the content of the original (anterior) discourse.

Because indirect forms of discourse presentation involve paraphrasing, they are seen as being less faithful to the (perceived) original than direct forms. They combine the original (anterior) discourse with the (posterior) discourse within the reported clause and allow the presenter to insert evaluations, judgements, or extra information into what is being presented (in the reported clause). The voice of the text producer therefore merges with the voice of the other person being presented which has the effect of blurring the point of view distancing the reader from (i) the original discourse, and (ii) the person that produced it.

Activity 10.1 Transpose Direct Speech into Indirect Speech

Test out your knowledge of indirect forms of discourse presentation by transposing the direct speech used in Figure 10.1 into indirect speech:

> "What are you still doing here at this time?"

We give our answer at the end of the chapter.

Reporting clauses

The stretches of text that introduce discourse presentation are often referred to as reporting clauses because they tend to be clausal structures and contain a reporting verb such as 'said', 'wrote' or 'thought'. Reporting clauses are an important aspect of discourse presentation because of the extra information they can provide about the original (anterior) discourse situation, including:

- mode of anterior discourse – indicated, for example, via reporting verbs (e.g. 'said', 'thought', 'wrote');
- attribution of source of original – typically who spoke, thought, wrote;
- the speech/writing/thought act performed – (e.g. 'promised', 'threatened') (see Chapter 4);
- manner – indicated, for example, by verb choice (e.g. 'shouted') and adverbs (e.g. 'loudly');
- emotive states – indicated, for example, by adverbs (e.g. 'angrily').

It is important to remember that reporting clauses are part of the posterior discourse. This means that they are formulated by the person doing the presenting and pertain to their point of view. Therefore, the language choices for rendering the speech/writing/thought act, manner, and emotive states are largely in the hands of the presenter and how they evaluate the original discourse and its producer. Even the choice of reporting verb can be subjective. For example, when introducing spoken discourse presentation, instead of choosing the neutral reporting verb 'said', other verbs such as 'blustered' could be chosen to suggest a more negative attitude toward the original speaker. Such **evaluative** choices can be important since they can be biased and influence readers' view of the producer of the original discourse. They can also provide information about the **attitude** of the person doing the presenting toward the original words or the original text producer (see Thompson 1996: 507–522).

Other linguistic structures are often used to introduce the presentation of other people's words and thoughts. Consider the following examples and, before reading on, identify the words that act like a reporting clause by introducing or signalling discourse presentation.

(12) One of the suggestions is that the amount offered by Cold Weather Payment is raised to address this crisis.

(*Express* online, London, 20/01/2022)

(13) The eventual declaration by the Minister of Finance that President Buhari does not want Nigerians to suffer, hence the suspension of the implementation of subsidy removal, came as the icing of the cake.

(*This Day*, Lagos, 30/01/2022)

(14) According to the documents, the waivers are related to work aimed at turning Iran's heavy-water Arak reactor into a less-dangerous light-water reactor

(*Wall Street Journal* online, 05/02/2022)

Extracts (12) and (13) are examples of Indirect Speech, where the noun phrases 'One of the suggestions' and 'The eventual declaration by the Minister of Finance' signal indirect discourse presentation. Extract (14) contains Indirect Writing presentation where the adverbial 'According to the documents' introduces the propositional content of the original discourse.

When analysing direct and indirect presentation it is important to consider both the content of the reported clause and the choice of reporting verb and to remember that the presentation of other people's discourse is controlled by the person doing the presenting.

Activity 10.2 Discourse presentation in naturally occurring conversation

Look at the extract below taken from the Santa Barbara Corpus of spoken conversations, which demonstrates how words spoken by other people can be included in a conversational turn. The extract is part of a longer conversation between two male friends (Fred and Richard) where Fred is sharing a story about his shift at the factory he works at. Identify the discourse presentation and any reporting clauses (or other signalling structures).

FRED: yeah, and so, he comes and says, well, he goes, I don't know if you've, if you've, packed this or not. You know. On your production card, all it says, you know, is that you did three thousand sheets, but you did . . . but you didn't pack it. So I go, yeah, I go look man, there they are. You could see, there's my name, stamped right on there. I just didn't put it down. And he goes, and what are you doing in the cafeteria so late. I'm just going, aw man, this is the pits man.

(SBC047, *On the Lot*)

Free Indirect Speech, Writing, and Thought (FIS/FIW/FIT)

(15) One farmer quietly admits he worries about the growing numbers of racial minorities; another enjoys hearing new accents at the grocery store.

(Asia News Monitor, 01/02/2022)

(16) 'What does it mean, just a woman?' he [Cipriano] said, quickly, sternly. She hung her head. What did it mean? What indeed did it mean? Just a woman!

(*The Plumed Serpent*, D. H. Lawrence, 1926)

Free Indirect Speech, Writing, and Thought sit between direct and indirect forms of discourse presentation on the cline shown in Table 10.1. They combine anterior and posterior discourses but tend to be anchored to the presenter's viewpoint. Unlike Indirect forms of discourse presentation, Free Indirect Discourse presentation is 'free' from reporting clauses and has no stable set of formal features, which makes it notoriously difficult to identify. Typically, though, verb tense and pronouns are, as with Indirect forms, aligned to the presenter, while other features such as lexis (e.g. dialect, colloquialisms), terms of address, discourse markers (e.g. 'Oh'), punctuation (e.g. exclamation marks), syntax (e.g. incomplete sentences) and mood (e.g. interrogatives) are, as with Direct forms, aligned to the original speaker/writer/thinker.

In our view, the underlined section of (15) is Free Indirect Speech. It is 'free' because there is no reporting clause to introduce what appears to be indirect speech presentation of 'another' farmer. Arguably, 'another' can be viewed as an incomplete reporting clause (something like: 'another farmer says that they . . . '). Often, it is the immediate co-text that plays a crucial role in identifying Free Indirect forms such as whether some other form of discourse presentation occurs immediately before or after. In (15) the FIS is preceded by IS, and this steers the reader to understand that more speech (the underlined part) is being presented rather than some observation made by the writer. Sometimes, though, it is not clear whose point of view is being presented and consequently it can be difficult to ascertain whether evaluative language and other markers of subjectivity relate to the posterior or anterior discourse.

Example (16) shows instances of Free Indirect Thought (underlined). We suggest that the two questions and the exclamation are the protagonist's (Kate Leslie) thoughts to herself as she hangs her head and thinks about the question asked by Cipriano (a Mexican general). Like (15), these examples of Discourse Presentation are Free because there are no reporting clauses, and they combine features of Direct and Indirect presentation. Both questions are structured as interrogatives, so retain the same form as (we imagine) the storyteller would have used in the original (anterior) discourse, but the verb tense is back-shifted ('did') and therefore aligns with the posterior discourse. The internalised exclamation is grammatically incomplete and includes an exclamation mark, perhaps indicating the strength of her thought. The example shows how Free Indirect forms blend features of both Direct and Indirect presentation, which is why these forms are positioned as they are on the DP cline.

The effect of Free Indirect Discourse depends on whether it is spoken, written, or thought. According to Semino and Short (2004: 83–85), Free Indirect Speech (FIS) distances us from the original discourse and can indicate the presenter's evaluative point of view towards the discourse and/or the person that produced it (see also Short 1996: 308; Leech and Short 2007: 268–270). Such distancing and point of view effects may lead to irony, humour, or present an ideological stance. Free Indirect Thought (FIT), however, brings us *closer* to the original thinker by providing access to their thoughts, which may lead to a sense of intimacy and empathy (Semino and Short 2004: 124; see also Short 1996: 315).

Presentation of Speech, Writing, and Thought Acts (PSA/PWA/PTA)

(17) She [Grace Tame] spoke of continuing her campaign to end sexual abuse against children and others through education and legal reform.
(NCA NewsWire, 25/01/2022)

(18) The organisers of the protest have called for the forceful elimination of all Covid-19 restrictions and vaccine mandates . . .
(*Evening Standard*, 31/01/2022)

(19) On Friday, she [Carrie Lam Cheng Yuet-ngor] ordered an investigation into the conduct of the officials who attended the party.
(*South China Morning Post*, 11/01/2022)

(20) Australia has accused WeChat of taking down Prime Minister Scott Morrison's account and redirecting his followers to a site that claims to provide information for Chinese Australians.
(CNN Business, 25 January 2022)

(21) It [pro-Beijing newspaper Ta Kung Pao] also blamed Cathay Pacific aircrew for triggering the fifth wave of infections by violating home isolation rules.
(*South China Morning Post*, 11/01/2022)

The next category of discourse presentation is Presentation of Speech/Writing/Thought Act (PSA/PWA/PTA).[5] These types of discourse presentation differ from the indirect forms we discussed above because, rather than having a two-clause structure, they comprise a reporting word (prototypically a verb) followed by a prepositional or noun phrase which contains a **summary** of the discourse being presented. The information relating to the content of the original discourse is therefore not a separate clause but is embedded into the reporting clause. In example (17), the reporting word is 'spoke' which is followed by a prepositional phrase beginning with 'of'. Similarly, in (18) 'have called' is the reporting verb phrase and this is followed by a prepositional phrase beginning with 'for'.[6]

Examples (19), (20), and (21) illustrate that some reporting words can indicate the illocutionary force of the original discourse (e.g. 'ordered', 'accused', 'blamed') and thus the speech/writing/thought act being performed. These sorts of reporting verbs therefore help convey part of the content of the original discourse (Thompson 1996: 517). It is worth remembering, though, that the person presenting the discourse chooses the reporting word so is also indicative of their evaluation of the original discourse which may be biased and designed to steer the reader's/hearer's opinion.

Presentation of a speech/writing/thought act (PSA/PWA/PTA) does not present the propositional content of original discourse but only a *summary*, so typically the original (anterior) discourse cannot be reconstructed. This then is different from Direct forms, which ostensibly renders the original discourse verbatim, and Indirect forms, which paraphrase the original, typically using some of the same words. The amount of information in the summary can differ considerably. Semino and Short (2004: 52–53) found that in news texts the indications of content could be lengthy and detailed. Example (20) contains the largest amount of summary information in a prepositional phrase consisting of 23 words (including 'of'). The summary is presented from the point of view of the text producer (the presenter) who controls the lexical choices used to summarise the original discourse and the summary may be interspersed with additional information and opinions not in the original discourse. There is therefore greater potential for the merging of anterior with posterior discourse with this type of discourse presentation. For example, in (20) we might wonder whether the use of 'claims', which casts doubt on the information contained on the website, stems from the original discourse, or was added by the text producer.

In their original conception of this type of discourse presentation, Leech and Short (2007: 260) say that it is "on a par with other kinds of action". This is partly because, structurally, the summary of what is said, written or thought is embedded in the same clause as the reporting word. Thompson (1996: 517) suggests that this is likely to place the focus on the communicative act or event rather than the content, making the content of the original discourse less salient.

Presentation of Speech, Writing, and Thought (PS/PW/PT)

(22) European officials have been scrambling to secure backup energy supplies in the event that a conflict disrupts flows from Russia, enlisting the help of the U.S. and talking with gas producers such as Qatar and Azerbaijan.
(*Wall Street Journal*, New York, 01/01/2022)

(23) President Uhuru Kenyatta on Thursday held one-on-one talks with Rwanda's President Paul Kagame who was in the country on a working visit.
(AllAfrica.com, 03/02/2022)

(24) Johnson attended the party and gave a speech, it is understood, but he left after a few minutes.
(*Daily Mail*, 02/02/2022)

(25) Warnings issued after group fined for luring 4m croc out of Proserpine River
(ABC Premium News, Sydney 02/02/2022)

(26) He [Pete Docherty] mumbled darkly and incoherently between songs.
(*Sunday Herald*, Glasgow, 25/09/2005)

(27) A Salvation Army leader threatened his wife after she caught him having sex with a co-worker in the religious charity's office. [. . .] The dad shouted and swore before following Sara when she ran from the premises in tears.
(*Daily Record*, Glasgow, 03/02/2022)

(Note: Discourse presentation is underlined in examples 22–27)

Presentation of Speech/Writing/Thought (PS/PW/PT) are the most minimal types of discourse presentation, and the categories recognise that sometimes we are told *only* that speech, writing, or thought occurred. As the examples above (22–27) demonstrate, with PS/PW/PT we are not given any details about the content of the anterior discourse. So, in (22) we know that European officials have been talking with gas producers, but no details are given about the content of the talk (although we can probably infer from the rest of the sentence that the general topic of conversation was gas and its supply!). There is no summary either, as would be the case for PSA/PWA/PTA.

PS, PW, and PT are manifest in a variety of forms. In example (22), the 'ing-form' of the speech-verb 'talk' indicates that spoken discourse has occurred. In example (23) it is the noun phrase 'one-on-one talks' (which is the direct object of the verb 'held') that informs us of a spoken interaction. Similarly, in (24) and (25) it is the nouns 'speech' and 'warning' that reference anterior discourses and not the verb forms 'gave' and 'issued'. With (24), the discourse is obviously spoken, however in (25) 'warnings' could be written and/or spoken.

The plural form nonetheless suggests reference to multiple discourses. Example (26) demonstrates that words that reference the manner of production (in this case a verb form – 'mumbled') can also signal the presence of an anterior discourse (in this case spoken). Finally, example (27) highlights that some lexical choices can indicate the illocutionary force of the discourse. The verb form 'threatened' summarises the overall force of the salvation army leader's verbal output (similar effects can also be achieved with nouns, e.g. 'threats'). The use of 'swore' strongly suggests that expletives were used and therefore constrains and/or suggests possible options for what the man said.

Notice that in (22) that while the speech verb ('talking') is followed by a prepositional phrase ('with gas producers') this is not an example of PSA because rather than giving information about the content of the discourse, the phrase serves to tells us who the other parties involved in the talking were. The lack of any sort of summary of or content from the anterior discourse helps us see that this Discourse Presentation is unlike any that we have seen so far in this chapter and is a case of PS.

With presentation of speech, writing and thought (PS/PW/PT), the text producer is apparently in complete control of the presentation of discourse, and we are furthest away from the original speaker/writer/thinker and their words. The distancing effect is demonstrated particularly well in Example (27) where we are not privy to the content of the abuse. All we are told is that a person shouted, threatened, and swore, but we are not given any hint of anything that was said. With these forms, then, there is only the reporting word, which is chosen by the text producer, and these alone provide information about the original discourse. It is, however, possible for the choice of verb to hint at the content or provide the essence of what was said (or written or thought).

Activity 10.3 Josh gives his opinion

The following sentence is taken from a UK daily newspaper. Does the sentence contain any Discourse Presentation? If so, can you identify which kind? What, if any, are the effects of the language choices? We give our answers at the end of the chapter.

Hollywood actor Josh Hartnett has waded in on the Downing Street controversy and Boris Johnson's actions during lockdown.

Daily Mirror (UK), 01/02/2022

Summary

The categories of discourse presentation discussed in this section provide a framework for identifying and analysing discourse presentation in texts. Each of the different categories in the framework express varying degrees of 'interference' (Leech and Short 2007: 260, 276) by the text producer, as well as claims to the faithfulness of the reporting of the supposed original utterance. The categories, which we summarised in Table 10.1, form a continuum ordered according to "[. . .] the amount of 'involvement' of (i) the original speaker in the anterior discourse and (ii) the person in the posterior discourse presenting what was said in the anterior discourse [. . .]" (Semino and Short 2004: 10). The continuum ranges from categories at the bottom of the table to the direct discourse presentation categories at the top of the table, which apparently involve only the original speaker. Anything lying in between these two extremes is a combination, in varying proportions, of the original speaker and the person presenting the discourse. Moving up the table through the categories coincides with a gradual transition in viewpoint, shifting more and more from the point of view of the person presenting the discourse, to the viewpoint of the original speaker/writer/thinker.

Activity 10.4 Discourse presentation from news story on the BBC website

Below is an example of discourse presentation taken from a news story that concerns the resignation of a UK TV historian from the Mary Rose Trust following comments he made during an interview on a YouTube channel. First read an extract of the statement made by the Trust.

(A) we were appalled to hear Dr Starkey's public comments on slavery today. Mary Rose Trust is a charity that exists for the benefit of everyone and we have zero tolerance for such comments. The board of the Mary Rose Trust has therefore accepted Dr Starkey's resignation

(The Mary Rose @MaryRoseMuseum, 6:48pm, Thursday 02 July 2020)

Now read the reporting of the statement in the news story.

(B) The Mary Rose Trust said it was "appalled" by Starkey's comments, adding on Thursday evening they had accepted his resignation.

(BBC News, 03 July 2020: 'David Starkey resigns from university role over slavery comments', https://www.bbc.co.uk/news/entertainment-arts-53279273)

Answer these questions:

i. Establish what type of discourse presentation is being used in (B). Spell out the formal features that lead you to your decision.
ii. Comment on the word in quotation marks in the news story.
iii. Say whether you think the discourse presentation is faithful to the original (A).

We provide our responses at the end of the chapter.

Attribution of source of original discourse

Earlier in this chapter we saw that one of the functions of reporting clauses (and other reporting structures) that 'signal' discourse presentation is to attribute the source of the original (anterior) discourse. As such, attribution relates to what is known as **evidentiality** which is, according to Aikhenvald (2004: 3), "a linguistic category whose primary meaning is source of information". Aikhenvald goes on to say that for many languages, evidentiality is a grammatical system realised, for example, through morphology. English, however, has no such system; instead, it has numerous lexical ways in which the source of information can be expressed, which include attribution in reporting clauses. Aikhenvald (2004: 10) stresses, though, that these lexical means are not the same as a grammatical category, not least because they are non-obligatory lexical choices.[7] That means that when another discourse (and therefore another voice) is incorporated into a discourse the text producer can choose whether and how to attribute the source. Exploring these choices, via the framework presented in this chapter, can be important for discourse analysis because Discourse Presentation and, more specifically, attribution can be used, for example, to legitimate actions and practices.

Legitimation

Legitimation refers to providing justification for doing something. In his work on discourse and social practices, van Leeuwen (2008: 105) suggests that legitimation is the use of language to answer the questions '"Why should we do this?" and/or "Why should we do this in this way?"' For example, consider the following invented conversation between two people:

A: We must wear face coverings in public buildings.
B: Why must we?
A: Because medical experts say it helps to stop the spread of Covid.

In our example, person A legitimises her assertion by referring to medical authority via Indirect Speech (or Indirect Writing). According to van Leeuwen (2008: 106–109), "**legitimation through authorization**" can be achieved by attributing discourse to those in a role of authority, (e.g. teacher, parent), those who have expert authority (e.g. scientists, medics), role models (e.g. celebrities, 'influencers'), and impersonal authorities (e.g. laws, rules). So, we often rely on others' speech (or writing) to legitimise what we say. In general, reference to another discourse can validate our own experiences, provide support for our claims, and help to substantiate and increase the credibility of our own stories and opinions.

Faithfulness

We have established that people can present the words (written or spoken) and thoughts of other people. You may have been in the situation when someone has quoted your own words back to you, telling you that 'you said this' or 'you said that', but they get what you said wrong; they misquote you! You might reply with something like 'I never said that!' Or maybe they don't quote you but present what you said in their own words (paraphrase) which does not quite capture the essence of what you said. In that situation you might respond with 'That's not what I meant!' You may have also seen occasions when people say that they were quoted out of context. The point is that when we quote other people (and when other people quote us) or present the gist of what was said, it is usually quite important that we do it accurately and honestly. This is known as being faithful to the original, and the notion of **faithfulness** is a crucial element of Discourse Presentation. As readers or listeners, it is important for us to have confidence that when other people's words (and thoughts) are presented they are faithful to the original.

For Short et al. (2002: 328) faithfulness refers to "specifying as accurately as is feasible in context the precise communicative content of the discourse being reported" and involves "the reproduction of the lexical items and grammatical structures used in the anterior discourse". Different kinds of discourse presentation bring with them different assumptions about their faithfulness to the content of the original discourse.

With Direct presentation, the assumption is that the words in the quotation marks are quoted faithfully. However, this assumption can vary depending on the type of discourse being presented (speech, writing, thought) and the context of the presenting situation. Quoting someone's spoken words is quite hard to do from memory. Indeed, to be accurate you would need to make a recording of the speech and then listen back to it very carefully, and possibly transcribe it. As far as we know, this is not normal everyday practice, so if you quote someone during a naturally occurring conversation, it is likely that your interlocutor will understand that your direct presentation of someone else's words might not be fully accurate because you are quoting from memory. However, when we see or hear direct presentation of speech in, for example, a news report, we expect the news producer to have taken steps (such as making a transcription from a recording) to ensure an accurate rendering of the other person's words. Our assumption, then, is that in 'high stakes' contexts (e.g. news, police reports, academic writing) more care will have been taken to render the original discourse faithfully. A key contextual difference between (for example) everyday conversation and news report is that it is unlikely to be a matter of great concern if you do not quote entirely accurately what your friend said to you, but there could be serious consequences, even legal ones, if you misquote someone in a news report (and other contexts such as academic writing).

The faithfulness associated with indirect presentation is less than that with direct presentation simply because there is no claim being made that what is presented is verbatim. However, there is still an *expectation* that the propositional content is faithful to the original. This sort of faithfulness can be more difficult to assess and, because the person who is doing the presenting manipulates the original by, for example, changing some words or missing some words out, we can never be sure how close we are to the original unless we have access to it. Once again, we might make assumptions about faithfulness claims based on who is doing the presenting. For example, we might assume that news outlets are more diligent than conversational partners, and we might trust some news outlets more than others. It is worth remembering, though, that any presentation of any kind, including direct forms, is mediated by the text producer because the text producer can choose (i) what to quote and (ii) the surrounding co-text that frames the quote. Activity 10.5 invites you to look at a real-life example of DP where faithfulness was an issue.

Activity 10.5 Fake news!

'Fake news' is defined by Young-Brown (2020: 5) simply as "any news story that contains false information on purpose". Similarly, Allcott and Gentzkow (2017: 213) describe it as "news articles that are intentionally and verifiably false, and could mislead readers". These definitions highlight that fake news is false information that pretends to be true and that it is intentional. The term 'fake news' was brought to the fore by Donald Trump during his presidential campaign and eventual reign and emerged as a key sociopolitical phrase[8] with a meaning broader than the previous definition suggests. Farkas and Schou (2018), for example, suggest that the term is used by left-wing liberals to critique right-wing politics and media outlets and then by the right-wing (especially Trump himself) to discredit mainstream media. They write that prior to becoming president, "Trump had insinuated that the term 'fake news' was a political construct created in order to attack and delegitimise his presidency". They go on to say that once in office:

> he began what would become a continuous and highly systematic use of the "fake news" [. . .] to attack and delegitimise what he saw as his direct opponents: mainstream media. Trump started using the term to lash out at media companies [. . .]
>
> (Farkas and Schou 2018: 306)

Bearing in mind the view of Farkas and Schou, look at the tweet below by Donald Trump and the reporting of it on the *Washington Post* and CNN websites.

On 29 October 2018 Donald Trump, in the role of US President, tweeted the following (sentences numbered for ease of reference).

> (1) There is great anger in our Country caused in part by inaccurate, and even fraudulent, reporting of the news. (2) The Fake News Media, the true Enemy of the People, must stop the open & obvious hostility & report the news accurately & fairly. (3) That will do much to put out the flame . . . of Anger and Outrage and we will then be able to bring all sides together in Peace and Harmony. (4) Fake News Must End!

In the news, on the same day, the *Washington Post* printed this on its website:

> President Trump lashed out anew Monday at the news media, calling it "the true Enemy of the People," and he again blamed what he called "fraudulent" reporting for anger [. . .]
>
> (https://tinyurl.com/mr3dkrdd)

NBC, on its news web pages, posted a story about the tweet in which they said the following.

> Trump used Twitter Monday morning to rip the media as "the true enemy of the people" and blame the press for "great anger" in the U.S.
>
> (https://tinyurl.com/z7h9keu3)

Now, consider whether the news reports were faithful to the original discourse. Give reasons for your conclusions. Following that, consider what, if anything, analysing discourse presentation and faithfulness can contribute to the discussion of 'fake news'.

Conclusion

In this chapter we have discussed in detail the idea of discourse presentation and that it introduces other voices into a discourse. Discourse presentation can provide other opinions and views and the help to legitimate and validate your own ideas. Our main aim in this chapter was to introduce a framework for the analysis of discourse presentation that will enable you, as discourse analysts, to identify different types of discourse presentation in texts. This is an important step in any analysis before further evaluative and interpretative steps can be made. We have also discussed how the way in which the discourse is framed by the person presenting it can affect how the original, anterior discourse is viewed by hearers and readers. This is especially true of minimal discourse presentation categories (e.g. Presentation of Speech), but also where reporting clauses (and other signals) include subjective and evaluative language.

Further reading

Semino and Short (2004) is a book length discussion using corpus data of the SW&TP framework used in this chapter.

For discussion of the application of the same framework to spoken data see McIntyre et al. (2004), and to historical data see McIntyre and Walker (2011, 2012) and Walker and McIntyre (2015).

Fairclough (2003: Chapter 3), who discusses discourse presentation from a Critical Discourse Analysis perspective, relates reported speech to the notion of intertextuality.

Walker and Karpenko-Seccombe (2017) provide an analysis of a BBC news report using Short's (2012) version of the Leech and Short framework.

Answers to activities

Activity 10.1 Transpose Direct Speech into Indirect Speech

"What are you still doing here at this time?" Jules asked.

Some options that we came up with are:
(i) Jules asked Ginny what she was still doing there at that time.
(ii) Jules wondered what Ginny was still doing there at that time.
(ii) Jules questioned Ginny about still being there at that time.
(iv) Jules gently quizzed Ginny about her continued presence there at that ungodly hour.

Notice that in options (i) and (ii) 'are' shifts in tense to 'was'. In option (i) the pronoun 'you' changes to 'she' while in (ii) and (iii) Ginny's name is used. In all options the deixis changes to be appropriate to the posterior discourse so 'here' becomes 'there' and 'this' becomes 'that'. In (iv), we have taken more liberties with the paraphrasing of the original and converted 'still doing here' to 'her continued presence there', and 'at this time' to 'at this ungodly hour'. Readers may like to think about whether (iv) remains faithful to the original.

Activity 10.2 Discourse presentation in naturally occurring conversation

Hopefully, you will have noticed that the extract largely involves Fred presenting part of a conversation he had with someone else at the factory (his line manager) and contains some of the words apparently spoken by the manager as well as some of Fred's own words in response. We can spot the conversational turns that are from an earlier discourse because they are introduced by verb phrases such as 'he comes and says', 'he goes', and 'I go'. If you listen to the spoken transcript (available at the Santa Barbara website), you will hear that Fred also signals that he is presenting his manager's words by impersonating his manager's voice. You may have also noticed that in the last orthographic sentence of the extract, Fred appears to tell Richard what he was thinking during his conversation with his manager. His thoughts, which are apparently 'aw man, this is the pits man', are introduced with 'I'm just going'. While 'going' is not specifically a verb of thought, and 'go' is used earlier in the extract to introduce speech, we reasoned that (i) it is unlikely that Fred said these words out loud to his manager, and (ii) the progressive aspect which encodes ongoing action suggests the thoughts are happening during the spoken conversation or at least while the manager is speaking.

Activity 10.3 Josh gives his opinion

'Waded in' is used metaphorically (and idiomatically) to mean intervene. We can wade into a debate, meaning that we intervene to give our two pen'orth[9] (another idiom meaning give one's opinion). In this headline, then, it seems likely that 'waded in' refers to some sort of discourse produced by Josh Hartnett and is therefore an example of Presentation of Speech (PS).

To use 'waded in' to refer to someone giving their opinion has rather negative connotations because it sounds like they are intervening forcefully and possibly uninvited. It possibly makes Josh look like he is 'sticking his nose in' where it's not wanted. To assess whether the *Daily Mirror* is offering us a true and fair rendering of Josh's contribution, we need to see the original, anterior discourse. We also need to appreciate the context. Josh was being interviewed about his new TV series, and the interview followed on from an item concerning the controversial story concerning parties being held at 10 Downing Street during a nationwide Covid-19 lockdown in the UK. After exchanging greetings, the interview starts by Susanna asking Josh whether he has been gripped by what is happening at in the UK government and whether those involve in the parties should be afraid. Josh replies as follows.

Josh: [H] ((laughs)) how can you not ↘be [Hx] er it's it's all that's on the ↘news (.) er (.) yeah I mean it's of ↑course↑ they should be afraid (.) this (.) this doesn't look ↘good people were people were having a very difficult time at that ↘time [H] (.) it's (.) it's hard to believe that they ↘were (. .) living it ↗↘up

[1.0]

The intonation contour and pause suggests that Josh has finished what he had to say and that this is a Transition Relevant Place (TRP) in the conversation. Susanna takes the floor at this point, saying that the parties have "appalled" and "shocked" everyone. She then moves on to ask Josh about his new TV series (which is the main purpose of the interview). Did Josh wade in, or was his opinion solicited by Susanna? We think that he was asked for his opinion, and he gave it, so 'waded in' seems to us like a misrepresentation of the original discourse.

Activity 10.4 Discourse presentation from news story on the BBC website

(A)

1	2
The Mary Rose Trust said	it was "appalled" by Starkey's comments,
adding on Thursday evening	they had accepted his resignation.
3	4

The presentation in (A) has the following structure:

- reporting clause (1), which contains the past tense form of the verb 'say';
- subordinated clause (2), which contains the **propositional content** of what was said, with the pronoun *it* and a past tense form of the verb 'be' aligned to the news report (the posterior discourse);
- another reporting clause (3), which contains the -ing form of the verb 'add';
- another subordinated clause (4), which contains more propositional content with the pronoun *they* and the past-tense form of the verb 'have' aligned to the posterior discourse.

The structure of the sentence, along with the choice of pronouns and verb tense in the subordinated clauses, makes it an example of indirect discourse presentation. The fact that the written words from a tweet are being presented, makes it Indirect Writing (IW). Notice, though, that the word 'appalled' is placed in quotation marks indicating that the IW also contains the Direct presentation of one of the words used by the Trust. This phenomenon of embedding direct quotation within indirect presentation is not unusual in news reports and highlights (in this case at least) a word that definitely was used in the original discourse.

We can also assess whether the indirect presentation in the news report offers a faithful rendering of the propositional content of the Twitter message. One difference between the original tweet (anterior discourse) and the presentation of it in the news report (posterior discourse) is that the Trust says that they 'were appalled to hear' while the news report says that the Trust 'was appalled by'. Whether that difference is important (i.e. whether the original statement and the reported statement amount to the same thing) is a matter for conjecture.

Activity 10.5 Fake news!

To assess faithfulness, we need to assess lexical choices made by the news outlets when they are reporting Trump's verbal actions:

In the NBC extract: 'rip', 'blame'.

In the Washington Post extract: 'lashed out'; 'calling', 'blamed', 'called'.

First, we can consider whether Trump's tweet can be characterised as 'lashing out'. Whatever we decide, we need to appreciate that the characterisation is imposed on us by those presenting the words of Trump; it is their choice of words for depicting the verbal action that frame the presentation of what Trump said.

Both news outlets quote 'the true enemy of the people'; additionally, the *Washington Post* quotes 'fraudulent', while NBC quotes 'great anger'. The quoted words are definitely used in the original, so in that sense they are faithful. However, Trump equates 'the enemy of the people' with 'the fake news media'. He does this via what is known as **apposition** (we introduced this in Chapter 2). This is where two words or phrases (in this case, two noun phrases) are placed side by side, separated by a comma, and refer to the same entity (i.e. they have the same referent). By doing so, the two noun phrases form a relationship of equivalence whereby 'the fake news media' = 'the true enemy of the people'.[10] However, in the news reports, the label of 'the true enemy of the people' is assigned to 'news media' by the *Washington Post*, and just the 'media' by NBC, so both miss out the word 'fake'. This omission is important because it suggests that Trump was attacking all the media and not just those outlets that produce fake news (of course, one might wonder which news outlets Trump had in mind when he tweeted his message). To present Trump's use of apposition, the *Washington Post* uses the verb form 'calling', while NBC uses 'rip' (the meaning of which is probably something like 'verbally attack' or 'use verbal aggression'). These verb forms are suggestive of a particular speech act (or in this case, writing act) that might take the form of 'X is (a/the) Y' (e.g. you are the enemy). This is effectively what Trump is doing, but via apposition, which is (perhaps) a less obvious way of creating equivalence than an 'X is Y' structure.

Finally, both reports use a form of the verb 'blame'. This presents Trump's claim of causation (the causative structure 'caused in part') and we would need to decide whether forging a partial causative link between states and actions (anger caused by fake news) counts as allocating blame in the original Trump tweet. Additionally, NBC say that Trump blames 'the press', which he does not; rather he suggests a partial ('caused in part') link between anger and 'inaccurate' and 'fraudulent' 'reporting of the news'. So, NBC's report is not completely faithful. This example also shows the importance of context – it is not enough to take the exact words 'x, y, z' and quote them faithfully as 'the true Enemy of the People', 'fraudulent', and so on, as both sources have done here, but to render them accurately in the context of utterance. Faithfulness therefore also pertains to the immediate textual context of the presented discourse.

The example helps to show how faithfulness to the original speech writing (or thought) is a complex issue and can be quite difficult to assess. We can also see that faithfulness is important in news discourse, as it is in other discourses such as political and scientific discourses.

Notes

1 Also relevant is Bakhtin's (1981) concept of heteroglossia ('different tongues/languages').
2 The report of the Iraq Inquiry Executive summary is available at: https://assets.publishing.service.gov.uk/government/uploads/system/uploads/attachment_data/file/535407/The_Report_of_the_Iraq_Inquiry_-_Executive_Summary.pdf and is used in accordance with the Open Government licence, a copy of which can be found at: https://www.nationalarchives.gov.uk/doc/open-government-licence/version/3/
3 We introduce and use this corpus in our next chapter.
4 Even though we prefer the term 'presentation', the terms 'reporting clause' and 'reported clause' are well established and widely used, so we will continue to use them here.
5 Our view on PTA/PWA/PTA diverges from that of Semino and Short (2004) and aligns with Thompson's (1996) category of 'summary'.
6 If 'called for' is analysed as a phrasal verb, then the content of the original discourse is summarised in a noun phrase beginning with 'the'.
7 Aikhenvald (2004) points out that evidentiality simply refers to the source of information and has nothing to do with probability, reliability, commitment to truth, or providing proof, which are to do with **modality**. Aikhenvald explains that evidentially and modality are often misunderstood and overlapped in ways that are confusing.
8 For discussion of sociopolitical keywords, see Jeffries and Walker (2017).
9 Short for two pence worth.
10 For more on textually constructed relationships of equivalence, see Jeffries (2009: 51–65).

References

Aikhenvald, Alexandra Y. (2004) *Evidentiality*. Oxford: Oxford University Press.

Allcott, H. and Gentzkow, M. (2017) 'Social media and fake news in the 2016 election'. *Journal of Economic Perspectives*, 31(2): 211–236.

Bakhtin, M. M. (1981) *The dialogic imagination: Four essays*, ed. M. Holquist, trans. C. Emerson and M. Holquist. Austin, TX: University of Texas Press.

Clark, H. and Gerrig, R. (1990) 'Quotations as demonstrations'. *Language*, 66: 764–805. doi: 10.2307/414729

Fairclough, N. (2003) *Analysing discourse*. London: Routledge

Farkas, J. and Schou, J. (2018) 'Fake news as a floating signifier: Hegemony, antagonism and the politics of falsehood'. *Javnost – The Public*, 25(3): 298–314. doi: 10.1080/13183222.2018.1463047

Halliday, M. A. K. and Matthiessen, C. (2014) *An introduction to functional grammar* (4th edition). London: Routledge.

Jeffries, L. (2009) *Critical stylistics: The power of English*. Basingstoke: Palgrave Macmillan.

Jeffries, L. and Walker, B. (2017) *Keywords in the press: The New Labour years*. London: Bloomsbury.

Leech, G. and Short, M. (2007) *Style in fiction: A linguistic introduction to English fictional prose* (2nd edition). London and New York: Longman.

McIntyre, D., Bellard-Thomson, C., Heywood, J., McEnery, A., Semino, E., and Short, M. (2004) 'Investigating the presentation of speech, writing and thought in spoken British English: A corpus-based approach'. *ICAME Journal*, 28: 49–76.

McIntyre, D. and Walker, B. (2011) 'A corpus based approach to discourse presentation in Early Modern English writing'. *The International Journal of Corpus Linguistics*, 16(1): 101–130.

McIntyre, D. and Walker, B. (2012) 'Annotating a corpus of Early Modern English writing for categories of discourse presentation'. In F. Manzano (ed.), *Unité et Diversité de la linguistique*, pp. 87–107. Les Cahiers du Centre d'Etudes Linguistiques. Lyon: Atelier intégré de publication de l'Université Jean Moulin – Lyon 3.

McIntyre, D., Bellard-Thomson, C., Heywood, J., McEnery, A., Semino, E., and Short, M. (2004) 'Investigating the presentation of speech, writing and thought in spoken British English: A corpus-based approach'. *ICAME Journal*, 28: 49–76.

Semino, E. and Short, M. (2004) *Corpus stylistics: Speech, writing and thought presentation in a corpus of English writing*. London: Routledge.

Short, M. (1988) 'Speech presentation, the novel and the press'. In W. van Peer (ed.), *The taming of the text*, pp. 61–81. London: Routledge

Short, M. (1996) *Exploring the language of poems, plays and prose*. Harlow: Longman.

Short, M. (2012) 'Discourse presentation of speech (and writing but not thought) summary'. *Language and Literature*, 21(1): 18–32.

Short, M., Semino, E., and Wynne, M. (2002) 'Revisiting the notion of faithfulness in discourse presentation using a corpus approach'. *Language and Literature*, 11(4): 325–355.

Thompson, G. (1996) 'Voices in the text: Discourse perspectives on language reports'. *Applied Linguistics*, 17(4): 501–530.

van Leeuwen, T. (2008) *Discourse and practice: New tools for critical discourse analysis*. Oxford: Oxford University Press.

Walker, B. and Karpenko-Seccombe, T. (2017) 'Speech presentation and summary in the BBC News online coverage of a Russian TV interview with Vladimir Putin'. *CADAAD Journal*, 9(2): 79–96.

Walker, B. and McIntyre, D. (2015) 'Thinking about the news: Thought presentation in Early Modern English'. In P. Baker and T. McEnery (eds), *Corpora and discourse studies*. Basingstoke: Palgrave.

Young-Brown, F. (2020) *Fake news and propaganda*. New York: Cavendish Square.

11 Corpus linguistics and discourse analysis

Introduction

Corpus linguistics is the study of language using computers, specialised software, and large bodies of electronic data known as corpora (which is the plural of corpus). Corpus linguistic approaches and tools can help us to explore linguistic patterns in large samples of language data in ways that would be impossible to do manually. Since its beginnings in the 1960s, when computing technology started to become readily available, corpus linguistics has been enhancing our understanding of language and how it works. Discourse analysis using corpora is an exciting and developing area of study that is becoming increasingly important for informing our understanding of discourse. In this chapter, we will introduce some of the basic ideas, methods, and approaches from corpus linguistics.

Corpus linguistics

We will start by explaining what a corpus is, and then go on to describe what is meant by corpus linguistics.

What is a corpus?

A corpus (which is Latin for 'body') is a collection of naturally occurring language data that has been selected to be **representative** of a particular type of discourse or language variety. Corpora can be very large containing hundreds of thousands, millions, or even billions of words. Many ready-made corpora are available to use for research or, depending on what it is you want to investigate, you can create your own corpora. Corpora are analysed using specially designed computer software, and so corpus data must be stored electronically on a computer in a machine-readable format. That means, for example, that while a collection of VHS video tapes[1] containing cookery programmes from the 1990s holds quite a large sample of language data, it is not a corpus in the sense used in corpus linguistics because the spoken words on the tapes are not in the form of computer readable files. To turn such VHS relics into a corpus, the spoken

DOI: 10.4324/9781003351207-11

discourses (typically between presenter and viewer) that form a major part of the programmes would need to be transcribed onto a computer. In the same way, scanning written texts (e.g. magazines) and saving them as, say, JPEG or PDF files does not make a corpus because these sorts of file format do not render the language data (the words) machine-readable. To create a corpus, then, the words from the original discourse need to be transcribed and stored on a computer in machine-readable (usually plain text) format.

What is corpus linguistics?

Corpus linguistics is the study of language using corpora and specially designed computer tools. According to Biber et al. (1998), corpus linguistics is also empirical, meaning that it is interested in actual language patterns observed in data (and not what you think the language patterns might be or should be) and requires both quantitative and qualitative analysis. So, corpus linguistics is not just about counting language features, which computers are very good at, but also looking at the computer-generated results, and using analytical frameworks or models from other areas of linguistics to make sense of the results. Like all computer-generated results (whether they are x-rays, graphs, or word frequencies), they require human interpretation, which means that corpus linguistic approaches do not dispense with the linguist!

Corpus linguistics and discourse analysis

Combining discourse analysis with corpus linguistics involves:

a) getting a big sample of discourse data onto a computer and using computer tools to analyse that data to find patterns that tell us something about the language use within the sample;
b) using the analytical frameworks from discourse analysis to help analyse and make sense of those results and patterns.

Corpus linguistic approaches (including building corpora and using corpus tools) can help to analyse a lot more discourse data than would be possible manually and help to explore patterns in the data that might provide an insight into the discourse(s) under investigation. The effectiveness and success of corpus linguistic approaches depends largely, in the first instance, on the quality of your data and there are some important principles that need to be considered (see Chapter 12 for more about data collection generally). While these principles relate to any data collection in any research and are not just to do with corpora, **sampling**, and **representativeness** have become watchwords in corpus linguistics. In the following sections we will discuss these important ideas in more detail.

Sampling, representativeness, and language variety

We have established that corpora tend to be defined as a representative sample of a language variety. Within this definition there are three important concepts that need further consideration: language variety, sampling, and representativeness.

Language variety

In the early days of corpus linguistics, researchers aimed to represent national languages (for example, British English), or periods of languages (for example, Early Modern British English). However, over the years, the scope of corpus linguistics has broadened, and corpora now also contain more constrained language varieties such as the language of a particular genre (e.g. print news media) or even the output of a single author (e.g. the novels of Charles Dickens).

As discourse analysts, we can think of a corpus as representing a discourse or collection of discourses which can be spoken or written. For example, we might have a corpus which contains transcribed spoken discourse consisting of samples of spoken interactions from a variety of different contexts. A corpus might also aim to represent a more narrowly defined discourse and contain, say, spoken discourse from just one context. For example, the Hansard Corpus at English-Corpora.org contains transcribed spoken interactions between politicians in the UK houses of parliament (the House of Commons and the House of Lords) and is therefore constrained by several factors including location and membership (only elected members may speak). Defining what counts as the discourse you are investigating is an important step in any research project, not least corpus research.

Sampling

Depending on the language variety or discourse you are investigating, sampling is extremely important. Say, for example, you are investigating email interactions, it would be practically impossible to collect every email ever written and sent in the world. Consequently, no matter how big your corpus, it could never contain every email. This is where sampling comes in. The idea with sampling, in theory at least, is to collect enough examples of a discourse type to represent the entirety of that discourse. So, if we are interested in studying emails, we would collect enough emails to represent the entirety of email discourse. The entirety of whatever phenomenon is being studied is usually referred to as the **population**, and as you might imagine, sampling requires knowledge of the population you are sampling from (for example, what sorts of emails are out there) as well as careful planning and a systematic approach to data collection. Figure 11.1 aims to show this idea using shapes. The large circle depicts the whole population, but within that population there is variety (shown by different shapes) which might be to do with sociocontextual factors such as age, gender, purpose, domain (e.g. business, education, social). Ideally, if we want to create a sample that represents the whole population, we need to collect examples of all the shapes that make up the population (Sample A). This would require knowledge of the population and what it comprises. We would need to decide how many examples of each different shape we needed in our sample and whether the proportions of shapes in our sample reflect the proportions in the population (e.g. if squares are the most frequent shape in the population, do we have more squares than any other shape in our sample?). Sample B in Figure 11.1 contains only one shape and, furthermore, the shape is the least frequent in the entire population. This is an extreme example, but one that might occur if, for example, the researcher's knowledge of the population extended only as far as their own discourse community and their data collection was limited by their knowledge of the population. The sample therefore only represents the discourse community from which it was drawn, and any findings are not representative of the wider population.

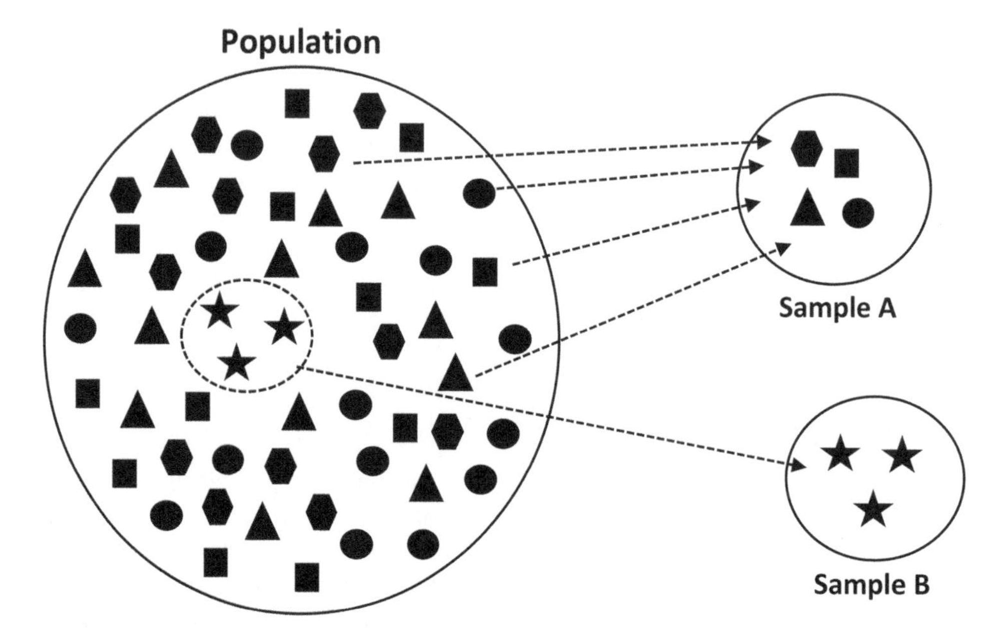

Figure 11.1 Sampling

Suppose we wanted to create a corpus of emails that represented the whole population of emails, we would have to think about the range and sort of emails we would need to collect. By that we mean things like the language the emails are written in (e.g. English, French, Japanese), the social situation in which the emails are created (e.g. at work between colleagues), and the purpose of the email (e.g. workplace admin). We might choose to collect only emails that are written in English,[2] that reflect three different social situations and purposes: personal ones between friends and family, professional ones between colleagues (or between employer and employee), and business emails between customers and clients. We might decide to exclude (for reasons we would need to make clear) advertising and spam email. These choices, which are based on our knowledge of emails, become the parameters which define (and inevitably restrict) our data and our corpus. We would also need to think about how many emails to collect and from whom, whether to collect whole email messages or extracts, and whether to collect equal amounts of email data from the different contexts. We would, of course, also need to obtain the consent of the email producers to use their emails for data (we discuss consent and ethics in Chapter 12).

Conversely, to take another example, if we were interested in examining witness statements from just one particular incident using corpus techniques, then our corpus would be much more constrained. That is because there would be a finite number of witness statements and once collected no more would be produced. So, depending on the size of the case and the number of witness statements collected, the corpus could easily hold every single example of that discourse.

Representativeness

The idea of sampling and using our knowledge of the language population to produce an informed sample, is that we want a corpus that represents the whole of the population. In Figure 11.1, Sample A represents the population more successfully than Sample B, because the former contains a better spread of different shapes from the entire population whereas the latter is far more restricted containing only one shape. Creating a corpus that aims to be a representative sample is important because if we want to make generalisations about the population from which our sample was drawn then they will only be reliable if our corpus is a fair and representative sample of the population. We will return to this point in the sections that follow below.

Corpus not always required!

It is worth acknowledging at this point that we do not need to build a corpus to use corpus linguistic methods and tools. We can explore any group of texts or a single text using corpus tools. Whatever way we choose to use corpus tools, we always need to be clear about our research aims and aware that any results, while possibly indicative of wider trends, might not be generalisable beyond the data.

Using corpus methods to analyse corpora

In this section, we introduce the main analytical methods used in corpus linguistics that are typically offered by corpus software.

Word frequency analysis

Word frequency analysis is a useful quantitative observation we can make about discourse data that shows the frequencies of all the different words in a corpus. Corpus tools tend to present word frequencies in two ways:

- **raw frequency** – shows the number of observed occurrences of each word in the corpus;
- **relative frequency** – shows the number of occurrences of each word divided by the total number of words in the entire corpus. The result of this calculation can be a very small number and typically, depending on the size of the corpus, it is multiplied by 100 to give a percentage (%), by 1,000 to give a per thousand frequency (‰), or even by a million to give a per million frequency (/mill).

Word frequencies and language change across time

Frequency analysis can be used to investigate lexical change across time (i.e. diachronic change). We are going to demonstrate this idea using a ready-made corpus called the Corpus of Historical American English (or COHA for short). COHA is available via a web-based interface (details are at the end of this chapter) and contains 475 million words of written American English (AmE) produced from 1820 to 2010. Importantly, the corpus is divided into 20 sub-corpora, one for each decade (see Table 11.1). This subdivision makes the corpus useful for studying language change over time.

Imagine, now, that you are interested in the modal auxiliary verb 'shall' and whether its usage has declined, risen, or stayed about the same over time (you might have your own intuitions about this). COHA, with its almost 200 years' worth of written data, can provide us with some insight on this. The raw and relative frequencies of 'shall' in each of the sub-corpora are shown in Table 11.1 along with the size of each sub-corpora. The graph in Figure 11.2 plots the relative frequency of 'shall' for each decade represented by the sub-corpora that make up COHA and shows a decline in the use of 'shall' in AmE (as represented by COHA) over time. COHA, then, enables us to explore diachronic lexical change. As far as 'shall' goes, we could explore the frequencies of this modal verb in other corpora (such as a corpus of British English) to see if a similar trend occurs (for corpus explorations of modal auxiliary verbs in different corpora see, for example, Leech 2003 and Biber 2004).

Notice that in Figure 11.2 we used the relative frequencies of 'shall' in each subsection of the corpus. We calculated the relative frequencies by first dividing the raw frequency of 'shall' by the number of words in the sub-corpus and then multiplying the result by 1 million to give the frequency per million words of data. This process is sometimes referred to as **normalising** the results and is necessary when comparing frequencies from datasets of different sizes. Normalising the frequencies takes into account the different sizes of the sub-corpora by presenting frequencies relative to the size of the data in which they occur.

Table 11.1 Raw and relative frequencies of 'shall' by decade in COHA

Decade	Sub-corpus Size	Raw Freq.	Relative Freq./mill.
1820	6,981,389	8727	1250.04
1830	13,711,287	14100	1028.35
1840	15,807,047	16916	1070.16
1850	16,536,003	15405	931.60
1860	16,936,560	15381	908.15
1870	18,788,467	14764	785.80
1880	20,067,205	15942	794.43
1890	20,426,783	14818	725.42
1900	21,977,250	13422	610.72
1910	23,103,098	10893	471.50
1920	25,700,422	10325	401.74
1930	27,707,879	8343	301.11
1940	27,399,750	6960	254.02
1950	28,661,274	5759	200.93
1960	29,122,676	5850	200.87
1970	28,829,225	4474	155.19
1980	29,851,580	3588	120.19
1990	33,149,318	2863	86.37
2000	34,821,812	2133	61.25
2010	35,452,806	1624	45.81

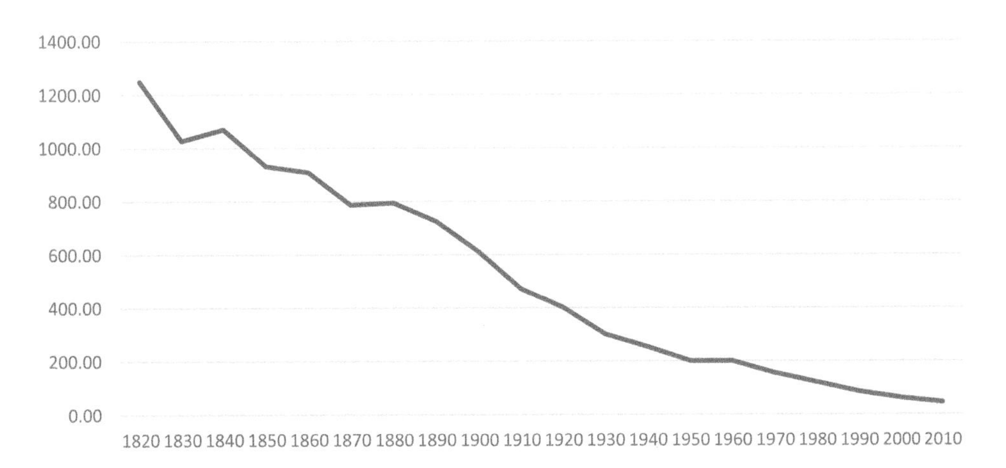

Figure 11.2 Frequency of 'shall' over time in COHA

Wordlists ranked by frequency

Corpus tools can provide a list of all the different words in a corpus (known as **types**) ranked by their frequency. Such wordlists can offer a way of viewing a corpus that we could not achieve by simply reading the data which can indicate: (i) the most common topics contained in a corpus; and (ii) the frequent grammatical structures used in the data. Words ranked by frequency can therefore suggest a focus for further analysis. This idea is illustrated by Activity 11.1 which requires you to consider the top 50 most frequent words (shown in Table 11.2) in a corpus that contains 3.5 million words in total.

Activity 11.1 The top 50 most frequent words

Before reading on, take a moment to look at the information in Table 11.2 and consider what (if anything) the top 50 most frequent words in our mystery corpus tells you about the data.

The table is set out in three columns with the first column showing the rank of the word (1–50), the second column contains the word, and the third column shows the raw frequency. We say more about the corpus and what it contains below.

Table 11.2 Top 50 most frequent words in the mystery corpus

Rank	Word	Raw Freq.
1	The	202018
2	And	120495
3	A	92170
4	To	80006
5	Was	65807
6	In	56144
7	We	50196
8	I	48650
9	Of	46057
10	For	39198
11	Is	38921
12	Hotel	36648
13	It	33774
14	Room	30155
15	With	26658
16	Very	25296
17	Were	24528
18	At	23984
19	You	21998

Rank	Word	Raw Freq.
20	This	21817
21	But	21710
22	On	20391
23	Our	20293
24	Had	20030
25	That	18971
26	Staff	17992
27	My	17885
28	As	17789
29	Not	16564
30	Are	16297
31	Have	15221
32	London	15151
33	From	14596
34	Stay	14134
35	All	13572
36	So	12742
37	Great	12492
38	Service	12481
39	Be	12332
40	There	12323
41	n't	12285
42	breakfast	11697
43	Which	10954
44	Good	10899
45	Would	10788
46	They	10709
47	's	9907
48	One	9891
49	Us	9497
50	An	9325

We can reveal that our mystery corpus contains online reviews for London hotels downloaded from a review website. We will refer to this corpus as the London Hotels Reviews Corpus (**LHRC** for short). The reviews relate to nine of the most expensive London hotels (e.g. The Dorchester) and 11 cheaper/lower budget hotels. A breakdown of the review data, including the number of words devoted to reviewing each hotel, is shown in Table 11.3.

Looking back at the top 50 most frequent words in Table 11.2, the non-grammatical words 'hotel', 'room', 'staff', 'London', 'stay', 'service', 'breakfast' provide clues about the corpus data, and these words give some indication of what the reviews are about and are suggestive of the sorts of things that provoke comment. Grammatical words are also important for understanding more about

Table 11.3 Constituent word totals for London Hotels Review Corpus (LHRC)

Top end		Cheaper end	
Name	words		words
Bulgari	44341	Apex	247342
Corinthia	365227	A to Z	10166
Dorchester	218839	City View	2107
Lanesborough	38767	Hartley	4122
Mandarin	135053	London Guest House	28229
Rembrandt	346226	Marble Arch	2538
Savoy	725460	Mondrian	471862
Wellesley	47886	Newham	30155
45 Park Lane	30527	Rhodes	135784
		Ridgemount	150200
		Xenia	143290
Totals	**1,952,326**		**1,225,795**
Grand Total		**3,178,121**	

a discourse. For example, in the LHRC the fifth most frequent word is 'was', which could indicate a prevalence of *X was Y* syntactic frame. This makes sense if we consider the sorts of comments that are likely in a review: 'The hotel/breakfast/room/service *was* good/great/awful', and so on. Additionally, the pronoun 'we' is slightly more frequent than 'I', possibly suggesting that fewer reviewers were travelling alone, and/or that reviewers write the review from the perspective of their couple/group status. All these things are worth investigating further yet it would have taken a very long time to assess these frequencies manually. Further investigation of individual words usually involves looking at concordance lines, which is the topic of our next section.

Concordance analysis

Concordances are generated by corpus linguistic software and provide a way of investigating how a word (or phrase) in a corpus is used. A **concordance** is a list of all the occurrences of a lexical item under investigation (a single word or short phrase) along with some of its surrounding co-text. This provides a view of the word in its linguistic environment (its co-text) and can allow us to observe patterns in the data.

Figure 11.3 shows an extract of a concordance for the word 'was' in the LHRC. The figure shows just the first 20 concordance lines out of a possible 65,807 and they are listed in the order in which they appear in the corpus (notice that all the occurrences are from reviews for the same hotel – The Apex). The concordance in Figure 11.3 shows the word under investigation in the centre with some co-text either side. This format is sometimes known as a **KWIC** view

1	of prosecco and a lovely comfortable room. Bed	was	very comfortable. Would definitely stay there aga	ApexLondon.txt
2	booked 1 night DBB choosing this hotel as it	was	so close to the Barbican where my daughter	ApexLondon.txt
3	so close to the Barbican where my daughter	was	graduating. We stayed Sunday night and I have	ApexLondon.txt
4	arrival to a room with a balcony which	was	great as it was also our wedding anniversary	ApexLondon.txt
5	with a balcony which was great as it	was	also our wedding anniversary and we enjoyed sitti	ApexLondon.txt
6	with everything you need eg iron etc. Dinner	was	tasty as was breakfast. City streets were busier	ApexLondon.txt
7	need eg iron etc. Dinner was tasty as	was	breakfast. City streets were busier the following	ApexLondon.txt
8	Staff friendly. rooms are Clean and the bathroom	was	pretty big. Only negative was breakfast which is	ApexLondon.txt
9	and the bathroom was pretty big. Only negative	was	breakfast which is served at the table and	ApexLondon.txt
10	ilities including a rubber duck! My one complaint	was	the bed which was beyond firm - very hard,	ApexLondon.txt
11	duck! My one complaint was the bed which	was	beyond firm - very hard, no give at all	ApexLondon.txt
12	like sleeping on a plank of wood. This	was	a shame as we didn't get a	ApexLondon.txt
13	rried in the city. Conveniently located the hotel	was	in fact a haven of calm with some	ApexLondon.txt
14	spacious and the external balcony access and area	was	one of the best features - it was great	ApexLondon.txt
15	area was one of the best features - it	was	great to sit out and read or have	ApexLondon.txt
16	ouse facilities were excellent and the room décor	was	modern and well considered. Would not think twice	ApexLondon.txt
17	the staff to be very helpful. room service	was	very good. transport to other parts of london	ApexLondon.txt
18	are both short walks away. the room itself (117)	was	very good, with a very comfortable king size	ApexLondon.txt
19	etc. the outlook from the first floor room	was	not attractive, but i wasn't staying here	ApexLondon.txt
20	closed on the weekend. as a result, it	was	very quiet the weekend i stayed, which is	ApexLondon.txt

Figure 11.3 KWIC view of 'was'; first 20 concordance lines out of 65,807

which stands for **Key Word In Context**. That is essentially what a concordance is. Here, *key word* is the lexical item under investigation and *context* means some of the co-text (or words) either side of the key word (we will introduce another type of keyword later in the chapter). The amount of co-text is known as the *concordance window* and in Figure 11.3, the window is 50 characters either side of 'was'. Some corpus tools allow the window size to be adjusted to suit your needs.

The 20 concordance lines in Figure 11.3 help to give a sense of how 'was' is used in the LHRC. As we mentioned earlier, 'was' is likely to feature in *X was Y* constructions, where *X* is the grammatical Subject, *Y* its Complement, and *was* operates as a copular verb. In Figure 11.3 we can see that this is the case in 19 out of the 20 lines (in line 3 'was' is an auxiliary verb). We can also see in the small sample that these clausal structures are used for evaluating things like bed, breakfast, view from the room, and location. However, Figure 11.3 shows just a small fraction of the 65,807 occurrences of 'was' in our data and as analysts our job is to assess the data systematically and rigorously rather than choose a few examples that help to support any hypotheses we might have about the data. Any such analysis of concordances is largely manual and so can be quite daunting, especially when faced with thousands of lines (in our case 65,807). In the following sections, we will consider some methods for handling the analysis of concordance lines.

Sorted concordances

Many corpus tools can sort concordances alphabetically based on the words to the left and/or right of the search term. Alphabetical sorting of concordances lines can help considerably with data analysis. We illustrate this in Figure 11.4 which shows the first 20 concordance lines of 'was' from the LHRC with alphabetical sorting switched on.[3] We can see that we get a different set of concordance lines to those shown in Figure 11.3 because now they have been ordered differently (recall that in Figure 11.3 we saw the first 20 concordance lines for 'was' without any sorting). The alphabetical re-ordering has pushed to the top of the list a different set of 20 occurrences of 'was' out of the total 65,807 – notice that the filenames in the 'File' column show that the occurrences are from different files, and none are from reviews of the Apex Hotel. Sorting, then, does not alter the data, it just changes the way we see it.

If you look carefully at Figure 11.4, you will see that the occurrences of 'was' are ordered, in the first instance, alphabetically by the first word following 'was' (i.e. one word to the right). So, we can see all the instances of 'was' when it is followed by 'awful', then 'awkward', then 'awoken' and finally 'back'. The concordances also incorporate a second level of sorting which places these results alphabetically using the second word following 'was' (i.e. two words to the right). So, for example, if you look at concordance lines 3 to 11 you

1	mattress springs through the material, it	**was**	awful. We made a more comfortable bed for him	Savoy.txt
2	complaint I would make was the porridge	**was**	awful. We also had the lunch time buffet/Carvery	Rembrandt.txt
3	of the premises. | The only instance where it	**was**	awkward (and slightly funny) was when we were	Mondrian.txt
4	fit, and being a tall man it was not ideal and it	**was**	awkward especially at night. However, The room	Rembrandt.txt
5	slight slope as you go in the bathroom door which	**was**	awkward for a person who has mobility problem	Rembrandt.txt
6	very center of the bedroom with no tools in hand	**was**	awkward; his explanation of repairing the ceiling	Savoy.txt
7	roomy bath, and comfortable furniture. Nothing	**was**	awkward, nothing was disappointing, nothing was	corinthia.txt
8	boutique. | However -- the check-in experience	**was**	awkward. They porters are wearing polo shirts	Mondrian.txt
9	some nuts and they were very nice about it, but it	**was**	awkward when they brought the tray out and had	Lanesborough.txt
10	The overall setup of the lobbies and the room	**was**	awkward, with little mapping and pointers toward	Dorchester.txt
11	my room by security. With respect to the guests, I	**was**	awoken at all hours on Saturday night by loudly	Mandarin.txt
12	vice was prompt. However, I stayed 3 nights and	**was**	awoken by a loud party on two of the nights. My	Savoy.txt
13	early morning hours of my first night at the hotel I	**was**	awoken by a group of women talking loudly and	Savoy.txt
14	i had was i believe a faulty valve, so at 5 am i	**was**	awoken by a load noise and the sound of gushing	Savoy.txt
15	in Los Angeles and sleep with my windows open I	**was**	awoken multiple times to loud late night traffic. I	Newham.txt
16	the tailors nearby at 9am on a Saturday and dress	**was**	back in my room before 11:30am. I also wanted	Dorchester.txt
17	from my recent experience it is not as good as it	**was**	back in the day. Housekeeping is not getting the	Savoy.txt
18	place to stay. The last review I wrote for The Savoy	**was**	back in July where things didn't go to plan and I	Savoy.txt
19	twice to celebrate special occasions. Our first visit	**was**	back in 2014 and the next in 2015. It's a shame	corinthia.txt
20	there is little choice really. Randomly the aircon	**was**	back on the auto selection by the time morning	Mondrian.txt

Figure 11.4 KWIC view of 'was' sorted alphabetically

will see that 'awkward' is followed by 'and' on line 3 (the open bracket is ignored), 'especially' on line 4, 'for' on line 5, and so on. Alphabetical sorting can expose patterns of usage of words in corpus data and in the next section we will explore a possible analytical 'next step' where we assign to categories any patterns we find.

Categorising results

It is often useful to categorise the language feature under investigation in some way based on its usage or function within the concordance lines and therefore the corpus data. Any such categories are selected or created by the analyst for the purpose of the analysis of the data in hand (i.e. **ad hoc**) and are often suggested by the data itself (sometimes referred to as **data-driven**). Categories need to be well defined and based on some sort of analytical framework, and the concordance data should be treated systematically using these categories (we talk more about systematicity in Chapter 12).

For example, if we consider the use of 'was' in the LHRC, one possible classification we could apply is whether 'was' is used as a copular or auxiliary verb. In Figure 11.4 we can see these two uses in action. Lines 11 to 15, which group together 'was' followed by 'awoken', are examples of 'was' being used as an auxiliary verb in passive constructions, where 'awoken' is a past participle. The other 15 lines are examples of 'was' as a copular verb. These two grammatical categories relating to the use of 'was' are based on linguistic description established within grammars of English and offer a potentially useful starting point for systematically analysing concordances of 'was' in the LHRC. Activity 11.2 asks you to try out applying this categorisation to some more data from the LHRC.

Activity 11.2 Copular and auxiliary 'was'

Below are ten short extracts from the LHRC corpus each containing an instance of 'was' (underlined). For every example, decide whether the underlined 'was' is used as a copular or auxiliary verb. Give reasons for your answer. Are some examples harder to categorise than others? If so, why?

(i) Our room was lovely, very chic and absolutely spotless.
(ii) The room was badly dated, a bit tattered, smelled weird, and had unsightly stains
(iii) As promised, I was called once the room became available at 14:00
(iv) Our room was called the Beauchamp Suite.
(v) The wifi was absolutely brilliant and very fast.

(vi) I was disappointed by the food though.
(vii) every restaurant in the hotel was fully booked for lunch.
(viii) The room was fully equipped with lots of unique extra touches.
(ix) Continental breakfast was included in our rate.
(x) My bed was positioned at an angle which was a little funky.

Answers are at the end of the chapter.

Other ad hoc categories we could employ in the analysis of 'was' include, for example, grouping occurrences of copular 'was' by the grammatical part of speech (e.g. adjective, adverb, noun) of the Subject Complement (i.e. the word or phrase that follows 'was'). The occurrences of copular 'was' followed by an adjective could then be further analysed to look at, for example, whether the adjective is positive (e.g. 'good'), negative (e.g. 'awful'), or neutral (e.g. 'big') and/or whether there are any patterns relating to the subjects they describe. For example, do certain grammatical subjects (e.g. 'the bathroom') attract particular types of adjective, such as adjectives of size (e.g. 'big'). In this way, a corpus analysis first provides a focus from which we can carry out more detailed analysis using linguistic models to categorise and further understand the discourse the data represents.

A concordance is an essential tool that provides a window onto the data allowing us to explore it in ways that would not be possible manually. Concordances help to identify patterns for further analysis, which might involve grouping occurrences of lexical items in a principled way (perhaps informed by existing linguistic models) that are suggested by the data itself. In the next section we move on to another essential corpus method for data analysis that is made possible by tools: comparison.

Making comparisons between corpora

So far, we have seen how word frequencies in corpora can offer some insight into the discourses they aim to represent. However, to know whether such frequencies are 'normal' or peculiar to the data under investigation and therefore noteworthy, we need a reference point against which we can compare them. For example, in our corpus of hotel reviews (LHRC) we saw that the words 'the' and 'and' were the top two most frequent words (see Table 11.2), but we do not know whether these frequency rankings are unique to written hotel reviews or normal in written discourse generally. To help find out, we need to compare the findings from the LHRC (our **research corpus**) with word frequencies from another corpus (a **reference corpus**).

There are numerous ready-made corpora that can act as a comparator against which word frequencies can be evaluated. Some of these corpora can be downloaded (sometimes for a fee) while others are only available via web-interfaces that allow you to interrogate them but not download the data. COHA, the corpus we met earlier in the chapter, is one such example (we list others at the end of this chapter). If a suitable ready-made reference corpus is not available, then you can build your own, provided you have access to the data you need. Deciding which reference corpus to use is a matter of balancing what is practical and what available data fits best as a point of reference.

Choosing a suitable reference corpus

Comparing a research corpus against a reference corpus helps to highlight potentially distinctive language features in the research data and the discourse it represents. The features that are highlighted will depend to some extent on the choice of reference corpus, which will be driven by a combination of research aims and what is practical and possible. The reference corpus aims to act as a norm or yardstick against which the research corpus is evaluated.

When choosing a reference corpus, it is often a good idea to match contextual aspects of the corpus data and the populations they represent. To help with this it can be useful to create a list of discourse parameters (see Chapter 1) that relate to your data. For example:

Event	Leaving a review for a hotel.
Time	21st century (2012).
Purpose	Reviewing; informing other potential customers; complaining; commending.
Participants	Reviewers (everyday customers) and readers of reviews (potential customers); hoteliers.
Code	Different varieties of English depending on nationality of reviewer.
Medium	Electronic web-based forum.
Mode	Written.

These parameters are variables which potentially affect language choices. We can consider which parameters, or variables, we want to investigate in relation to language choices. So, say we are interested in the effect purpose and medium has on language choices in the data, we would aim to build a reference corpus that matches the other parameters. Matching discourse parameters in the data is one way of controlling variables that might affect language use, and this can help to reduce 'noise' in the results. By 'noise' we mean results that are not connected to the focus of the research aims, which is to find out about language features associated with online hotel reviews. So, for example, if we were to use a corpus of spoken discourse for our reference point, then we are likely to get results that highlight difference that relate to written versus spoken discourse. Similarly, if we were to compare our hotel reviews against a corpus of 18th-century British English (BrE), we would find out something about the differences between 21st-century and 18th-century BrE. The idea then is to try to match discourse parameters that do not relate to your research interests.

We aimed to match the mode of the discourse under investigation (written) and the language (code). Because the hotel reviews in the LHRC were posted by a variety of English speakers including those whose first language is not English, we built a reference corpus that contains examples of many different English varieties from around the world (e.g. UK English, US English, Indian English, etc.). To achieve this breadth of variety (which we hoped would go some way to match the breadth of variety in our corpus), we combined several small corpora to form our reference corpus.

We used ten corpora from the International Corpus of English (ICE) family of corpora, each of which have a similar structure and aim to represent different varieties of English from around the world. The corpora are around 1 million words each and contain both (transcribed) spoken and written data. Our reference corpus contains the written sections from those ICE corpora that are freely available for download: ICE Canada, East Africa, Hong Kong, India, Ireland, Jamaica, Nigeria, Philippines, Singapore, and USA. As well as these corpora, we also used the 1-million-word Freiburg, Lancaster, Oslo, Bergen (FLOB) corpus of written British English. The resulting super-corpus of 11 different varieties of English (hereafter ICE-FLOB[4]) contains approximately 5.8 million words. Table 11.4 provides summary details.

Table 11.4 ICE-FLOB reference corpus

Constituent corpus	No. of words
ICE Canada written	435170
ICE East Africa written	802341
ICE Hong Kong written	498924
ICE India written	438694
ICE Ireland written	424186
ICE Jamaica written	415198
ICE Nigeria written	386405
ICE Philippines written	452198
ICE Singapore written	436339
ICE USA written	435155
FLOB	1128063
Total	**5, 852, 673**

Comparing LHRC against ICE-FLOB

Table 11.5 sets out the top 20 most frequent words in LHRC and those in ICE-FLOB. Take a moment to look at the information in the table and consider whether the comparison helps to offer further insights into the reviews data. The frequencies in Table 11.4 are per 1,000 words (denoted by the symbol ‰), which was calculated by dividing the raw frequency by the total number of words in the corpus and multiplying the result by 1,000. This makes the frequencies from the two corpora (which differ in size) comparable.

Note: Choosing the first 20 words as a cut-off is purely a matter of convenience; we could have decided just as easily to show the first 23 or 127 words. The choice then is completely arbitrary because it is not made on any principled basis other than it is a round number that fits easily onto the page and gives enough information for us to talk about.

If we assume that ICE-FLOB provides a reference point for international varieties of written English including British English, then comparing the ranks and word frequencies of the words can help to show what language features are particular to the hotel reviews in our data. Looking at the information in Table 11.5

Table 11.5 Top 20 words by frequency in LHRC and ICE-FLOB

	LHRC		ICE-FLOB	
Rank	**Word**	**Freq ‰**	**Word**	**Freq. ‰**
1	the	63.45	the	62.16
2	and	37.85	of	32.56
3	a	28.95	to	26.53
4	to	25.13	and	26.46
5	was	20.67	a	22.17
6	in	17.63	in	20.18
7	we	15.77	is	11.34
8	I	15.28	that	9.92
9	of	14.47	for	9.65
10	for	12.31	it	7.79
11	is	12.23	I	7.34
12	hotel	11.51	on	6.83
13	it	10.61	as	6.78
14	room	9.47	s	6.65
15	with	8.37	was	6.58
16	very	7.95	be	6.39
17	were	7.70	with	6.33
18	at	7.53	are	5.52
19	you	6.91	by	5.16
20	this	6.85	he	4.80

tells us that 'the' is the most frequent word in both corpora (and the relative frequencies are very similar), so the LHRC data are not special in having this as the most frequent word. However, 'and' has a noticeably higher ranking and relative frequency in the LHRC list, and this could be indicative of a syntactic style prevalent in our online reviews. We can also confirm that the relative frequency of 'was', which we mentioned above, is considerably higher in LHRC, which might also be indicative of a recurring syntactic structure. The comparison also highlights that (unsurprisingly) 'hotel' and 'room' have a high ranking in the LHRC data. Additionally, we can see that in the review data 'very' is the 16th most frequent word, whereas in the ICE-FLOB it is ranked 104 (so not shown in the table) with a relative frequency of around one occurrence per 1,000 words.

The comparison between two datasets where one is used as a point of reference can be useful in highlighting lexical and possibly syntactic features that are peculiar to a discourse and can offer a good starting point for further investigation. The next step in an analysis is to investigate these lexical items within the data to establish how they are used and whether their usage is distinctive of that discourse. This next stage is achieved (certainly in the first instance) using concordance lines.

Keyness and keywords

In the previous section, we made manual comparisons between word frequencies in the LHRC (our research corpus) and ICE-FLOB (our reference corpus). By using ICE-FLOB as a comparator, we were able to observe differences in word frequencies between our review data and a corpus of general international English and use our own judgement to decide whether the differences were salient and worth further investigation. However, a substantial problem with this method of judging saliency is that it is subjective. A further and equally sizeable problem is that we only evaluated differences for the 20 most frequent word types and not <u>all</u> the word types in the corpus.

A more principled and systematic way of comparing frequencies and deciding which differences are noteworthy is to use statistical testing to calculate what are known as **keywords**. Keywords are those words that are **over-represented**[5] in the research corpus by comparison with a reference corpus and are determined by comparing word frequencies using statistical tests. Many corpus tools will compute keywords automatically using either **statistical significance** or **effect size** calculations, or a combination of both.

Statistical significance

Simply put, statistical significance refers to results that are assessed as important or noteworthy using statistical tests. Results that are statistically significant are said NOT to have happened by chance but have been caused by some factor that is particular to the population from which the sample was drawn. Just what that factor might be and whether it is peculiar to the population is for the analyst to investigate. Statistically significant results, then, are those highlighted as being potentially important and worthy of further investigation. Keywords are those words in a corpus whose frequencies are found to be significantly different from the corresponding word frequencies in the reference corpus.

Statistical significance depends on what is known as **hypothesis testing.** Recall that at the start of this chapter we discussed the idea of corpora being a representative sample from an entire population. When we calculate keywords, we are making a comparison between two corpora and therefore (if we assume the corpora are representative samples) two populations. Hypothesis testing relates back to the populations from which the corpora were sampled and a default assumption that there is no difference between them. Consequently, any differences in word frequencies observed in the corpora are assumed to be due to sampling error or chance. This default assumption is called the **null hypothesis** and is denoted by H_0. The **alternative hypothesis,** which is denoted by H_1, is that any observed differences in the corpus data *do* reflect a true or real difference in the populations. To summarise:

H_0: There is no difference between two populations the data came from, and any observed differences in the data are due to sampling error or chance rather than a true difference between the populations.

H_1: There is a true difference between the two populations, so observed differences in the data relate to differences in the population.

The idea of hypothesis testing is that the null hypothesis holds true unless there is sufficiently strong evidence against it to reject it. This is where significance testing comes in. A significance test, of which there are many to choose from, is a mathematical calculation that provides us with evidence by computing the probability of getting a result if the null hypothesis were true. If the probability is high, then that is evidence to accept the null hypothesis and reject the alternative. However, if the calculation returns a low probability, then that is evidence to reject the null hypothesis and accept the alternative hypothesis. When we do that, we are saying that the result is statistically significant. To summarise:

High probability that the result would have been obtained if H_0 were true = Evidence to accept H_0 and reject H_1; result not significant.

Low probability that the result would have been obtained if H_0 were true = Evidence to reject H_0 and accept H_1; result is significant.

If we relate this idea back to our LHRC and ICE-FLOB corpora, the default assumption is that there is no difference between the two populations from which these two corpora were drawn. Population here refers to the discourses that the two corpora represent, and difference refers to persistent patterns of language use within the discourses. So, H_0 assumes there is no pervading difference in language use between the online review discourse and the various discourses in ICE-FLOB. If we reject H_0 then we make an inference about the populations – that they are different in relation to persistent language choices. We might also make an inference about the contextual variables that influence such language choices (such as medium, purpose, producer/receiver). These inferences might become additional hypotheses that are explored further. For instance, we might hypothesise that the language is influenced by some non-random factor in the discourse such as being online, or by the purpose of reviewing.

Statistical tests provide a numerical indication of the probability of the results being obtained if the null hypothesis were true. The probability is suggestive of the confidence with which we can reject the default assumption of there being no difference. Later in this section, we will discuss what level of probability counts as sufficient evidence to confidently decide whether to reject the null hypothesis or not.

A popular significance test used in linguistics for calculating keywords is **log-likelihood** (Dunning 1993). This test was designed especially for text analysis and corpus research and is the test we will refer to over the rest of our discussion of keywords. With log-likelihood, the higher the number returned from the calculation, the lower the probability that the result would have been obtained if H_0 were true. Results with a high log-likelihood (LL) are therefore potentially statistically significant, due to differences in the populations, and worthy of further investigation.

Statistical significance tests help to establish that a difference exists between a research corpus and a reference corpus. They do not, however, give an indication of the scale of the difference between observed results. To do that we need to use **effect size** calculations, which we will look at next.

Effect size: measuring the scale of the difference

While statistical significance tests indicate the confidence with which we can say that our results are not a chance happening, they do not tell us whether a difference is big or small. Consequently, keywords investigations increasingly incorporate a second statistic known as **effect size** because this measures the scale of the difference between results (known as the **effect**). Whereas significance testing is a type of **inferential statistic** because it allows us to make inferences about the population from which a representative sample was drawn, effect size is a

descriptive statistic which means it simply describes the data. The basic idea with effect size is that small differences are less important and therefore less worthy of further investigation than big differences.

As with significance testing, there are many different measures of effect size to choose from, and each one returns a value that indicates the scale of difference between results. **Log ratio,** for example, was developed by Andrew Hardie especially for keyword research (see Hardie 2014). With log ratio, a value of 1 means that the frequency in the research corpus is twice as big as in the reference corpus; a log ratio of 2 means that the difference is four times as much, and so on (see Table 11.6). Therefore, the higher the number returned by the log ratio calculation, the bigger the scale of difference.

Table 11.6 Scale of frequency difference between research and reference corpora based on log ratio of relative frequencies (after Hardie 2014)

Log ratio of relative frequencies	Frequency in research corpus compared with Reference corpus
0	Frequency in research and reference corpora is the same
1	2 times more frequent in research corpus
2	4 times more frequent " " "
3	8 times more frequent " " "
4	12 times more frequent " " "
5	16 times more frequent " " "
. . .	. . .

Keyness

Associated with keywords is the notion of **keyness** which, according to Scott and Tribble (2006), is "a quality words may have in a given text or set of texts, suggesting that they are important" (Scott and Tribble 2006: 55–56).[6] Important words for discourse analysts are those which are indicative of language use that is peculiar to the discourse under investigation and therefore symptomatic of a contextual variable associated with that discourse. However, as Scott and Tribble state, keyness only suggests importance and so offers a starting point for further investigation of particular words in a corpus. So, keywords are potentially important, and their importance is indicated in the first instance by statistical tests but then evaluated by further investigation. We will return to this point later in this chapter.

What counts as a keyword? Using statistical cut-offs to decide

In combination, significance testing and effect size offer a principled way in which to establish which words in your data are key. Fortunately, corpus tools will carry out the calculations for us, so we do not need to do them manually (we do not have space here to show the formulae, but see 'Further reading' below). Statistical tests and effect size calculations both return numerical results, but we still need to know which values count as enough evidence against the null hypothesis and therefore offer enough confidence for us to reject it. For this we require what are known as **critical values**.

The result from a statistical test can be seen from two points of view; they indicate:

(i) the probability that the result would have occurred if the null hypothesis were true;
(ii) the level of confidence you have that a result is significant.

The lower the probability of getting the result if H_0 is true, the more confidently we can infer the result is due to a true difference in the population from which the data was drawn. To summarise:

low probability that the result would have been obtained if H_0 were true	=	**high confidence** that we can assume the result is significant.

The analyst decides on the level of confidence at which they are happy to reject the null hypothesis. The **critical value** is the line you draw in your results below which you say 'I do not have sufficient evidence to reject the null hypothesis, so these results are not significant', and above which you say 'I do have sufficient evidence to reject the null hypothesis so these results are significant'. The idea of a critical value, then, is that anything that falls below a chosen value is ignored; anything on or above the value is accepted as a keyword. Different statistical calculations have different critical values that relate to particular levels of confidence. The critical values for log-likelihood (LL) are shown in Table 11.7. The table shows that an LL score of at least 15.13 means that the probability of obtaining that result if H_0 were true (i.e. no difference in the populations from which the data were drawn) is very low at 0.01%, which means we can be 99.99% confident that the result is significant. A result with a LL score of at least 10.82 brings with it slightly less confidence of significance at 99.9%.

Table 11.7 Log-likelihood critical values (based on Rayson et al. 2004)

Log-likelihood critical value	Probability of getting result if H_0 true (%)	Level of confidence that result is significant (%)
3.84	5	95
6.63	1	99
10.82	0.1	99.9
15.13	0.01	99.99

When calculating keywords, the usual practice is to set a level of significance below which results are ignored. This means setting a minimum statistical score (in our case log-likelihood) for the results. With log-likelihood, if you want to be very confident about your results, then you set the minimum value high at, say, 15.13. Any results returned with a LL score lower than that are ignored.

Keywords can also be calculated using effect size calculation such as log ratio. However, there are no agreed critical values for this statistic and here researchers must rely on their own judgements. We choose to ignore any keywords with a log ratio of less than 1 which means we only look at keywords that are at least as twice as frequent in the research corpus as they are in the reference corpus. Applying this cut-off therefore eliminates keywords where the scale of difference is very small.

NOTE: Keywords can also be restricted using frequency cut-offs, which means deciding on a minimum raw frequency in the research corpus below which keywords are eliminated. This is rather different from using significance results because it has nothing to do with hypothesis testing, probability, or confidence. Instead, researchers must decide whether limiting results using frequency is useful for answering their research questions. For example, keywords that have a low raw frequency in the research corpus might be eliminated because they are unlikely to form patterns across the whole corpus and therefore unlikely to be indicative of language patterns in the discourse the corpus is representing.

Keywords in LHRC

Let's now return to the comparison between frequencies from LHRC and ICE-FLOB. We carried out a keyword analysis of the LHRC and, using AntConc (Anthony 2022), automatically compared all the words and their frequencies in the LHRC corpus against the corresponding words and frequencies in the ICE-FLOB corpus. We delimited our results using the following cut-offs: log-likelihood of 10.83 (so, our level of confidence in the differences is at least 99.9%), log ratio of 1 (so, keywords that are at least twice as frequent as those in the reference corpus), and raw frequency of 100, which we judged to be sufficient to observe meaningful patterns in the data. The comparison produced 1,028 keywords, which is a lot of keywords to assess. By assess we mean establish whether a keyword is symptomatic of discourse under investigation and tells us something about the linguistic nature of the data. This is a crucial step in any keyword analysis because while a difference might be statistically significant, it does not necessarily mean that it is telling us something important about the discourse we are investigating. We therefore aim to work out whether a keyword is not just statistically significant but also interpretatively significant.

Ideally, then, we need to work through each keyword in the list systematically looking at their co-text in detail using concordance lines. However, this can be time-consuming, and when there are thousands of keywords, impractical. Therefore, we will discuss methods for dealing with large numbers of keywords, which we will do using just the first 20 keywords in the LHRC for illustrative purposes. Table 11.8 shows the first 20 keywords listed in order of their log likelihood (LL) score.

Table 11.8 Keywords in LHRC when compared against ICE-FLOB

		LHRC		ICE+FLOB			
Rank	Keyword	Freq.	‰	Freq.	‰	LL	LR
1	hotel	36647	11.51	533	0.09	71694.5	7.0
2	room	30155	9.47	1637	0.28	51680.2	5.1
3	we	50196	15.77	17130	2.93	43680.0	2.4
4	was	65807	20.67	39764	6.79	32488.4	1.6
5	staff	17992	5.65	1343	0.23	29051.8	4.6
6	very	25296	7.95	6054	1.03	27419.7	2.9
7	london	15150	4.76	832	0.14	25872.0	5.1
8	stay	14134	4.44	751	0.13	24262.2	5.1
9	breakfast	11697	3.67	161	0.03	22894.5	7.1
10	stayed	8913	2.80	205	0.04	16848.9	6.3
11	rooms	8915	2.80	266	0.05	16459.0	5.9
12	great	12492	3.92	2132	0.36	15820.1	3.4
13	service	12481	3.92	2129	0.36	15809.5	3.4
14	our	20293	6.37	7925	1.35	15804.1	2.2
15	location	8635	2.71	348	0.06	15407.4	5.5
16	bar	7883	2.48	285	0.05	14252.1	5.7
17	i	48650	15.28	41442	7.08	13389.7	1.1
18	savoy	5790	1.82	5	0.00	12024.2	11.1
19	friendly	6444	2.02	208	0.04	11797.3	5.8
20	lovely	5984	1.88	172	0.03	11085.2	6.0

In Table 11.6, ‰ = per thousand frequency, LL = log-likelihood, and LR = log ratio

Like concordances, placing keywords into groups is often a useful starting point for an analysis. Groupings can be driven (in the first instance) by the grammatical class of the keywords. For example, looking at our top 20 keywords, three are pronouns ('we', 'I', and 'our') and these grammatical words are suggestive of the personal nature of reviews with the reviewer being present within the review. Nine of the keywords are common nouns ('hotel', 'room', 'staff', 'stay', 'breakfast', 'rooms', 'service', 'location', 'bar') and these indicate the discourse topic of the data and potentially the focus of many of the comments in the reviews data. For this reason, such keywords are sometimes referred to as 'aboutness' (Phillips 1989) keywords (see Scott 2000; Scott and Tribble 2006). There are also two proper nouns ('London' and 'Savoy'), both of which are indicative of the content of the corpus. It is usual for proper nouns to be keywords in any corpus comparison and often they are of low interpretative value. Three of the keywords are adjectives ('great', 'friendly', 'lovely') as well as one adverb ('very') and these are indicative of the evaluative nature (or purpose) of the discourse that the corpus represents. That three positive adjectives are in the top 20 keywords could suggest that the reviews in the corpus contain more positive evaluations than negative or that there is greater lexical variety used for negative evaluation therefore reducing the frequencies of individual negatively evaluative words. Finally, there are two verbs: 'was', which is indicative of repeated syntactic structures within the data; and the lexical verb 'stayed', which is another example of an aboutness keyword.

Keywords might also suggest categories that are semantic rather than grammatical. For instance, we could form groups such as 'food and drink', 'room, fixtures, and fittings', 'facilities', and so on depending on what other keywords are in the list. We could also have categories such as 'positive evaluation' and 'negative evaluation'. Whatever we decide, placing a keyword into a category requires investigation of the keyword in its surrounding co-text using concordance lines. Even when assigning keywords to grammatical categories this is required. For example, before categorising 'service' we ascertained that in the data it is always used as a noun rather than a verb, often as part of a two-word phrase 'room service'.

Intra-corpus comparison

As well as utilising a reference corpus for comparison, it can sometime be useful to carry out intra-corpus comparisons, whereby different sections of the same corpus are compared against each other. Whether this is possible or useful will depend in the structure of the corpus under investigation. With our data, we could split the LHRC on the basis of the price/star-rating of the hotels with nine being 'top-end' and the remaining 11 being 'cheaper-end'. Intra-corpus keyword comparisons are carried out in much the same way as described above.

We compared the nine top-end hotel reviews against those of the cheaper-end hotels, and vice versa to obtain two sets of keywords. These are shown in Activity 11.3, which asks you to guess which keywords belong to which group.

Activity 11.3 Comparing subsets of the London Hotels Reviews Corpus (LHRC)

Which set of keywords do you think are from the reviews of top-end hotels and which from the cheaper-end hotel reviews? Give reasons for your answer.

List A: clean, small, modern, friendly, views, very, room, great, walk, tube, helpful, rooftop, breakfast, shower, balcony, owners, owner, bus, good, nice, on, prosecco, free, floor, beans, close, definitely, stairs, location

List B: afternoon, tea, service, pool, butler, spa, experience, deco, beautiful, concierge, sandwiches, luxury, foyer, suite, scones, world, the, best, cakes, dinner, grand, truly, wonderful, history, treat, elegant, pianist, doormen, class, flowers

Once you know which keywords belong to which subcorpus, consider whether there is anything that is consistent in top end/cheaper-end hotel reviews?

Our answers are at the end of the chapter.

Collocation

We met collocates earlier in the book in Chapter 3. Collocates are those words that tend to occur near to the word under investigation (sometimes referred to as the **node word**; see Sinclair et al. 2004: 10). The term 'collocation' is usually attributed to J. R. Firth (1957) and relates to the co-occurrence relationships that words are involved in. Different discourses and different discourse topics will produce different patterns of collocation for a word, and corpora and corpus tools can help to explore these patterns.

Calculating collocates

Collocates are calculated within a **collocation window**, which is a span of words either side of the node word. The window can usually be set in the computer tool being used and differently sized windows can be chosen to suit your analytical focus. Sinclair et al. (2004: 35) suggest the optimum window is four words before and after the node word which, when the node word is included, gives a nine-word collocation window.

Collocates of words can be assessed using raw frequencies. So, for example, Table 11.9 shows the top ten collocates (out of over 2,500) of 'was' in the LHRC within a nine-word window (i.e. four words either side of the node word).

We can see in Table 11.9 that the most frequent collocate of 'was' is 'the', co-occurring a total of 42,871 times: 27,033 to the left of 'was'; 15,838 to the right. To illustrate left and right co-occurrence of 'the' with 'was', Figure 11.5 shows two examples from the corpus. In the figure, the collocation window is indicated by a rectangle and any word that occurs within that window counts as a collocate.

Frequency can help us to assess the salience of collocates for a word. However, as Table 11.9 shows, many of the high-frequency collocates are grammatical

Table 11.9 The most frequent collocates of 'was', 4L-4R

Rank	Collocate	Total Freq.	Freq. Left	Freq. Right
1	the	42871	27033	15838
2	and	24746	11120	13626
3	a	14405	3159	11246
4	room	12156	10341	1815
5	it	11943	9985	1958
6	i	9189	5685	3504
7	to	8175	2670	5505
8	very	7797	1180	6617
9	in	7533	4094	3439
10	was	6380	3190	3190

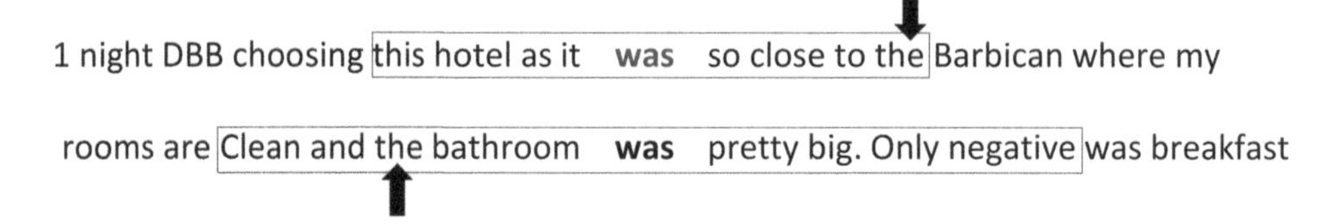

1 night DBB choosing this hotel as it was so close to the Barbican where my
rooms are Clean and the bathroom was pretty big. Only negative was breakfast

Figure 11.5 Examples of 'the' as right- and left-hand collocates of 'was'

words which are also likely to collocate with lots of other words. That means we cannot be sure whether these co-occurrences are peculiar to 'was' or happen with lots of other words in the data. For that reason, other statistical measures can help us to assess whether a collocate of the node word is noteworthy or not.

Some statistics, such as log-likelihood, compute the confidence with which we can assume that there is an association between two words. Other statistics evaluate the strength of association between two words (i.e. the node and its collocates). For example, **mutual information** (MI) is a statistic common to many corpus tools and assesses strength of attraction between words by looking at the other company the node word and the collocate in question keep within the corpus (see Clear 1993: 280; Manning and Schütze 1999: 182). So, while 'the' and 'was' may occur together a lot in the LHRC, we know that both 'the' and 'was' frequently hang around with lots of other words. So, in order to assess whether 'the' and 'was' have a particularly close association, the co-occurrence of these two words is compared against their co-occurrence with the other words in the corpus.

Church and Hanks (1990) recommend using a combination of statistics to calculate collocates. First, a measure of strength of association (e.g. MI) and then a measure of the confidence with which we can assume that there is an association (e.g. log-likelihood). This method helps to eliminate low frequency collocates which are potentially chance co-occurrences.

Using statistical cut-offs to decide what counts as a collocate

As with keywords, the usual practice with collocates is to set statistical levels below which results are ignored. For example, if MI is used, the lowest score that is indicative of a strong association is 3 (see Stubbs 1996; Hunston 2002). For log-likelihood any of the critical values shown in Table 11.7 can be used. Minimum raw frequencies can also be used on the basis that low frequency collocates might not be indicative of patterns that run through the whole corpus and are therefore less important as a feature of the discourse under investigation.

Statistically salient collocates of 'was' in LHRC

Using AntConc, we calculated collocates for 'was' again, but this time using statistical measures. AntConc uses combination of MI and log-likelihood (the LL critical value is pre-set to 3.84). So, MI is calculated first and then LL, and any collocates that do not achieve an LL score of at least 3.84 are eliminated. We also applied an MI cut-off of three and a minimum raw frequency cut-off of 20 to eliminate low frequency collocates. These settings produced a list of 917 collocates. Table 11.10 shows the first ten collocates of 'was' (out of 917) in order of frequency.

Table 11.10 The most frequent 4L-4R collocates of 'was' with an MI above 3 and an LL above 3.84

Rank	Collocate	Total Freq.	Left Freq.	Right Freq.	MI
1	the	42871	27033	15838	3.36
2	and	24746	11120	13626	3.31
3	room	12156	10341	1815	4.28
4	it	11943	9985	1958	4.09
5	i	9189	5685	3504	3.19
6	very	7797	1180	6617	3.90
7	our	5726	4009	1717	3.77
8	but	5400	2619	2781	3.59
9	breakfast	4930	4107	823	4.35
10	that	4369	2778	1591	3.48

We have listed the collocates in Table 11.10 in order of frequency for ease of comparison with Table 11.9. Using the information shown in Table 11.10 we can see that 'the' and 'and' are not only the most frequent collocates but are also attracted to 'was' because they have an MI score that is above the minimum required. Also, because AntConc uses LL to assess confidence of association, we can be reasonably confident that there is an association between 'was' and these words. However, the highly frequent collocates 'a', 'to', 'in', and 'was' that were in Table 11.7 do not appear in Table 11.8 because these are not statistically salient when assessed using a combination of MI and LL. Instead, 'but', 'breakfast', and 'that' have now moved into the top ten. The collocates shown in Table 11.10 are therefore both high in frequency and have statistical salience so we can be reasonably confident that these associations are not chance happenings. As we mentioned earlier, high-frequency collocates are likely to be indicative of patterns of language use that extend across much of the corpus.

Once collocates are calculated (of which there might be many), manual effort is required to make sense of the results, usually achieved by returning to concordance lines. As we discussed in the section above, any such manual analysis might involve creating data-driven categories, which can help to ascertain collocational tendencies and patterns.

N-grams

N-grams (sometimes referred to as lexical bundles or multi-word expressions) are contiguous sequences of words where a single word is a 1-gram, a two-word sequence is a 2-gram, a three-word sequence is a 3-gram; and so on. N-grams are calculated by corpus tools, which can rapidly search for repeated sequences of n words (imagine trying to do that manually!). Typically, the number of words in a sequence (the 'n') is specified by the analyst, and results can be filtered based on frequency and range, which is the spread of n-grams across the files that make up a corpus. So, a minimum frequency and range can be specified which will instruct the corpus tool to disregard: (i) low frequency n-grams which are likely to be of limited use for discourse analysis; and (ii) n-grams that appear in only a small number of the files that make up the corpus. N-grams have been studied extensively in both spoken and written discourses by corpus linguists (see, for example, Biber and Conrad 1999; Cortes 2004), with Biber and Barbieri (2007: 270) describing them as "important building blocks in discourse".

N-grams in the LHRC

Using AntConc, we calculated 3-grams (i.e. three-word sequences) in the LHRC with a minimum frequency of 20 and a range of at least 15 out of 20 files, meaning that the 3-gram had to appear in at least 75% of the files that make up the corpus for it to be included in the results. This produced a list of 1,143 3-grams, the top ten of which are shown in Table 11.11. Four of these 3-grams (the first, fifth, seventh, and tenth) have a range of 20 so appear in all of the corpus files; the rest have a range of either 17, 18, or 19, so are well spread across the data.

The 3-grams shown in Table 11.11 reiterate the importance of clauses that contain a form of the verb 'be' in the data, as well as the (unsurprising) foci of the reviews ('room', 'hotel', 'staff'). Concordances can be used to explore n-grams further. For example, looking at the first 3-gram in Table 11.11 we found the most frequent word immediately to the left of 'the room was' was 'very', and the most frequent words following that were 'clean', 'comfortable', 'small', or 'spacious'.

Table 11.11 The top 20 3-grams in the LHRC

Rank	3-gram	Freq.	Range
1	the room was	3422	20
2	the hotel is	2977	19
3	one of the	2122	17
4	we had a	2090	18
5	the staff were	2036	20
6	of the hotel	1924	19
7	in the room	1738	20
8	the rooms are	1646	19
9	stayed at the	1548	18
10	our room was	1477	20

Note that the higher the value of 'n' in an n-gram, the fewer n-grams that are returned in a search. So, for example, using the same parameters we searched for 4-grams in the LHRC and this returned just 156 results, none of which occurred across the full range of the corpus.

We do not have space here to discuss our n-grams further, but we can observe that sequences of words can provide yet another window on our data that would have been impossible to obtain manually. Each n-gram also provides a 'way in' to a large dataset providing a focus for further, more detailed analysis.

Conclusion

Rather than a sideline followed by only those analysts interested in computers, corpus linguistic approaches are coming more and more to the forefront of Discourse Analysis. This is because there are several advantages that come with using corpus data, including the following.

- Corpus data gives access to quantitative information about language, which can often be used to support qualitative analysis.
- Insights into language gained from corpus analysis are often generalisable in a way that insights gained from the qualitative analysis of small samples of data are not.
- Using corpora forces us to acknowledge how language is really used (which is often different from how we think it is used).
- Exploring large datasets using corpus tools can be enlightening and open new avenues of research.

Computer tools provide a quantitative way into large amounts of data as well as the means to explore the data qualitatively. However, the analyst needs to find ways to assess the results in a systematic and rigorous way to establish which results are important for the analysis of discourse. Often there are too many results to be assessed so the analyst needs to establish principled ways in which to reduce the data or make selections that do not amount to 'cherry-picking'. That means integrating linguistic models and frameworks in corpus analysis to make sense of the computer-generated results.

This chapter has provided only a brief snapshot of some of the analytical approaches possible using corpora and corpus tools. We limited our discussion to one online corpus (COHA) and one corpus tool (AntConc) as these are freely available and reasonably straightforward to use. There are many other tools available, of course and we encourage readers to explore the possibilities of discourse analysis using corpus linguistic approaches. We provide some examples below.

Further reading

Read more about choosing a suitable reference corpus in Scott (2009).

Readers interested in knowing how log-likelihood is calculated can find details on the Lancaster University website at this URL: http://ucrel.lancs.ac.uk/llwizard.html
Tip: type 'log likelihood wizard' into your search engine.

An explanation of the log ratio calculation can be found on Andrew Hardie's blog: http://cass.lancs.ac.uk/log-ratio-an-informal-introduction/
Tip: type 'Andrew Hardie log ratio' into your search engine

For an overview of the statistical measures we have introduced, see also McIntyre and Walker (2019), chapter 5.

Corpus tools

AntConc (Anthony 2022) – Free-to-download software for corpus analysis: http://www.laurenceanthony.net/software.html

Wmatrix (Rayson 2009) – Online corpus annotation and analysis tool (requires registration): https://ucrel.lancs.ac.uk/wmatrix

Wordsmith Tools (Scott 2022) – The corpus analysis tool that made the notion of keywords popular (available to download for a small fee): https://lexically.net/wordsmith

Sketch Engine (Kilgarriff et al. 2014) – A powerful online corpus analysis tool which allows you to upload your corpus to a server and carryout various quantitative analyses, including those we have described in this chapter. https://www.sketchengine.eu/

Corpora

British National Corpus (BNC)

100 million words of written and spoken British English from a variety of discourse situations from the early 1990s. Freely available with restrictions via BNCWeb (hosted by Lancaster University, UK at http://bncweb.lancs.ac.uk/bncwebSignup/user/login.php). Also, at English-Corpora.org (see below).

Brown Family of corpora

- Brown – 1 million words of 1960s written American English
- LOB (Lancaster-Oslo-Bergen) – 1 million words of 1960s written British English
- FROWN (Freiburg-Brown) – 1 million words of 1990s written American English
- FLOB (Freiburg-LOB) – 1 million words of 1990s written British English

All available to purchase as part of the ICAME Corpus Collection (http://clu.uni.no/icame/newcd.htm) and freely available with restrictions via CQPweb (see below).

CQPweb (Corpus Query Processor)

Online concordancer hosted by Lancaster University, UK that gives access to numerous corpora including English corpora (e.g. BNC, Brown Family) and South and East Asian language corpora (e.g. Thai National Corpus): https://cqpweb.lancs.ac.uk

English-Corpora.org

Online concordancer (https://www.english-corpora.org) that gives access to numerous very large corpora including:

- *Corpus of Contemporary American English (COCA)* – 560 million words of written American English from 1990 to 2017
- *Global Web-Based English (GloWbE)* – 1.9 billion words of textual varieties of English from 20 different countries

- *News on the Web (NOW)* – Monitor corpus of over 6 billion words of web-based newspapers and magazines from 2010 to the present time; updated daily

International Corpus of English (ICE)

A collection of parallel corpora of different Englishes worldwide, for comparative studies. Some of the corpora are available to download for free (under licence). Further details are at the project website: http://ice-corpora.net/ice/.

Log-Likelihood and effect size calculator

Log-Likelihood wizard (http://ucrel.lancs.ac.uk/llwizard.html)

The LHRC

We prepared the LHRC using a dataset built by PromptCloud. The data was downloaded from Kaggle and used under a creative commons license CC BY-SA 4.0 (https://creativecommons.org/licenses/by-sa/4.0/). For the purposes of writing this chapter, we edited the data to remove non-English contributions.
https://www.kaggle.com/datasets/PromptCloudHQ/reviews-of-londonbased-hotels

Answers to activities

Activity 11.2 Copular and auxiliary 'was'

In many of the examples it is not straightforward to decide whether 'was' is acting as a copular or as an auxiliary. These are the examples where 'was' is followed by a participle form of a verb. This is because we tend to say 'was' + past participle of a verb = passive construction (in which case, 'was' is an auxiliary verb). However, participle forms of verbs can also function as adjectives (known as participle adjectives). For example, compare 'the motivated donkey' and 'the donkey was motivated (by a carrot)'; 'motivated' is adjectival in the former but a verb in the latter. So, not everything that looks like a passive construction is actually . . . a passive construction. So, when analysing 'was' + past participle, the issue is differentiating between participle forms when used as a verb (e.g. 'I was called') and when used as an adjective (e.g. 'the hotel was fully booked'). In other words, we need to decide whether the participle is acting as a verb, or acting as an adjective. If it is acting as a verb, then the 'was' that accompanies it is auxiliary, and if it is acting as an adjective, we can say that the 'was' is copular.

Examples (i), (iii), and (v) are reasonably straightforward to analyse:

(i) Our room was lovely, very chic and absolutely spotless. **Copular**
(iii) As promised, I was called once the room became available at 14:00 **Auxilliary**
(v) The wifi was absolutely brilliant and very fast. **Copular**

In both (i) and (v) 'was' is copular with a 'standard' adjective in Complement position; in (iii) 'was' is auxiliary forming a passive construction with the past participle 'called' ('I was called' presumably by someone, telephonically).

The other examples pose more of a problem and, when analysing, it can help to keep in mind the following:

- participle form is acting as an adjective when describing a state of being (e.g. the room was dated);
- participle acting as a verb when describing actions (e.g. I was called).

So, if 'was' + participle describes an action, we can say that 'was' is auxiliary. However, to make things complicated, 'was' + participle acting as a verb can also describe states of being! (e.g. 'I was disappointed'). To help out, Huddleston and Pullum (2002) provide some further tests that can be used to identify how participle forms of verbs are being used. For verbal usage:

V1. Can a by-phrase that identifies the agent of the action be inserted into the example without significantly altering the meaning?
V2. Can an active version of the example be constructed?

For adjectival usage:

A1. Can the words 'too' or 'very' be inserted without significantly changing the meaning,
A2. Can 'was' be replaced with verbs like 'seemed', 'appeared', 'looked', 'remained'.

Using these tests, we analysed the rest of the examples as follows (we have put the test that helped in brackets):

(ii) The room was badly dated, a bit tattered, smelled weird, and had unsightly stains **Copular (A1 and A2)**
(iv) Our room was called the Beauchamp Suite. **Auxiliary** (**V1** 'by the hotel'; **V2** 'the hotel called the room the Beauchamp Suite')
(vi) I was disappointed by the food though. **Auxiliary** (**V1** – the by-phrase is already there for us; **V2** 'the food disappointed me'; however, **A1** 'I was very disappointed by the food'; but **A2** 'I seemed/appeared/looked/ remained disappointed by the food' changes the meaning). Our view is that the by-phrase pushes for an auxiliary interpretation.

(vii) every restaurant in the hotel was fully booked for lunch. **Copular** (**A2** e.g. 'remained fully booked'); cannot construct an active alternative '*X fully booked every restaurant for lunch')

(viii) The room was fully equipped with lots of unique extra touches. **Copular** (**A2** e.g. 'seemed fully equipped')

(ix) Continental breakfast was included in our rate. **Auxiliary** (**V2** 'our rate included breakfast'/ 'the hotel included breakfast in our rate')

(x) My bed was positioned at an angle which was a little funky. **Auxiliary** (**V1** 'the bed was positioned at an angle by the hotel'/ and **V2** 'the hotel positioned the bed at an angle'; BUT A2? Does 'the bed seemed/appeared/ looked positioned at an angle' carry the same meaning? We felt it did not, so opted for auxiliary.

This activity highlights that notionally straightforward categories are sometimes anything but and need to be informed by existing theoretical approaches and research. While some of the interpretations seemed counterintuitive, we were guided by the analytical framework set out by Huddleston and Pullum (2002). In this way, a framework can help produce a consistent analysis.

Activity 11.3 Comparing subsets of the hotel review corpus

List B is from the top-end hotels. The keywords that perhaps indicate top-endness are words that may be perceived to have higher social class connotations (see Chapter 5): 'pool, 'butler', 'spa', 'concierge', 'suite', and 'pianist'. 'History' might also be an indicator since the top-end hotels tend to have a long history.

The consistencies between the two lists relate to the class of keywords rather than the words themselves. Both lists contain adjectives – indicating that both sets of reviews evaluate – and reference to food and meals. The difference is, of course, in the adjectives actually used (e.g. 'good'/'great' vs 'best'; 'nice' vs 'beautiful') and the types of food ('tea'/'scones' vs 'beans'). The inconsistencies relate to, for example, the cheaper-end keywords indicating that proximity to/types of transport is/are mentioned a lot (e.g. 'walk', 'tube', 'bus'). Each of these keywords would need to be investigated using concordance lines to check out these intuitions.

Notes

1 Video tapes are ancient artefacts for recording television programmes pre-internet and Smart TV era.
2 There are many varieties of English (British English, Australian English, American English, and so forth) so this restraint on the data would need to be refined further in a study.
3 We used AntConc to do this with our data.
4 Yes, we also thought it sounded like an ineffectual anti-hero from an X-Men comic book.
5 Negative keywords can also be calculated, and these are words with a significantly low frequency by comparison and therefore under-represented in the research corpus. We do not

have space to deal with negative keywords in this chapter, but the principle behind them is the same as positive/over-represented keywords.

6 The notion of keyness extends beyond keywords. For example, key-clusters are statistically significant strings of words, and Wmatrix (Rayson 2009) can calculate key grammatical and semantic categories.

References

Anthony, L. (2022) AntConc (Version 4.2.0) [computer software]. Tokyo: Waseda University. Accessed 10 July 2023. https://laurenceanthony.net/software.html

Biber, D. (2004) 'Modal use across registers and time'. In A. Curzan and K. Emmons (eds), *Studies in the history of the English language II: Unfolding conversations*, pp. 189–216. Berlin: Mouton de Gruyter.

Biber, D. and Barbieri, F. (2007) 'Lexical bundles in university spoken and written registers'. *English for Specific Purposes*, 26, 263–286.

Biber, D. and Conrad, S. (1999) 'Lexical bundles in conversation and academic prose'. In H. Hasselgard and S. Oksefjell (eds), *Out of corpora*, pp. 181–190. Amsterdam: Rodopi.

Biber, D., Conrad, S. and Reppen, R. (1998) *Corpus linguistics: Investigating language structure and use*. Cambridge: Cambridge University Press.

Church, K. W. and Hanks, P. (1990) 'Word association norms, Mutual Information and lexicography'. *Computational Linguistics*, 16(1): 22–29.

Clear, J. (1993) 'From Firth principles: computational tools for the study of collocation'. In M. Baker, G. Francis, and E. Tognini-Bonelli (eds), *Text and technology: In honour of John Sinclair*, pp. 271–292. Amsterdam: John Benjamins.

Cortes, V. (2004) 'Lexical bundles in published and student disciplinary writing: Examples from history and biology'. *English for Specific Purposes*, 23, 397–423.

Dunning, T. (1993) 'Accurate methods for the statistics of surprise and coincidence', *Computational Linguistics*, 19(1): 61–74.

Firth, J. R. (1957) *Papers in linguistics 1934–1951*. London: Oxford University Press.

Hardie, A. (2014) 'Log ratio: An informal introduction'. Blog post: ESRC Centre for Corpus Approaches to Social Science (CASS). Accessed 23 March 2022. http://cass.lancs.ac.uk/log-ratio-an-informal-introduction

Huddleston, R. D. and Pullum, G. K. (2002) *The Cambridge grammar of the English language*. Cambridge: Cambridge University Press.

Hunston, S. (2002) *Corpora in applied linguistics*. Cambridge: Cambridge University Press.

Kilgarriff, A., Baisa, V., Bušta, J., Jakubíček, M., Kovář, V., Michelfeit, J., Rychlý, P., and Suchomel, V. (2014) 'The Sketch Engine: Ten years on'. *Lexicography*, 1: 7–36.

Leech G. (2003) 'Modality on the move: the English modal auxiliaries 1961–1992'. In R. Facchinetti, F. Palmer, and M. Krug (eds), *Modality in contemporary English*. Berlin: Mouton de Gruyter

Manning, C. D. and Schütze, H. (1999) *Foundations of statistical natural language processing*. Cambridge, MA: MIT Press.

McIntyre, D. and Walker, B. (2019) *Corpus stylistics: Theory and practice*. Edinburgh: Edinburgh University Press

Phillips, M. (1989) *Lexical structure of text*. Discourse Analysis Monograph 12. Birmingham: English Language Research.

Rayson, P. (2009) Wmatrix: A web-based corpus processing environment. Computing Department, Lancaster University. Accessed 21 April 2022. http://ucrel.lancs.ac.uk/wmatrix

Rayson, P., Berridge, D., and Francis, B. (2004) 'Extending the Cochran rule for the comparison of word frequencies between corpora'. In G. Purnelle, C. Fairon, and A. Dister (eds), *Le poids des mots: Proceedings of the 7th International Conference on Statistical analysis of textual data (JADT 2004)*, Vol. II, pp. 926–936. Louvain-la-Neuve: Presses universitaires de Louvain. Conference held in Louvain-la-Neuve, Belgium, 10–12 March 2004.

Scott, M. (2000) 'Focussing on the text and its key words'. In L. Burnard and T. McEnery (eds), *Rethinking language pedagogy from a corpus perspective*, Vol. 2, pp. 103–122. Frankfurt: Peter Lang.

Scott, M. (2009) 'In search of a bad reference corpus'. In D. Archer (ed.), *What's in a word-list? Investigating word frequency and keyword extraction*, pp. 79–91, Farnham, Surrey: Ashgate Publishing.

Scott, M. (2022) *WordSmith Tools version 8* (64 bit version) Stroud: Lexical Analysis Software. Accessed 10 July 2023.

Scott, M. and Tribble, C. (2006) *Textual patterns: Key words and corpus analysis in language education*. Amsterdam: John Benjamins.

Sinclair, J., Jones, S., Daley, R., and Krishnamurthy, R. (2004) *English collocational studies: The OSTI report*. London: Continuum.

Stubbs, M. (1996) *Text and corpus analysis*. Oxford: Blackwell.

12 Doing a project in discourse analysis

Introduction

In this final chapter, the focus is on the practicalities of doing discourse analysis. The 'analysis' part of discourse analysis is only part of the process because there are other considerations when conducting an analysis of any discourse. These include how to select and handle data, how to approach the analysis of data methodologically, what ethical concerns need to be addressed and how to address them, and how to define and then refine your research idea into a question that is manageable and valid. In keeping with the 'practical' focus in this book, the chapter includes some ideas for doing research in discourse analysis.

Thinking about discourse as the focus of a project

Throughout this book, we have considered discourse as language in use that needs to be analysed within its social, political, ideological, interpersonal, and cultural contexts. There are an infinite amount of situational contexts in which discourse occurs. Therefore, whatever discourse you choose to analyse, your methodological approach must be one that is consistent and appropriate within the context you are working in. In this chapter, we will discuss some of the issues you need to consider when designing and executing a research project. We will consider data collection and some of the ethical concerns involved with using other people's discourses and then go on to discussing how to develop a research idea and formulate research objectives and questions. We will finish by outlining the process of writing up your research, which is a separate process from doing your research. We will start though with an overarching concern that embraces a whole project from design to dissemination: systematicity.

Systematicity and the three Rs of research

A systematic analysis is one that is organised and well-structured and deals with all the data involved in the research in the same way. To help achieve systematicity, Simpson (2014: 4) suggests the three Rs of doing research: rigour, retrievability, and replicability.

DOI: 10.4324/9781003351207-12

- **Rigour** means being thorough and careful in your analysis and accounting for all your data rather than simply 'cherry-picking' examples that help to support your hypothesis (if you have one). Rigour can be helped by using an analytical framework to help structure your analysis.
- **Retrievability** means making explicit and explaining the framework, principles and terminology that are used to organise your analysis. It also means making explicit how you reached your conclusions, describing the steps you took to get from the data to an interpretation, and providing evidence to support your claims. Retrievability is therefore concerns being transparent about your design, data, logic and reasoning, and the route to your conclusions. In this way, other scholars looking at your research will not have to take you at your word because they can see for themselves what you did.
- **Replicability** is achieved through retrievability – when your methodology, framework, and terminology are retrievable, other researchers can see what you did and how you did it, and can replicate your study. This means that, given the write-up of your project, other scholars can replicate your research and potentially verify your results or your method.

Say, for example, that you wish to analyse the discourse of hotel reviews using a corpus (as we did in Chapter 11) and that you are interested in the verb-form 'was' when it is used as a copular verb in Relational-Intensive clauses (see the Transitivity framework discussed in Chapter 9). As we saw in Chapter 11, a corpus approach can quickly provide us with a list of all the occurrences of 'was' in a corpus. However, to differentiate between copular 'was' and 'was' when used as an auxiliary verb, we need some criteria (drawn from existing grammars of English) to inform our categorisation. These criteria become our framework for analysis of 'was' in the data which need to be applied **systematically** and **rigorously** to every occurrence. Describing the categories used for the analysis, referencing the grammar that inform the criteria, and explaining the process of working through the data makes the research **retrievable** and **replicable**. Therefore, anyone wanting to do a similar analysis would be able to examine the source used to establish the criteria, examine (and maybe critique) the categories, and perform a similar analysis.

Ethics

The second important factor in discourse analysis is an ethical one. Each discourse context may carry different constraints ranging from how freely you can access the data to how appropriate it is to share the data publicly. Additionally, you should consider what ramifications exist for the producers of that data if it is studied or shared, and what gains you receive from analysing it.

Guidelines for ethics can be found on numerous websites, such as: the British Association of Applied Linguistics (BAAL); UK Research and Innovation (UKRI);

Professional and ethical codes for socioeconomic research in the information society (EU): National Council on Ethics in Human Research (Canada); and the Association of Internet Researchers (AoIR). The ESRC, which is part of UKRI, summarise what is meant by ethical research using these six core principles:

1. research should aim to maximise benefit for individuals and society and minimise risk and harm;
2. the rights and dignity of individuals and groups should be respected;
3. wherever possible, participation should be voluntary and appropriately informed;
4. research should be conducted with integrity and transparency;
5. lines of responsibility and accountability should be clearly defined;
6. independence of research should be maintained and where conflicts of interest cannot be avoided they should be made explicit.

(UKRI 2021)

We can see from these principles that ethics permeates all aspects of research from project design and data collection to the analysis and reporting of results. It also covers how we as researchers should conduct ourselves within the research and wider communities.

Let's consider data in terms of ethics. Data for discourse analysis might include, for example, naturally occurring conversations, interviews, focus group discussions, or social media interactions. When data is collected from people, the notion of ethics, particularly relating to ESRC/UKRI principles 2, 3, and 4 above, becomes important because data collection of this nature is bound by ethical guidelines summarised by BAAL:

> Applied linguists should respect the rights, interests, sensitivities, privacy and autonomy of their informants in all research contexts, including those in which users' rights are not so clear-cut, such as easily accessible internet sites.
>
> (BAAL 2016)

The latter part of the quotation hints at the increasing amount of data that is gathered from the internet, and the ethical questions that collecting and using such data can raise (for a discussion about using the internet for research purposes, see Larner 2014).

Informed consent

BAAL states that "the cornerstone of ethical research" is **informed consent**. This is the practice of obtaining consent from informants (participants) to use their discourse as data **prior** to the data being collected and **after** they have been informed about the research as fully as is practically possible. Informants can therefore make an informed decision about whether they wish to participate in the research or not. Gathering examples of discourse data from informants without their knowing – known as covert research – is now acknowledged as ethically unacceptable. This is different from conducting research with your participants' consent but where you do not share full details of the study's aims because it might compromise the data collected (see the section on 'Observer paradox' below).

Obtaining informed consent is reasonably straightforward with some forms of data. For example, collecting spoken discourse from informants in focus groups requires the analyst to select or solicit the informants in the first place, at which point they can be presented with all relevant information concerning the research study. This information should include what happens after the study (e.g. how you will use the data). However, informed consent becomes less straightforward in some situations when collecting, for example, spoken discourse data in a public place because it is likely to be impossible to locate all the people who might appear on the recording whose language might potentially end up in the data. Additionally, depending on the context, there may be extra challenges for securing informed consent because there might be more than one party involved. For example, in forensic situations there may be additional data protection issues that constrain data collection from host organisations or institutions such as the police or court. If you wanted to analyse the discourse of police interactions with witnesses, you need the informed consent of witnesses to both observe their interaction and collect the data from that interaction, but you will also need the consent of the police force who will want to know for what purposes the data will be used, how it will be stored, for how long, and who has access to it. In Appendix 2, we have included a sample document that seeks informed consent from participants willing to take part in a study involving data collection using the discussion group example that we outlined in Case study 12.1. Appendix 1 shows a sample statement declaring consent for a study.

Informed consent can also be difficult to obtain when data is downloaded from online forums, chatrooms, and other forms of electronic social media (ESM), such as Twitter and Facebook. For example, in this book we referenced Twitter users and we wrote to the authors to ask for their consent to use their posts, but they did not respond. Even though their utterances are publicly available (the account holders have public profiles and one of the tweets was subsequently picked up by the press) we felt, nonetheless, that the right thing to do (ethically) was to inform them of our (pedagogic) use of their tweets. This brings us to the notion of 'implied consent' (Martin and Knox 2000), which is where participants are offered the opportunity to say that they do not want their contributions to be used as data, and if no reply is received then consent is implied.

A more general point about using publicly available material is whether consent is needed, since much of what can be found on the internet is arguably in the public domain. The general guide here is that if the discourse data is password-protected, then it is not for wider public consumption and cannot be used without consent. Doing things like signing up to a chatroom and 'lurking' to collect data could be viewed as covert research and a form of deception, because the researcher is posing as a 'normal' chatroom user. This is viewed as an ethically questionable research practice.[1] In certain online situations it might not be clear who the participants are or how to contact them, so asking for consent is likely to be difficult. Additionally, if there are thousands of participants (e.g. certain Twitter feeds), then the task of asking for consent might become extremely difficult and practically impossible. While there appear to be no specific guidelines on how to deal with these sorts of problems with obtaining consent for these kinds of internet data, generally, researchers should do what they reasonably can to inform participants about the research and how their data will be used and give them the opportunity to withdraw.

Observer paradox

Aside from the practicalities of gaining consent, a significant problem with informed consent is what is known as the observer's paradox (Labov 1972). This is where discourse participants are aware that they are being studied or 'observed' and change their linguistic performance because they are conscious that their language production is 'on show' and under scrutiny. If such changes in performance occur in informants' production of otherwise naturally occurring discourse, this can skew results and, at worse, make the data unusable.

One option to help alleviate the observer's paradox is a form of covert research known as **justified deception**. This is where some details about the specific purpose of the research are withheld from informants until after the data is collected. In such situations, participants would know that their language is being studied (or some aspect of their contributions is informing the research), but they would not know what aspect until the data has been collected. For example, in Case study 12.1, which we discuss below, the speech habits of students under formal and informal conditions were studied, but the linguistic phenomenon that was being investigated was not shared with informants prior to the data collection in case they were primed in some way to use (or avoid) the phenomenon during the data collection period.

With justified deception, the research is not wholly covert in the sense that we describe above, but only partly so. The UKRI guidance addresses the issue of covert research as follows.

> covert research should only be used when no other approach is possible, where it is crucial to the research objectives and design, or where overt observation may alter the phenomenon being studied. The broad principle should be that covert [. . .] research should not be undertaken lightly or routinely. It is only justified if important issues are being addressed and if matters of

social and/or scientific significance are likely to be discovered which cannot be uncovered in other ways.

(UKRI 2021)

So, in certain special, socially significant (but unspecified) circumstances, research that does not fully disclose the aims of the study is allowable but should be handled carefully to address the key ethical consideration set out by BAAL, quoted above.

Anonymity

Also important in data collection from informants is the right to anonymity, so even where informed consent is obtained (or implied), the data must be anonymised. This can also raise several practicalities, not least if there is a considerable amount of data. The extent of the anonymisation must also be considered (for example, any place or institutional names, or other personal names mentioned) so that there is no way in which participants can be identified by their contributions.

In summary, there are numerous guidelines for ethical research that can be consulted if there is any doubt about whether research practices are ethical or not, particularly around data collection from informants.

Case study 12.1

Research question: Does 'prestige' manifest in our speech?
This is a rather general research question, so we need to narrow it down to answer it. One of the ways we can do this is by testing a hypothesis in a sample of language users. To do this, we will need:

a) a discourse community in which to test whether prestige exists;
b) some linguistic variables to test for prestige (and linguists need to agree what counts as a prestige marker to make the research retrievable and replicable);
c) and some speech environment(s) that represent differing speech styles in which prestige is likely to be more or less manifest.

One possible answer . . .
In a Belfast High school, one of the authors of this book set up a small focus group discussion with teenage male students on the topic of 'mobile phone use'. This was in 2003 when mobile phones were pre-smartphone and certainly not as widespread as they are today. The participants were told that the point of the discussion group was to share thoughts on owning and

using mobile phones and their consent was sought and secured for the audio recording of the discussion group and its use in a research study. While the experiment was indeed seeking to collect their thoughts, this was only as a vehicle for eliciting and assessing the use of two linguistic variables conventionally considered to mark prestige in English: the presence of '**-ing**' [-ɪŋ], as in 'go**ing**' vs its absence, as in 'go**in**' (see Chapter 1), and the presence of the standard '**th**' [ð] as in 'bro**th**er' versus its absence as in 'broer'. The school was located in what is perceived to be a working-class area, so the discourse community was more likely to exhibit non-standard features such as '-ing dropping'. It was hypothesised that prestige markers would be largely absent in informal speech.

The point of the study was to test a version of Labov's 'fourth floor' experiment (1972) in which he elicited casual and emphatic utterances of the rhotic [r][2] across three New York department stores distinguished by social class (lower, middle, high). Labov wanted to test whether the presence of the prestige marker [r] aligned with the perceived prestige attached to the store – so higher-class stores would result in more [r] whereas lower-class stores return less [r]. In the school experiment in Belfast, the goal was to elicit as many utterances as possible of words containing the variables [-ɪŋ] and [ð] in two speech situations, formal and informal, and then to analyse the presence or absence across the two situations for patterns that discriminated the two styles. Formal styles were assessed by getting the students to read aloud. Essentially, this was done by the researcher asking the students to select a piece of paper from a pile containing short statements that included words containing the linguistic variables which they were to read out loud to serve as a discussion starter. Two such examples read 'My brother keeps stealing my phone', and 'My mother hates me texting at the dinner table', and so on. This was the 'formal' condition, so-called because students are likely to be more conscious of the way they speak when reading aloud to a small audience than when they are spontaneously speaking to each other in a group discussion. The presence or absence of the variables in formal speech could then be tested. The discussions that followed, some very animated, would then provide the data for informal speech. The discussion talk satisfied the 'informal' or 'casual' condition.

Results from the high school experiment

'**-ing**' [-ɪŋ]: Results showed a marked disparity between formal and informal speech in every instance of '-ing'. This variable was dropped 100 per cent of the time during the informal discussion yet was present in most instances of the (formal) reading aloud condition.

'**th**' [θ], [ð]: Results showed a marked disparity between formal and informal instances of '**th**': it was dropped in most instances during the informal discussion (e.g. [ˈbrʌðər]>[ˈbrʌʔər]), yet it was present in all but one instance of the reading aloud condition.

A really interesting finding from the research was that in the formal condition the same student resorted to non-standard forms, dropping 'ing' and 'th' (so from [ð] to [ʔ]) which may indicate covert prestige of the non-standard forms in all conditions. Covert prestige is when non-standard forms of a language are given more value than the standard forms amongst specific social groups. This means that the speaker may have believed that using non-standard variants in the formal condition may have gained him some kudos with his peers. It would be interesting to test whether this student used these non-standard forms in the formal condition in one-to-one readings without his peers listening in!

We concluded that in defaulting to standard forms (higher prestige) in the formal condition, students were aware of the social differences of both forms and that the presence of these variables signalled overt prestige. Their absence, therefore, may serve to connect them to their peer speech community reinforcing their social bonds, and so constitute covert prestige.

A final word on the ethical considerations of this study: by not telling the students what speech phenomenon was being studied we preserved the integrity of the data. As all but one of the participants used the standard forms in the formal condition it suggests that they were conscious of the formality constraints on speech styles and adjusted their speech accordingly. If we had told them what linguistic phenomena was being elicited and why, they may well have changed their informal speech behaviour, too.

Copyright

If you are collecting and storing discourse data, sharing your data, building a corpus, and/or publishing your work along with your data, then you might need to think about copyright. Copyright protects the work of others and gives them the exclusive right to use it (e.g. print or publish it). If you want to use work that is in copyright, then you must ask the rights holder's permission. For example, the 'Norn Iron' T-shirt image in Chapter 1 is included with permission from the source 'Norn Iron Tees'. Images are not the only medium that requires copyright permission. Whether you use news discourse, advertising discourse, or political discourse, for example, you need to check whether you need permission from the rights holder(s). Copyright laws are different in different parts of the world, so you need to check carefully whether you need to consider copyright or not. In the US, for example, copyright extends across the owner's lifetime plus another 50 years, although with works published before 1978 where the copyright was renewed after 28 years, the period of copyright after the death of the owner is 75 years. In the EU, copyright extends across the owner's lifetime, plus another 70 years.

Provided that the research is for non-commercial purposes, it is possible to use short extracts of discourse for research under what is known as **fair dealing** (or **fair use**). Fair dealing permits the use of extracts without needing permission, and currently allows up to 400 words from a journal article or book chapter, but no more than a total of 800 words from an edition of a journal, or a whole book. For other genres, including newspapers and magazines, no such fair dealing possibilities exist, and permission must always be sought. If you are not intending to make a profit from your research, then there is a good chance that permissions will be granted, but without permission you cannot legally use and disseminate data.

Developing a research project

A research project that examines and analyses discourse is no different from any other research project in the social and pure sciences: they all require planning and design. The planning can begin with a series of questions, as follows.

- What do you want to find out and why?
- What are your research questions?
- What data do you need to answer those questions?
- Can you access the data?
- Are there any other problems with collecting the data?
- How will you analyse the data?
- How will you present your findings?
- Does your data reveal anything worth reporting?
- If you do answer your questions, are your findings generalisable?

Any project in discourse analysis should have clear research aims and research questions that frame the research and help to direct it. The analysis of your discourse data will aim to answer your research questions and achieve your research aims. Research projects should begin with a hypothesis from which follows a question or questions. Our example case study begins with a broad question, which is developed until it becomes a measurable, testable hypothesis (see Figure 12.1).

Deductive and inductive research

So, how should you approach your research? Two possibilities are inductive research (sometimes called 'bottom-up') and deductive research (conversely, 'top-down'). **Inductive** research is where you look for patterns in your data with no prior hypothesis about the possible patterns that might occur. Using our earlier example of the hotel reviews data this would mean reading through the data to see what, if any, patterns occur and how such patterns were categorisable. For example, you might notice that 'super' occurs very often as an adverb (e.g. 'super fun') in reviews of higher-end hotels but rarely in lower-end hotels and this might lead you to hypothesise that 'super' marks prestige. You can then select

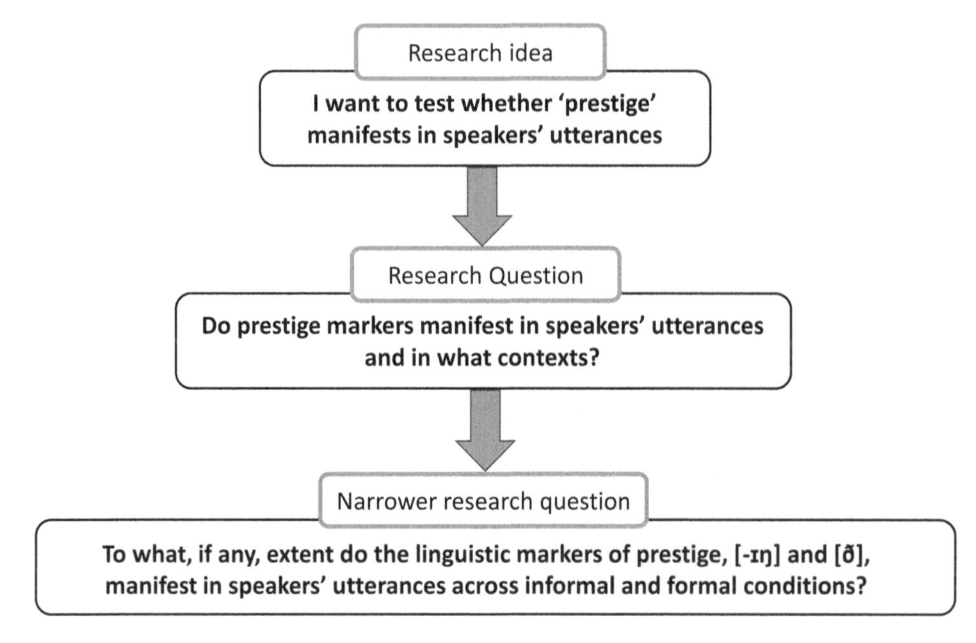

Figure 12.1 Refining a research question

this variable and study its occurrence in the data. These patterns might lead to the formulation of a hypothesis. **Deductive** research is where you start with a hypothesis – that the adverbial function of 'super' is a marker of prestige' – and study the data to assess whether your findings support this hypothesis or not. It's important to note that disproving a hypothesis is as informative and helpful as proving a hypothesis. Research can be a combination of both inductive and deductive approaches.

Hypotheses

Hypotheses might be formulated based on our intuitions, or they might stem from the literature on whatever topic you happen to be interested in, or something else such as some previous research or observations as in our case study. Intuitions about the phenomenon you are investigating can be important for formulating hypotheses. Intuitions might be based on personal observations, knowledge, and might develop previous research. For example, the hypothesis that people from a lower social class speak differently in formal and informal situations could come from your intuitions (or observations) about discourse:

> I have a feeling (or I have witnessed) that people use standard English when they are more self-conscious of their speech than when they are not.

Conversely, it could come from existing research, for example:

> William Labov conducted an experiment in the 1970s that found differing speech styles across different social classes and I want to test it in a new speech community with different variables to see if the phenomenon of social stratification exists in that speech community.

The idea of a hypothesis is that it aims to explain a particular phenomenon. For example, imagine that you are a European naturalist working in the 1700s and someone sends you the stuffed remains of a duck-billed platypus. You have never seen anything like it; you observe that the animal has a bill and webbed feet like a duck, but a fur coat and tail more like a beaver. You might hypothesise based on your knowledge of the natural world that the person who sent you the animal is playing a practical joke on you, that the animal has been faked by a talented taxidermist and does not exist.[3] That the animal is fake is the hypothesis that explains what you are observing.

A hypothesis must also be testable. That is, a hypothesis must be formulated in such a way as to make it possible, after appropriate analysis, to reject it as an explanation of the phenomenon under investigation. This idea of rejecting a hypothesis is known as falsification, whereby we do not try to prove a hypothesis to be correct; instead, we try to find data that forces us to reject the hypothesis. So, to test our duck-billed platypus hypothesis, we would need to sail to Eastern Australia (it is the 1700s, remember, so we're going by boat) and look around for a real, naturally occurring duck-billed platypus. As soon as we observe one, then we can reject our hypothesis that the stuffed specimen scaring the neighbours from our home office window is a fake (no matter how painful and damaging to our reputation that might be).

Activity 12.1 Testing hypotheses

Suppose you hypothesise that vocabulary size makes the discourse in a particular tabloid newspaper (Tabloid A) distinctive from other newspapers. How would you test that hypothesis?

Before reading on, consider the following questions (we have offered answers to the first few).

- Q.1 What do you want to find out and why?
- Answer: Whether vocabulary size makes the discourse in a particular tabloid newspaper (Tabloid A) distinctive from other newspapers.

- Q.2 What are your research questions?
- Answer: Does vocabulary size serve as a marker of discursive distinctiveness in a tabloid newspaper?

- What data do you need to answer those questions?
- Can you access the data?
- Are there any other problems with collecting the data?
- How will you analyse the data?
- How will you present your findings?
- Does the data reveal anything worth reporting?
- Are the findings generalisable?

Objectives and research questions

Using the activity question above, if we hypothesised that the discourse in a particular tabloid newspaper (Tabloid A) is distinctive from other newspapers in terms of vocabulary size, an over-arching or global research question might be:

Is the size of the vocabulary in Tabloid A distinctive from other newspapers?

The question raises other questions which we would first need to answer before we can:
(i) either reject or confirm our hypothesis; and
(ii) posit an answer to our over-arching research question.

To determine what these other questions are, we need to think about what our research objectives are. These might be as follows (O = Objective):
O1: Determine the size of the vocabulary of Tabloid A and of other newspapers.
O2: Collect a sample of the discourse in Tabloid A.
O3: Collect a sample of discourse from other newspapers
O4: Count the number of words in both samples.
O5: Determine the number of different words in the samples.

To achieve these objectives, we need to answer the following research questions (RQs):
RQ1: What is the vocabulary size of (i) Tabloid A, and (ii) other newspapers? [Addresses O1]
RQ2: What counts as a representative sample of Tabloid A? [Addresses O2] (see Chapter 11 for how to ensure representativeness in sampling)
RQ3: What counts as a representative sample of other newspapers? [Addresses O3]
RQ4: How many words are in each sample? [Addresses O4]
RQ5: How many different words are in each sample? [Addresses O5]

RQ1 is the global research question. The answer to this question can only be posited after the other research questions have been answered. The other questions can be seen as local research questions (see McIntyre and Walker 2019: 123–124). Answering local research questions enables us to achieve objectives and therefore decide whether to reject or confirm the initial hypothesis. Whether we reject or confirm our hypothesis is determined by the answer to our global research question (RQ1).

Research questions help to direct your analysis as well as indicate to your reader what it is you are looking for (and what you are not looking for). You do not have to wait until you have decided on your data before start to develop research questions; you can be thinking of questions before that, and those questions might dictate the sorts of data you need to look at and eventually collect.

To summarise, one way to start thinking about research questions is to decide what it is you want to know. If you have a hypothesis about a discourse, then this could be stated as a question. It is perfectly normal for research questions to start off quite general but then become more honed to address, say, specific discourse practices (see Figure 12.1). Do activity 12.2 which invites you to devise research questions from a hypothesis about advertising discourse for gambling websites.

Activity 12.2 Hypothesis and research questions

Suppose you are interested in the advertising discourse of a gambling company and how they present . . . well . . . gambling and how it positions you as a potential gambler. These general ideas about what it is that you want to know can be seen as the aims of your project. From your aims you can develop a research question or questions that help you to achieve your aims. So, if your hypothesis is that 'gambling advertising highlights the autonomy of the gambler' (i.e. appears to put the gambler in control), then what research questions could you ask?

Defining terms

An important step in any research project is to define as clearly as possible the phenomenon that you are investigating. This links back to the three Rs we mentioned earlier, which require that you define the terminology you are using so that everyone is clear what you are researching and what your terms refer to. For example, if you are interested in researching pauses in stand-up comedy, then you first need to make clear what is meant by the term 'pause'. This might seem intuitively simple, but as we saw in Chapter 4, a pause is only a pause if it lasts for more than a certain length of time. Furthermore, a pause is not a fixed length, so your research might need to monitor and account for different lengths of pause. Similarly, say we are investigating whether a particular discourse is formal or informal (as in our Case study 12.1), we need to be very clear what these terms mean, and which linguistic features combine to create formality/informality. The same goes for the term 'prestige' and what counts as markers of prestige in a particular language – we might use conventional examples of prestige markers suggested in previous scholarly research, for example. Research projects that do not define terms clearly are not **replicable** because it is not clear what is being researched.

Controlling variables

It is important in any research project that variables are controlled. Variables are things that might affect your results. If you want to know what has caused your result (which variable) you need to be clear which variables are in play when you do your research. So, for example, if you hypothesise that females swear less than males in spoken discourse you need to be aware of and control the other variables that might be in play when it comes to collect your data. Variables are either **dependent** or **independent** and research aims to investigate the effects of independent variables on dependent variables. In our swearing example, the *amount of swearing* is the dependent variable (i.e. the thing being tested) and the research aims to establish what effect, if any, the independent variable *speaker gender* has on that. Speaker gender is not the only independent variable that might affect the amount of swearing in spoken discourse. Other independent variables, such as age and socio-economic background of the speaker, might influence the amount of swearing. If these other variables are not controlled (e.g. by only using speakers from the same age group in the research) then it will be difficult to draw conclusions from the results because it will not be clear which independent variable is affecting the dependant variable and thus causing the results. This means making sure that the males and females you collect data from are of a similar age, socioeconomic background, and discoursing in the same or similar context (e.g. at home with friends). Additionally, you will also need to define what you mean by swearing (see discussion above), and for that you might need to use an existing taxonomy of swearwords (see, for example, McEnery 2005).

Data

As we have observed throughout this book, discourse data can be written, spoken, or images (or multimodal). Remember, though, that spoken data must be transcribed first. The data you collect will aim to answer your research questions and fulfil your research aims. One question that is often asked by students is: How much data do I need for a project? The amount of data you need depends on what you are aiming to do. One fairly short piece of discourse data can be enough, but it rather depends on what your aims are. Some projects will make more than one example of discourse a necessity. For example, you might want to carry out a comparison between discourses from different newspapers or different politicians on the same topic. So clearly you need more than one set of data to do that. Or you might want to investigate the way in which someone presents someone else's discourse by comparing the original (anterior) discourse against the posterior discourse (see Chapter 10). Again, you would need more than one text for that. In the school Case study (12.1) the whole discussion from which the data was derived took about 30 minutes. It took about four hours to transcribe. Be warned – transcribing data can take a very long time even for a few minutes' worth of talk! The data you need and what you do with it will be directed by what it is you are trying to find out.

Analysing your data

Discourse data can be analysed using any number of linguistic tools and approaches, some of which we have outlined in this book. You need to approach your analysis in a systematic and rigorous way. You need to go through all the data bit by bit looking for all the occurrences of whatever discourse feature you have chosen to focus on. Even though you might have a hypothesis about what you expect to find in the data, you need to be quite open-minded about whether you will find it, or not. This is very important.

You are not doing an analysis that sets out to find features that support your hypothesis about the data, you are doing an analysis that goes through all your data looking for all the features that you are looking for.

You cannot ignore or 'cherry-pick' examples to suit your hypothesis. You need to take all occurrences of a feature into account. Once you have been through all the data then you can see whether there are any patterns and begin to think about how the discourse makes meaning. If your analysis supports your initial ideas, then that's something you can report. But if it does not, then that is still something to report – and, as we said earlier, actually might be of greater interest. Doing systematic and rigorous analyses means that you might find things that you did not anticipate. And you gain a more detailed and more in-depth understanding of the discourse.

Writing up your research – doing academic discourse

If you write up your research (why wouldn't you?), your report should bring together data collection, your analysis, how you went about it and what you found. The report should have a clear structure that is detached from the messy stuff that you might have experienced while you were doing the research. Let's just take a look now at what your report might include.

Introduction

You should have an introduction where you set out what you are doing and your research questions. You may want to contextualise your study.

Methodology

- You need to talk about your method of analysis and maybe your method for collecting data in the first place.
- You could state how and why you collected your data, how much you collected, if you experienced any problems. As a minimum you should say what your data is and where it came from.
- You should also say how you went about your analysis. It is important to say, for example, that you went through looking for the feature that you were interested in and that you looked for every single example of that feature. Or if you took another approach and focused on some part of the data or one participant in the data, then you need to say that and explain why.
- Try to show that you have been as objective as possible and tried as much as possible to avoid your own biases about the data. Your readers need to know that you have been systematic and rigorous and that you have not just looked through for the interesting examples that help you to make the point you want to make or that satisfy your hypothesis about the data. One of the best ways of assessing objectivity is to ask questions of your own study as if you were its greatest critic.

Analysis, results, and discussion

Here you present the results of your analysis, talk about what you found, and suggest the impact of what you found. For example, you can discuss any patterns you found. At the discussion stage, you write about your results in a narrative format, as a kind of story about your data that makes sense. So, you have two different processes and two different skills: doing the analysis on one hand, and then writing up what you did and what you found in your analysis on the other. Try not to do them both together at the same time. You could (should!) include any tables or figures of data in your narrative of the analysis so that you can flesh out the results of your findings for your reader. Remember to keep the reader with you – do not assume they will know what you did or how you did it. You need to tell them!

Conclusion

Conclusions can be hard to write. They might also be boring to write because you are repeating yourself, but try not to make them boring to read. It is important that you draw out the main findings and reiterate what is important about your research. Don't just copy and paste bits from other parts of your study into the conclusions. Try to start with a blank piece of paper and try to summarise your study just from your memory and say what it is you found out. You can then fill in the detail if you need to once you have got the basic structure down. You should also return to your research questions and reflect on whether you answered your questions or not. Make it easy for your reader to see that you have kept the focus on the research questions that you started with.

Appendices

If you want to include additional materials relevant to the analysis, you could add them as appendices. These might include ethical permissions and participant consent forms, or longer stretches of data.

Conclusion

In this chapter we have considered some of the issues that need to be addressed before, during, and after conducting analyses of discourse. These include ethical concerns such as getting consent from participants, clearly informing participants in your study what their contribution will be, what you will do with the data you collect, and who will see it. We also offered suggestions regarding discourse contexts in which you might want to conduct analyses. We encouraged you to think about your own motivation for conducting discourse analysis – what kinds of questions you are seeking to answer, who or what will benefit from your analysis, and what you (and others) will learn from doing (and reading) your study. One of the key takeaways from this chapter is that your research must observe the three Rs: *rigour*, *replicability*, and *retrievability*. Finally, we offered a structural template for presenting your research. In the appendices, we offer a sample document for acquiring informed consent from participants in your study, along with a sample 'information for participants' document. When your study involves other humans or their language use (as it invariably will!), you need to ensure that it is crystal clear about what you are aiming to do and why. Following these guidelines means that you, too, will be very clear about your role. Good luck!

Further reading

For more on doing project and for project ideas try Wray and Bloomer (2012); the latest edition includes guidance on doing research on computer-mediated communication.

For more on ethics and social media, see Townsend and Wallace (2017).
For more on testing hypotheses and designing research questions, see McIntyre and Walker (2019), chapter 4.

Answers to activities

Activity 12.2 Hypothesis and research questions

Hypothesis: gambling advertising highlights the autonomy of the gambler.

RQ1: Does gambling advertising present gamblers as having autonomy?

For this RQ you would need to ask: How does gambling advertising discourse suggest that gamblers have control? One way you could investigate this is through transitivity choices. So, you could ask more specifically: Do the transitivity choices of the text producer suggest that the gambler is in control? Of course, if this were your project, it would be helpful to make sure from the outset that it's clear what you mean by 'in control'! This might be done by stating whether gamblers are Actors in Material-Intention processes in the advertising discourse. This might indicate that they have agency over their actions rather than being acted upon. Further questions that you would need to answer your research question would relate to which data to collect and how much. You might focus on one company or collect the adverts produced by several.

Notes

1 Note that 'research practice' is different from forensic investigations. An example of the latter is a police operation in which decoy participants are deployed to act as real participants in online chatrooms in investigations into cases involving, for example, child exploitation.
2 Rhotic /r/ or 'rhoticity' is the term given to the pronunciation of the post-vocalic /r/ sound in words like 'car' and 'worked'. In some speech communities the /r/ is absent (i.e. not voiced) – these are 'non-rhotic' pronunciations. In other speech communities the /r/ is voiced – these are 'rhotic' pronunciations. Culturally, and depending on where you are geographically, rhoticity can carry prestige. In Labov's New York study rhoticity was a marker of prestige. Rhoticity is not to be confused with the rotating cooking method of roasting meat.
3 True story (sort of) – At the end of the 1700s, the biologist George Shaw struggled to accept that the specimen of a duck-billed platypus he had been sent was legitimate.

References

BAAL (2016) Recommendations on good practice in Applied Linguistics. Accessed 12 April 2023. https://baal.org.uk/wp-content/uploads/2016/10/goodpractice_full_2016.pdf

Labov, W. (1972) 'Some principles of linguistic methodology'. *Language in Society*, 1(1): 97–120.

Larner, S. (2014) *Forensic authorship analysis and the world wide web*. Basingstoke: Palgrave Macmillan.

Martin, J. I. and Knox, J. (2000) 'Methodological and ethical issues in research on lesbians and gay men'. *Social Work Research*, 24(1): 51–59.

McEnery, T. (2005) *Swearing in English. Bad language, purity and power from 1586 to the present*. London: Routledge.

McIntyre, D. and Walker, B. (2019) *Corpus stylistics: Theory and practice*. Edinburgh: Edinburgh University Press.

Simpson, P. (2014) *Stylistics: A resource book for students* (2nd edition). London: Routledge.

Townsend, L. and Wallace, C. (2017) 'The ethics of using social media data in research: A new framework'. In K. Woodfield (ed.), *The ethics of online research*, pp. 189–207. Advances in Research Ethics and Integrity, Vol. 2. Bingley, Yorkshire: Emerald Publishing Limited.

UKRI (2021) Framework for research ethics. Accessed 12 April 2023. https://www.ukri.org/councils/esrc/guidance-for-applicants/research-ethics-guidance/framework-for-research-ethics/our-core-principles/#contents-list

Wray, A. and Bloomer, A. (2012) *Projects in linguistics and language studies*. London: Routledge.

Appendices

Appendix 1 Sample statement declaring consent for a study

1. Informed consent and ethical considerations in a forensic linguistic study of police–witness interactions.

DECLARATION OF CONSENT for participation in:

[Project Title]

I confirm:

- that I have been satisfactorily informed about the study;
- that I have received answers to any questions I have asked;
- that I have had the opportunity to carefully consider my participation in this study;
- that I am voluntarily participating.

I agree that:

- the data collected will be obtained for the purposes of the research study for which it was intended

- if the data is to be used for additional research studies, that I am informed beforehand, and my permission will be sought

I understand that:

- I have the right to withdraw my consent for the use of the collected data.

Name participant: ________ Date of birth: ___/___/____ (dd/mm/yyyy)

Signature: ____________________ Date, place: ___/___/____, ___________

If using audio or video, or both, this can be added:

Declaration on data reuse **to be completed after the data collection has taken place**
(please tick the appropriate boxes and sign at the bottom):

(1) Do you consent to us sharing the collected audio and video recordings with other researchers for the current research project?

[ ] Yes, I agree. [ ] No, I do not agree.

(2) Sometimes, image and/or audio recordings are also shown in scientific lectures or lessons. Do you consent to us using the audio and/or video recordings for these purposes?

[ ] Yes, I agree. [ ] No, I do not agree.

Signature: ______________________ Date: ________________

Appendix 2 Information for participants

Information for participants

[Project title]

1. Introduction

You have indicated your willingness to participate in a scientific study taking place in [PLACE] using data obtained from a discussion group which will be analysed at [PLACE]. This document contains all information you need when deciding if you want to take part in the study. You are kindly asked to read this document attentively.

The study has been approved by the Ethics Committee of [XXXXX], which is part of [PLACE] University. At any point, you are free to decide to opt out of this study.

2. What is the background and aim of this research?

Language use is studied intensively at [RESEARCH CENTRE]. The aim of this research is to [collect consumers' views on the use of mobile phones with the purposes of understanding how people talk in peer groups about mobile phone use].

3. How is the research conducted?

I, [NAME], will be requesting [to audio-record a 30-minute focus group discussion in which you will be participating]. These recordings will be fully anonymised to protect the privacy of all concerned. All data collected will be analysed at [RESEARCH CENTRE].

4. What is expected of you?

Your participation in a 30-minute focus group discussion on consumer behaviour relating to mobile phones. We will ask you to read aloud a one-line prompt from a card to generate discussion. The cards will contain statements about mobile phone use (e.g. 'My brother looks at my phone when I am watching TV'). We will record the 30-minute session. We will seek your consent to record it.

5. What are the possible advantages and disadvantages of taking part in this research?

Participating in this study may lead to us learning useful knowledge about how people talk about mobile phone use. There are no disadvantages to the study.

6. Voluntary participation

Your participation is voluntary. If you decide not to take part in the research, you do not need to do anything, nor sign any document. You do not have to explain why you decide not to participate in the research. If you do decide to participate, you have 24 hours to withdraw participation. If you decide to stop participating at any of the points mentioned above, I will destroy any notes that I made based on the audio file. I will not include your contribution in the research.

7. What happens with the data that we collect?

Spoken data is recorded on a voice recorder and stored in encrypted files on protected servers at [NAME] university. Written data collected in this research will be stored in complete anonymity on protected servers of [NAME] University. Your personal data are taken care of by the lead researcher, [NAME]. In case you would like to update your details, you can contact me at the email address: [EMAIL]. Only the research team will have access to the data.

We are obliged to keep the anonymised research data for [NUMBER] years. By participating in this research, you are giving us permission for us to do that. If you do not want us to keep these anonymised details, you can choose not to take part in this research.

9. Approval for this research

Ethics Committee of the [RESEARCH CENTRE] has approved this research. In case you have any concerns regarding the procedures associated with this research, you can contact the secretary: [NAME], phone: [NUMBER], email: [EMAIL]

10. More information on this research?

Would you like to have more information on this research? Please feel free to contact [NAME] on [EMAIL].

Index